The Green Crypto Handbook

The Green Crypto Handbook is a practical guide exploring how blockchain can address the $11 trillion climate finance gap through more transparent, accountable green asset systems. Using the Environmental Finance Stack framework, it maps green finance layers from environmental measurement to market dynamics, showing where blockchain can redesign processes for better environmental outcomes. Drawing on nearly a decade of real-world experience with green blockchain initiatives, the book combines environmental science, financial innovation, and digital governance insights and offers a structured methodology for evaluating blockchain's role in making green systems more credible and equitable.

Features

- Introduces the Environmental Finance Stack framework to analyze green finance system layers systematically.
- Explains how tokenized green assets work, what governance challenges regenerative finance must overcome, and how blockchain technologies can be harnessed.
- Provides real-world case studies from Web3 and ReFi projects like Regen Network, translating theory into practice through detailed, practitioner-informed examples.
- Delivers practitioner insights from authors with nearly a decade of field experience and access to global sustainability networks.
- Bridges blockchain and environmental governance with academic rigor while maintaining accessibility.

This book is for professionals and researchers working at the intersection of environmental sustainability and blockchain. It's also an excellent resource for graduate and advanced undergraduate students who are familiar with sustainability or blockchain, and taking courses in environmental governance, political economy, ecological economics, and digital innovation; as well as environmental activists, sustainability consultants, innovation strategists, and general readers interested in climate solutions and the evolution of decentralized technologies.

The Green Crypto Handbook

Blockchain for Sustainability Professionals

Patrick Rawson and Louise Borreani

CRC Press
Taylor & Francis Group
Boca Raton London New York

CRC Press is an imprint of the
Taylor & Francis Group, an **informa** business

Cover: Background image credit goes to Matt Str (@matt039_yt on Unsplash)

First edition published 2027
by CRC Press
4 Park Square, Milton Park, Abingdon, Oxon, OX14 4RN

and by CRC Press
2385 NW Executive Center Drive, Suite 320, Boca Raton FL 33431

CRC Press is an imprint of Taylor & Francis Group, LLC

This Open Access chapter was funded by Ecofrontiers.

ISBN: 978-1-041-25893-3 (hbk)
ISBN: 978-1-041-25894-0 (pbk)
ISBN: 978-1-003-74847-2 (ebk)

DOI: 10.1201/9781003748472

Typeset in Times
by KnowledgeWorks Global Ltd.

Ecofrontiers

To Sloterdijk, our primary source of inspiration in work and in life.

Contents

Preface

This handbook emerges from our work at Ecofrontiers, a research organization focused on digital technologies and ecological systems. Since 2021, we have advised central banks, international organizations, and foundations on how public blockchains intersect with environmental finance. That advisory work revealed a persistent gap: sustainability professionals increasingly encounter blockchain-based solutions but lack the conceptual framework to evaluate them.

The Green Crypto Handbook addresses that gap. Whether you work in corporate sustainability, environmental consulting, conservation finance, or climate policy, you will encounter tokenized carbon credits, decentralized verification systems, and blockchain-based supply chain tools with increasing frequency. Some will be legitimate innovations; others will be greenwashing dressed in technical jargon. This book provides the tools to distinguish between them.

We approach the subject through a layered model, moving from the material substrate of computation through data structures, institutional arrangements, protocol design, asset creation, and finally market dynamics. Each layer presents distinct sustainability considerations and decision points. Understanding these layers requires engaging with technical details that sustainability professionals have historically been able to avoid—but can no longer.

The emergence of artificial intelligence as a general-purpose technology adds urgency to this project. AI systems are increasingly deployed alongside blockchain infrastructure for environmental monitoring, verification, and prediction. The same analytical framework that helps professionals evaluate blockchain claims—attending to ecological realities, data provenance, institutional arrangements, and market dynamics—applies equally to AI-augmented climate finance tools. We address these intersections throughout the book.

This is not a book advocating uncritical adoption of blockchain technology. Nor is it a dismissal. It is a practical guide for professionals who must make informed decisions about when public blockchains can genuinely advance sustainability goals—and when they cannot.

Patrick Rawson and Louise Borreani
ecofrontiers.xyz

About the Authors

Patrick Rawson is co-founder of Ecofrontiers, a research organization at the intersection of digital technologies and ecological systems. He has consulted for Giga/UNICEF on connectivity infrastructure, and serves on Sostento's Crypto Advisory Board, a non-profit providing free ridesharing for underserved patients. He previously was CEO of Curve Labs, a Berlin-based blockchain venture studio. There, his work included program coordination for the Celo Foundation's regenerative finance initiative, as well as foundational research and design work for tokenized carbon credits and decentralized commerce systems. Today, his research spans spatial economics, AI for institutional design, and climate-intelligent infrastructure.

Louise Borreani is a blockchain and Artificial Intelligence governance scholar, with a special focus on environmental policy and finance. She is the co-founder of Ecofrontiers, where she conducts research on how emerging technologies can be integrated into environmental governance and financial infrastructures. She has worked on Kolektivo, a suite of Web3 tools enabling local communities to develop regenerative economies, and on Regen Atlas, an open-source registry aggregating and classifying tokenized green assets. She has presented her research on environmental crypto-assets at Banque de France (Le Lab) and the Central Bank of Uruguay. She is a graduate of Freie Universität Berlin and Sciences Po Paris, with an academic background in environmental policy and institutional economics.

Acknowledgments

This book would not have been possible without the generosity, insight, and encouragement of many individuals who contributed their expertise, reviewed early drafts, and helped bring this project to life.

We would like to thank, in no particular order: Dr. Jacques-André Fines-Schlumberger, Ataberk Casur, Alp Ergin, Timothy Gieseke, Mihai Hrimiuc, Fabian Scherer, Dr. Erik Bordeleau, Jeff Emmett, Theodor Beutel, Rubin Russel, Pedro Parrachia, Dr. Daniel Villa Monteiro, Marcus Levine, Raz Pulurian, Christoph Wünsche, Dr. Julian Granados, the ReFai Sicilia and CarbonCopy teams. Your contributions—whether through thoughtful feedback, operational support, rigorous review, or spirited conversation—have shaped this work in ways both large and small.

This book stands on the shoulders of a vibrant community of researchers, builders, and practitioners who challenge conventional thinking and contribute tirelessly to public knowledge. The fields of blockchain, sustainability, and regenerative finance are defined by open inquiry and collaboration, and we are grateful to be part of that tradition.

We are also indebted to our editorial team at Taylor & Francis for their guidance and professionalism throughout the publication process.

Finally, our deepest gratitude goes to our families and friends, who have supported us with patience and understanding through the many years of research and writing that went into this book. Your encouragement sustained us when the work was hardest, and we could not have done it without you.

1 Introduction

Sustainability professionals will encounter blockchain in their work. Many already have: a carbon credit platform promising radical transparency, a supply chain tool claiming immutable provenance, a tokenized conservation project seeking investment. The question is not whether practitioners will face these tools but whether they can evaluate and use them effectively. The World Economic Forum puts it directly:

> Conventional methods cannot be relied on to tackle perhaps the biggest-ever threat to humanity. Global climate infrastructure, tools and coordination technologies are needed to keep pace with the changing planetary ecosystem, transcend borders and span social, economic, cultural and governmental domains. This is where blockchain can help.
>
> **World Economic Forum (2023)**

But how does one know when it actually helps, and when it is greenwashing dressed in technical jargon?

The stakes are high. Climate finance currently reaches approximately $1.9 trillion per year but must scale to $7.4 trillion annually through 2030 to meet Paris Agreement targets—an investment gap exceeding $5 trillion per year (Naran et al. 2025). The agrifood system generates an estimated $12.7 trillion in annual hidden costs through health and environmental externalities (FAO 2023); the electricity sector, $11.6 trillion (Sovacool, Kim, and Yang 2021). Investment in nature-based solutions must nearly triple from current levels to reach the $542 billion per year needed by 2030 (UNEP 2022), while real-world asset tokenization is projected to reach from $3.5 to $10 trillion by the same date (21.co 2023). Over half of climate finance already comes from the private sector (Climate Policy Initiative 2023), but scaling requires instruments and infrastructure that current arrangements have not produced. These figures represent both opportunity and risk. Capital is seeking credible green assets. The question is what makes an asset credible—and whether blockchain infrastructure can provide that credibility where traditional systems have failed.

The current system for producing green assets has structural problems that sustainability professionals know well. High fixed costs of verification exclude many community-led initiatives from carbon markets. Multi-year timelines from project initiation to credit issuance place intense liquidity pressure on local stewards, particularly in the Global South where access to capital is already constrained. Powerful standard-setters concentrate authority, imposing high barriers to entry while imposing methodologies that may favor large-scale industrial projects over community-based alternatives. Over-the-counter market structures limit price transparency and restrict access to established trading desks. Data formats remain fragmented across registries, impeding the interoperability that would allow assets to flow efficiently to buyers. Meanwhile, investigations reveal that many existing green assets lack

DOI: 10.1201/9781003748472-1

material basis—avoided deforestation credits issued for land that faced no credible threat, renewable energy certificates for projects that would have been built regardless, baselines inflated to maximize credit generation rather than measure actual impact, etc.

Blockchain does not automatically solve these problems. A fraudulent measurement, once recorded on a blockchain, is simply a record of fraudulence. Immutability of a ledger says nothing about the quality of the claims it's processed. But blockchain infrastructure can, when properly designed, reduce verification costs, automate compliance, create new forms of institutional accountability, and open global markets to actors previously excluded. The practitioner's task is to distinguish genuine capability from technical theater.

This book provides the tools for that distinction. It offers a structured framework—the Environmental Finance Stack—for professionals who must make informed decisions about when public blockchains genuinely advance their sustainability goals, and when they do not.

THE PRACTITIONER'S CHALLENGE

Sustainability professionals face a distinctive evaluation problem. Blockchain projects present themselves with technical terminology that obscures rather than clarifies: smart contracts, tokenomics, decentralized autonomous organizations (DAOs), zero-knowledge proofs. Yet beneath the jargon lie fundamental questions about measurement, governance, and market access that practitioners already know how to ask. The challenge is translating blockchain claims into answerable questions.

Consider a carbon credit offered on a blockchain platform. The platform claims the credit is "immutably verified" and "transparently tracked." But what does this mean in practice? Immutability refers to the ledger, not the underlying claim. Transparency of transactions tells nothing about the quality of the original verification. Both claims require understanding the technical design tradeoffs the underlying blockchain has made—it may simply be a centralized database advertising itself as an immutable ledger. Furthermore, the practitioner must look beyond the blockchain layer to the measurement infrastructure, the institutional arrangements, and the methodologies that produced the credit in the first place.

Practitioners need a framework that maps blockchain capabilities to sustainability requirements. Greenwashing risk is real. The problem is not unique to blockchain-based assets, but blockchain does not automatically solve it either; it is no substitute for rigorous measurement and credible institutional oversight. What blockchain can provide, when properly designed, is infrastructure for traceability, automated compliance, and reduced transaction costs. Practitioners need to know which questions to ask to exploit these advantages. The Environmental Finance Stack provides that framework.

THE ENVIRONMENTAL FINANCE STACK

The Environmental Finance Stack (see Figure 1.1) is a multi-layered framework for evaluating how green assets are produced, governed, and exchanged. Each layer

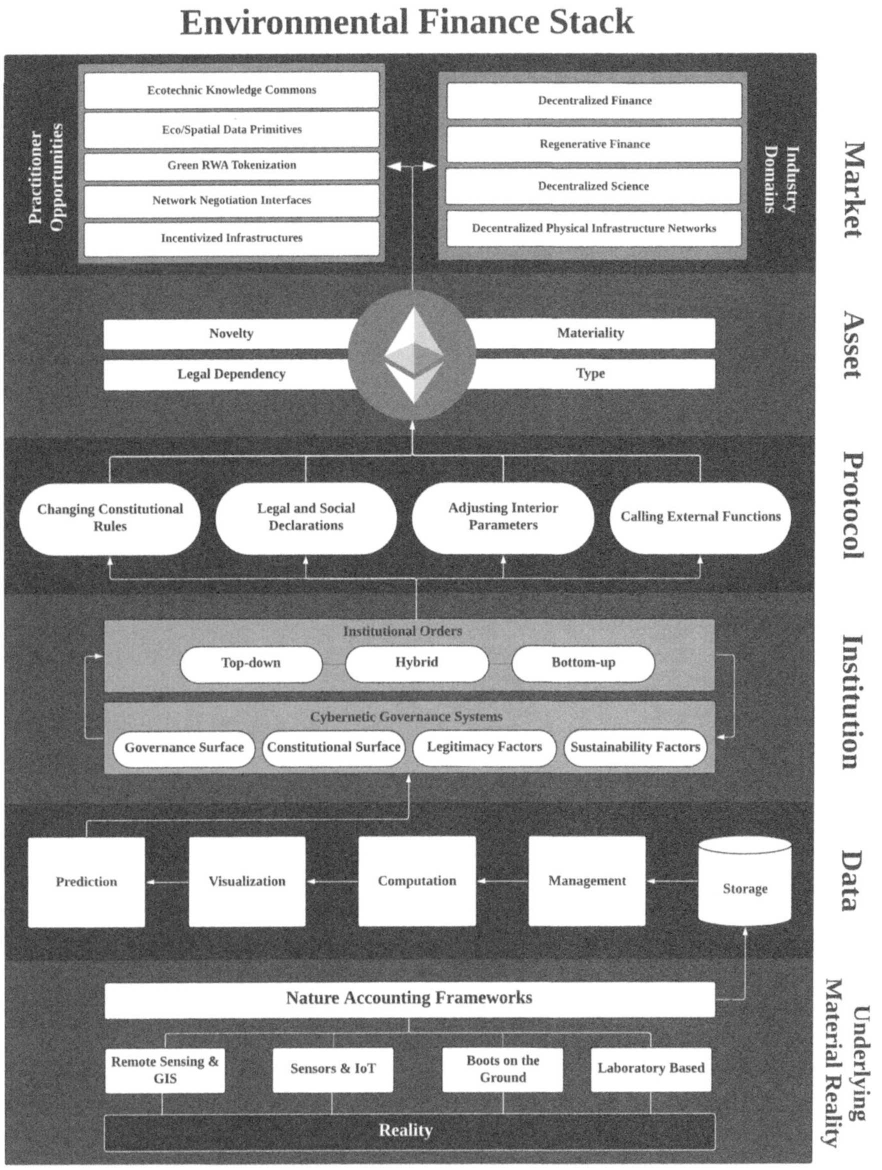

FIGURE 1.1 The Environmental Finance Stack, showing the six layers from underlying material reality to market dynamics.

Source: **Diagram by the authors.**

addresses a distinct practitioner question. Together, they provide a systematic method for due diligence on any blockchain green finance project or tool.

The six layers of the Stack roughly correspond to six practitioner questions, demonstrated in Table 1.1.

TABLE 1.1
The Environmental Finance Stack and Corresponding Practitioner Questions

Layer	Practitioner Question
Underlying Material Reality	What measurement technology backs a sustainability claim?
Data	Where is claim data stored and who controls it?
Institution	Who governs this system and how?
Protocol	What rules determine how green assets are created?
Asset	What am I actually exchanging?
Market	Where can green assets trade, and at what cost?

Source: Table by the authors.

The Stack is designed to be read from the bottom up. Each layer depends on the one beneath it: an asset's credibility rests on the protocol that created it, which rests on the institution that governed it, which rests on the data that informed it, which rests on the measurement that produced it. Skipping a layer means missing the questions that layer was built to ask.

At the base lies the **Underlying Material Reality:** the biophysical world from which all environmental claims derive. This layer encompasses the full spectrum of environmental observation technologies. Remote sensing and geographic information systems provide planetary-scale monitoring of forest cover, land use change, and atmospheric composition. Internet-of-things sensor networks track local conditions: soil moisture, air quality, water flow, biodiversity indicators. Field-based surveys and citizen science initiatives contribute ground-truth data. Laboratory and genomic analysis provide molecular-level verification. Each technology has characteristic strengths and limitations; combining them requires understanding their respective domains of validity.

The credibility of any green asset ultimately rests on the quality of observation and measurement at this layer. A carbon credit claiming sequestration in a Brazilian forest depends on how that sequestration was measured: satellite imagery, ground plots, allometric equations, or some combination. The precision and accuracy of these measurements, their spatial and temporal resolution, and their validation against independent sources all determine whether the claim has material grounding.

The Data Layer translates material observations into structured digital records. It covers five interconnected functions: storage, management, computation, visualization, and prediction (see Figure 1.2). Storage determines where data lives and who can access it. Management encompasses standardization, quality control, and interoperability across systems. Computation transforms raw observations into derived metrics: carbon stock estimates, biodiversity indices, water quality scores. Visualization makes complex environmental data accessible to decision-makers. Prediction uses historical patterns to forecast future states, increasingly through machine learning and AI models trained on vast troves of environmental data.

When data is stored on decentralized systems like the InterPlanetary File System (IPFS), it gains persistence and censorship resistance, but these properties say nothing

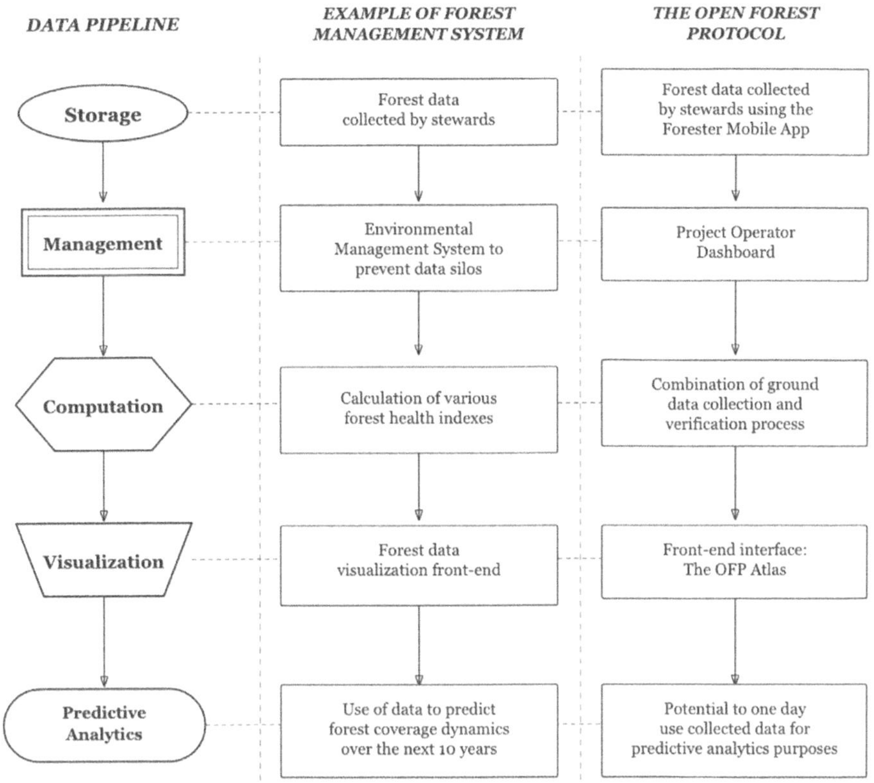

FIGURE 1.2 The data pipeline for environmental finance, showing the flow from storage through prediction. The Open Forest Protocol example illustrates how blockchain infrastructure integrates with this pipeline. Throughout the pipeline, cryptographic hashes ensure data integrity: if data is altered after recording, the hash changes, revealing tampering.

Source: **Diagram by the authors.**

about its data quality or management practices. AI is increasingly embedded in specialized compute systems to ensure the verifiability of its outputs. Visualization is becoming more fluid as open interfaces feed into and display disparate environmental data sources in fluid context. Prediction is shifting from private compute environments to open market-based oracles. With so many rapid developments at hand, the Data chapter's pipeline grounds practitioners so they can evaluate and identify data infrastructure gaps regardless of whether they leverage blockchain or traditional architectures.

The Institution Layer encompasses the organizations, rules, and norms that interpret and formalize environmental data into protocols, a category that Ostrom terms the "rules-in-use" governing commons (Ostrom 1990). This is where raw data becomes credentialed claims, and funding is distributed to green projects and initiatives.

Traditional institutions have dominated carbon market certification, imposing methodologies, verification requirements, and registry rules that determine project access. These institutions concentrate industry power: they decide what counts as a valid carbon credit, who can produce one, and how much it costs to enter the system. Their high upfront verification costs and long timelines reflect institutional governance design choices, not technical necessities.

Blockchain enables new organizational forms that innovate on these industry dynamics. The Institution chapter analyzes how cybernetic governance principles (feedback loops, requisite variety, self-regulation) apply to emerging blockchain-based institutions (crypto-institutions, or DAOs). It examines coordination problems that have long constrained environmental action, including the Prisoner's Dilemma and free-rider dynamics, and demonstrates how enhanced crypto-institutional properties like transparency, immutability, and programmability can reduce these coordination costs. DAOs, as organizational primitives, encode governance rules in smart contracts, making decision-making transparent and legible. Onchain treasuries enable automated fund disbursement based on verified environmental outcomes. The chapter moves across three scales: building-level prototypes testing governance primitives, bioregional financing facilities coordinating across watersheds, and planetary-scale architectures where AI agents help institutions navigate complexity that exceeds human cognitive capacity.

The Protocol Layer standardizes how green assets are created and governed. In traditional markets, this means certification methodologies and registry rules: the specific procedures that determine how measurements become credits. In blockchain systems, protocols are encoded in smart contracts: self-executing code that enforces rules automatically. When a verification condition is met, the contract mints tokens without requiring human intervention. When a violation is detected, the contract can freeze assets or trigger dispute resolution. These automated mechanisms reduce transaction costs and discretionary gatekeeping, but they also encode assumptions that may be difficult to modify once deployed.

The Protocol chapter introduces a fourfold framework for understanding protocol operations: changing governance parameters, legal and social declarations, interior parameter-setting (operational settings), and external functions (interactions with other systems). A four-primitive surface matrix maps reversibility against transferability to classify different green crypto-asset types that protocols produce. The chapter examines how carbon credit issuance mechanisms, biodiversity verification protocols, and renewable energy certificate systems encode their rules at this layer.

The Asset Layer is where green assets take form as tradable objects. Traditional environmental assets include carbon credits, renewable energy certificates, and conservation easements. Blockchain enables new asset forms: tokenized carbon credits with embedded provenance data, fractionalized natural capital ownership, parametric insurance contracts that pay out automatically when environmental triggers are met, and dynamic assets that update their properties based on real-time monitoring data.

The Asset chapter provides a comprehensive taxonomy: over 20 categories of green crypto-assets organized by type and subtype, and characterized by three design properties. Composability means assets can be combined: a carbon credit can be bundled with a biodiversity premium and a community benefit certificate. Adaptability means assets can evolve: new verification data can update the asset's metadata without requiring reissuance. Material modularity means assets can be unbundled: the carbon sequestration component can be separated from the land tenure component. The chapter includes case studies across all categories.

The Market Layer addresses where and how green assets circulate. Legacy carbon markets operate through over-the-counter desks with limited price transparency and restricted access. Trades are negotiated bilaterally, with prices discoverable only to participants. Settlement takes days. Counterparty risk requires credit assessment and legal agreements. These friction costs are significant: transaction costs for small projects can exceed the value of the credits themselves.

Blockchain enables automated market makers and decentralized exchanges with 24/7 global access. Anyone with an internet connection can trade. Prices are transparent, determined by algorithmic curves rather than opaque negotiations. Settlement is near-instantaneous compared to traditional T+2 timelines. Smart contracts reduce certain forms of counterparty risk by holding assets in escrow until both sides of a trade are confirmed. These efficiency gains are real, though they introduce new risks: smart contract vulnerabilities, liquidity fragmentation across platforms, and regulatory uncertainty.

The Market chapter examines the scale of the challenge: annual climate finance reached approximately \$1.3 trillion in 2021–2022 but must scale to \$8–9 trillion annually by 2030 (Climate Policy Initiative 2023). The chapter argues that materiality is the foundation of market legitimacy—green assets must be fully auditable, transparent, and credible about their underlying material claims. The chapter concludes by mapping actionable opportunities across three domains: regenerative finance, which applies Web3 tools to socioecological impact; decentralized science, which opens research funding and data sharing beyond traditional gatekeepers; and decentralized physical infrastructure networks, which coordinate distributed energy, sensor, and connectivity assets. For practitioners seeking entry points, the chapter surveys industry trends and innovations, equipping professionals with a map of where opportunity exists.

CROSS-CUTTING CONCERNS

The Stack provides the evaluative framework. But three cross-cutting concerns shape how practitioners will apply it at the time of writing: the shift from legacy to digital verification systems, the materiality principle that distinguishes genuine green assets from greenwashed labels, and a regulatory landscape that increasingly demands both climate integrity and crypto-asset disclosure. The following sections address these foundations before the chapter closes with reading paths for different professional contexts.

DIGITAL MONITORING, REPORTING, AND VERIFICATION (MRV)

MRV is the infrastructure that makes environmental claims credible. Traditional MRV systems face serious bottlenecks: verification costs are high, multi-year timelines from project initiation to credit issuance create liquidity gaps, and outdated technologies inhibit scaling.

	Legacy	Open Forest Protocol
Verification cost	Starting at $50,000 USD	Free
# of entities verifying a project	1	Dozens to (ultimately) hundreds
Minimum project size	1,200 Ha (3,000 Acres)	No minimum
Time to value creation	Approximately 2-5 years	Exactly 1 year
Credit transparency	Opaque	Immutably trustless & transparent
Data re-verification and update	Every 3-4 years	Every year
Project financing options	Fragmented and Opaque	Integrated and smart-contracted

FIGURE 1.3 Comparison of legacy MRV and digital MRV systems, showing efficiency gains in verification capacity and cost.

Source: **Ruch-Kamgar (2023).**

Digital MRV (dMRV) systems combine remote sensing, IoT (Internet of Things) sensors, and blockchain infrastructure to automate verification processes (see Figure 1.3). The throughput improvement is striking: dMRV systems can process ten projects per day per verification officer, compared to legacy systems' annual throughput of 100–150 projects (SustainCERT 2023). Marginal per-project verification costs drop from tens of thousands of dollars to a fraction of that. Project minimum sizes disappear; a community forestry initiative managing 50 hectares can participate on the same platform as an industrial reforestation project covering 50,000 hectares.

The architecture of a typical dMRV system illustrates how the Stack layers integrate. At the base, satellite imagery from sources like the Sentinel program provides continuous monitoring, while ground-level IoT sensors measure soil carbon, canopy density, or water quality, and mobile applications allow local stewards to submit geotagged observations. This multi-source data flows into distributed storage systems and through computer vision models that detect cover changes and estimate sequestration or biodiversity indicators.

From there, verification networks—whether traditional certification bodies adapting to digital workflows or blockchain-native validator networks with staked collateral—review the processed data. Smart contracts encode the rules: if validators approve a measurement, if satellite imagery confirms no deforestation, if ground sensors report adequate conditions, then credits are minted or funding allocated. The resulting tokens carry embedded metadata linking back to verification evidence and can be traded on decentralized exchanges or burned for offsetting.

At present, major standards bodies have active working groups on digitization. Gold Standard and Verra are developing dMRV frameworks that specify how remote sensing evidence can supplement or replace traditional field verification (Carbonmark 2025). Smart contracts on blockchain networks like Polygon and Base auto-issue credits when verification conditions are met. Token standards like ERC-20 embed verification metadata directly in the asset, making provenance queryable by any party.

The efficiency of dMRV does not guarantee quality. dMRV is infrastructure, not a substitute for judgment. It amplifies whatever quality standards are embedded in its design. A poorly calibrated satellite model, once deployed, will produce systematically biased estimates across every project it monitors. The practitioner's task remains evaluation: does the underlying measurement technology produce reliable data? Do the institutional arrangements ensure accountability? Does the protocol encode appropriate rules? Are there mechanisms for detecting and correcting errors?

MATERIALITY AS FOUNDATION

A principle runs through this book: green assets must verifiably connect to physical reality. This principle provides the evaluative standard for all green finance. An asset's credibility depends on the strength of its connection to the material conditions it claims to represent. Without that connection, an asset is not green; it is merely labeled green.

Environmental commodification has its own history. Carbon pricing reflects a certain form of market logic, framing nature as capital. Here runs a real risk: the tendency to reduce ecological systems to oversimplified metrics, and the potential for financial instruments to displace rather than complement direct conservation action. Yet the alternative—refusing to price environmental outcomes—does not prevent ecological degradation. Capital flows according to market signals; if nature has no price, it has no standing in the systems that need to allocate investment to close the climate investment gap.

This book demands that economic claims have physical substance, verifiable data, and accountable institutions. A carbon credit should correspond to actual sequestration, measurable through validated methods, maintained over verified time periods. A biodiversity asset should reflect documented species presence, habitat quality, or ecosystem function. A renewable energy certificate should trace to specific generation, metered and timestamped.

Blockchain provides infrastructure for traceability. It is a database with certain key properties: immutability, transparency, decentralization. Immutable records prevent retrospective modification of claims and transparent transactions allow independent audit, while automated compliance reduces discretionary gatekeeping. Still, these properties are not substitutes for measurement and scientific process. The question for practitioners is always: what measurement technology backs this claim? If the answer is "satellite imagery processed through validated models with ground-truthing protocols and independent verification," the claim has strong material grounding. As such, a rigorous dMRV system on a blockchain produces credible assets. If the answer is "self-reported data uploaded to a blockchain," then credibility is sharply limited.

Green finance is moving toward stronger materiality. Institutional buyers increasingly demand third-party verification. The Science Based Targets initiative requires emissions reductions to align with climate science (Science Based Targets initiative 2024). MiCA regulations require crypto-asset whitepapers to disclose environmental impacts (European Parliament and Council 2023). Practitioners who understand the material basis of environmental claims will be better positioned as standards tighten.

COMPLIANCE AND REGULATIONS

The regulatory environment for blockchain-based green finance has matured considerably since the early 2020s. Two developments are particularly significant for practitioners: the operationalization of Article 6 of the Paris Agreement and the full application of the Markets in Crypto-Assets regulation in the European Union.

Article 6 establishes the international framework for cooperative climate action. Sixty-three Parties are engaged in bilateral cooperation, with 169 projects operating under Article 6.2 mechanisms (Article 6 Partnership 2025; UNFCCC 2025). The Article 6.4 mechanism, successor to the Clean Development Mechanism, has received transition requests from 1,389 CDM project activities. COP29 in 2024 adopted further guidance on cooperative approaches.

For practitioners, Article 6 creates both opportunity and constraint. Projects that meet Article 6 standards gain access to international carbon markets with recognized corresponding adjustments—the mechanism that prevents double-counting of emissions reductions across jurisdictions. The low 9% approval rate for CDM project activity transition requests, however, indicates that standards are stringent (Article 6 Partnership 2025). Projects must demonstrate additionality, permanence, and avoidance of harm, with verification by accredited bodies.

MiCA provides "the world's most comprehensive legal framework for crypto-assets" (InnReg 2025). Full application begins mid-2026, with no further grace periods. Environmental disclosure is mandatory: crypto-asset white papers must report total annual electricity consumption in kilowatt-hours. For assets exceeding 500,000 kWh, enhanced disclosure requirements apply: renewable energy share, energy intensity per transaction, and greenhouse gas emissions.

The combination of Article 6 and MiCA creates a regulatory environment where environmental claims about blockchain assets face scrutiny on both the climate and the crypto sides. A tokenized carbon credit that claims to represent verified emissions reductions must satisfy both climate integrity standards and crypto-asset disclosure requirements. The days of vague sustainability claims are ending. Practitioners should expect increasing demands for documentation, third-party verification, and quantitative disclosure.

Beyond Europe, regulatory frameworks are developing unevenly. The United States remains fragmented, with the SEC, CFTC, and state regulators asserting overlapping jurisdiction. Developing countries, particularly those rich in biodiversity and carbon stocks, are crafting approaches that balance environmental protection with economic opportunity. The lack of global harmonization creates both risk and opportunity: risk of regulatory arbitrage and inconsistent standards, opportunity for innovative jurisdictions to establish leadership.

The Environmental Finance Stack provides a framework for meeting regulatory demands regardless of jurisdiction. Each layer maps to a category of regulatory concern: material and data layers must satisfy environmental integrity and auditability standards; institutional and protocol layers must demonstrate governance adequacy and compliant procedures; asset and market layers must meet disclosure, trading, and settlement requirements. By ensuring each layer withstands examination, practitioners build structures that adapt as regulations develop.

A SNAPSHOT IN MOTION

This book captures a field in rapid evolution. The specific projects, platforms, and statistics cited throughout will date. What persists is the methodology: the Environmental Finance Stack as an analytical framework that applies regardless of which projects succeed or fail. The questions remain constant even as the answers change. What measurement technology backs this claim? Where is data stored? Who governs the system? These questions will be as relevant ten years from now as they are today.

Honest framing requires acknowledging uncertainty. Blockchain technology remains volatile, both technically and economically. Regulatory frameworks are still developing. The climate crisis itself introduces unpredictable dynamics. Projects that appear promising may fail; projects that seem marginal may scale. The 20-year timeline for steel industry transitions (IEA 2020) suggests that infrastructure transformations of this magnitude require patience.

AI adds another dimension of rapid change. Large language models, computer vision systems, and predictive analytics are being integrated into environmental monitoring at accelerating pace (Kaack et al. 2022). The same evaluation principles apply: attend to training data quality, institutional arrangements, and material grounding. AI does not change the fundamental questions; it adds new technical layers that require the same kind of rigorous assessment.

The authors are acutely aware that the present is already slipping into obsolescence. What follows is not a definitive map but a snapshot of a system still taking shape. The value lies not in the specific claims but in the framework for evaluating claims as sustainability and green finance continues to evolve.

HOW THIS BOOK WORKS

The book is structured so that sequential reading provides the most comprehensive understanding, but practitioners with specific tasks can navigate directly to relevant layers. Different professional contexts demand different entry points into the Stack.

Carbon project developers, particularly those managing community or smallholder initiatives, would enter the Stack from the bottom. Their pressing question is whether a credible path exists from forest measurement to tradable credit without prohibitive verification costs. They need Chapter 2 (measurement infrastructure) and Chapter 3 (data systems), then Chapter 6 (asset composition) and Chapter 7 (market access). Chapters 4 and 5 serve as reference when evaluating specific institutional and protocol designs.

Governance and policy professionals enter through the institutional layers. Climate policy advisors designing Article 6 implementation strategies and protocol designers building DAOs for environmental coordination both need Chapter 4 (institutional governance) and Chapter 5 (protocol design). Chapter 7 provides market context

TABLE 1.2
Reading Paths by Practitioner Profile

Practitioner	Entry Question	Core Path	Reference
Carbon project developer	Can my project reach markets?	Ch 2 → 3 → 6 → 7	Ch 4, 5
ESG/impact fund analyst	Is this asset investable?	Ch 6 → 7 → 2	Ch 4, 5
Climate policy advisor	How should we regulate this?	Ch 4 → 5 → 7	Ch 2
Protocol/DAO designer	How do I design this right?	Ch 4 → 5 → 6 → 2	Ch 3
Corporate sustainability director	Which credits are defensible?	Ch 7 → 6 → 2	Ch 5

Source: Table by the authors.

for policy implications. Chapter 2 provides essential grounding—governance that ignores measurement quality produces poorly performing green assets.

Financial actors (ESG fund analysts evaluating green asset portfolios, corporate sustainability directors procuring offsets for Scope 3 compliance) would enter from the top of the Stack and work downward. Chapter 6 (asset taxonomy) and Chapter 7 (market dynamics) provide the entry point. Due diligence requires tracing each asset backward through the protocol, institutional, data, and material layers that produced it.

Table 1.2 maps these reading paths by practitioner type.

For readers arriving with a task rather than a role, there are three fast-tracks through the book:

1. **Evaluating a specific carbon credit or green token:** Start with Chapter 2—is the underlying measurement credible? Then Chapter 6—what is this green asset actually composed of? Work outward from there as needed.
2. **Designing governance or protocol mechanics for a green project:** Chapter 4 provides the coordination theory, Chapter 5 the encoding framework. Read Chapter 2 before deploying anything: governance that ignores measurement quality is ignoring the principle of materiality.
3. **Full due diligence on a blockchain-based environmental platform:** Read sequentially. Each layer reveals what the layer above it hides. The Stack is designed so that skipping a layer means missing the questions that layer was built to ask.

Each chapter concludes with practical implications for sustainability professionals, and various case studies. The goal throughout is not to promote blockchain adoption but to provide the tools for rigorous evaluation. The Environmental Finance Stack equips practitioners to make that determination systematically.

The climate finance gap persists because current institutional arrangements were not designed to close it. Pricing externalities and building sustainable infrastructure demand financial instruments and coordination mechanisms that existing systems have not produced. Blockchain technology, properly understood and critically evaluated, offers capabilities that may contribute to meeting these challenges. This book provides the framework for determining when that contribution is real.

The next chapter begins where all environmental claims must begin: with the underlying material reality of the biophysical world and the technologies and taxonomies used to observe, measure, and classify it.

REFERENCES

21.co. 2023. "The State of Tokenization." https://www.21.co/research/the-state-of-tokenization. Accessed March 2026.

Article 6 Partnership. 2025. "A6 Partnership." https://a6partnership.org/. Accessed March 2026.

Carbonmark. 2025. "How dMRV and Smart Contracts Help Build Trust in Carbon Markets." https://www.carbonmark.com/post/how-dmrv-and-smart-contracts-help-build-trust-in-carbon-markets. Accessed March 2026.

Climate Policy Initiative. 2023. "Global Landscape of Climate Finance 2023." November 2023. https://www.climatepolicyinitiative.org/publication/global-landscape-of-climate-finance-2023/. Accessed March 2026.

European Parliament and Council. 2023. "Regulation (EU) 2023/1114 on Markets in Crypto-Assets (MiCA)." Official Journal of the European Union L 150: 40–205.

FAO. 2023. The State of Food and Agriculture 2023: Revealing the True Cost of Food to Transform Agrifood Systems. Food and Agriculture Organization.

InnReg. 2025. "Markets in Crypto-Assets Regulation (MiCA) Updated Guide (2026)." https://www.innreg.com/blog/mica-regulation-guide. Accessed March 2026.

International Energy Agency. 2020. "Iron and Steel Technology Roadmap: Towards More Sustainable Steelmaking." https://www.iea.org/reports/iron-and-steel-technology-roadmap. Accessed March 2026.

Kaack, L.H. et al. 2022. "Aligning Artificial Intelligence with Climate Change Mitigation." Nature Climate Change 12: 518–527.

Naran, B. et al. 2025. Global Landscape of Climate Finance 2025. Climate Policy Initiative.

Ostrom, Elinor. 1990. Governing the Commons: The Evolution of Institutions for Collective Action. Cambridge University Press.

Ruch-Kamgar, Dariusch. 2023. "A Primer on the Intersection of Carbon Credit Markets and Web3." Open Forest Protocol, August 2023. https://docsend.com/view/ctp8zj4e427z7tgh.

Science Based Targets initiative. 2024. "SBTi Corporate Net-Zero Standard." Version 1.2. https://sciencebasedtargets.org/net-zero. Accessed March 2026.

Sovacool, B.K., J. Kim, and M. Yang. 2021. "The Hidden Costs of Energy and Mobility: A Global Meta-Analysis and Research Synthesis of Electricity and Transport Externalities." Energy Research & Social Science 72: 101885.

SustainCERT. 2023. "Digital Verification Solutions for Carbon Markets Could Fast-Track Climate Action." https://www.sustain-cert.com/news/digital-verification-solutions-for-carbon-markets-could-fast-track-climate-action. Accessed March 2026.

UNEP. 2022. "State of Finance for Nature 2022. United Nations Environment Programme." https://www.unep.org/resources/state-finance-nature-20220. Accessed March 2026.

UNFCCC. 2025. "Article 6 Cooperative Approaches." https://unfccc.int/process-and-meetings/the-paris-agreement/article-6/article-62/carp/cooperative-approaches. Accessed March 2026.

World Economic Forum. 2023. "Blockchain for Scaling Climate Action." World Economic Forum.

2 The Underlying Material Reality

Scientific Observation Technologies and Their Relationship to Environmental Accounting

At the bottom of the environmental finance stack is the *underlying material reality*, the diverse family of planetary systems described by the natural sciences from which all financial abstractions are derived. Through human tools of observation and measurement, society translates the physical world into data. The economy—operating with inherent biases—produces technologies for these measurements and their integration into accounting frameworks legible to human institutions. Austin Wade Smith, Executive Director of the Regen Foundation, highlights that the observations and knowledge gathered from nature are not merely data points or research findings; they are epistemic *commons* foundational to human self-perception and value systems, emerging directly from human interactions with the living world (Wade Smith 2023). While this is not a book on the epistemology of nature or science, these first principles must be acknowledged as the basis by which environmental finance is conceived of as accounting technology.

Environmental finance is rooted in how we interpret and quantify nature, but the methods used to create environmental assets differ from traditional scientific research. Unlike open-ended studies of ecosystems, this work is goal-driven, aiming to identify specific outcomes—such as regeneration or protection—that can be standardized and financed. This methodological divergence emphasizes *observation over experimentation*. The ability to accurately observe the underlying material reality is essential for any accounting system that seeks to report on and expand the economic value generated from it.

Environmental observation and data collection are processes that gather information about the various spheres of the natural world, such as the biosphere (life on earth) or hydrosphere (water on earth). They involve measuring and recording raw environmental parameters such as the moisture content of soil, the biomass of vegetation, or the concentration of atmospheric greenhouse gases. Key observational objectives include developing a deeper understanding of material reality in its current state, continuously evaluating changes and trends against

DOI: 10.1201/9781003748472-2

historical baselines, assessing the impacts of human activities on these changes, and making scientific decisions around its use. Observation must therefore produce reliable scientific insights that objectively gauge the success of various management, conservation and restoration efforts. Accordingly, objective measurement standards—such as those applied in carbon stock assessment—must reflect an appreciation for both *accuracy* and *precision*. While precision relates to the repeatability of measurement results, accuracy denotes the true reflection of stock changes in the environment. It is crucial to recognize that these two aspects do not always align and that one can achieve consistent measurements (high precision) that may not accurately represent the actual changes (low accuracy) (Hamburg 2000).

BOX 2.1 DEVELOPING OPERATIONAL ACCOUNTING RULES IS KEY TO ENVIRONMENTAL ASSET PRODUCTION

Such rules offer a structured methodology for quantifying and monitoring the health and value of these assets, ensuring that production is both sustainable and verifiable. Here is an example of operational accounting rules for measuring changes in ecosystem carbon in forestry-offset projects.

- Changes in living aboveground biomass must always be measured in forestry-offset projects.
- Belowground living biomass can be estimated from aboveground living biomass. Generalized root/shoot ratios can be used as long as conservative ratios are applied.
- Not all changes in soil carbon stocks need to be measured, only those for which there is a possibility the stock is declining.
- The necromass pool need not be measured except when there has been a recent disturbance.
- To ensure that inaccurate techniques do not lead to overestimating of carbon stock changes, imprecise estimates should be discounted.
- There should be no required level of accuracy associated with estimates of carbon stock changes, but the creditable carbon should be discounted proportional to the uncertainty.

Source: Hamburg (2000)

Consider the issues of precision and accuracy in the complex interplay of energy exchanges among plants, animals, and humans within socioecosystems. Such complexity demands tailored approaches to data collection sensitive to these unique fluctuating energy flows, diverse species interactions, and varying socioecological conditions and their relations. Furthermore, socioeco-systems operate at distinct spatial and temporal scales that must be recognized and respected to ensure meaningful and effective intervention. To take a specific example, in the context of carbon stock measurement (see Box 2.1), ecosystems can be divided into carbon pools—aboveground and belowground biomass, nec-romass, and soil carbon. The relationships between these pools are essential to grasp, as they can shift with changes in ecosystem type and management practices (Hamburg 2000). The conversion of forested land to agricultural uses results in complex alterations in carbon distribution among these pools. In this instance, recognizing existing system dynamics and the effect of land use change is critical for accurately estimating material carbon stocks, and will inevitably affect their accounting.

Following observation and raw data collection, the evaluation of restoration projects increasingly focuses on measuring key ecological indicators—diversity, vegetation, and ecological processes—integral to accounting and governance operations higher up in the environmental finance stack (Prasad 2021). Natural capital accounting specialist Timothy M. Gieseke notes that these indicators move through "the entire data supply chain to support each of the stakeholders" pursuing "sustainability values"—not only in the ethical sense of the term, but also in the *assignment of financial value* for each sustainability factor (Gieseke 2016). With this understanding, the more complex material indicators are to measure and produce, the more speculative their proposed value is. This relationship between measurement complexity and market access is the organizing principle of this chapter, and the reason it surveys observation technologies and accounting frameworks in detail. Each measurement choice constrains or enables the financial instruments that can be built upon it. The capacity to accurately and precisely measure the underlying material reality has a cascading effect throughout the layers above in the environmental finance stack. For example:

- The quantification of tCO2e—tons of carbon dioxide equivalent—from the destruction of the industrial gas hydrofluorocarbon-23 is relatively straightforward. This ease of measurement has led to its inclusion in the stringent legal frameworks of the Kyoto Protocol's Clean Development Mechanism, which allows countries to fund greenhouse gas emissions-reducing projects across national boundaries and claim corresponding emissions reductions. This expands market access and volume via state recognition and spending.
- In contrast, despite forest carbon accounting being grounded in more than a hundred years of observational research and practice to produce tangible and predictable measures, (Hamburg 2000) afforestation and reforestation (A&R) projects remain complex to measure. They struggle to establish concrete baselines for tree growth, prove the permanence of carbon sequestration, and enforce precise monitoring. This complexity has historically relegated A&R projects to voluntary carbon markets, which, while not legally binding and far smaller in volume, offer more flexibility for carbon reduction claims (Bumpus 2011).

- Consider a final example: the restoration of any water resource—the most valuable and life-giving natural capital—necessitates a comprehensive understanding of multiple factors, from the structural composition of the site to the historical conditions prior to degradation. This includes acknowledging, finding, and leveraging many types of data, from land use to hydrological regimes, nutrient fluxes, and the site's topography. One can appreciate how the complexity of these systems compounds the challenge of acquiring and interpreting the data required to substantiate a water restoration project's value claims in order to be finance-worthy!

On the other hand, an absence of data undermines the legitimacy and political appetite for green asset production. While discussed at length in Chapter 4, note that green assets produced without proof of positive ecological and material change risk hurting public confidence in the institutions that produce them. In the carbon market especially, "implementation of poorly quantified pathways (in relation to their GHG mitigation efficacy) could give the false impression that they… [balance] fossil emissions" (Buma, Gordon, and Kleisner 2024). To go to market with any green asset, a "precautionary approach" must be taken "until the scientific foundations are strengthened" (Buma, Gordon, and Kleisner 2024). Table 2.1 presents pivotal questions that should be considered before initiating measurement of the underlying material reality.

TABLE 2.1
A Non-Exhaustive Table of Pivotal Questions That Should Be Considered Before Initiating the Measurement of Underlying Material Reality

Category	Example of Relevant Questions
General Inquiry	What are the specific material parameters that need to be measured? How will these parameters provide insights into the current state and trends of the environmental system? What historical baselines will the new data be compared against? How will human impacts on these parameters be assessed?
Data Management	What data collection and measurement technologies will be employed? How will the collected data move through the supply chain to support stakeholders? What are the ethical and financial values associated with the environmental parameters? How will the data contribute to global initiatives (e.g., Global Stocktake)?
Legal and Methodological Frameworks	What legal and accountability frameworks are applicable to the data being collected? What standards of accuracy and precision are required for the measurements? Are there specific carbon pools or other ecological components that must be measured?
Ecological Considerations	How will complex factors such as land use, hydrology, and nutrient fluxes be integrated? What spatial and temporal scales are relevant for the ecosystem in question? How does the natural self-designing capability of the ecosystem influence data collection?

Source: Table by the authors.

This complexity reveals that despite the foundational role of the underlying material reality in the environmental finance stack, our grasp of this reality is surprisingly limited. Modern restoration ecology is itself in flux, having pivoted from striving to return ecosystems to their historical states to emphasizing adaptability and ongoing socioecological system resilience (Truitt et al. 2015). Ecosystems are now changing faster than at any point in human memory, influenced by natural disturbances, climate volatility, and other anthropogenic factors (Prasad 2021). As a result of this rate of change, new ecological challenges and phenomena are arising daily, such as infectious diseases and the proliferation of invasive species, which complicate attempts to solidify our baseline understanding of ecosystems.

Significant data gaps persist and widen as conditions change. Marine and coastal areas are of particular concern—the earth is 71% water, and marine observation gaps significantly hinder comprehensive ecosystem accounting (Dvarskas 2019). Data deficiency in developing countries compounds the problem, with research funding sporadic and often earmarked for specific issues. According to Pyšek et al. (2008), a disproportionate concentration of environmental information is published in more developed countries, suggesting a geographical bias in our understanding of the material world (Sagarin and Pauchard 2010). Compounding this bias, the aggregation of indigenous and traditional knowledge—which have accumulated deep insights into ecosystem management over time—remains limited (Capel 2014). Take, for example, the recently discovered 175 new species within the lichenized fungal family Graphidaceae, or the additional 1,800 species pending identification—a reminder that environmental finance often builds on incomplete catalogs of the very ecosystems it seeks to protect (Lücking et al. 2014).

Projections indicate that by the close of the twenty-first century, a substantial fraction of the global population will grapple with severe climatic conditions, including extreme heat, limited food availability, and heightened mortality rates attributable to climate change (Ripple et al. 2023). The need for effective environmental finance arises from this rapid deterioration of the climatic conditions that largely benefit humankind. Technological advances—of which innovation in accounting is paramount—are rapidly needed for these ends. Without them, "Hothouse Earth" becomes highly likely: a potential future climatic state where the climate system exceeds a critical tipping point leading to self-perpetuating, irreversible warming beyond human control (Rocky Mountain Institute 2023).

The gap in foundational environmental and ecological data, as well as the rapidly changing conditions that constantly seek to widen this gap, is more than an academic concern; it has practical implications for environmental finance and asset production. The effectiveness of interventions aimed at conservation, restoration, and sustainable use of natural resources depends on a nuanced understanding of socioecological dynamics. Without grasping the species composition, ecological interactions, anthropogenic, and environmental processes at play, efforts to produce effective green assets risk being based on incomplete or erroneous assumptions, undermining intended outcomes and sustainability.

Bridging this knowledge gap demands innovation, advanced observational tools, and new accounting frameworks capable of continuously observing, measuring, interpreting, and valuing the natural world. New technologies—from satellite-based remote sensing to AI-driven ecological modeling—are translating ecosystem complexity into actionable insights. These tools enable deeper, real-time understanding of environmental conditions, species behavior, and ecosystem health at unprecedented scales. The following sections, geared towards sustainability practitioners who are wrestling with these challenges, survey the key technologies reshaping how nature is observed, documented, supported, and ultimately, financed.

TECHNOLOGIES TRANSLATING NATURE

The technologies surveyed in this section serve a specific function in environmental finance: they are *oracles*—the mechanisms by which physical reality becomes legible to financial systems. In traditional markets, this translation happens through auditors, certifiers, and registries. In Web3, the oracle problem is explicit: blockchain guarantees data immutability once recorded, but cannot guarantee that recorded data accurately reflects physical reality. A smart contract—a program that runs on the blockchain—can verify that a carbon credit was issued, but not that the forest it represents actually exists. Each technology choice carries different costs, trust assumptions, update frequencies, and vulnerability to manipulation. Chapter 3 will dive deeper into these oracle design trade-offs: for now, it's enough to know what options exist. As shown in Figure 2.1, environmental observational technologies fall into four broad categories, from macro to molecular:

- **Remote Sensing and Geographic Information Systems (GIS)**: Remote sensing consists of satellite imagery, aerial photography, and other long-range sensing technology that gather data over large areas. GIS is the corresponding framework for gathering, managing, and analyzing spatial and geographic data.
- **Sensors and Internet of Things (IoT)**: Networks of physical devices equipped with sensors that collect and exchange data in real-time.
- **Boots on the Ground**: Direct, on-site human observation and data collection involving physical presence and manual effort.
- **Laboratory-Based**: Collected environmental samples analyzed in a lab setting using various scientific methods and instruments.

For green asset production, the incorporation of multiscale approaches that leverage the power of observational data from multiple tools and techniques simultaneously is becoming more common. Such multiscale studies recognize the limitations of single-scale observations for explaining complex ecological phenomena. For example, monitoring plots over varied temporal intervals—be it daily, seasonally, annually, or over decades—yields stronger insights into the dominant processes at each time scale (Sagarin and Pauchard 2010).

Selecting the right measurement approach involves weighing cost, scalability, and credibility. Remote sensing offers broad coverage at low marginal cost but may lack the granularity required for compliance-grade verification. IoT sensors provide continuous, real-time data streams well-suited to smart contract integration, but require infrastructure investment and maintenance. Field surveys deliver

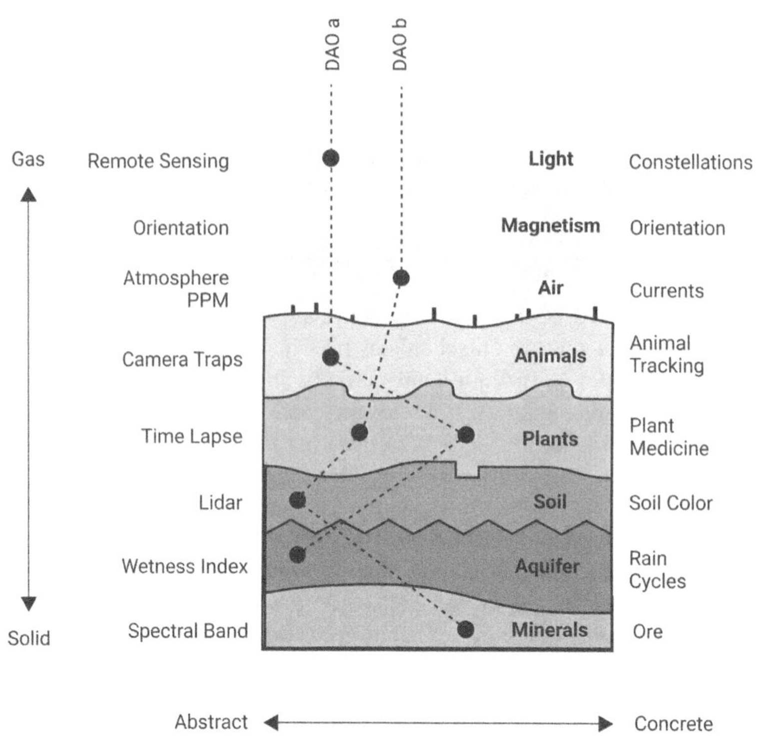

FIGURE 2.1 Environmental observation tools and methods, ranging from abstract to concrete; from gaseous to solid states. The data they collect and the insights they produce inform stakeholders and drive decisions within global sustainability frameworks such as the Global Stocktake, offering both ethical and economic valuations of Earth's natural capital.

Source: **Wade Smith (2023).**

high-fidelity ground truth essential for calibrating other methods, while laboratory analysis provides the molecular-level precision needed for emerging biodiversity and eDNA-based assets. Most green asset projects will ultimately combine multiple approaches—the key is matching measurement strategy to verification requirements and target market.

REMOTE SENSING AND GIS

Remote sensing encompasses the utilization of satellite imagery, aerial photographs, and light detection and ranging (LiDAR) technologies to assess land use and ecosystem responses, such as forest cover and crop productivity. These technologies include:

Satellites: Satellites continuously collect data about the Earth's surface through their equipped sensors. Data collected includes land cover, vegetation health, ocean color, and surface temperatures. Different satellites have different capabilities, such as high-resolution imagery or specific spectral bands for environmental monitoring.

Limitations: Managing a fleet of satellites is a complex operational problem. Balancing competing requests from various users under practical and physical constraints compounds this challenge (Cordeau and Laporte 2005). Furthermore, the optimization of the selection and scheduling of satellite observations by competing users must be taken into consideration (Tangpattanakul, Jozefowiez, and Lopez 2015).

Aerial Photography and Drones (UAVs): UAVs collect high-resolution images and data over specific areas. Drones are particularly useful for hard-to-reach or dangerous locations and can be equipped with sensors to collect environmental data that many satellites cannot.

Limitations: The absence of accurate positional data and the influence of atmospheric disturbances such as turbulence and wind can impact the stability and precision of UAVs during data collection (Miller and Miller 2015). AI integrations, particularly deep learning algorithms, are one key strategy for improving UAV performance (Santos et al. 2022).

Radar (including Synthetic Aperture Radar, or SAR): Provides data on surface characteristics, even in cloudy or night-time conditions. Useful for mapping land surfaces, monitoring deforestation, and detecting changes in the Earth's surface.

Limitations: One significant challenge is distinguishing the radar signal of the target from the ground backscatter (Brunzell 1999). Radio frequency interference in SAR observations can severely impair image quality (Meyer, Nicoll, and Doulgeris 2013).

LiDAR: Emits laser pulses to measure distances to the Earth's surface, creating high-resolution maps of land topography, vegetation structure, and even ocean depths. LiDAR technologies can notably be used to measure forest carbon (see Figure 2.2).

Limitations: LiDAR struggles with the attenuation of the laser signal as it travels through the atmosphere (Collis 1970). LiDAR backscattered signals suffer from interference by various noise sources (Sivakumar 2007).

GIS, unlike remote sensing, refers to comprehensive data systems that capture, store, analyze, and present spatiotemporal data. GIS tools cover large geographical areas while providing insights into their physical, biophysical, and chemical characteristics. GIS software is commonly used for creating land use and land cover maps. The process involves analyzing satellite imagery and aerial photographs within GIS platforms to classify land cover types—essential for urban planning, environmental conservation, and tracking land use change. GIS also plays a key role in wildlife conservation efforts.

Example GIS software includes ArcGIS and QGIS. ArcGIS offers a comprehensive suite of tools for mapping and spatial analysis (ArcGIS 2024). Quantum GIS is a free and open-source software supporting various vector, raster, and database formats (QGIS 2025). GIS and its critical role as an environmental data technology are discussed at length in Chapter 3.

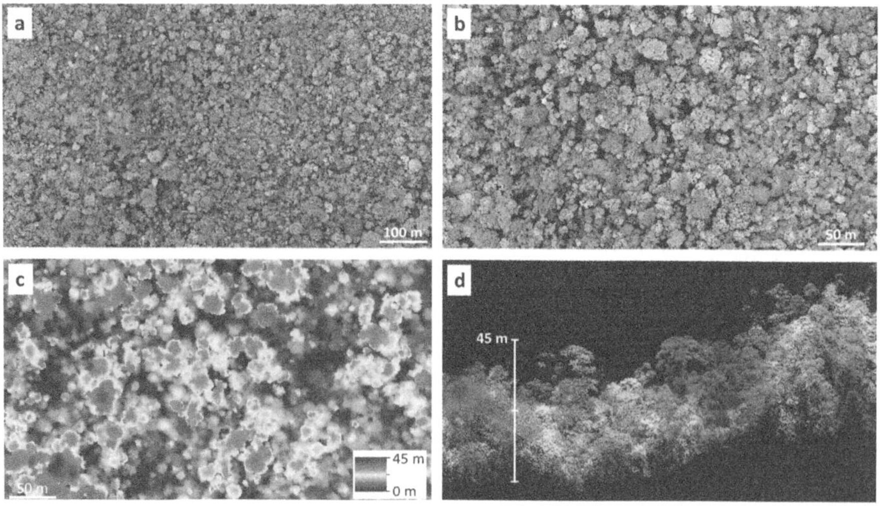

FIGURE 2.2 Using LiDAR to identify High Carbon Stock forest at the concession level: (a) Aerial overview of a forested area provides a broad view of the canopy. (b) Targeted aerial close-up of the selected area within the red outline. (c) LiDAR-derived canopy height model with colors transitioning from cool (low) to warm (high elevation). (d) 3D LiDAR visualization showing detailed topography and tree structure, with height indicated by color gradation.

***Source*: Raison et al. (2015). Licensed under Creative Commons. https://www.researchgate.net/figure/How-LiDAR-can-be-used-to-identify-High-Carbon-Stock-forest-at-the-concession-level_fig3_323622030**

SENSORS AND IOT

Sensors are devices or instruments that detect and measure physical properties or changes in the environment and convert them into comprehensible signals. Sensors capable of gathering real-time environmental data are advancing monitoring and data collection practices (Gao and Zhang 2021). *IoT sensors* are sensors designed for integration into IoT ecosystems. One analysis of 640 IoT projects found them to be generally aligned with the realization of the UN Sustainable Development Goals (SDGs) (Abdul Salam 2020). Table 2.2 provides an overview of different sensor types available for environmental data collection.

The proliferation of sensors coupled with other observational technologies has driven recent innovation across environmental and ecological domains:

- **Agriculture**: Precision agriculture uses sensors for soil moisture, nutrient levels, and crop health monitoring (Rehman et al. 2022).
- **Air Quality Monitoring**: Networks of sensors deployed across urban and industrial areas provide real-time data on pollutants (Zhang and Srinivasan 2020).
- **Water Quality and Management**: Sensors track parameters like pH, turbidity, and contaminants in water bodies (Park, Kim, and Lee 2020).

- **Wildlife Conservation**: Sensors and tracking technologies are being used to monitor the movements and health of wildlife (Dulari et al. 2020).

Many pilot studies are being deployed that combine Web3 with sensors, exploring how decentralized infrastructure can address persistent challenges in environmental monitoring, such as data provenance, stakeholder coordination, and incentive alignment. For example, the BLCK IOT project monitored 20 lions in Kenya using Helium, a decentralized wireless IoT network incentivized by the Helium Network Token. Beyond enabling real-time tracking of endangered species, the project demonstrated how blockchain-based sensor networks can establish tamper-evident data trails—critical for building trust between conservationists, researchers, local communities, and potential funders of conservation assets. The collected wildlife data feeds directly into habitat protection decisions and anti-poaching efforts (BLCK 2022).

Glow demonstrates how sensor-based verification can scale to production-grade renewable infrastructure through what is known as a DePIN (Decentralized Physical

TABLE 2.2
A Bird's Eye View of the Different Types of Sensors Available Today for Environmental Data Collection

Type	Example	Description
Environmental Sensors	Air Quality Sensors	Measure pollutants like CO_2, NO_2, SO_2, or particulate matter.
	Water Quality Sensors	Monitor parameters such as pH, temperature, dissolved oxygen, turbidity.
	Soil Sensors	Measure soil moisture, temperature, pH, and nutrient content.
Weather and Climate Monitoring	Weather Stations	Provide data on atmospheric conditions including temperature, humidity, and wind.
IoT Networks	Connected Sensor Networks	Networks that communicate with each other and with a central system.
	Remote Data Transmission	Sensors with wireless communication (Wi-Fi, Bluetooth, LoRaWAN).
Specialized Monitoring	Acoustic Sensors	Monitor sound levels; important for noise pollution and wildlife monitoring.
	Optical Sensors	Monitor algal blooms or changes in forest canopy density.
Wearable and Portable	Personal Monitoring Devices	Collect data on exposure to environmental factors like air quality.
Data Loggers	Data Loggers	Record environmental data over time for wildlife studies or microclimates.
	Telemetry	Automatic transmission of data from remote sensors for analysis.

Source: Table by the authors.

Infrastructure Network) model. Solar farms in the Glow network are verified through multiple layers: IoT sensors measuring actual electricity production, satellite imagery confirming panel installation, AI analysis, and physical audits—all published onchain. Their multi-layer verification approach—where no single data source is trusted and consensus emerges from agreement across satellites, sensors, AI models, and human validators—represents an emerging architecture for addressing the oracle problem (Glow 2024).

BOOTS ON THE GROUND

Boots-on-the-ground refers to traditional, hands-on methods of gathering environmental data directly from the field—on-site observations, measurements, and sample collection by researchers or field workers. Despite technological advances, boots-on-the-ground methods remain vital for ground-truthing remote data and capturing localized insights.

FIELD SURVEYS

Many environmental asset production processes have inherited these manual methods, having been designed before satellite, remote sensing, and blockchain technologies were widely available (Rocky Mountain Institute and Climate Collective 2023). Traditional environmental asset producers still rely mostly on field surveys (see Table 2.3), though these methods are slowly being phased out for more performant, lower-cost options.

TABLE 2.3
A Bird's Eye View of the Different Types of Field Surveys Historically Used for Environmental Data Collection

Type	Example	Definition
Biological Surveys	Biodiversity Assessments	Documenting the variety of species in a given area.
	Vegetation Surveys	Assessing plant communities: their distribution, density, and species composition.
	Wildlife Monitoring	Observing and recording wildlife, including bird counts and mammal tracking.
Physical Surveys	Topographic Surveys	Mapping the terrain of an area, including its contours and elevations.
	Hydrological Surveys	Studying water flow, water levels, and hydrological features.
Human-Environment Studies	Land Use Surveys	Documenting how land is being used and altered by human activities.
	Socioeconomic Surveys	Gathering information on how local communities interact with their environment.

Source: Table by the authors.

PARTICIPATORY APPROACH

The *participatory approach* involves recruiting community members, citizen scientists, and stakeholders to gather environmental data. As early as 2010, Sagarin and Pauchard underscored that observational methods in ecology were increasingly within reach of non-experts:

> Data can come from anywhere. Observational approaches to ecology allow far more openness in data assimilation than do controlled experiments. Data collected by independent parties (eg non-scientists, enthusiasts) can have unexpected implications when they are analyzed under larger conceptual frameworks.
>
> **Sagarin and Pauchard (2010)**

Participatory initiatives include:

- **Citizen Science Projects**: Individuals contribute by collecting data on species sightings, weather patterns, pollution levels through mobile apps. Example: eBird, developed by the Cornell Lab of Ornithology (Cornell Lab of Ornithology 2019).
- **Community-Based Monitoring**: Local communities observe and record environmental changes. Example: The Arctic Community-Based Monitoring Network (Arctic Council 2015).
- **Participatory Mapping**: Community members create maps of their local area, document land use, and take stock of natural resources. Example: Mapping for Rights by Rainforest Foundation UK (Rainforest Foundation UK n.d.).
- **Data Sharing Networks (DSN)**: Systems designed to facilitate information exchange across organizations. Example: Murmurations, a distributed DSN that enables regenerative economy projects to share standardized information about their activities—effectively creating discoverability infrastructure for impact initiatives that can interface with Web3 coordination tools (Murmurations 2024).

Web3 protocols are extending participatory approaches by adding token-based incentive layers that directly compensate data collectors. GainForest exemplifies what is called a 'Measure-to-Earn' model: local stewards use offline-capable smartphone apps, camera traps, and drones to collect forest data, which is validated by AI algorithms analyzing satellite imagery. When AI confirms tree growth or forest protection, smart contracts automatically release payments—eliminating intermediaries and ensuring funds reach communities directly. An XPRIZE Rainforest semifinalist, GainForest addresses both the cost problem of traditional MRV (which typically runs $20,000–30,000 for on-ground inspection) and the equity problem of who benefits from environmental data collection (GainForest 2023; Solana Foundation 2023).

LABORATORY-BASED

Laboratory-based methods involve analyzing environmental samples in a controlled lab setting to obtain detailed information about their composition and characteristics.

This approach includes chemical, microbial, biochemical, molecular, and genomic analyses using delicate instruments and specific techniques.

- **Chemical data collection techniques** are essential for assessing ecosystem health and identifying pollutants. By detecting contaminants like heavy metals and pesticides in soil, water, air, and biological samples, they help prevent costly health crises and environmental disasters.
- **Microorganisms** are unseen laborers driving critical ecosystem services—soil fertility, waste decomposition, oxygen production, and carbon dioxide removal. Understanding microbial functions can yield significant economic benefits—microbes play a pivotal role in bioremediation, and could potentially save billions in cleanup costs (Kour et al. 2022). In agriculture, harnessing beneficial microbes can reduce the need for chemical fertilizers, leading to cost savings and sustainable farming practices (Miransari 2011).
- **Molecular and genomic techniques** are crucial for studying biodiversity, detecting pollutants, monitoring ecosystem health, and understanding genetic makeup across environments. Certain Web3 projects, such as SimplexDNA, have experimented with incentivizing collection of molecular and genomic data, aiming to address the challenge of biodiversity observation at scale. Using environmental DNA (eDNA) analysis, scientists can non-invasively identify organisms and their spatiotemporal patterns (Thomsen and Willerslev 2015). For the XPRIZE Rainforest Competition, SimplexDNA surveyed 60 hectares of rainforest and produced over 12 million DNA sequences in just 72 hours (ETH BiodivX 2023), demonstrating the throughput possible when molecular observation is combined with distributed coordination.

ENVIRONMENTAL INDICES

An *environmental index* serves as a quantitative measure that transforms complex environmental data into a format that is more comprehensible and actionable, and is a downstream byproduct of raw data observed by the technologies surveyed above. Environmental indices distill measurements into quantifiable metrics, but nonetheless represent a compression of the original data. An air quality index collapses dozens of pollutant measurements into a single number; a biodiversity index reduces the complexity of species interactions to a scalar value. This is important for practitioners to take into account, as the choice of index determines which ecological signals pass through to financial logic and which are filtered out. Some examples of well-known indices:

- **Biodiversity Indices** provide insights into the diversity within ecosystems (e.g., Shannon Diversity Index, Simpson's Diversity Index).
- **Water Quality Indices** amalgamate various parameters to present an overarching view of water health (e.g., WQI).
- **Air Quality Indices** convey the quality of air and its implications for human health (e.g., AQI).

- **Soil Quality Indices** evaluate aspects such as soil fertility and contamination levels.
- **Ecological Footprint Indices** measure human demand on natural resources against the Earth's capacity to regenerate them.

For environmental finance and green asset production, indices play a critical role bridging the gap between raw environmental data and the financial instruments built upon them. They are key building blocks or *primitives* for creating conditional or programmable green assets; from them, many types of green assets can be structured and traded, translating environmental values into economic terms. In a Web3 context, these indices themselves become oracle inputs—the data feeds that trigger smart contract execution. Their compression helps create the interface that makes environmental data programmable: a biodiversity index crossing a threshold might release conservation payments; a water quality index could adjust the terms of a parametric insurance contract. The precision and reliability of the underlying index thus directly determines the viability of the financial instrument built upon it.

EXISTING NATURE ACCOUNTING FRAMEWORKS

Efforts to valuate nature have produced frameworks and taxonomies that classify and quantify nature in economic terms, typically expressed in fiat currencies such as USD. As Wade Smith observes, "ecological state is a form of knowing the wellbeing of the living world which is legible and thus actionable within anthropogenic systems like law, economy, policy, information technology" (Wade Smith 2023). These frameworks serve essential accounting purposes, enabling structured estimation of cost relationships between economic and environmental activities. For green asset design, these frameworks represent both constraints and opportunities: they define what measurement approaches will be accepted as credible, but they also provide templates for structuring novel assets and asset classes. Understanding which frameworks govern a target market is essential for practitioners—a carbon credit destined for compliance markets must meet SEEA-aligned measurement standards, while voluntary markets may accept alternative frameworks.

PUBLIC FRAMEWORKS

These frameworks are developed by public institutions for governmental and public application. Similar to the relationship between voluntary carbon markets and compliance markets, many frameworks that begin in academic or private settings are later adopted by public institutions for application. The most established public framework is the UN's System of Environmental-Economic Accounting (SEEA), illustrated in Figure 2.3, which operates through a baseline unit of measurement, employing space and time as quantifiable dimensions for environmental data (United Nations 2025). Table 2.4 summarizes different types of nature accounting frameworks used by governments.

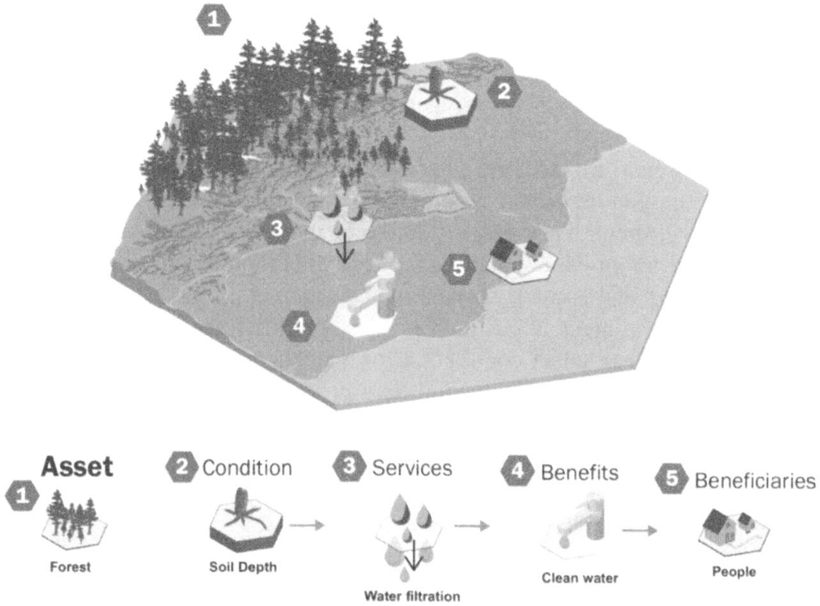

FIGURE 2.3 The UN SEEA framework attempts to comprehensively integrate economic and environmental data to support policy analysis.

***Source*: United Nations (2025).**

OTHER FRAMEWORKS

Other Nature Accounting Frameworks consist of non-public approaches to systematically incorporate the value of nature and ecosystem services into accounting systems (see Table 2.5, for example, indicators). The development of these frameworks generally follows several key steps:

1. **Identification of Ecosystem Services**: This involves identifying the various services provided by nature, such as provisioning services (food and water), regulating services (air quality and climate regulation), supporting services (nutrient cycling and soil formation), and cultural services (recreational and spiritual benefits).
2. **Data Collection and Ecological Assessment**: Academics collect, aggregate, and analyze environmental and ecological data to understand the present condition and evolving trends of natural resources.
3. **Valuation of Ecosystem Services**: This step assigns monetary values to ecosystem services, typically using non-market valuation techniques such as contingent valuation (CVM) or choice modeling (CM) (Koetse, Brouwer, and van Beukering 2015). These techniques are highly generalizable and applicable across a broad range of ecosystem services. CVM allows for the estimation of both *use* and *nonuse* ecosystem value. It involves asking individuals how much they would be willing to pay for specific environmental changes

TABLE 2.4
Different Types of Nature Accounting Frameworks Presently Used by Governments to Understand the Environment in Economic Terms

Type	Example	Public Institutional Adoption	Key Focus
Environmental Economics Accounting	SEEA provides a comprehensive framework for integrating economic and environmental data.	UN	Integration of economic and environmental data for holistic policy analysis.
Physical Accounting	The UN Framework for the Development of Environmental-Economic Accounts.	UN	Quantification of environmental assets in physical terms (e.g., water volume, forest area).
Monetary Environmental Accounting	The EU's Environmental Accounting and Material Flow Accounting framework.	EU	Valuation of environmental resources in monetary terms to inform economic policies.
Ecological Footprint Accounting	National governments use the Ecological Footprint as a tool.	Switzerland, Japan, Germany, UK, others	Sustainability assessment by measuring demand on Earth's ecosystems.
Biodiversity Accounting	The CBD encourages countries to develop national biodiversity accounting frameworks.	190 of 196 CBD parties	Biodiversity measurement and impact on conservation efforts.
Integrated Environmental and Economic Accounting	The Green National Accounting System integrates environmental considerations.	US, China, Norway, Australia, Canada, Indonesia, UK	Comprehensive accounting merging traditional economic indicators with environmental costs.
Climate Accounting	The IPCC provides guidelines for national greenhouse gas inventories.	190+ countries party to UNFCCC	Emissions tracking for climate policy.

Source: Table by the authors.

or improvements and building a counterfactual value assessment from their responses. It's useful for assigning a value to ecosystem services not currently traded in markets, such as biodiversity conservation or recreational benefits. Similarly, CM has gained prominence as it offers an alternative to CVM by presenting respondents with choices between different scenarios involving changes in ecosystem services and their associated costs (Guimarães et al. 2014).

4. **Integration with Economic and Financial Systems**: The assigned values are integrated into existing economic and financial frameworks.
5. **Development of Indicators and Reporting Standards**: Academics develop indicators and standards to report on environmental contributions to the economy.
6. **Policy and Management Implications**: These frameworks ultimately inform policy-making and business strategies.

TABLE 2.5
This Table Presents Example Indicators Used for Assessing the Value of Regulating and Supporting Ecosystem Services Provided by Coastal Environments

Ecosystem Service	Limited Function	Strong Function
Sediment Retention	Little or no natural vegetation stabilizing shoreline zones	Dense vegetation widespread along shoreline, enhancing sediment anchoring
Hydrological Regulation	Wetlands and mangrove habitats are missing	Continuous wetlands/mangrove belts supporting consistent water flow regulation
Foreshore Protection	Coral reefs or sandstone formations absent	Extensive reef systems acting as robust coastal shields
Pollutant Breakdown	Lack of natural filtration ecosystems	Well-established natural filters delivering effective pollutant assimilation
Habitat Provision	Mangrove forests, resting zones, and coastal rainforests are absent	Multiple, overlapping transitional habitats fostering ecosystem resilience

Source: Table by the authors.
Note: Ecosystem services are generally classified according to ranges that measure functionality, such as the range of limited to strong function.

Example non-public frameworks include *Accounting for Nature*®, which measures, certifies, and communicates changes in the condition of environmental assets such as native vegetation, soils, fauna, freshwater, and marine ecosystems. It is recognized for its scientific credibility and is used to inform better investment, policy, and management decisions in natural capital (Accounting for Nature 2025). Whitten et al. propose a practical, intervention-biased matrix-based approach that identifies low hanging fruits to capitalize on readily accessible opportunities for enhancing ecosystem services, estimating the potential economic benefits resulting from their increased provision (Whitten et al. 2003). One last well-known example is the Ecosystem Services Valuation (ESV): a method for quantifying and valuing ecosystem services. The key components of ESV are the identification of services by determining which ecosystem services are provided by a particular natural area; the quantification by measuring the extent or quantity of these services, and finally the valuation by assigning economic value to these services, either through market-based or non-market-based methods (Costanza, d'Arge, and de Groot 1997).

Finally, the authors note the usefulness of spatial frameworks for ecosystem service valuation, as they help capture the service flows from sources to beneficiaries, incorporating geographical aspects of both supply and demand. These frameworks help visualize the complex spatial interactions between ecosystems and economic activities, highlighting how changes in one can affect the other over different spatial scales. By providing a spatially explicit assessment of ecosystem services, these frameworks can inform more targeted and effective resource management decisions. They facilitate understanding of the supply of ecosystem services in relation to the spatial distribution of demand, and help identify critical areas for conservation or restoration by highlighting regions where ecosystem services are most needed or most at risk.

Spatial frameworks are of particular interest for green asset design because ecosystem services rarely align with property boundaries or administrative units. A forest upstream provides flood control and water filtration to communities downstream; a wetland on one parcel delivers nutrient cycling benefits across an entire watershed. Spatial frameworks help identify these mismatches—cases where the providers of ecosystem services are not the same as the beneficiaries, creating both challenges and opportunities for payment mechanisms. For Web3 applications, spatial considerations directly affect smart contract design: a parametric insurance product for flood risk must define its geographic scope; a biodiversity credit must specify the spatial unit being protected; a water quality token must establish which monitoring points constitute valid oracle inputs. The six transfer types shown in Figure 2.4 and detailed in Table 2.6 illustrate the range of spatial relationships that frameworks must accommodate.

Finally, *temporal frameworks* address *when* ecosystem services are delivered—a critical consideration often overlooked. A 2019 analysis found that only 2% of ecosystem services research accounts for temporal changes (Rau et al. 2020). For Web3 applications, temporal dynamics directly affect oracle design: a carbon sequestration smart contract must specify measurement intervals; a biodiversity credit might require seasonal verification windows; parametric insurance triggers must define observation periods. The choice of temporal resolution—daily, seasonal, annual—determines both verification costs and claim credibility. Just as spatial frameworks

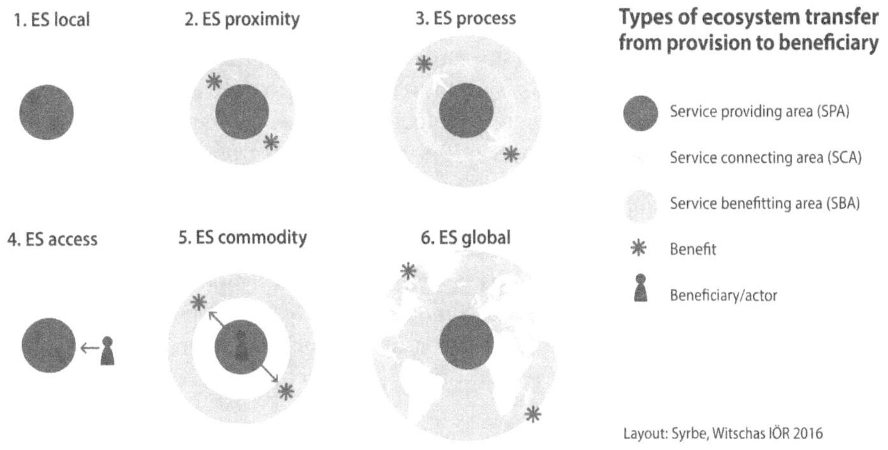

FIGURE 2.4 This spatial framework visualizes the six types of ecosystem service transfers from provision to beneficiary, highlighting different spatial relationships.

***Source*: Syrbe and Grunewald (2017). Licensed under Creative Commons.**

TABLE 2.6
Types of Ecosystem Service Transfers

Type of ES Transfer	Definition (Syrbe and Grunewald 2017)	Example
ES local	Ecosystem services that provide benefits mainly at the area where they are generated.	Shade provided by a tree
ES proximity	Benefit is not derived at the same point as its origin; therefore, the distance is crucial.	Pollination services in agricultural landscapes
ES process	Arises where movements reach the beneficiary by natural processes at distance.	Water filtration provided by a wetland upstream
ES access	A beneficiary can get to an ecosystem and enjoy the ES there if they can reach it.	Urban recreation in public parks
ES commodity	Goods (timber, meat, fruit, etc.) transported to a final consumer with shared benefits.	Trade of timber
ES global	Relevant when the benefit of a service is global and cannot be restricted spatially.	Carbon stored by a seagrass meadow

Source: Adapted from Syrbe and Grunewald (2017).

reveal mismatches between service providers and beneficiaries, temporal frameworks expose mismatches between when services are generated and when they are measured or monetized.

CONCLUSION

The technologies, frameworks, and methodological considerations surveyed in this chapter constitute the measurement infrastructure upon which all green assets ultimately rest. The core insight is that blockchain-based environmental finance does not escape the constraints of physical measurement—it inherits them. The credibility of a tokenized carbon credit, biodiversity unit, or water quality asset depends entirely on the robustness of the observation systems feeding data to the chain. Decentralized protocols like GainForest, Open Forest Protocol, and Glow demonstrate that moving verification onchain does not eliminate the need for robust physical measurement infrastructure—it changes who performs and verifies those measurements, and how the incentives are aligned. As subsequent chapters will demonstrate, the protocols and smart contracts governing green assets must be designed with explicit awareness of measurement uncertainty, spatial variability, and temporal dynamics. The underlying material reality, in all its complexity, is not merely a technical detail to be abstracted away—it is the foundation upon which the entire environmental finance stack must be built.

REFERENCES

Accounting for Nature Ltd. 2025. "Framework." https://www.accountingfornature.org/framework. Accessed March 2026.

ArcGIS. 2024. "ArcGIS Online." https://www.arcgis.com/index.html. Accessed March 2026.

Arctic Council. 2015. "Community Based Monitoring." https://arctic-council.org/news/community-based-monitoring/. Accessed March 2026.
BLCK. 2022. "Lion Conflict Mitigation." https://blck-iot.com/project/kwt-conflict-mitigation. Accessed March 2026.
Brunzell, H. 1999. "Detection of Shallowly Buried Objects Using Impulse Radar." IEEE Transactions on Geoscience and Remote Sensing 37: 875–886.
Buma, B., D. R. Gordon, K. M. Kleisner, et al. 2024. "Expert Review of the Science Underlying Nature-Based Climate Solutions." Nature Climate Change 14, no. 4: 402–406.
Bumpus, Adam G. 2011. "The Matter of Carbon: Understanding the Materiality of TCO2e in Carbon Offsets." Antipode 43, no. 3: 612–638.
Capel, Celine. 2014. "Mindfulness, Indigenous Knowledge, Indigenous Innovations and Entrepreneurship." Journal of Research in Marketing and Entrepreneurship 16, no. 1: 63–83.
Collis, R.T.H. 1970. "Lidar." Applied Optics 9: 1782–1788.
Cordeau, J., and G. Laporte. 2005. "Maximizing the Value of an Earth Observation Satellite Orbit." Journal of the Operational Research Society 56: 962–968.
Cornell Lab of Ornithology. 2019. "eBird—Discover a New World of Birding." https://ebird.org/home. Accessed March 2026.
Costanza, Robert, Ralph d'Arge, Rudolf de Groot, et al. 1997. "The Value of the World's Ecosystem Services and Natural Capital." Nature 387: 253–260.
Dulari, Pawitar et al. 2020. "Internet of Things (IoT) to Study the Wild Life: A Review." Journal of Biological and Chemical Chronicles 6, no. 2: 11–15.
Dvarskas, Anthony. 2019. "Experimental Ecosystem Accounting for Coastal and Marine Areas." Marine Policy 100: 141–151.
ETH BiodivX. 2023. "Reportage XPrize 2023 with DNA of Music." YouTube, June 9, 2023. https://www.youtube.com/watch?v=0gJPW-Bgh6A. Accessed March 2026.
GainForest. 2023. "What is GainForest's Measure-To-Earn Technology?" Substack, December 6, 2023. https://gainforest.substack.com/p/what-is-gainforests-measure-to-earn. Accessed March 2026.
Gao, Feng, and Xiaoyang Zhang. 2021. "Mapping Crop Phenology in Near Real-Time Using Satellite Remote Sensing." Journal of Remote Sensing 2021: 8379391.
Gieseke, Timothy M. 2016. Shared Governance for Sustainable Working Landscapes. CRC Press.
Glow. 2024. "What is Glow?" Glow Blog, July 9, 2024. https://glow.org/blog/what-is-glow. Accessed March 2026.
Guimarães, Maria H. et al. 2014. "Using Choice Modeling to Estimate the Effects of Environmental Improvements: When the Purpose Modifies the Tool." Ecological Economics 108: 104–114.
Hamburg, Steven P. 2000. "Simple Rules for Measuring Changes in Ecosystem Carbon in Forestry-Offset Projects." Mitigation and Adaptation Strategies for Global Change 5, no. 1: 25–37.
Koetse, Mark J., Roy Brouwer, and Pieter J. H. van Beukering. 2015. "Economic Valuation Methods for Ecosystem Services." In Ecosystem Services: From Concept to Practice. Cambridge University Press.
Kour, Divjot et al. 2022. "Microbe-Mediated Bioremediation: Current Research and Future Challenges." Journal of Applied Biology and Biotechnology 10, no. Suppl. 2: 6–24.
Lücking, Robert et al. 2014. "One Hundred and Seventy-Five New Species of Graphidaceae." Phytotaxa 189, no. 1: 7–38.
Meyer, F., J. Nicoll, and A. Doulgeris. 2013. "Correction and Characterization of Radio Frequency Interference Signatures in L-Band SAR Data." IEEE Transactions on Geoscience and Remote Sensing 51, no. 10: 4961–4972.

Miller, A., and B. Miller. 2015. "Stochastic Control of Light UAV at Landing with the Aid of Bearing-Only Observations." Proceedings of SPIE 9875: 98750Y.

Miransari, Mohammad. 2011. "Soil Microbes and Plant Fertilization." Applied Microbiology and Biotechnology 92, no. 5: 875–885.

Murmurations. 2024. "The Murmurations Protocol." https://murmurations.network/. Accessed March 2026.

Park, Jungsu, Keug T. Kim, and Woo H. Lee. 2020. "Recent Advances in Information and Communications Technology (ICT) and Sensor Technology for Monitoring Water Quality." Water 12, no. 2: 510.

Prasad, M. N. V. 2021. Handbook of Ecological and Ecosystem Engineering. Wiley.

Pyšek, Petr, Vojtěch Jarošík, Philip E. Hulme, et al. 2008. "Geographical and Taxonomic Biases in Invasion Ecology." Trends in Ecology and Evolution 23, no. 5: 237–244.

QGIS. 2025. "Spatial without Compromise." https://qgis.org/. Accessed March 2026.

Rainforest Foundation UK. n.d. "Mapping for Rights." https://www.rainforestfoundationuk.org/our-projects/mapping-for-rights/. Accessed March 2026.

Raison, J. et al. 2015. The High Carbon Stock Science Study: Independent Report from the Technical Committee, Part 3: Gabon Case Study. High Carbon Stock Science Study.

Rau, Anna-Lena et al. 2020. "Temporal Patterns in Ecosystem Services Research." AMBIO 49: 1377–1393.

Rehman, Amjad et al. 2022. "A Revisit of Internet of Things Technologies for Monitoring and Control Strategies in Smart Agriculture." Agronomy 12, no. 1: 127.

Ripple, William J. et al. 2023. "The 2023 State of the Climate Report: Entering Uncharted Territory." BioScience 73, no. 12: 841–850.

Rocky Mountain Institute. 2023. The Applied Innovation Roadmap for Carbon Dioxide Removal. RMI.

Rocky Mountain Institute and Climate Collective. 2023. Voluntary Carbon Market Landscape Guide. RMI and Climate Collective.

Sagarin, Raphael, and Aníbal Pauchard. 2010. "Observational Approaches in Ecology Open New Ground in a Changing World." Frontiers in Ecology and the Environment 8, no. 7: 379–386.

Salam, Abdul. 2020. Internet of Things for Sustainable Community Development. Springer.

Santos, R. et al. 2022. "Applying Deep Neural Networks to Improve UAV Navigation in Satellite-less Environments." In 2022 International Young Engineers Forum (YEF-ECE), pp. 63–68. IEEE.

Sivakumar, V. 2007. "De-noising LiDAR Signal Using Wavelet Technique." In SPIE Proceedings, edited by U. N. Singh, vol. 6681, p. 66810O. SPIE. https://doi.org/10.1117/12.739450. Accessed March 2026.

Solana Foundation. 2023. "Case Study: GainForest Brings Transparency to Climate Preservation Efforts Using Blockchain Technology." https://solana.com/news/case-study-gainforest. Accessed March 2026.

Syrbe, Ralf-Uwe, and Karsten Grunewald. 2017. "Ecosystem Service Supply and Demand—The Challenge to Balance Spatial Mismatches." IJBS 13, no. 2: 148–161.

Tangpattanakul, P., N. Jozefowiez, and P. Lopez. 2015. "A Multi-Objective Local Search Heuristic for Scheduling Earth Observations Taken by an Agile Satellite." European Journal of Operational Research 245, no. 2: 542–554.

Thomsen, Philip F., and Eske Willerslev. 2015. "Environmental DNA—An Emerging Tool in Conservation for Monitoring Past and Present Biodiversity." Biological Conservation 183: 4–18.

Truitt, Amy M. et al. 2015. "What Is Novel About Novel Ecosystems." Environmental Management 55, no. 6: 1217–1226.

United Nations. 2025. "System of Environmental-Economic Accounting (SEEA)." seea.un.org/Introduction-to-Ecosystem-Accounting. Accessed March 2026.

Wade Smith, Austin. 2023. "Commons Sense—The Social Life of Ecological ↔ Digital Linkages." Mirror.xyz, June 28, 2023. https://paragraph.com/@austinwadesmith/commons-sense-the-social-life-of-ecological-digital-linkages. Accessed March 2026.

Whitten, Stuart, James Salzman, Dave Shelton, and Wendy Proctor. 2003. "Markets for Ecosystem Services: Applying the Concepts." CSIRO, February 2003.

Zhang, He, and Ravi Srinivasan. 2020. "A Systematic Review of Air Quality Sensors, Guidelines, and Measurement Studies for Indoor Air Quality Management." Sustainability 12, no. 21: 9045.

3 Data Layer
Blockchain's Digital Twin

Data is essential for measuring the success of ecosystem conservation and restoration efforts, or any applied sustainability initiative. Data ultimately legitimizes all sustainability strategies that use green assets, as well as the institutions that originate them. As infrastructure, the Data Layer converts analog complexities into actionable digital intelligence for evidence-based interventions. It is not merely a repository of information—a collection of facts, numbers, symbols that describe objects, their characteristics and conditions (Stankov 2020). On the contrary, it is a dynamic lattice of interacting components that store, sort, compute, visualize, and forecast present and future ecological states of the underlying material reality.

This chapter details these components and their roles in producing green assets. It starts by detailing green data use cases, or the problems the Data Layer is trying to address. Following this, the chapter presents a detailed *data pipeline* that moves progressively through data storage, management, computation, visualization, and prediction to detail the components that support these use cases. The chapter closes with a practitioner-focused decision framework and two case studies illustrating how leading projects have navigated infrastructure choices. For sustainability practitioners evaluating Web3 infrastructure, this chapter provides both conceptual foundations and practical guidance—mapping the green *data pipeline* while addressing a core question: how do I choose the right data architecture for my green asset project?

For practitioner reference, Appendix A at the end of this chapter (Table 3A.1) provides a glossary of data terminologies used throughout.

THE BIG PICTURE: WHAT IS ENVIRONMENTAL DATA USED FOR?

The central argument of this book posits that environmental data substantiates the production of green assets (Figure 3.1), that is, assets whose financial abstraction can improve the ecological state of the underlying material reality. Ultimately, to understand what types of green assets will be created, one must inquire into the diverse applications for which environmental data is employed. We identify three high-level categories of use cases, whose boundaries are fuzzy and contingent on specific use cases:

1. **Natural Asset and Ecosystem Management:** These use cases range from biodiversity conservation (management of ecosystem services) to agro-commodity production (management of ecosystem assets). Precision agriculture, for instance, is an agricultural management approach that systematically gathers, processes, and analyzes spatiotemporal and individual

DOI: 10.1201/9781003748472-3

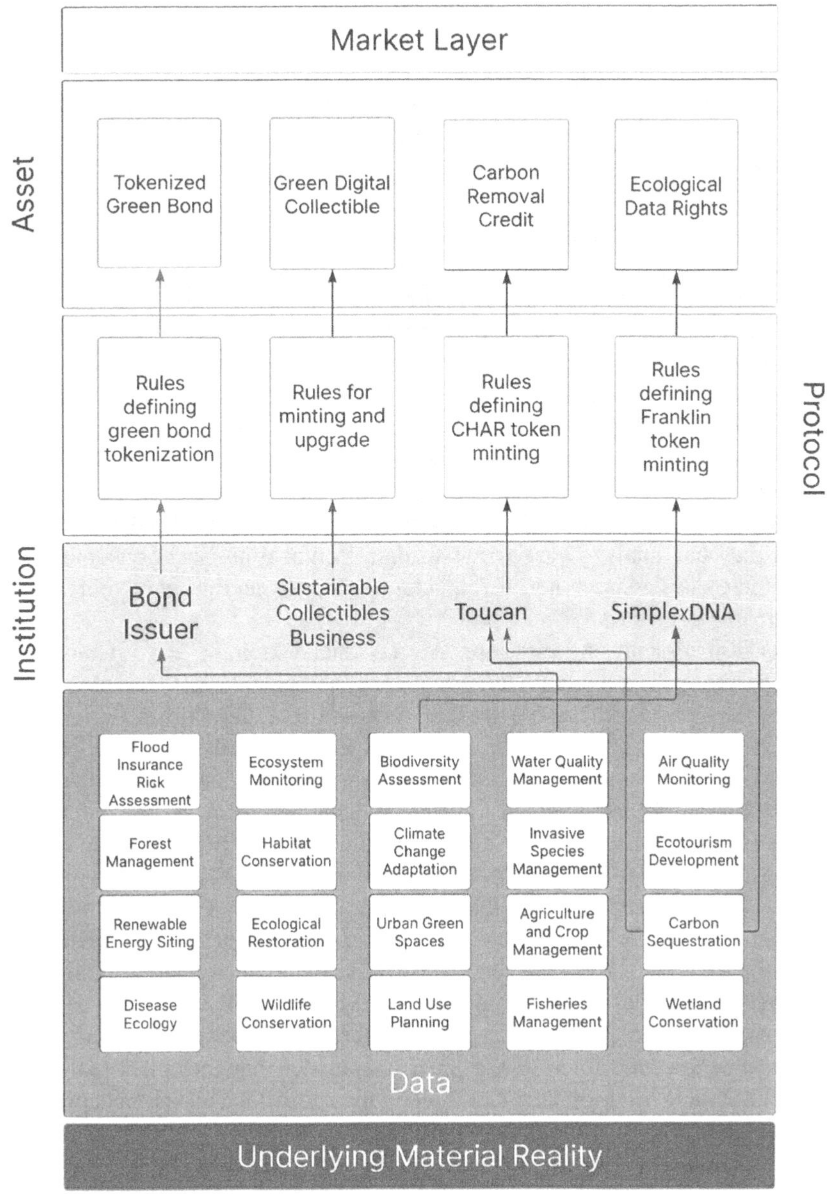

FIGURE 3.1 Four green crypto-asset production pathways showing how environmental data flows from the underlying material reality through institutions and protocols to produce tokenized assets including green bonds, digital collectibles, carbon removal credits, and ecological data rights.

***Source*: Diagram by the authors.**

practitioners' data to enhance natural asset use efficiency, productivity, quality, and sustainability (Mercy Corps Ventures 2024). Like other use cases in this category, this data is refined to produce tooling known as Environmental Decision Support Systems (DSS): computerized, amalgamated models that help select optimal management solutions and actionable strategies from competing economic, social, and environmental viewpoints (Salam 2019).

2. **Cyberphysical Systems:** By using environmental data, all types of cyberphysical infrastructures—such as supply chains or renewable energy systems—can be configured for greater energy and resource efficiency and fewer negative externalities. Green logistics ranges from optimizing transportation routes to measuring and utilizing sustainable materials for production, packaging, and transport. It also encompasses the integration of renewable energy sources in transportation and storage facilities. For these systems, blockchain as an immutable ledger technology enhances transparency and traceability for verifiable sustainability metrics (Takyar 2022). DSS also play a crucial operational role here, as they can analyze vast arrays of data in real-time (fuel consumption, vehicle emissions, material impacts) to identify and propose more sustainable equilibria.
3. **Territorial-scale Adaptation:** At the intersection of ecosystems and cyberphysical systems is territorial and bioregional-scale planning that encompasses both. In the book *Ecosystem and Territorial Resilience: A Geoprospective Approach*, Malé and Lagier detail the Métropole de Lyon's initiative to provide an interactive planning platform—called the MUG—which integrated territorial challenges into computerized models (Malé and Lagier 2020). MUG illustrates what a fully integrated data pipeline looks like at territorial scale: storage of multi-domain datasets, management across institutional silos, computation of scenario models, visualization for stakeholder engagement, and prediction of territorial evolution. The tool analyzes interrelations and interactions within the territorial fabric, transcending compartmentalized planning approaches. Singapore's Virtual Singapore project offers a parallel example at national scale: a dynamic three-dimensional city model that integrates real-time environmental sensor data, urban planning parameters, and climate projections into a unified digital twin, enabling scenario testing for heat island mitigation, flood management, and green infrastructure siting (National Research Foundation Singapore 2022). These types of platforms become critical as bioregional-scale coordination and portfolio design becomes a critical issue for institutional place-based coalitions—to be discussed in Chapter 4.

These three categories become clearer at finer resolution. Within each are specific use cases: concrete applications that make it possible to trace the pathways through which green assets are produced—not in abstraction, but grounded in material and infrastructural data realities.

THE ENVIRONMENTAL DATA PIPELINE

The production of green assets depends on a fully functioning environmental data pipeline: a set of progressive data processes—storage, management, computation, visualization, and prediction—and their constituent technical components that transform environmental data into actionable insights. As surveyed in Chapter 2, data acquisition from the underlying material reality—through satellites, sensors, field surveys, and participatory observation—feeds this system and is its starting point.

Each stage builds on the outputs of the previous one: raw observations must first be stored reliably, then managed according to standards that enable interoperability. Following this, computational models can extract actionable intelligence through indicators and indexes. These outputs are visualized for stakeholders through dashboards and maps, and ultimately feed predictive models that inform forward-looking decisions.

The pipeline's steps are not strictly linear or synchronous: certain data processes may traverse multiple steps simultaneously, and throughout this chapter, discussion of one step may encompass aspects of another. Nonetheless, the pipeline provides the organizing framework for understanding how environmental data is progressively refined into the basis for green asset production. See Table 3.1 for a comparison of the traditional and Web3 approaches across the data pipeline.

Consider data gathered from fisheries management, such as fish populations, which is used to enforce catch limits. The same data supports the production of

TABLE 3.1
Compares Traditional and Web3 Approaches Across the Five Data Pipeline Stages Using Forest Management as an Example

	Pipeline Stage				
	Storage	**Management**	**Computation**	**Visualization**	**Prediction**
Traditional Forest Management	Forest data collected by stewards → Data Server	Environmental Management System to prevent data silos	Calculation of various forest health indexes	Forest data visualization front-end	Use of data to predict forest coverage dynamics over next ten years
Open Forest Protocol (Web3)	Forest data collected via Forester Mobile App → IPFS	Project Operator Dashboard	Combination of ground data collection and verification	Front-end interface: OFP Atlas	Potential to use data for predictive analytics

Note: The traditional row shows a conventional forest management system with centralized data servers and siloed databases. The Web3 row illustrates the Open Forest Protocol (OFP), a decentralized monitoring, reporting, and verification platform for forestry projects that uses IPFS for storage and provides transparent data access through public interfaces. OFP is discussed in detail as a case study later in this chapter.

Source: Table by the authors.

tokenized blue bonds that finance sustainable fishing practices. The bond parameters—interest rates, coupon schedules—can be coupled to the enforcement of catch limits, provided its underlying data pipeline is well designed. Wetland conservation data—critical for biodiversity measurement and flood mitigation—can be used to produce tokenized ecocredits that value ecological services and co-benefits beyond mere carbon sequestration. Cyberphysical systems, similarly, require integrated datasets to determine optimal locations for wind, solar, and geothermal projects. Tokenized power-purchasing agreements could use these datasets to underwrite long-term renewable energy contracts whose contents adjust based on dynamic performance tracking.

Today, there exist many high-level sociotechnical challenges in optimizing the data pipeline:

- **Environmental data storage and management is generally siloed and centralized.** A 2022 paper highlights that the current climate data accounting supporting the Global Stocktake (GST)—a global overview of where the world stands in terms of climate action—is fragmented and insufficient (Open Earth Foundation, Data-Driven EnviroLab, and Camda Secretariat 2022). The GST's data infrastructure requires enhanced interoperability and aggregation across data silos—isolated data repositories that are centrally stored and accessible to a limited number of institutionally accredited individuals within specific regulatory regimes. The agriculture sector has similar issues, dealing with the unsolved challenge of developing a library of crop types and management options that is sufficiently varied and detailed that a more open and interoperable data approach could remedy (Armstrong 2020).
- **Data pipeline infrastructure is expensive for institutions.** High costs associated with data collection, limited technological capabilities in certain regions, and the absence of coordinated efforts delimit data production. The EU's Copernicus Programme—the most comprehensive Earth observation system in operation—commands a budget of approximately €4.7 billion for the 2014–2021 period, illustrating the scale of investment required to maintain just one centralized environmental monitoring infrastructure (European Commission 2021). At the project level, ground-based monitoring stations can cost tens of thousands of dollars per year to operate, while satellite-derived datasets require substantial processing infrastructure that remains beyond the reach of most institutions in the Global South (World Bank 2023). The resulting cost asymmetry means that the regions most vulnerable to environmental degradation are often the least equipped to produce the data needed to effectively intervene.
- **Environmental data—the pipeline's foremost input—is scarce.** The lack of complete, accurate, and timely environmental data hampers the ability for institutions and researchers to make informed governance decisions that execute smart policies. The World Meteorological Organization found that only 26% of weather stations across Africa met WMO reporting requirements as of 2019 (WMO 2020). The Global Climate Observing System

has similarly identified persistent gaps in Essential Climate Variables—the core measurements needed to monitor climate change—particularly for ocean and terrestrial systems in developing regions. These observation gaps propagate through the entire data pipeline: without reliable inputs, downstream computation, visualization, and prediction become unreliable or impossible—much less green asset design and production.

The remainder of this chapter examines each pipeline stage—and how decentralized alternatives are beginning to address these constraints. For each stage, we survey across traditional centralized approaches and emerging Web3 technologies, revealing how blockchain-based solutions can mitigate the interoperability, cost, and scarcity challenges that currently limit environmental data systems.

DATA STORAGE AND MANAGEMENT

The first pipeline process, storage, refers to the recording and retaining of digital information using technology. This includes saving data to hard drives, solid-state drives, memory cards, magnetic tape, or cloud-based servers. The focus of storage is on how and where data is physically or digitally kept, ensuring that it remains reliable, complete, and available over time.

The choice of storage solution varies depending on factors like data volume, the need for quick access, and the importance of data security or reliability. For example, for internet-of-things (IoT) data, it is difficult to manage the vast amounts of recorded data and metadata, such as its attributed ownership, allowed usage, sharing, and sensitivity. These concerns are critical in the context of green asset production, where data integrity, accuracy, and reproducibility may play significant roles defining asset properties, such as supply. Consider an elastic (supply is adjustable) carbon credit token whose supply depends on verified sequestration metrics for a specific region. Its underlying sequestration proofs must be accurate and reproducible across databases to minimize its risk profile. Similarly, the territorial boundaries—spatial data—defining where sequestration occurs must remain consistent. Without this data integrity across systems, the credit cannot maintain its market value or credibility.

CENTRALIZED STORAGE

Major environmental programs—including the Copernicus Programme (Copernicus 2025a) and NASA's Earth Science Data System (Earth Science Data Systems, NASA 2019)—use centralized databases for storage purposes, keeping data in a single location such as a data center or cloud environment. These centralized systems enforce uniform data standards across contributors—essential when satellite imagery from different sensors must be comparable for atmospheric, marine, and terrestrial monitoring. This architectural centralization simplifies governance, security, and compliance—a meaningful advantage when managing sensitive environmental datasets subject to international agreements. And by consolidating data in one place, centralized architectures enable the integrated analytics and trend identification that underpin large-scale environmental assessments like the IPCC's reports.

These advantages, however, carry corresponding risks. Dependence on a single storage location creates a single point of failure: if a data center goes offline, all downstream applications—from real-time monitoring dashboards to asset verification systems—lose access. Rapidly increasing data volumes pose scalability challenges, as expansion requires costly infrastructure investment and strategic planning. Of particular concern to environmental practitioners is that centralized systems concentrate control over data access, creating political dependencies on the institutions that operate them.

The Copernicus Programme, the flagship Earth observation initiative of the EU, exemplifies centralized data storage for environmental data. Operating with the European Space Agency, the program uses Sentinel satellites and in situ IoT sensors to gather comprehensive environmental data. Copernicus systematically acquires data regarding atmospheric, marine, and terrestrial (eco)systems. Its data storage system is optimized to efficiently handle the vast influx of data from multiple sources, ensuring availability and integrity. It employs a combination of on-premises data centers and cloud-based solutions. This hybrid approach supports data scalability and resilience, accommodating an ever-increasing volume of environmental data. The centralized data repository is equipped with user-friendly interfaces and APIs, enabling data retrieval and promoting the widespread use of Copernicus data in environmental research and applications (Copernicus 2025b).

NASA's ESDS similarly maintains centralized repositories optimized for atmospheric research and earth science applications (NASA 2025). However, there are past examples of political administrations attempting to destroy critical climate data, highlighting the vulnerability of centralized systems to political interference. In 2017, scientists scrambled to archive EPA climate data amid fears of its removal during the U.S. administration transition (Calma 2021), and more recently, the National Security Archive has documented ongoing removal of climate information from government websites (Santarsiero 2025). These episodes underscore a structural risk of centralized data custody: political authority over storage infrastructure can translate into authority over the data itself.

CENTRALIZED MANAGEMENT

The second data pipeline process, management, encompasses the methods and systems used to store, organize, and access stored data. Environmental Data Management (EDM) is a critical discipline that deals with the handling of data related to various aspects of environmental research, standardization, regulation, and asset production. A data standard, for example, is a set of rules and guidelines that ensures consistency, interoperability, and accuracy when sharing and managing data across different platforms; management is used to produce and enforce these standards.

As noted earlier, regulatory agencies often accumulate extensive data concerning environmental issues within their jurisdictions, but these datasets are frequently collected in silos, being shared and analyzed in a manner that is disorganized and uncoordinated—if not entirely unilateral. Accordingly, EDM systems tend to utilize enterprise-style data management architectures—characterized by their centralization of storage, compute, governance, and security functions—through which politically centralized institutions search, sort, exchange, and analyze large volumes of environmental data. In most cases, these software systems are optimized toward regulatory and compliance purposes enforced by state institutions rather than any sort of overarching green or sustainable imperative.

Recognizing demand for accessible Copernicus data, the European Commission initiated in 2017 the Data and Information Access Services (DIAS). DIAS addresses the need for centralized data access control and processing capabilities, enabling utilization of Copernicus data for value-added services and app development. DIAS aims to offer a unified platform that integrates data access with robust processing infrastructure. DIAS helps avoid individual users or organizations storing and managing their own copies of this extensive dataset. In an endeavor to stimulate competition and foster creative solutions, the Commission has mandated a minimum of three distinct DIAS each operated by different consortia. This strategy ensures diversity and enshrines user choice, enhancing the overall effectiveness of the management service (Copernicus 2025c).

While DIAS demonstrates the advantages of centralized infrastructure for complex datasets, most institutions lack the state resources to build comparable management systems. In digital agriculture, for example, critical farm data—ranging from crop yields to soil conditions—has heightened concerns over data security, and by extension, data privacy. The involvement of actors across the agricultural value chain who use location data for analytics and business model development—such as vendors and digital agriculture service providers—intensifies the risk of security breaches and data vulnerability. To address these privacy concerns, traditional methods like obfuscation—which involves replacing exact location data with ambiguous information—pose their own set of technical challenges. They may in fact impede the functionality of geographic services due to reduced precision, and are far from foolproof against location deduction attacks. This highlights the market need for more advanced mechanisms to safeguard privacy and location information without compromising accuracy. Technical innovation is necessary to address these challenges, and Web3 is addressing these market gaps.

THE BLOCKCHAIN TURN

Decentralized data storage and management techniques encompass methodologies for dispersing digital information across their networks, rather than centrally consolidating it. By employing a constellation of independent nodes, these techniques mitigate security risks associated with single points of failure and enhance data resilience against censorship or systemic failure.

Cryptographic protocols and consensus mechanisms help ensure data integrity, privacy, and accessibility, providing clear direction for infrastructural innovation. Public blockchain ledgers, as core technical infrastructure, are cryptographic state machines distinguished by the fact that no single entity controls read-write operations, ensuring a technically decentralized approach to data storage and management. Generally, information stored on public blockchains is verifiable and auditable, providing enhanced transparency and trustworthiness; more importantly, it is immutable: once recorded, data cannot be altered retroactively. According to the

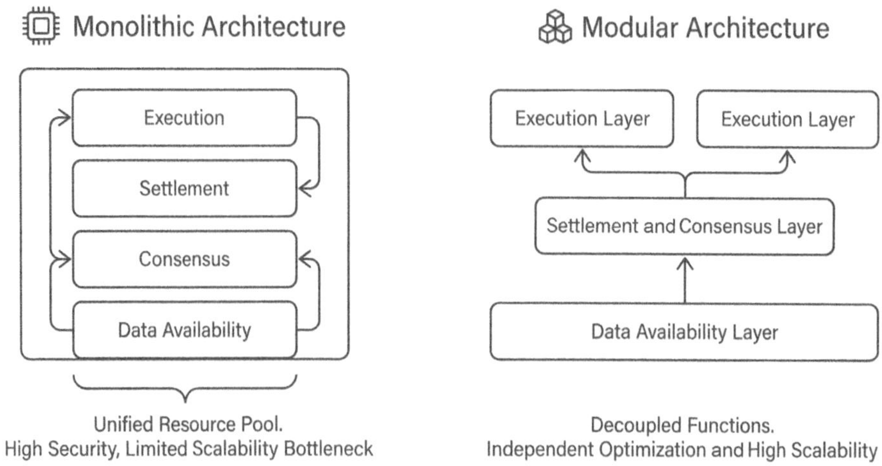

FIGURE 3.2 Blockchain architecture can be modular (separating functions across layers) or monolithic (integrating all functions in a single L1). Key layers include: Data Availability (ensures data accessibility), Consensus (achieves network agreement), Settlement (records transactions), and Execution (processes smart contracts).

***Source*: Diagram by the authors.**

Rocky Mountain Institute, environmental data packages backing green assets should be able to pass three critical tests: credibility (data is precise, reliable, and scientifically valid), efficiency (data is well-managed, usable, timely, and shareable), and governance (data has strong oversight, grievance resolution, and independent vetting) (Sahay et al. 2024). Ultimately blockchains satisfy these three requirements, with their layered architecture shown in Figure 3.2.

Public layer one (L1) blockchains refer to the basic cryptographic ledgers upon which additional layers and functionalities can be built—such as Ethereum. Unlike private blockchains—which are more like federated databases—public L1s are open-source and accessible to all users by default. In this sense, referring to private blockchain systems as "blockchains" is misleading, as they lack the verifiable guarantees only public blockchains provide. L1s are foundational primitives responsible for validating and recording transaction (tx) data and are integral to overall security and architectural decentralization. They tend to lack scalability (tx speed, or finality, as well as throughput) by design, instead concentrating on optimizing architectural decentralization and economic security.

With this in mind, L1s are not viable data storage solutions for large datasets. Their volume limitations are far too restrictive for the vast and complex datasets associated with environmental monitoring, which often include large-scale imagery, comprehensive datasets, and detailed IoT sensor readings, making onchain storage impractical. Nonetheless, the choice of L1 as a consensus mechanism is critical for institutions and projects focused on the production of high quality green assets, who must consider that:

- **The L1's type of consensus mechanism and the mechanism's corresponding environmental impact can undermine material claims.** Proof of stake (PoS) is favored for green crypto projects due to its dramatically lower energy consumption compared to proof-of-work. In PoS, the validation of txs and the creation of new blocks are generally based on the stake (or the amount of cryptocurrency held) by a validator, rather than computational power.
- **The L1 should balance the dichotomy between transparency and privacy, securing sensitive information while being rich in programmable expression.** This balance is essential for producing green assets, as any compromise in data security or privacy may detrimentally impact project environmental objectives. An example of a compromise between transparency and privacy could occur when a conservation project's location data for an endangered species is made transparent to demonstrate the project's impact, but inadvertently exposes at-risk populations to poachers. To achieve this balance, the blockchain must support smart contracts: programs that run on the blockchain. The vibrancy of an L1's development community and ecosystem—and the extent of its privacy-supporting culture—provides invaluable support and resources. Green projects aiming to leverage these network effects would benefit immensely by building in the Ethereum ecosystem—the largest privacy-focused public blockchain ecosystem today (Electric Capital Partners 2024).
- **Green assets tied to real-world assets face regulatory requirements from state authorities.** A blockchain that is secure, credibly neutral, and can provide 100% liveness guarantees is critical for them to maintain their value and avoid legal and operational overhead. The long-term viability and developmental roadmap of the chosen blockchain is critical in this respect as well, as green asset tokenization is a long-term endeavor. A solution that is interoperable with many open-source technologies has better long-term prospects; tokenization of green assets often involves interactions across different blockchain networks and diverse institutions. A key interoperability aspect to consider is data portability—the right to own and carry user-generated data across the internet.

Layer 2 (L2) solutions are built on top of L1 blockchains to enhance scalability and efficiency. In principle, these secondary "layers" manage txs off the main chain, easing the load on the base layer and enabling faster txs at lower costs, all while inheriting the security and decentralization of the underlying L1. In the context of environmental data, L2s offer a unique combination of scalability, security, and trustworthiness. They can better handle more complex and frequent txs than L1 at lower cost. A short survey of L2 solutions is available in Appendix B (Table 3B.1).

DECENTRALIZED STORAGE

In Web3, data storage tends towards P2P models, where data availability is propagated through a network of nodes instead of a centralized server. There exist many

TABLE 3.2
Decentralized Storage Comparison

Solution	Type	Mechanism	Environmental Application
IPFS	Content-addressed P2P	Cryptographic CIDs for content verification	Globally available environmental datasets, governance metadata
Filecoin	Incentivized storage	Proof-of-replication and proof-of-spacetime	Long-term integrity of critical environmental data
Arweave	Permanent archive	One-time payment endowment model	Immutable environmental records and audit trails
Storj	Encrypted object storage	End-to-end encryption with node distribution	Sensitive environmental data with privacy requirements
Sia	Contract-enforced storage	Blockchain-based host contracts	Secure distributed storage with redundancy

Source: Table by the authors.

technical architectures that blend these models depending on the properties of the data or the use case it supports. Many Web3 applications adopt hybrid architectures, storing tx data onchain while maintaining larger content offchain in decentralized storage networks.

As a result of this hybrid architecture, decentralized storage solutions exist as practical alternatives to centralized storage. These P2P networks of nodes simultaneously assume a blend of client and server roles, eschewing the need for any centralized oversight. They maintain blockchain's ethos of decentralization, yet afford the scalability and flexibility needed to handle large and complex data sets. Table 3.2 compares the key features of well-known decentralized storage solutions.

IPFS (INTERPLANETARY FILE SYSTEM)

The InterPlanetary File System (IPFS) is a protocol and network designed to create a content-addressable, P2P method of storing and sharing hypermedia in a distributed file system. IPFS allows users to host and receive content in a decentralized manner. Unlike traditional HTTP-based web services where files are found by their location (URL), IPFS identifies files based on their content using cryptographic hashes known as Content Identifiers (CIDs). CIDs ensure that any change in the content results in a different identifier. This mechanism allows the network to locate and verify data with greater efficiency and reliability.

Snapshot, a leading blockchain governance platform, stores votes on IPFS with cryptographic signatures to ensure tamper-proof governance records (IPFS Docs 2022). One concrete example of a green Web3 project employing IPFS is Regen Network, which stores and references metadata related to its governance. CID-addressed metadata uploaded to IPFS is used in proposal JSON files, which detail the actions to be executed by the Regen Ledger if the proposal passes (Regen Ledger Documentation 2024).

FILECOIN

As a repairable storage system, Filecoin embeds preservation mechanisms to maintain and repair decentralized data integrity throughout its lifecycle. Unlike other solutions that might focus on object storage, database functionalities, or content delivery, repairable storage is uniquely suited for handling vast volumes of files, like detailed environmental reports, high-resolution satellite imagery, and extensive research documents. This specialization ensures that each file is stored redundantly across multiple nodes, enhancing data durability and accessibility.

Repairable storage proactively monitors the health of data, employing self-healing processes to automatically rectify corrupted or lost information. In the context of environmental projects, this means that the raw data underpinning tokenized assets such as carbon credits or biodiversity offsets is not only securely stored but also remains readily accessible and verifiable. This transparency affords stakeholders the ability to track and validate the source and integrity of each file, ensuring the data's reliability as a foundation for environmental asset valuation.

Filecoin integrates multiple proof protocols to provide ongoing assurance of data integrity (Filecoin Docs 2024). If these proofs lapse, the network enforces corrective actions, including data replication to alternative reliable nodes, reinforcing data reliability and availability. In the context of green asset production, Filecoin Green's CO2. Storage is designed to enable transparency of the comprehensive material attributes underlying green assets. It is a decentralized storage solution for structured data based on content addressed data schemas for environmental assets, such as Renewable Energy Credits, Carbon Offsets, and geospatial datasets (Filecoin Green Documentation 2022).

ARWEAVE

Arweave uses a decentralized network to provide collective data storage that users tap into by paying upfront for perpetual storage. Arweave's design attempts to ensure that stored data becomes immutable, situating it for applications where data integrity and permanence are required (Williams et al. 2023). Despite both being Decentralized Repairable Storage systems, Filecoin and Arweave differentiate themselves from each other in that Arweave focuses on this permanency, while Filecoin is designed for general-purpose, flexible data storage. Over time, both have gradually added compute layers to their platforms. Filecoin introduced FilecoinVM to integrate with Ethereum and has evolved into a multi-faceted platform that now supports storage, retrieval, compute, and programmability, while Arweave launched Smartweave and AO, its execution layer, to enable programmability (AR.IO 2025; Filecoin 2025).

These systems provide credibility and traceability for green crypto-assets by ensuring data fidelity and persistence. In environmental applications, data integrity is essential since it underpins asset value. For instance, tokenized forest carbon credits could be based on data tracking long-term forest health. Permanent storage ensures this data provides a reliable foundation for tracking carbon sequestration over time.

DECENTRALIZED OBJECT STORAGE: STORJ AND SIA

In decentralized object storage systems, information is structured as discrete entities, also known as objects. Each object encapsulates the data content, which may range from conventional files to more intricate structures such as JSON or XML documents, augmented by a variable set of metadata and a unique identifier. This structuring as objects aims to enhance flexibility and scalability compared to file-based storage systems for more precise control over data, including sophisticated capabilities for metadata processing, indexing, and the ability to perform complex data transformations.

Storj is a decentralized cloud storage protocol that emphasizes privacy and security through end-to-end encryption, treating each file as an object that is split into smaller, encrypted segments distributed across multiple worldwide nodes. Its architecture is meant to provide high availability and durability of data, alongside efficient retrieval times. Providers can rent out unused storage space, turning their own devices into nodes; they are compensated for their storage contributions with tokens pegged to USD-denominated payouts (Storj Labs 2025).

Sia is a similar platform where each object is treated independently; object encryption, distribution, and retrieval are managed separately. Sia employs blockchain to enable txs and enforce contracts between network clients and hosts. Users rent storage space from a global network of hosts, who are compensated by the platform's cryptocurrency, for offering their disk space. Data is divided into chunks, encrypted, and then distributed across nodes for redundancy and security (Sia Foundation 2025).

A NOTE ON PLANT-BASED DATA STORAGE

Non-Fungible Plants (NFPs) are an experimental technology intersecting biotechnology and digital assets. NFPs refer to living plants that are engineered to store digital files—specifically non-fungible tokens (an "NFT" is a unique blockchain asset representing verifiable ownership)—within their DNA. This innovative and peculiar idea uses the storage capacity of DNA to embed digital information, proposing an organic method of data preservation.

While highly experimental, the relevance of NFPs is varied: NFPs represent a tangible and natural form of storing and validating green data. For instance, a plant could hold data about its own carbon sequestration capabilities, biodiversity value, or even the ecological conditions of its habitat. As physical and living representations of NFTs, NFPs add a layer of emotional and ecological connection absent from the virtual, serving as a novel approach to raising awareness and promoting conservation efforts (GYOC 2022).

Web3 DATA MANAGEMENT PRIMITIVES

Web3 data engineering requires understanding core primitives that enable efficient data management across blockchains. Table 3.3 summarizes six essential primitives—indexers, relayers, resolvers, bridges, governance mechanisms, and oracles—each addressing specific challenges in building decentralized applications for environmental data management.

TABLE 3.3
Summary of Web3 Data Management Primitives

Primitive	Function	Example
Indexers	Scan and structure blockchain data for efficient retrieval and querying	The Graph
Relayers	Enable crosschain communication by transmitting messages and proofs	IBC-Relay
Resolvers	Translate human-readable names to machine-readable blockchain addresses	ENS
Bridges	Enable crosschain asset transfers and smart contract interactions	Wormhole
Governance	Community-centric data management through decentralized autonomous organizations and Data Unions	Protocol Guild (Protocol Guild 2024)
Oracles	Primitives that report offchain data for onchain use.	Chainlink

Source: Table by the authors.

INDEXERS

Indexers scan and structure blockchain data for efficient retrieval and querying. They parse the blockchain, cataloging events, txs, and states (Envio 2023). This transforms linear blockchain data into a format optimized for rapid searches and complex queries. Indexers enable decentralized applications (dApps) to access specific data points without scanning the entire chain. They retrieve targeted information—historical txs, smart contract events, wallet balances—enhancing Web3 UX.

The Graph is a well-known decentralized protocol for indexing and querying blockchain data in use by some green crypto projects today, such as Toucan Protocol (The Graph 2025; Toucan Protocol 2025). Its subgraphs define which data from the blockchain is indexed and how it is stored. Developers create subgraphs by defining a schema of the data they are interested in, along with the smart contract events that a Graph Node should listen to retrieve this data. The subgraph is then deployed to The Graph network, where it is indexed by the network's nodes (indexers) and made queryable via GraphQL (The Graph 2025).

RELAYERS

A blockchain relayer is a system or service that enables communication between different blockchains or between a chain and external system by transmitting messages, txs, or proofs across networks. They are bridges, enabling crosschain functionality such as asset transfers, data synchronization, or smart contract interactions without requiring full trust in a centralized party. Relayers may observe events on one chain and submit cryptographic proofs or messages to another. They also play a role in systems using meta-transactions or account abstraction, which allow users to interact with a blockchain without holding a blockchain's native token to pay tx gas fees—a small cryptocurrency charge paid to interact with the blockchain. Many relayers aggregate and optimize txs to enhance gas efficiency and overall tx throughput.

RESOLVERS

In Web3, resolvers are fundamental to decentralized naming services like the Ethereum Name Service (ENS). Their primary role is the translation of human-readable domain names, such as "example.eth," into machine-readable formats, e.g., Ethereum addresses (0xABC…). This role is analogous to that of the Domain Name System (DNS) in the conventional web, which translates domain names into IP addresses. Unlike traditional DNS which is limited to IP address resolution, a Web3 resolver can interpret various types of records, including cryptocurrency addresses, IPFS content hashes, and other arbitrary data. Domain owners maintain autonomy to update or modify resolver smart contracts, allowing for dynamic changes in mapped addresses or data in a secure, decentralized manner.

Beyond naming services, resolvers play a critical role in the hosting and access of decentralized websites on IPFS, linking ENS names to IPFS hashes. For environmental projects, resolvers could map human-readable names like "rainforest-project-2024.eth" to project wallets, carbon credit contracts, and verification data—creating transparent, accessible identities for green assets. They also serve as decentralized identifiers, streamlining authentication and identity verification for Web3 AI agents and applications.

BRIDGES

Bridges enable blockchain processes to be offloaded or managed across other execution environments. There exist different types of bridges:

- **Simple Bridges** enable the transfer of assets, such as tokens, from one chain to another. They typically involve locking assets on one chain and minting corresponding tokens on another chain, with the bridge reporting these values. Tokenized carbon asset projects like Toucan have developed simple bridges to port carbon tokens across blockchain networks and centralized carbon API providers such as Puro.earth (Toucan 2023). As mentioned above, many relayers are themselves simple bridges.
- **Smart Contract Bridges** allow for more complex interactions, such as executing smart contracts across different blockchains. They enable not just asset transfers but also dApp functionality across chains.
- **Augmented Bridges** offer enhanced functionalities and use cases. One example is Wormhole, which enables the creation of multichain exchange platforms that draw on liquidity from various interconnected chains. Wormhole also allows for unified governance across different networks, where votes from disparate chains can be consolidated for collective decision-making (Wormhole 2025).

GOVERNANCE

The largest-scale uses of data today are extremely siloed, not just within corporate or institutional boundaries but even by individual privacy policies. The movement to allow data sharing even for clear public interest cases, such as public health or the curing of diseases, has been held out for years under a variety of names and yet has made very little progress either in the private sector or in open standards-based collaborations (Weyl et al. 2024). This is unfortunate, as data sharing can improve the product offering of green assets; data sharing among agricultural or climate insurance stakeholders, for instance, can reduce premiums and expand market access (Mercy Corps Ventures 2024, 44).

Web3 offers innovative and community-centric approaches to environmental data management and governance to break these barriers. As Mercy Corps Ventures has identified, blockchain Data Unions and other decentralized autonomous organization (DAO) governance primitives are collaborative solutions that allow users to collectively monetize their personal data due to their intrinsic properties:

> Data governance and ownership… are fundamentally built into how blockchains function. Data governance refers to the systems and processes that ensure data is high quality, usable, secure and private…. Data ownership determines who decides these rules—who decides when data is shared and for what purposes, if data can be modified, and when data access should be removed. The governance rules are transparently shared with all users of the blockchain… There is an unprecedented opportunity for data to be owned and managed by individual users, and specifically the climate-vulnerable communities who could benefit the most.
>
> **Mercy Corps Ventures (2024)**

DAOs can engage and incentivize groups to produce, enhance, and share datasets. Imagine, for example, community-owned Environment APIs—an initiative currently being explored by organizations like Google (Anderson 2023). The design of blockchain-based governance systems requires its own detailed practitioner walkthrough, and is a key focus of Chapter 4.

ORACLES

At their core, Web3 oracles are primitives that bridge otherwise disconnected external data to blockchains (see Figure 3.3). They supply API data to smart contracts, enabling them to execute and respond to real-world events or conditions, e.g., temperature readings, carbon prices, flight statuses, etc. This is necessary for dApps that dynamically interact with real-world conditions, such as green bonds, where yield rates can be automated based on oracle-reported sustainability metrics. Properly designed oracles responding to or anticipating real-world conditions can revolutionize entire sectors by increasing the speed and reducing the cost in which green finance is deployed.

Arbol's proposed parametric insurance mechanism illustrates this use case: it pays out based on the occurrence of predefined weather events (like a certain amount of rainfall or temperature level) rather than traditional claims processes. The data is provided by Chainlink, an oracle provider, and is used to automate insurance contracts. If a farmer purchases insurance for drought conditions and Chainlink's oracles confirm the drought per smart contract parameters, a payout is triggered (Arbol 2022). This streamlined integration enhances transparency, reduces the risk

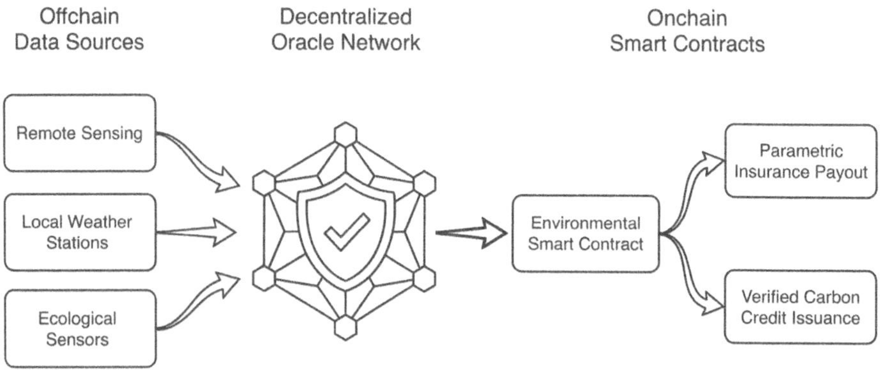

FIGURE 3.3 Decentralized oracle networks connect smart contracts with real-world data. This is critical for environmental data, as it ensures that climate-related metrics—like carbon prices or weather conditions—can be verified and used onchain with high integrity.

***Source*: Diagram by the authors.**

of manual errors, and accelerates the payout process. The winners are those farmers and other parties exposed to climate risks who can now hedge more effectively against potential losses due to adverse conditions.

Good oracle design is a hotly contested field in a process of ongoing innovation as security assumptions are constantly challenged by live production environments. Oracles come in many shapes and sizes; they vary in their levels of decentralization, immutability, compatibility, latency, track record, cryptoeconomic guarantees, attack costs, and trust assumptions. While oracles add substantial value to blockchains by bridging them with external data—such as centralized APIs or cloud-stored databases—they also introduce critical trade-offs, including vulnerabilities related to latency, manipulation, and cost (Bank for International Settlements 2023). The next wave of oracle development is likely to emphasize minimizing trust assumptions, increasing data reliability, and improving both speed and security of delivery (Bank for International Settlements 2023). Table 3.4 categorizes principal oracle types and their applications.

Oracles do not resolve the issue of poor input data, where monitoring, reporting, and verification (MRV) data being entered onto the blockchain is of dubious quality. Blockchains improve data transparency, but do not bridge scientific gaps in identifying what to measure and how to measure it. Simply put, if unhelpful dMRV data from the underlying material reality is collected, an oracle that reports it is itself unhelpful. Oracles themselves do not remedy the scientific need for measuring the right material things in the first place.

Several specialized oracle mechanisms have been deployed in the energy and environmental sectors. Shamba Network integrates Chainlink oracle technology to supply verifiable climate and agricultural data (Shamba Network 2022). DIMO is a vehicular DePIN that allows users to collect, manage, and monetize vehicle data using sensors; its oracle infrastructure ensures that telemetry data submitted to smart contracts is verifiable and tamper-resistant (DIMO Foundation 2025). DIVA

TABLE 3.4
Categorizes Principal Oracle Types and Their Applications

Oracle Type	Description	Example
Software-based	Programs that gather and verify data from digital sources like APIs and databases	Chainlink
Hardware	Physical devices or networks that collect real-world data directly to blockchain, e.g., IoT sensors measuring pollution levels, soil moisture, or carbon readings	W3bstream (2025)
Human	Use community consensus where humans serve as data validators	Kleros (2025)
Trustless	Use ZKPs to prove data accuracy without revealing underlying information. Can serve various offchain compute functions as well	zkOracles, RISC Zero (Algaba 2023)

Source: Table by the authors.

Protocol is a decentralized platform for creating and settling data-driven financial derivatives, using oracles to deliver external information to smart contracts. In the environmental space, this could allow for conditional payouts based on ecological metrics, such as temperature anomalies or biodiversity indexes. DIVA Donate, a project built on DIVA, uses this mechanism to distribute donations based on climatic conditions verified through oracle-fed data (DIVA Donate 2023).

COMPUTATION

Computation encompasses the systematic methods for extracting actionable insights from datasets—ultimately generating models: mathematical abstractions of environmental, socioecological, and climatic systems that identify patterns and simulate dynamics. One useful way to conceptualize ESG modeling is as a pyramid structure, in which environmental data aggregates upward from granular observations to portfolio-level assessments. At the base sit fine-grained, sub-asset-level measurements, successive tiers aggregate these into assets, corporate institutions, and portfolios, until the apex represents national-level ESG performance. Each tier depends on verified data computed from the levels below, enabling multi-scale analyses that account for spatial, organizational, and systemic complexity (Almond et al. 2023). These models inform decision-making for the Institution Layer—albeit with some degree of uncertainty.

Web3 introduces three computational advantages: automatic provenance tracking, since blockchains record every tx and computational step; trust-minimized offchain execution, where complex computations run outside the blockchain but submit verifiable results back to it; and improved reproducibility, since provenance records make it possible to re-run or audit any computation. The data oracles discussed in the previous section can be extended to computation: rather than simply relaying external information to smart contracts, computation oracles execute processing offchain.

They can run environmental models, aggregate sensor data, compute environmental indexes, and return verified results onchain. This enables complex environmental analyses that would be infeasible to perform directly on a blockchain.

Model complexity is not without trade-offs. Simple models are easier to validate but often lack nuance, while complex models are more representative of the phenomena they seek to represent yet harder to calibrate and verify. The combination of remote sensing and AI is pushing the complexity frontier of ecological modeling by integrating large-scale, multi-source datasets. Trade-off bottlenecks in calibration and verification are being addressed through advanced AI models that learn from unlabeled data and adapt across regions (Almond et al. 2023). The Verifiable Compute and AI × Web3 subsections below address how blockchain infrastructure is supporting these innovations in calibration and verification.

The most normative aspect of modeling is understanding and selecting what to measure and use as input for production and parameterization for some green asset. Consider institutional biodiversity impact reporting, where Sustainability-Linked Bond and Loan Principles recommend relevance (material to the issuer's operations and environmental impact), practicality (is trackable), benchmarking (following industry-recognized standards), and verifiability for reporting (World Bank Group 2024, 7). Few, if any of these principles are straightforward material observations: they are subjective and contestable recommendations. Similarly to how practitioners must decide what and how to measure the underlying material reality, institutions must determine through their governance what to model and how to model it (with what form of compute). They typically do so through a financial lens.

For example, the most well-known environmental models that produce green assets are the many integrated assessment models (IAMs) that calculate the social cost of carbon (SCC). The SCC is derived from IAM outputs that model the atmospheric changes resulting from each additional ton of emitted carbon and project its consequent economic damages and changes to human wellbeing. The SCC, expressed in monetary fiat terms, represents the value of damages avoided by mitigating carbon emissions. It measures the difference between the impact of unabated carbon emissions and the lesser damages that would result from emission reduction efforts (Metcalf and Stock 2017).

While the SCC is regarded as a standard of objectivity in policy, its calculation also highlights the boundaries of modeling as it presents the common trait of being inherently subjective and contestable. This is partly because the SCC can only be based on sectors of the economy for which reliable data exists to predict climatic impacts, such as changes to agricultural yields, sea level rise, coastal property loss, and changes to labor productivity. Consequently, its calculation often overlooks many critical industries and aspects of human wellbeing that cannot be quantified in conventional economic terms, due to the absence of adequate data. This point of failure is frequent in environmental models, and reinforces the axiom that which is not measured, is not accounted for.

The following subsections survey four domains of computation that are expanding what can be modeled and verified for green asset production: spatial computing, which grounds environmental models in geographic reality; verifiable compute, which extends blockchain's trust guarantees to offchain processing; the convergence of AI and Web3, which aims to democratize access to machine learning infrastructure; and private compute, which enables collaboration on sensitive environmental data without exposure.

SPATIAL COMPUTING

Spatial computing integrates 3D and temporal information to bridge physical and virtual reality. Combining datasets such as soil, crop, and atmospheric conditions with spatial models supports more accurate, location-specific decision-making. Spatial computing applications for environmental work span scales from field to planet. At the field level, spatial models can optimize the co-location of natural assets on farms to enhance bird species richness and breeding activity (Valente, Zurlini, and Petrosillo 2025). At the planetary scale, NASA and IBM's Prithvi foundation model uses AI to automatically process satellite imagery for flood detection and land-cover classification (Jakubik et al. 2023). These integrations demand significant computational resources and meticulous spatiotemporal data preparation, highlighting the need for standardized data formats and interoperability protocols (Armstrong 2020; OGC 2025).

The scale and complexity of spatial data make manual analysis impractical, demanding advanced computational methods to uncover meaningful patterns. Unlike traditional datasets, spatial data exhibits unique traits like spatial autocorrelation—where nearby locations often share similar characteristics—and spatial heterogeneity, where relationships vary by location. These properties violate a common statistical assumption that data points are independent and identically distributed (i.i.d.), which means that measuring soil quality in one location tells one nothing about the adjacent one. This is clearly false for spatial data, increasing the risk of false or missed patterns when using standard analytical methods. In high-stakes fields like environmental monitoring and public policy, such errors can lead to costly outcomes, from misallocating resources to misinterpreting the spread of disease or pollution.

Spatial computing in Web3 rests on three primitives: Proof-of-Location (verifiable claims about where and when events occur), Verifiable Geocomputation (proof that spatial analyses were performed correctly), and Peer-to-peer Spatial Data Management (distributed storage with cryptographic integrity). Few spatial standards have emerged in Web3 thus far, even as decentralized networks increasingly require them for location-based applications that interact with the physical world. Web3's inherent features—immutability, programmability, and cryptographic verification—are well suited for managing spatial data, but realizing trust-minimized systems for environmental monitoring, land use, and urban planning depends on solving a fundamental problem: how to verify, onchain, that something happened at a specific place and time.

Figure 3.4 illustrates a reference architecture for spatial Web3 computing organized in four layers. The Data layer stores and indexes geospatial information in content-addressable, interoperable formats—standards like STAC and GeoDIDs that allow spatial datasets to be discovered and verified across systems. The Credibility layer addresses the core verification problem, aggregating independent evidence

Astral Stack

Application	Astral Location Services	• Location Proof Verification • Geospatial Policy Engine • Privacy-preserving evals
Platform	Astral Location Services	• Location Proof Verification • Geospatial Policy Engine • Privacy-preserving evals
Credibility	Astral Location Proof Framework	• Plugins library for signal collection • Evidence evaluation
Data	• Location Protocol • EAS / ATProto + IPFS • Astral Indexer	• IPFS-STAC • IPFS-optimized formats • GeoDIDs

astral.global

FIGURE 3.4 A reference architecture for spatial Web3 computing. The Data layer stores and indexes geospatial information in interoperable, content-addressable formats; the Credibility layer aggregates independent evidence signals into composite location proofs scored for reliability; the Platform layer executes verifiable spatial computations against those proofs; and the Application layer exposes these capabilities as services for location-aware dApps.

***Source*: Astral Protocol (2025).**

signals (device attestations, network measurements, sensor readings) into composite location proofs scored for reliability. The Platform layer executes verifiable spatial computations against those proofs—running geospatial queries in trusted execution environments or validating them through cryptographic proofs. The Application layer exposes these capabilities as services for location-aware dApps.

Central to this emerging spatial infrastructure is the concept of the location proof: a verifiable digital artifact that supports a claim about the timing and location of an observed event. A location proof bundles independent pieces of evidence—device attestations, network measurements, sensor data, signed observations from nearby devices—into a composite artifact whose credibility increases with the independence of its sources. Astral's framework formalizes this through three components: location claims (spatially referenced assertions with mandatory uncertainty bounds), location stamps (independent evidence from proof-of-location systems), and location proofs that combine stamps with claims to produce a credibility assessment—a confidence score between 0 and 1 that smart contracts can read and respond to (Astral Protocol 2025). The security model relies on the principle that forging two or three unrelated stamps simultaneously is substantially harder than forging one. The governing constraint is economic: the cost of forging a location proof should exceed the value of the tx it underpins. A neighborhood cleanup token might accept a single attested check-in, while a biodiversity credit worth thousands of dollars might demand a score above 0.9, combining satellite imagery, IoT sensor data, and social attestation from local rangers. Location proofs thus function as the spatial equivalent of what data oracles do for offchain information: they bridge the gap between physical geography and onchain logic.

Projects filling the Web3 spatial gap include the EASIER Data Initiative's Web3 Geospatial Dashboard, which aims to decentralize access and use of satellite imagery through a user-friendly interface integrating IPFS and Filecoin (EASIER Data Initiative 2024). The Astral Protocol is working to standardize location data attestations both onchain and offchain for location-aware dApps in finance, gaming, and environmental impact verification (Astral Protocol 2025). Cycloid, a hardware device enabling Ethereum txs over radio, enables offline interactions with blockchain-based spatial data (FOAM 2024). FOAM's Proof of Location uses terrestrial radio beacons and time-of-flight measurements to provide trustless verification of physical spaces without relying on GPS (Foamspace 2025). In remote wildlife monitoring, for instance, rangers could use Cycloid to verify their location and log environmental data in areas without cellular signal, ensuring tamper-proof records even offline. Once location is established, the next challenge is ensuring that the computations performed on spatial data are themselves trustworthy—the domain of verifiable compute.

VERIFIABLE COMPUTE

When computation moves offchain for scalability, a core trust problem emerges: how does a smart contract—or an auditor—know that an offchain carbon credit calculation, satellite classification, or biodiversity assessment was performed correctly? Traditional cloud computing offers flexibility but requires trusting the provider; blockchains offer trustlessness but limited programmability. Verifiable compute bridges this gap by enabling offchain execution with onchain-grade integrity guarantees (Algaba 2023; EigenLayer 2025).

Three key verification methods have emerged, each with distinct trade-offs for environmental applications:

- **Zero-Knowledge Proofs (ZKPs):** Cryptographic proofs that a computation was executed correctly, without revealing underlying data or requiring re-execution. Multiple proof systems exist, each offering different trade-offs between proof size, verification speed, and computational cost. Zero-knowledge virtual machines (zkVMs) compile standard programs into provable execution, meaning complex environmental models can produce verifiable outputs that smart contracts trust (Algaba 2023; Peng et al. 2025).
- **Trusted Execution Environments (TEEs):** Hardware-isolated enclaves that execute code in encrypted memory inaccessible to the host operator. Faster and cheaper than cryptographic proof generation, TEEs shift trust

from the computation operator to the hardware manufacturer—a meaningful but narrower trust assumption. Astral Protocol's Geospatial Policy Engine runs PostGIS (an open-source spatial database) inside a TEE, connecting the location proofs described in the previous section to verifiable spatial computation (Astral Protocol 2025). TEEs are well suited to high-throughput environmental tasks where cryptographic proving would be prohibitively expensive: real-time sensor data processing, geospatial analysis pipelines, and continuous monitoring systems (Poetic Technologies 2024).

- **Cryptoeconomic Optimistic Verification:** Outputs are assumed correct unless challenged during a dispute window; operators stake economic collateral that can be programmatically slashed (seized, or burned) for incorrect results. This form of verification is normally cheap, as costs are incurred only when challenges occur. The "pay only for security consumed" model means a routine sensor reading need not carry the same verification cost as a high-value biodiversity credit issuance.

These methods are complementary rather than competing, and most production systems layer them. For sustainability practitioners, the key design decision is whether a task requires integrity alone (proving the output is correct) or both integrity and privacy (hiding input data or model parameters). Carbon credit calculations, verified satellite image classification, and public MRV data typically need only integrity—ZKPs or optimistic verification suffice. Multi-institutional biodiversity data sharing, where no party wants to expose proprietary datasets, may additionally require privacy-preserving techniques beyond integrity guarantees alone. These trade-offs sharpen when the computation being verified is AI or machine learning inference, as the following section explores.

AI × Web3

AI and machine learning have become essential infrastructure for environmental work—emulating climate models, classifying satellite imagery, processing sensor streams, and optimizing resource use (Rolnick et al. 2022). Foundation models—AI systems trained once on vast datasets and then adapted to specific tasks like forecasting, image classification, or biodiversity assessment—have accelerated this shift, enabling environmental analysis at a fraction of previous cost (Cheema and Baioumy 2024). But this capability is concentrated. Two companies control 88% of AI-native company revenue; three cloud providers hold 63% of infrastructure; one chipmaker supplies 94% of data center GPUs (a16z crypto 2025). For sustainability applications where transparency and auditability are foundational, this concentration creates both an access problem and a trust problem.

Blockchain infrastructure—smart contracts, decentralized compute layers, tokenized incentive systems—offers mechanisms to decentralize AI development, verify model outputs, and distribute access to computational resources across open networks (Cheema and Baioumy 2024). Rather than trusting a single provider's API to classify satellite imagery correctly, a blockchain-based system can require cryptographic proof that the declared model was run on the declared data.

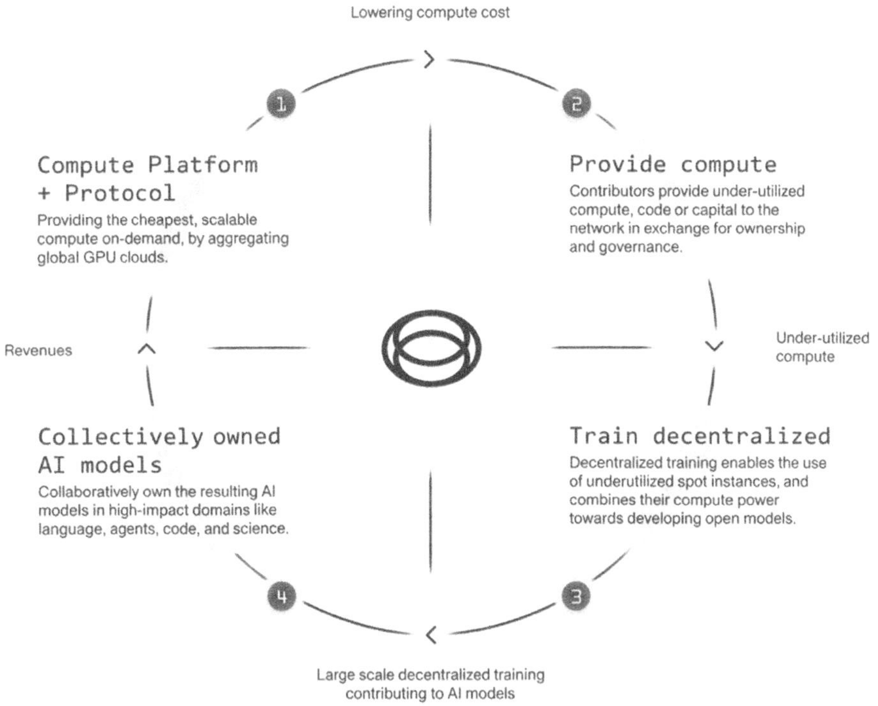

FIGURE 3.5 The decentralized AI compute flywheel: a protocol aggregates GPU resources from distributed contributors, who receive ownership and governance rights in return; these resources are combined for model training, producing collectively owned AI systems.

***Source*: Prime Intellect, Inc. (2024).**

Figure 3.5 illustrates the logic: compute platforms aggregate underutilized GPU resources via token incentives; contributors provide compute, code, or capital in exchange for ownership and governance rights; decentralized training combines distributed resources toward open models; and collectively owned AI systems emerge across domains. Decentralized compute platforms help commoditize AI resources in open markets, offering a pathway to overcome the resource concentration that constrains open-source AI development. For environmental applications, this means that a community monitoring deforestation or verifying carbon credits need not depend on a single cloud provider's model or pricing. Still, distributing computation across untrusted nodes sharpens the verification problem: how can a smart contract—or an auditor—confirm that an offchain computation was performed correctly without re-executing it?

Consider a carbon credit methodology backed by satellite image classification. Zero-knowledge Machine Learning (zkML) can produce cryptographic proof that the classification was performed correctly using the declared model, without revealing proprietary model parameters—extending the verification methods described in the previous section to AI inference. A critical prerequisite, however, is deterministic inference. He et al. (2025) demonstrated that AI inference endpoints produce different outputs depending on server load and batching—even with deterministic sampling settings—with varying batch sizes under concurrent requests, not floating-point arithmetic, as the primary cause. This matters because verifiable AI-driven MRV requires reproducible outputs: if two parties run the same model on the same satellite imagery and obtain different results, the verification proof is meaningless regardless of its cryptographic soundness. Specialized software designs can achieve deterministic inference at acceptable cost, and once this reproducibility constraint is met, zkML enables scalable, privacy-preserving ML workflows for blockchain-based environmental systems.

PRIVATE COMPUTE

Verifiable compute, described above, answers whether a computation was performed correctly. Private compute answers a different question: can multiple parties collaborate on sensitive data without exposing it? For sustainability applications, this distinction is practical. A carbon auditor verifying an emissions claim needs verifiable compute—a cryptographic proof that the declared methodology was applied to the declared data. A consortium of companies pooling supply chain data to calculate Scope 3 emissions without revealing individual operations needs private compute. Both rely on cryptography, but they solve different problems.

Two techniques are central. Secure Multi-Party Computation (SMPC) enables multiple parties to jointly compute a result—such as aggregate emissions across a supply chain—without any party seeing another's inputs. Fully Homomorphic Encryption (FHE) goes further: computation runs directly on encrypted data, so even the processor never sees plaintext, which is essential in contexts like sustainability reporting, healthcare, and finance where sensitive data must be processed without ever being decrypted (Almeida 2023). Blockchain implementations such as fhEVMs integrate FHE with the zero-knowledge proofs and trusted execution environments already described, enabling encrypted, private interactions with smart contracts (Archetype 2024). Federated learning extends this logic to AI: models train on environmental data distributed across locations—sensor networks, field stations, corporate facilities—without the data ever leaving its source.

These technologies expand the surface area for institutional collaboration on environmental data. Performance overhead remains the primary barrier to adoption (Hujara 2024), but the trajectory is clear: as environmental governance demands more data sharing across organizations, private compute determines what can be shared without unacceptable exposure. A simple heuristic: use verifiable compute when the question is "was this done correctly?" and use private compute when the question is "can we do this together without showing each other our data?"

VISUALIZATION

Visualization is the process by which complex data is transformed into visual content such as diagrams, graphs, and importantly, maps. This is essential for making information accessible, understandable, and usable across diverse domains and actors—including environmental science, finance, and technology—by enabling the identification of trends, patterns, and anomalies. In environmental and ecological contexts, where much of the subject matter is grounded in real-world phenomena, visualization bridges the gap between raw data and practical decision-making. Ultimately, visualization occurs through application and platform interfaces that pull from data sources to structure the content.

Over time, environmental data visualization has evolved out of a historical process of mapmaking into the heavy digital approach of the present day. In environmental contexts, the stakes of effective data visualization are particularly high. The way it is presented can influence public perception, inform policy, and guide scientific inquiry. Interfaces that are not easily accessible and utilizable by a general audience risk excluding the populations that have most to gain from the material data and predictions they display. Environmental science often necessitates interaction with non-scientific audiences, and visualizations are essential for translating complex ecological concepts into accessible narratives.

INTERFACES

The front-end is the interface layer where users directly engage with data—and, critically, where the transparency and verifiability built across the entire data stack either reaches the end user or doesn't. In environmental and climate applications, current interfaces are often rigid: fixed dashboards deployed by registries or project developers that determine what users see and what remains hidden. A carbon credit buyer evaluating a project, a community monitoring its watershed, or an auditor verifying MRV outputs all encounter the underlying data through the interface. Whoever controls the frame controls the interpretation. More malleable visual systems that support exploratory, localized, and user-remixable engagement with data would better serve practitioners—particularly when the underlying data is already verifiable and composable. Open, composable data demands open, composable interfaces; otherwise, the backend is decentralized while the experience remains centralized.

In Web3, several projects aspire to close this gap by developing interfaces that function on P2P networks without dependence on centralized servers. This enhances censorship resistance, reinforces user sovereignty, and allows direct interaction with the blockchain without intermediaries. Despite the availability of ENS and IPFS as decentralized front-end deployment options, they are not yet widely adopted—meaning that for most users, access to ostensibly decentralized systems still runs through conventional web infrastructure controlled by a single operator.

CONTENT

If the data layer stores verified measurements, the credibility layer scores their reliability, and the compute layer proves the analysis was performed correctly, then visualization content is what makes that entire provenance chain inspectable by non-technical users. The rich content of visualization—diagrams, graphs, dashboards, maps—populates the interfaces described above. But in the context of green asset production, the critical question is not what platforms exist but what visualization should *show* to close the trust gap between claimed and verified environmental impact.

Several platforms demonstrate what this looks like in practice. Naturebase (Figure 3.6) consolidates thousands of science-based data points—gathered

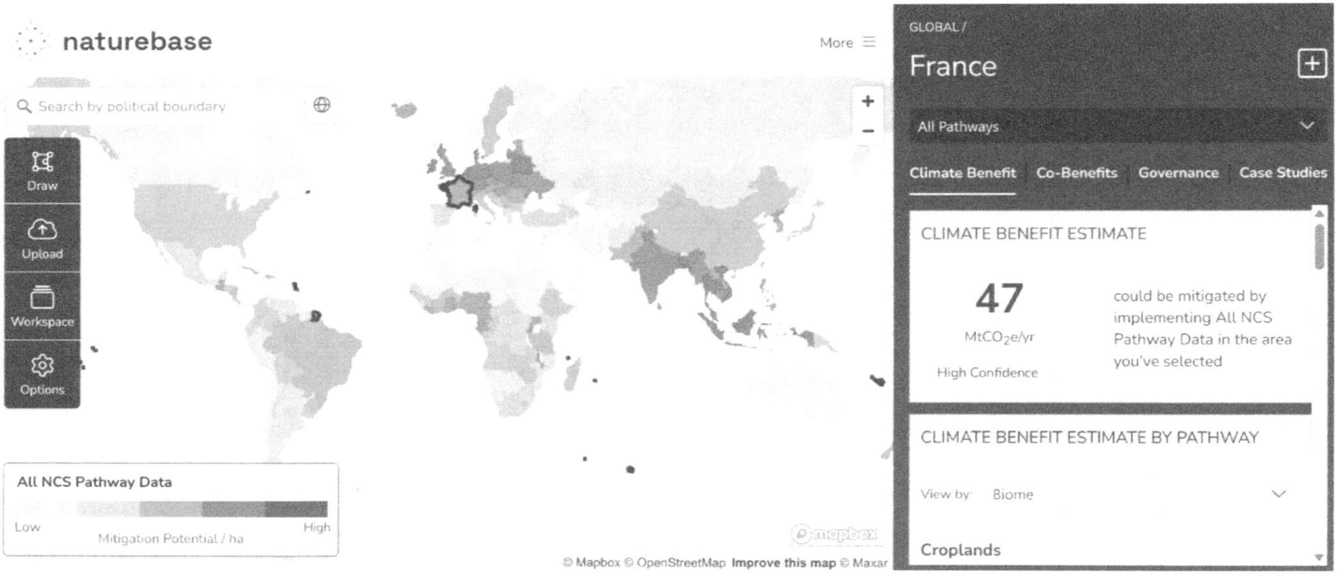

FIGURE 3.6 Naturebase platform visualizing climate mitigation potential for France. The estimate is produced by analyzing 20 conservation, restoration, and improved land management strategies across forests, wetlands, grasslands, and agricultural lands, combining geospatial data on applicable land areas with carbon flux estimates (tons of CO_2 sequestered per hectare). These analyses are constrained by safeguards to protect food security, fiber supply, and biodiversity conservation. The interface allows users to filter results by pathway, biome, and administrative boundary down to one-kilometer resolution—illustrating a design pattern in which methodology is transparent and data explorable rather than static.

***Source*: Naturebase.org.**

through satellite imagery and ML/AI—to visualize where and how high-integrity nature-based solutions can be implemented, displaying carbon mitigation, ecosystem health, and human well-being content at one-kilometer resolution worldwide (Naturebase 2025). Through satellite analysis and other forms of remote sensing, high-resolution maps can now illustrate territorial changes over time, helping users understand the effects of human pressures and build confidence in restoration efforts (Almond et al. 2023, 57). NASA Worldview offers access to over 1,000 satellite imagery layers with time-based animations, measurement tools, and customizable map layers for real-time monitoring and long-term environmental research (Smith 2024). ETH Zurich's Crowther Lab is developing SEED, a platform designed to tackle the complexity of biodiversity assessment through spatial visualization methods (Almond et al. 2023, 32). Beyond environmental monitoring, Grid Status created the first national Nodal Price Map to visualize Locational Marginal Prices in U.S. electricity markets, transforming highly technical market data into accessible insights (Grid Status 2024).

What distinguishes Web3 visualization from these examples is composability. Because onchain data is open and queryable by default, anyone can build a dashboard drawing from the same underlying verified data. Platforms like Dune Analytics, Nansen, and Glassnode use this pattern to interpret blockchain data, with Glassnode providing in-depth analysis supporting quantitative trading, risk management, and research. The environmental application is significant: a carbon credit dashboard could surface not just price and volume but each credit's verified satellite classification, location proof, and attestation history—making the full provenance chain from measurement to market visible to buyers in a single view. This marks the shift from static reports and dense spreadsheets to interactive platforms where complex methodologies are transparent and explorable rather than opaque. Looking ahead, emerging research on geospatial AI agents suggests that visualization content may increasingly be generated dynamically in response to practitioner queries rather than presented through fixed interfaces (Ahmadalipour 2025).

PREDICTION

Sisson and Ben-Meir (2024) argue that the value of data derives from its use in making predictions—predictions that enable more effective action when accurate. Figure 3.7 illustrates the full logic as a cybernetic loop: environmental systems are sensed, predictions generated, decisions made, actions executed, and feedback incorporated—closing the cycle between observation and intervention. Each stage of this loop is now being built with decentralized infrastructure.

Sense and Predict

Prediction draws on historical data and advanced analytics in statistics and ML/AI to execute simulations, scenario planning, and forecasting—techniques that assess the likelihood of future events and inform adaptive responses. Applications span long-range climate modeling, shorter-term early warning systems for flooding,

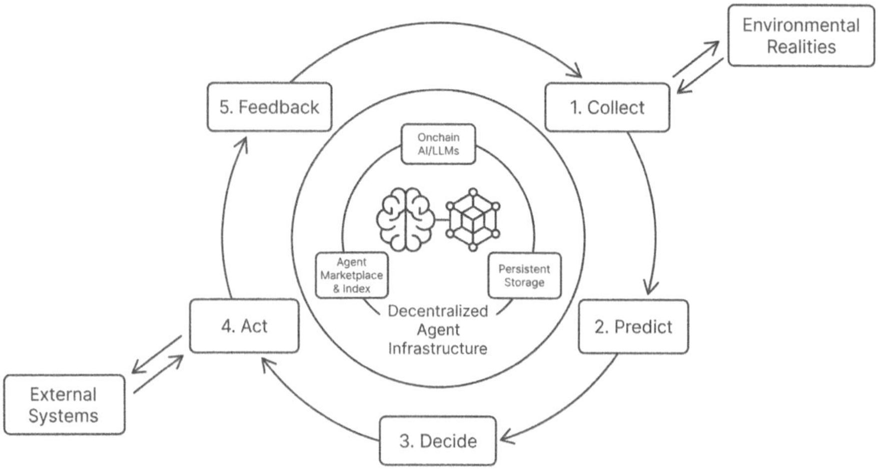

FIGURE 3.7 The cybernetic loop for decentralized environmental agents. Agents collect data from environmental realities, generate predictions, make decisions, act on external systems, and incorporate feedback—closing the loop between prediction and intervention. At the center, Decentralized Agent Infrastructure provides the enabling stack: onchain AI/LLMs for computation, persistent storage for data continuity, and an agent marketplace and index for coordination.

***Source*: Diagram by the authors.**

wildfires, and hurricanes, and tailored advisory services for climate-vulnerable end users such as smallholder farmers (Mercy Corps Ventures 2024, 8). A central focus is environmental risk: defined as the probability of loss shaped by hazards, vulnerability, and exposure. With $182.7 billion in U.S. weather and climate disaster costs in 2024 alone (NOAA NCEI 2025), insurers are pulling back from high-risk areas, and parametric coverage—driven by fast, data-based risk assessments—has emerged as a response. Floodbase, for instance, produces flood models that predict the size and damage of flood risk as inputs to parametric insurance policies (Floodbase 2025). Web3 decentralizes this prediction infrastructure: a data challenge co-organized by Ocean Protocol and Shamba Network deployed blockchain-based environmental oracles to forecast vegetation health in Marsabit County, Kenya, using historical Enhanced Vegetation Index data—producing models across multiple time horizons applicable to natural asset management (Ocean Protocol 2023). The advantage of decentralized prediction is that model inputs, parameters, and outputs can be made publicly auditable rather than locked inside proprietary systems, allowing stakeholders to evaluate not just the forecast but the methodology behind it.

Decide and Act

Prediction becomes most powerful when a model's output triggers an intervention rather than merely informing a human decision-maker. An AI agent is a software entity capable of perceiving its environment, making decisions, and taking actions to achieve specific goals—often with minimal or no humans in the loop (Gershuni 2025). Key interoperability infrastructure is emerging to support autonomous agent operations: the Model Context Protocol (MCP) provides a universal standard for AI tool integration with external systems; the ERC-8004 standard establishes onchain identity, reputation, and validation registries for agents, giving them portable, censorship-resistant identifiers (Backpack Exchange 2025); and the complementary x402 protocol enables automated agent-to-agent payments over HTTP. Together, these standards point toward an ecosystem in which AI agents own crypto wallets, interact with smart contracts, and execute operations independently—a shift already underway, with agents conducting the majority of transactions through Safe, a popular smart wallet, on Gnosis Chain on some days (Selva 2024). In an environmental context, a prediction oracle might assess the health of an agroecology project, identify a future risk such as crop shortfall, and trigger an automatic response—releasing emergency funds or adjusting farm management variables via smart contract—without waiting for human authorization.

Feedback and Governance

Onchain prediction markets and futarchy extend this logic by closing the loop's final gap: evaluating whether the intervention worked. Market-based instruments can pre-emptively forecast the impact of a decision, allowing agents to evaluate consequences before committing resources—and retrospectively assess outcomes to refine future behavior. This prescriptive power transforms oracles from passive data relays into active decision-makers, completing the feedback cycle from environmental sensing through prediction to autonomous intervention. But governing these agents—constraining their behavior through what Zargham and Nabben (2023) term a governance surface—becomes a central institutional design challenge, one that Chapter 4 addresses through the lens of cybernetic institutions and the coordination problems inherent to decentralized environmental governance.

PRACTITIONER GUIDANCE AND CASE STUDIES

The preceding sections surveyed the components of the environmental *data pipeline*—from storage and verification through oracles, computation, and visualization to prediction. For sustainability practitioners building green asset systems, this technical landscape presents a core challenge: which infrastructure choices are right for the project? Drawing on frameworks from the Rocky Mountain Institute and Climate Collective for evaluating data quality in carbon markets (Sahay et al. 2024), this section provides a decision framework organized around four key domains, and existing case studies for practitioners to review.

Storage: Where Does the Project's Environmental Data Live?

The fundamental choice is between centralized cloud storage and the decentralized alternatives surveyed above—IPFS, Filecoin, and Arweave. Centralized storage offers mature tooling and predictable costs but introduces single points of failure and censorship risk—a concern highlighted by documented attempts to remove climate data from government servers (Calma 2021; Santarsiero 2025). Decentralized storage provides censorship resistance and content-addressable verification through cryptographic hashes, meaning data integrity can be confirmed by anyone without trusting a central authority (Psaras et al. 2022), but requires understanding incentive dynamics and accepting higher technical complexity.

Security consideration: Centralized systems concentrate attack surfaces; decentralized systems distribute risk but introduce new vectors including malicious nodes and smart contract vulnerabilities.

Practitioner guidance: Use centralized storage for rapidly iterating prototypes and data requiring strict regulatory compliance. Transition to decentralized storage for production systems where audit trails and tamper-evidence are essential.

Verification: How Is the Environmental Data Validated?

Attestor networks rely on designated verifiers who cryptographically sign attestations—flexible but dependent on reputation. Validator staking requires verifiers to lock economic collateral that can be slashed for incorrect attestations, creating what the Regen Network documentation describes as digital signatures comparable to signing a legal document (Regen Ledger Documentation 2024). Cryptographic proofs provide mathematical guarantees through zero-knowledge techniques (Algaba 2023) but cannot verify that input data accurately reflects physical reality—the persistent "garbage in, garbage out" problem.

Security consideration: Attestor models face social engineering risks. Staking models face economic attacks if corrupting validators costs less than potential fraud profits. Cryptographic proofs shift trust to implementation correctness.

Practitioner guidance: For high-stakes credits with institutional buyers, multi-party verification with economic stakes provides the strongest guarantees. For community-scale projects, attestor networks with transparent reputation tracking offer accessible entry points.

Oracle Design: How Does Offchain Data Reach Smart Contracts?

First-party oracles operated by the data source eliminate intermediary trust but concentrate risk. Third-party oracle networks such as Chainlink aggregate data from multiple sources with economic incentives but introduce latency and fees. As the Ethereum documentation notes, oracles are essential for smart contracts that need to respond to real-world conditions—without them, contracts cannot access offchain data by design (Ethereum Foundation 2025).

Security consideration: Oracle manipulation is a leading attack vector in decentralized systems. Parametric insurance contracts triggered by weather data can be exploited if oracle feeds are corrupted.

Practitioner guidance: For parametric triggers and automated payouts, use decentralized oracle networks with multiple independent sources. Always implement sanity checks—contracts should reject data falling outside plausible ranges.

Chain Selection: Which Blockchain Hosts the System?

Application-specific chains such as Regen Ledger (built on Cosmos SDK) provide customized functionality including native ecocredit modules, but require maintaining validator sets and limit interoperability. General-purpose chains offer established ecosystems, developer tooling, and liquidity but may lack environmental-specific primitives. Among general-purpose options, Ethereum and its ecosystem of L2 rollups merit particular attention: Ethereum's EVM (Ethereum Virtual Machine) has become the dominant smart contract execution environment, supporting the largest developer community, the most mature privacy-preserving toolset, and the broadest DeFi composability of any public blockchain (Electric Capital Partners 2024). Green projects aiming to leverage these network effects benefit from interoperability with the Ethereum ecosystem, as discussed in the blockchain architecture section above. Interoperability protocols—including Inter-Blockchain Communication (IBC) for Cosmos-based chains and bridge infrastructure for EVM-compatible networks—expand functionality but introduce cross-chain attack surfaces.

Security consideration: Newer chains may have undiscovered vulnerabilities; established chains like Ethereum have battle-tested security but higher base-layer costs, offset increasingly by L2 scaling solutions. Bridges remain a persistent attack vector.

Practitioner guidance: If the project requires deep integration with environmental registries or specialized methodologies, evaluate application-specific chains. If the project needs broad market access, DeFi composability, and a mature privacy stack, the Ethereum ecosystem provides the strongest foundation.

RED FLAGS: WHAT PRACTITIONERS SHOULD AVOID

When evaluating Web3 data infrastructure, practitioners should watch for warning signs. These include single oracle dependency without redundancy or sanity checks, smart contracts handling environmental asset issuance that lack professional security audits, and opaque verification processes where verifier identities or attestation logic cannot be independently examined. Equally concerning are validator systems without economic or reputational consequences for incorrect attestations, infrastructure dependent on token incentives requiring perpetual growth to maintain security, and contracts with centralized upgrade keys that allow unilateral modification.

REGEN NETWORK

Regen Network provides modular blockchain infrastructure specifically tailored for ecological asset issuance and verification, including biodiversity credits. The architecture separates data storage from onchain governance and token logic, emphasizing

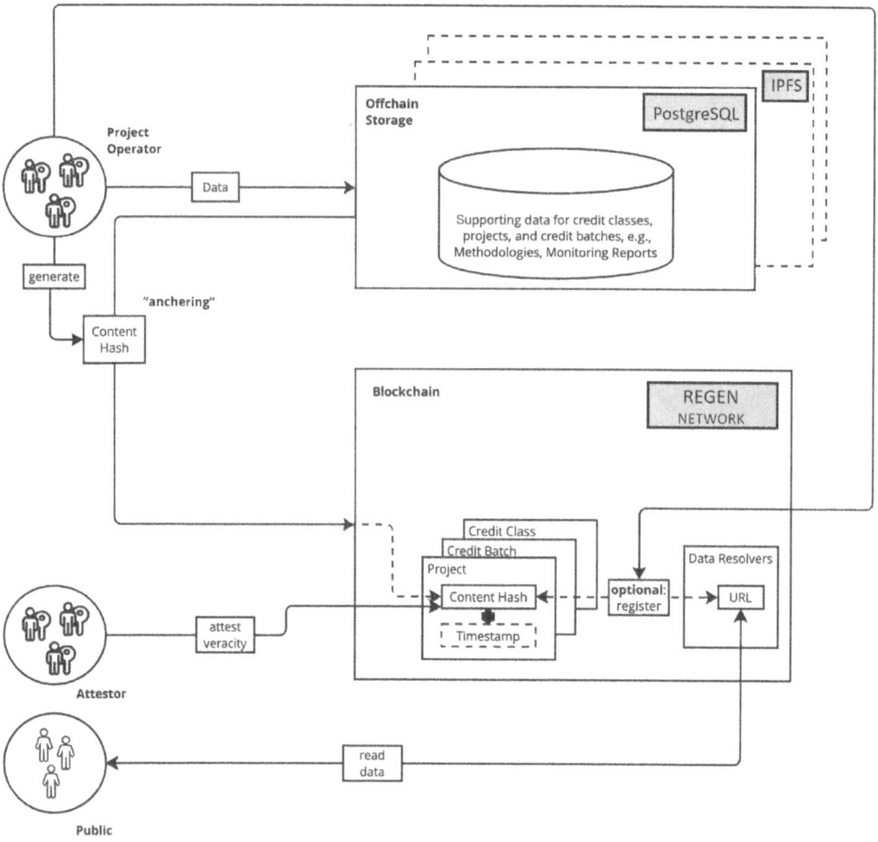

FIGURE 3.8 Regen Network data flow: Project Operators upload data to offchain storage (PostgreSQL, IPFS), generating content hashes anchored on Regen Ledger. Attestors verify data accuracy. Data Resolvers map onchain records to offchain locations via URLs, enabling public access while maintaining data integrity.

***Source*: Diagram by the authors.**

modularity and stakeholder flexibility. Figure 3.8 illustrates the Regen Network data flow architecture, showing how project data moves from operators through attestors to the public ledger, while Table 3.5 describes the Regen Network data pipeline.

Environmental data—including monitoring reports, geospatial imagery, and project metadata—is stored offchain using solutions like PostgreSQL and IPFS. References to this data are anchored on the Regen Ledger through content hashes—unique cryptographic representations of the data—ensuring that while the data itself remains offchain for scalability, its references are immutable and traceable. Data Resolvers then map onchain references to offchain storage locations via URLs, allowing public access to data when made available.

The Regen Ledger governs the state of ecological projects and credits, allowing tracking and referencing of project metadata over time. By default, project data is

TABLE 3.5
Outlines the Regen Network Data Pipeline from Storage Through Prediction

Pipeline Stage	Implementation Details
Storage	Project data (reports, geospatial imagery, metadata) stored offchain; storage can be centralized (PostgreSQL) or decentralized (IPFS)
Management	Operators create and manage projects on Regen Ledger; submit content hashes to anchor data; data private by default, made public by linking hash with pointer
Computation	Verification performed offchain by attestors who assess data accuracy and submit attestations onchain; impact evaluators theorized for resource allocation
Visualization	Interfaces allow exploration of projects, metadata, and attestation history; Registry and Explorer provide project transparency
Prediction	Not natively implemented but extensible; third-party tools could run predictions based on accessible offchain data

Source: Table by the authors.

private. Project operators must intentionally expose their data by submitting a reference hash to the chain. This design respects the data sovereignty of local stakeholders while enabling transparency through voluntary disclosure.

Data verification is performed by attestors—independent verifiers who cryptographically sign attestation txs submitted to the Regen Ledger, formally confirming the accuracy and validity of project data. This establishes a decentralized trust layer without necessitating full data availability onchain, focusing on verifiability through cryptographic commitments rather than computationally intensive onchain validation.

OPEN FOREST PROTOCOL

Optimized for the NEAR blockchain, Open Forest Protocol (OFP) enables transparent, decentralized, and tamper-proof MRV of reforestation and afforestation efforts. Its data architecture directly addresses issues of data integrity, accessibility, and equitable participation in carbon markets (Helen 2025). Figure 3.9 shows the Open Forest Protocol data flow, illustrating how MRV data is stored on IPFS and anchored to the NEAR blockchain. Table 3.6 details the Open Forest Protocol pipeline stages.

Like Regen Network, OFP employs a dual-layered data system combining onchain smart contracts with offchain decentralized storage. Each forest project is represented by an NFT on the NEAR blockchain, which encodes key metadata and links to raw project data stored on IPFS. An oracle mediates between signed txs and the NFT contract, bridging offchain data submissions to the onchain ledger—a concrete implementation of the oracle design patterns discussed in the framework section above.

System actors within OFP include Project Operators, who upload forest data through the Forester App, and Project Validators, who stake tokens and perform verification of submitted data. These actors interact with the blockchain through smart

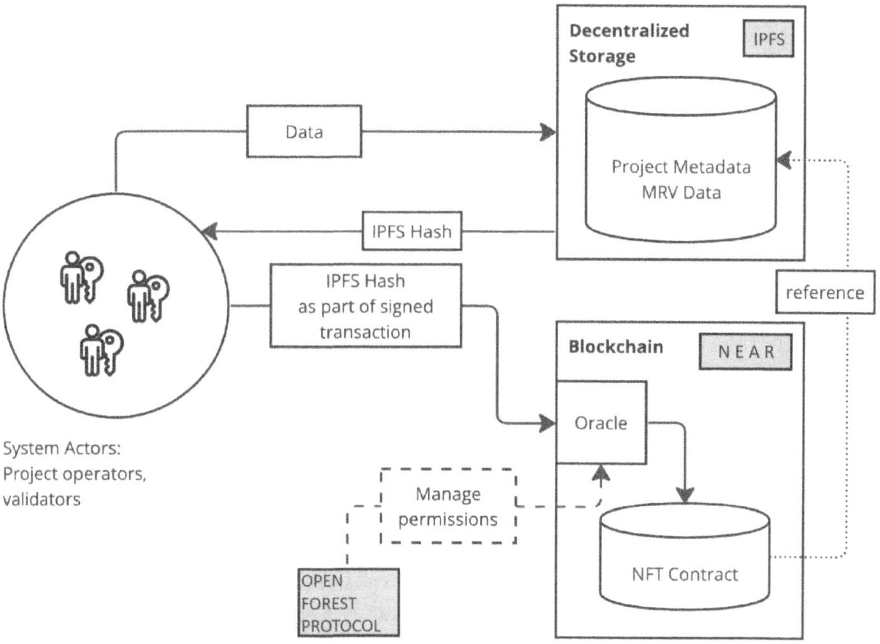

FIGURE 3.9 Open Forest Protocol data flow. Project operators and validators upload project metadata and MRV data to IPFS, generating an IPFS hash. This hash is included in a signed tx and submitted to the NEAR blockchain. The blockchain references the IPFS hash and stores it within an NFT contract, immutably linking it to project data. Permissions and access control are managed to ensure secure participation and verification by trusted actors.

***Source*: Diagram by the authors.**

TABLE 3.6
Details the Open Forest Protocol Pipeline Stages

Pipeline Stage	Implementation Details
Storage	Raw forest data (geospatial coordinates, photographs, environmental measurements) stored offchain using IPFS; smart contracts store IPFS hashes immutably
Management	Smart contracts on NEAR manage access control, project metadata, and references to IPFS data; NFTs represent forest projects and link to respective datasets
Computation	Validators review and verify project data via staking mechanisms; AI tools (species detection, tree health) integrated into Forester App for data collection
Visualization	Forester App dashboard provides visual access to project status, validator activity, and uploaded datasets; Open Forest Atlas enables community and funder transparency
Prediction	AI tools support early-stage pattern recognition (tree health, species identification); predictive modeling for carbon yield projections in development

Source: Table by the authors.

contracts, which enforce access control, validation procedures, and conditional issuance of carbon credits. OFP's ex-post credit issuance model ensures that only verified, already-sequestered carbon is eligible for tokenization—countering speculative crediting practices.

OFP integrates AI tools in its mobile app to automate species recognition and enhance field data collection, lowering MRV costs and increasing data accuracy. The decentralized and open nature of OFP's system fosters trust among stakeholders—such as funders, regulators, and local communities—by providing transparent and auditable data records. In one documented case, a Tanzanian forest project's continuous data submissions revealed signs of poaching activity, enabling early intervention—demonstrating how persistent, transparent environmental monitoring can yield conservation benefits beyond carbon accounting (Helen 2025).

In 2024, OFP's partnership with Celsia produced what the project describes as the first fully digital, immutable, and traceable carbon credits created using blockchain infrastructure from project inception through issuance and sale. Each credit's provenance is documented through the Open Forest Atlas and verified by third-party validators, allowing independent analysis of underlying claims, data, and methodologies—as demonstrated by Renoster's audit in late 2024. For local stakeholders, such as those managing the Reverde forests in Colombia's Valle del Cauca region, this transparency ensures that contributions are visible, recognized, and rewarded through automated credit distribution following verification (Mercy Corps Ventures 2024, 65–66).

REFERENCES

a16z crypto. 2025. "State of Crypto 2025: The Year Crypto Went Mainstream." a16z crypto, October 2025. https://a16zcrypto.com/posts/article/state-of-crypto-report-2025/. Accessed March 2026.

Ahmadalipour, Ali. 2025. "GeoLLMs and the Future of Climate-Tech Agents." GeoAI Unpacked (blog), September 3, 2025.

Algaba, Fran. 2023. "Introduction to Zero-Knowledge Machine Learning for Blockchains." https://franalgaba.medium.com/introduction-to-zero-knowledge-machine-learning-for-blockchains-c78ec97cf5a2. Accessed December 2025.

Almeida, Diogo. 2023. "A New Paradigm in Privacy: Homomorphic Encryption - Part 1." Lightshift Blog, November 2023.

Almond, Lucy, Jen Stebbing, Xavier Lorphelin, Daniel Swid, and Raviv Turner. 2023. The State of Nature Tech: Building Confidence in a Growing Market. MRV Collective.

Anderson, Jennifer. 2023. "Going beyond the Map: Introducing Environment APIs." Google Maps Platform.

AR.IO. 2025. "What Is AR.IO?" https://docs.ar.io/learn/what-is-ario/. Accessed December 2025.

Arbol. 2022. "Climate Tech Talk: Protecting Farmers with Parametric Crop Insurance." Chainlink Tech Talk. https://chain.link/techtalks/arbol-parametric-insurance. Accessed March 2026.

Archetype. 2024. "Privacy 2.0: The Present State of the Programmable Privacy Stack."

Armstrong, Leisa. 2020. Improving Data Management and Decision Support Systems in Agriculture. Burleigh Dodds Science Publishing.

Astral Protocol. 2025. "Introducing the Astral Protocol." Paragraph, April 2025.

Backpack Exchange. 2025. "ERC-8004 Explained: Ethereum's AI Agent Standard Guide 2025." https://learn.backpack.exchange/articles/erc-8004-explained. Accessed March 2026.

Bank for International Settlements. 2023. "The Oracle Problem and the Future of DeFi." BIS Bulletin No. 76.

Calma, Justine. 2021. "How Scientists Scrambled to Stop Donald Trump's EPA from Wiping out Climate Data." The Verge, March 2021.

Cheema, Alex, and Mohamed Baioumy. 2024. "AIxCryptoPrimer." February 2024. https://alexcheema.github.io/AIxCryptoPrimer.pdf. Accessed March 2026.

Copernicus. 2025a. "Accueil | Copernicus." https://www.copernicus.eu/fr. Accessed 23 May 2025.

Copernicus. 2025b. "Copernicus Data Space Ecosystem." https://dataspace.copernicus.eu/. Accessed 23 May 2025.

Copernicus. 2025c. "Data and Information Access Services." https://www.copernicus.eu/en/access-data/dias. Accessed May 2025.

DIMO Foundation. 2025. "Connect Your Car and Earn Rewards." https://dimo.co/?srsltid=AfmBOoqgyi8xrENggIl2hXapW3gT6ZdQbjzTDMqDSvpZB21SvbSsLVRX. Accessed December 2025.

DIVA Donate. 2023. "DIVA Donate." https://www.divadonate.xyz/. Accessed December 2025.

Earth Science Data Systems, NASA. 2019. "Earth Science Data Systems (ESDS) Program." Earthdata. https://www.earthdata.nasa.gov/esds. Accessed March 2026.

EASIER Data Initiative. 2024. "Web3 Geospatial Dashboard." https://easierdata.org/updates/2024/2024-01-24-dashboard-showcase. Accessed March 2026.

EigenLayer. 2025. "EigenCloud: Cloud-Scale Programmability, Crypto-Grade Verifiability." https://blog.eigencloud.xyz/eigencloud-technical-blog/. Accessed March 2026.

Electric Capital Partners. 2024. "Developer Report." https://www.developerreport.com/. Accessed April 23, 2025.

Envio. 2023. "What Is a Blockchain Indexer, and How Does It Simplify Data Retrieval for Web3 Developers?" Medium, August 2023.

Ethereum Foundation. 2025. "Oracles." https://ethereum.org/developers/docs/oracles/. Accessed December 2025.

European Commission. 2021. "Copernicus: The EU's Earth Observation Programme." Regulation (EU) 2021/696. Official Journal of the European Union L 170: 69–148.

Filecoin. 2025. "Smart Contracts: The FVM." https://docs.filecoin.io/smart-contracts/fundamentals/the-fvm. Accessed December 2025.

Filecoin Docs. 2024. "Proofs." Gitbook, October 2024. https://docs.filecoin.io/basics/the-blockchain/proofs. Accessed March 2026.

Filecoin Green Documentation. 2022. "CO2.Storage." Gitbook.io, October 21, 2022.

Floodbase. 2025. "Best-in-class Flood Models." https://www.floodbase.com/. Accessed December 2025.

FOAM. 2024. "Introducing Cycloid: Ethereum Transactions over Radio." Mirror.xyz, June 2024.

Foamspace Corp. 2025. "FOAM." https://foam.space/. Accessed December 2025.

Gershuni, Stepan. 2025. "Agent Economy Stack." Cyber•Fund Blog, April 2025.

Grid Status. 2024. "Analyzing LMPs with a Nodal Price Map." Grid Status Exports, August 2024.

GYOC. 2022. "Grow Your Own Cloud: Non-Fungible Plants." https://growyourown.cloud/non-fungible-plants/. Accessed March 2026.

He, Horace et al. 2025. "Defeating Nondeterminism in LLM Inference." Thinking Machines Lab, September 2025.

Helen, Amalia. 2025. "How Blockchain Could Help Build Trust in Nature Data." Edited by Cate Kelly. Nature Tech Collective, March 10, 2025.

Hujara, Markus. 2024. "The Muted Seven – 7 Things You Should Consider Re Confidential Compute." Greenfield, July 2024.

IPFS Docs. 2022. "Case Study: Snapshot & IPFS." https://docs.ipfs.tech/case-studies/snapshot/. Accessed March 2026.

Jakubik, Johannes et al. 2023. "Foundation Models for Generalist Geospatial Artificial Intelligence." arXiv:2310.18660.

Kleros. 2025. "Kleros Oracle." https://kleros.io/oracle/. Accessed December 2025.

Malé, Christine, and Thomas Lagier. 2020. "Simulating the Interactions of Environmental and Socioeconomic Dynamics at the Scale of an Ecodistrict." In Ecosystem and Territorial Resilience: A Geoprospective Approach, edited by Emmanuel Garbolino and Christine Voiron-Canicio, pp. 299–321. Elsevier.

Mercy Corps Ventures. 2024. Advancing Climate Resilience: Innovations in Data, Analytics and Artificial Intelligence in Emerging Markets. MCV.

Metcalf, Gilbert E., and James H. Stock. 2017. "Integrated Assessment Models and the Social Cost of Carbon: A Review and Assessment of U.S. Experience." Review of Environmental Economics and Policy 11, no. 1: 80–99.

NASA. 2025. "About the ESDS Program." NASA Earthdata. https://www.earthdata.nasa.gov/about. Accessed May 2025.

National Research Foundation Singapore. 2022. "Virtual Singapore." https://www.nrf.gov.sg/programmes/virtual-singapore. Accessed May 2025.

Naturebase. 2025. "Naturebase." https://app.naturebase.org/. Accessed December 2025.

NOAA NCEI (National Centers for Environmental Information). 2025. "2024: An Active Year of U.S. Billion-Dollar Weather and Climate Disasters." NOAA Climate.gov, January 10, 2025.

Ocean Protocol. 2023. "Announcing the Winners of Predicting Vegetation Health in Marsabit, Kenya Data Challenge." Medium, November 3, 2023.

OGC (Open Geospatial Consortium). 2025. "Standards." https://www.ogc.org/standards/. Accessed December 2025.

Open Earth Foundation, Data-Driven EnviroLab, and Camda Secretariat. 2022. "Digitally-Enabled Independent Global Stocktake (DIGS) Litepaper." https://www.openearth.org/. Accessed March 2026.

Peng, Zhizhi, Taotao Wang, Chonghe Zhao, Guofu Liao, Zibin Lin, Yifeng Liu, Bin Cao, Long Shi, Qing Yang, and Shengli Zhang. 2025. "A Survey of Zero-Knowledge Proof Based Verifiable Machine Learning." arXiv:2502.18535.

Poetic Technologies. 2024. Private Compute: The Future of Confidential Computing. Poetic Technologies.

Prime Intellect, Inc. 2024. "Introducing Prime Intellect Compute: The Compute Exchange." Prime Intellect Blog, July 1, 2024. https://www.primeintellect.ai/blog/compute. Accessed March 2026.

Protocol Guild. 2024. "Onchain Architecture." Protocol Guild Documentation. https://protocol-guild.readthedocs.io/en/latest/02-onchain-architecture.html. Accessed December 2025.

Psaras, Yiannis et al. 2022. "Why the Internet Needs the InterPlanetary File System." IEEE Spectrum, October 2022.

Regen Ledger Documentation. 2024. "Message-Based Governance Proposals." https://docs.regen.network/tutorials/. Accessed March 2026.

Rolnick, David et al. 2022. "Tackling Climate Change with Machine Learning." ACM Computing Surveys 55, no. 2: 1–96.

Sahay, Apoorva, Caitlin Smith, Bonnie Lei, and Sebastian Weeks. 2024. A Buyer's Guide to Carbon Credit Data Quality. RMI and Climate Collective.

Salam, Abdul. 2019. "Internet of Things in Agricultural Innovation and Security." In Internet of Things for Sustainable Community Development (pp. 71–112). Springer.
Santarsiero, Rachel. 2025. "Disappearing Data: Trump Administration Removing Climate Information from Government Websites." National Security Archive.
Selva, Jorge. 2024. "The Safe Case: How AI and Smart Accounts Will Revolutionize Crypto." Safe Blog, March 25, 2024.
Shamba Network. 2022. "Shamba Integrates Chainlink Oracle Technology to Power Parametric Insurance for Smallholder Farmers." Medium, November 9, 2022.
Sia Foundation. 2025. "Sia." https://sia.tech/. Accessed March 2026.
Sisson, David, and Ilan Ben-Meir. 2024. "Why Is There Data?" SSRN. https://doi.org/10.2139/ssrn.4933063
Smith, Joseph M. 2024. "Data Tool in Focus: NASA Worldview." NASA Earthdata, March 2024.
Stankov, Ivan. 2020. "Environmental Management Information Systems." IEEE Xplore. https://doi.org/10.1109/BulEF51036.2020.9326021
Storj Labs. 2025. "Node Operator Terms and Conditions." https://www.storj.io/node-operator-terms-conditions. Accessed March 2026.
Takyar, Akash. 2022. "Role of Web3 in Supply Chains and Logistics." LeewayHertz, November 2022.
The Graph. 2025. "The Graph Documentation." https://thegraph.com/docs/en/. Accessed December 2025.
Toucan. 2023. "Two-Way Bridge to Puro.earth | Biochar Credits." Toucan Protocol, October 2023.
Toucan Protocol. 2025. "Toucan Documentation." https://docs.toucan.earth/. Accessed December 2025.
Valente, Donatella, Giovanni Zurlini, and Irene Petrosillo. 2025. "The Spatial Distribution of Biodiversity." In Reference Module in Earth Systems and Environmental Sciences. Elsevier B.V. https://doi.org/10.1016/B978-0-443-21964-1.00027-6
W3bstream. 2025. "Build Decentralized Physical Networks Fast." https://w3bstream.com/. Accessed December 2025.
Weyl, Glen et al. 2024. "Plurality: The Future of Collaborative Technology and Democracy | Property and Contract." https://plurality.net/. Accessed March 2026.
Williams, Sam, Abhav Kedia, Lev Berman, and Sebastian Campos-Groth. 2023. Arweave: The Permanent Information Storage Protocol. Draft 17.
World Bank. 2023. State and Trends of Carbon Pricing 2023. World Bank. https://doi.org/10.1596/39796
World Bank Group. 2024. IFC Biodiversity Finance Metrics for Impact Reporting. International Finance Corporation.
World Meteorological Organization. 2020. 2020 State of Climate Services: Risk Information and Early Warning Systems. WMO-No. 1252. WMO.
Wormhole. 2025. "Build Multichain." https://wormhole.com/docs/. Accessed December 2025.
Zargham, Michael, and Kelsie Nabben. 2023. "Aligning 'Decentralized Autonomous Organization' to Precedents in Cybernetics." MIT Computational Law Report.

APPENDIX A: DATA TERMINOLOGIES

TABLE 3A.1
Data Terminologies Glossary

Term	Definition
Accuracy	The extent to which environmental data mirrors the actual values it is meant to represent; data is devoid of errors
Completeness	Measure of the totality of information required for comprehensive environmental assessment
Consistency	Homogeneity exists within and across datasets; all stakeholders view same coherent state
Timeliness	Data is recent; information is contemporary and relevant to current conditions
Relevance	Data is pertinent to a particular environmental inquiry or use case
Validity	Data adheres to predefined formats, standards, and acceptable value ranges
Uniqueness	Singularity of data records; duplications are avoided to maintain integrity
Integrity	Maintenance of data accuracy and consistency over time through lifecycle
Monitoring	Continuous observation and analysis of data to track changes over time
Reliability	The dependability of the data source; freedom from systematic bias or error
Reproducibility	The ability to consistently replicate results under same conditions
Precision	Relates to the granularity of the data; level of detail in measurements
Provenance	Documentation of the origin, history, and changes made to data over time
Traceability	The capacity to track the lineage of data through its entire lifecycle
Availability	Necessary data can be accessed as required by authorized stakeholders

Source: Table by the authors.

APPENDIX B: BLOCKCHAIN SCALING SOLUTIONS

TABLE 3B.1
Blockchain Scaling Solutions Comparison

Solution Type	Data Availability	Consensus	Settlement	Execution	Best For
Monolithic L1	L1	L1	L1	L1	Simple applications, maximum security
Rollup	L1	L1	L1	Offchain	High throughput with L1 security
Validium	Offchain (DAC)	L1	L1	Offchain	Privacy-focused applications
EigenDA Rollup	EigenDA	L1	Ethereum	Offchain	Ethereum-aligned DA with restaked security
Sovereign Rollup	External DA	Own consensus	Independent	Offchain	Chain sovereignty, custom governance
AVS-Secured Rollup	EigenDA	EigenLayer	Ethereum	Offchain	Shared security via restaking + EVM composability

Source: Table by the authors.

4 Institution Layer
Structuring Sustainable DAO Governance

The Institution Layer refers to the planet's institutional network and the institutionalization process. Institutions define the overarching legal and regulatory frameworks, scientific methodologies, and technical protocols that govern and delineate green crypto production—deemed *Institutional Protocols* in this book. These protocols filter and curate the Data Layer, then establish and enforce rules for its object representation as green crypto-assets. In short, institutions determine "techniques and procedures" that ultimately structure "the possible field of action" (Foucault 1982).

The authors' decision to position the Institution Layer above the Data Layer warrants explanation. Chapter 2 surveys the scientific observation technologies through which humans measure and translate the underlying material reality into data legible to institutions. Positioning the Institution Layer above this data reflects an institutional reorientation where new forms of institutions transcend conventional physical boundaries and find their accounting procedures embedded within the blockchain's techno-virtual infrastructure. In the environmental sector, these new crypto-institutions—also termed DAOs or cryptonetworks—are uniquely positioned to govern the underlying material reality and its computational shadow more efficiently. These efficiencies aim to leverage the abundance of "high-quality data" and the "enormous computing power" of the present to isolate key signals from material reality and determine appropriate responses (Hui 2024, 195). As Davidson, De Filippi, and Potts argue, blockchain-based coordination may enable new types of economic activity that were previously not able to be governed by firms, markets, or governments, "bringing economic coordination and governance institutions to spaces that are currently either poorly served or not served at all by extant coordination mechanisms" (Davidson, De Filippi, and Potts 2018).

The crypto-institutional offers a substrate for computational civilization to experiment with institutional design in support of the biosphere. This chapter examines these evolving design practices and concludes with a list of the requisite governance design considerations inherent to any green crypto-institutional project.

WHAT ARE CYBERNETIC INSTITUTIONS?

The cybernetic perspective on institutional design (Figure 4.1) involves applying the principles of cybernetics—such as networked systems, feedback loops, and self-regulation—to the creation, design, and management of institutions. This approach is relevant given the dominance of networked systems in the postindustrial economy:

 DOI: 10.1201/9781003748472-4

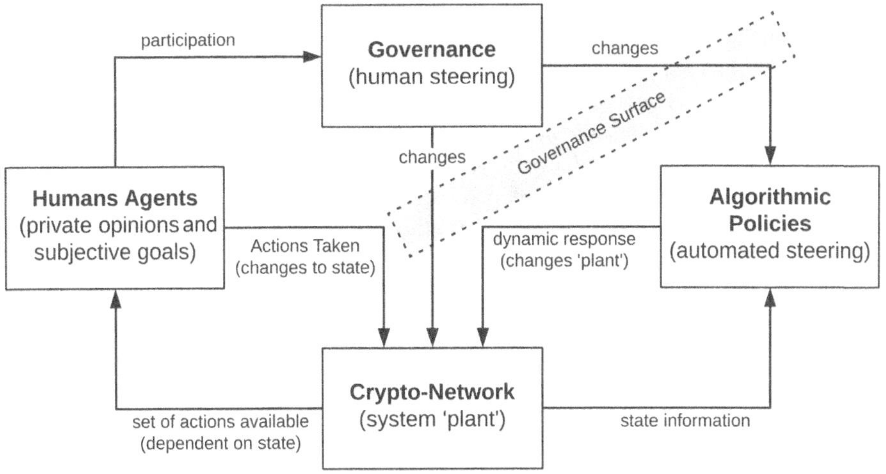

FIGURE 4.1 A governance surface is the set of parameters through which an organization's code may be modified—a variation of the cybernetic term *control surface*, dealing with variables directly affected by decision-making software in a feedback control system. Cybernetics is an interdisciplinary field studying systems, control, and communication in living organisms, machines, and organizations.

***Source*: Zargham and Nabben (2023). Licensed under Creative Commons. https://law.mit.edu/pub/dao-precedents-cybernetics/release/1**

economic production, once conceived as linear, is now deeply networked at both local and global scales (Jagoda 2016, 11).

Cybernetics abstracts system similarities into categories like sensors, controllers, and feedback loops to enhance adaptability and self-regulation, enabling effective responses to internal and external changes and the anticipation of future changes. Institutions apply these categories to achieve "requisite variety," cultivating a "wide enough range of behaviors" to thrive in dynamic environments (Zargham and Nabben 2023). Similarly, green institutions concern themselves with fashioning socioecological networks that are resilient, responsive, and materially goal-oriented. This is where blockchain's capacity for low-cost integration of heterogeneous data sources—from IoT sensors to satellite imagery to community reports—becomes relevant: institutions governing complex ecosystems need information channels that match that complexity.

Anticipatory cybernetic regulation is underpinned by institutional capacity to iteratively refine a *governance system*, whose mechanisms collectively render a *governance surface*. This surface constrains the possible future states of the institution, ensuring institutional resilience across time. A larger surface constrains fewer parameters, thus supporting more states, but increases the risk of undesirable states, while a smaller surface enhances certainty and reduces coordination costs for stakeholders. Of particular concern are the rules to change the rules, or an institution's *constitution*: a flexible constitution can radically expand the complexity of the governance surface and the future states an institution may take. For example, a DAO that allows any token holder to propose constitutional amendments has a larger governance surface than one requiring supermajority approval.

This governance surface enables recursive feedback: Do-Learn-Decide cycles where collective action produces outcomes, outcomes generate information, and information informs subsequent decisions. For green institutions, this loop connects environmental monitoring (data), institutional response (governance), and ecological outcomes (material reality) into adaptive systems.

Building on this foundational cybernetic framework, the operational strategies of firms become clearer. This transition from theory to application represents a critical shift: whether dealing with corporations or crypto-institutions, cybernetic principles must address the concrete challenge of operationalizing their governance to leverage their resources to achieve specific goals, such as fiat-denominated profits or positive ecological outcomes. Here, the focus shifts to minimizing coordination costs and reducing uncertainty. To this end, firms apply a "lens of efficient contracting" to navigate uncertainty, address asymmetric information, mitigate opportunism, and build trust (Tan, Merk, and Hubbard 2024). Reducing uncertainty becomes indispensable to institutional scaling—without it, coordination at scale is impossible, as the coordination problems in Table 4.1 illustrate (De La Rouvière 2024).

THE GREEN CRYPTOECONOMY

Crypto-institutions mark a structural shift in how societies can organize governance, environmental management, and economic production. At its core lie DAOs: blockchain-based governance surfaces that render predictable and transparent cybernetic systems. Functionally, what sets the decision-making processes of DAOs apart from traditional institutions is their unique programmable capability to make decisions to any degree afforded through the use of smart contracts. This simplifies the process of organizational design, streamlining the ability to manipulate governance surfaces—those points of institutional interaction where interior or exterior actors can influence, control, and interact with the system—as design objects.

Today, crypto-institutional governance is marked by rapid innovation in constitutional (process rules governing how rules change) (De Filippi et al. 2024, 25)—and non-constitutional governance mechanisms. Unlike most institutions today, DAOs' governance mechanisms are generally transparent, clear, and legible to their participants, constraining exploitation of the system by defining a well-bounded "field of action and possibility" in "smart contract code" (Dávila 2023, 226). This clarity delineates governance agent roles and capabilities, mitigating information asymmetries and principal-agent conflicts. The World Economic Forum observes that crypto-institutions—and by extension, their participants—"have the potential to offer greater transparency, trust, adaptability and speed over traditional organizational forms such as corporations" largely due to the properties they inherit from the immutability of blockchain code (World Economic Forum 2022).

These properties directly address prerequisites for ecosystem services markets. Murtough, Aretino, and Matysek identify seven characteristics required for

TABLE 4.1
Examples of Institutional Coordination Problems

Coordination Problem	Definition	Green Example
Prisoner's Dilemma	A situation in strategic interactions where entities, acting independently and rationally according to their self-interest, behave contrary to a collective's long-term best interest.	Short-term economic gains from high carbon emissions vs. the collective long-term benefits of reducing emissions.
Free Rider Problem	Entities consume more than their fair share or pay less than their fair share of the cost of a shared resource.	The Tragedy of the Commons as colloquially taught (Hardin 1968).
Moral Hazard	A situation where an entity can take risks because they know they will not have to face the full consequences of their actions.	Corporations may underinvest in proper environmental protection measures during a project if they believe they can shift the cleanup costs onto the public.
Negative Externalities	Costs suffered by a third party as a result of an economic transaction. In a transaction, the producer and consumer are the first and second parties, and third parties include any legible entity or resource that is indirectly affected.	Chemical manufacturing plants discharging waste into rivers, which does not affect their production costs directly but leads to water pollution affecting downstream communities and ecosystems.
Principal-Agent Problem	An entity (the "agent") is able to make decisions and/or take actions on behalf of, or that impact, another entity: the "principal."	State regulators (agents) might not always act in the best interest of the public (principals) due to industry capture.
Collective Action Problem	Entities would all benefit from a certain action, but it has associated costs making it implausible that any entity can or will undertake and solve it alone.	Anthropogenic climate change.
Information Asymmetry	One party in a transaction has more or better information than the other party, leading to poor decision-making and inefficiencies.	A firm might possess full knowledge of the environmental damage it causes, but if it does not disclose this information, it can continue harmful practices that others cannot challenge or mitigate.

Source: Table by the authors.
Note: The reduction of coordination costs incurred through these issues helps explain why institutions exist in the first place.

market formation: clearly defined property rights, verifiability, enforceability, value, transferability, low scientific uncertainty, and low sovereign risk (Whitten et al. 2003, xii). Crypto-institutions strengthen most of these: shared immutable databases ensure property rights are clearly defined and transferable at low cost;

transparency enables verification without auditor conflicts of interest; smart contract enforcement reduces transaction costs; and open liquidity environments create value propositions through accessible global markets. While sovereign risk remains jurisdictional, the global accessibility of cryptomarkets reduces dependence on any single government's decisions—uniquely enabling green capital formation at planetary scale.

When properly implemented, the properties in Table 4.2 combine to produce trustlessness—the emergent quality that distinguishes protocols from platforms. Shared databases enable public verification; open-source code ensures any operator can be replaced; transparency binds participants to protocol rules rather than private agreements. The Trustless Manifesto, co-authored by Vitalik Buterin, adds that users must control their own actions, transactions must resist censorship, and participation must remain accessible beyond technical elites (Weiss, Buterin, and Posner 2025). For sustainability practitioners, trustlessness addresses a persistent failure mode: environmental claims have been undermined by verification systems where auditors are paid by the entities they assess, and where greenwashing thrives because reputational trust substitutes for cryptographic proof.

For green crypto-institutions, these properties translate into specific design requirements: environmental data must be independently verifiable from public sources rather than relying on trusted attesters; carbon credit registries must permit any qualified verifier to challenge claims; and governance mechanisms must ensure that no single entity can unilaterally modify environmental accounting rules. Trustlessness in environmental finance means that the integrity of ecological claims depends on cryptographic proof rather than institutional reputation.

In summary, these distinctive properties of crypto-institutions help address the institutional coordination problems introduced at the beginning of this chapter. These properties stem from a "regression to code" (Hart, Lotti, and Shorin 2024) and the robustness provided by a shared, global, immutable public ledger. If these cybernetic benefits and institutional cost savings can be realized, then the trajectory of institutional evolution in the twenty-first century will bend toward the crypto-institutional. This institutional futurity—where governance becomes a quantifiable, adaptive tool for harmonizing the institutions that mediate social and ecological systems—and the practical design questions for its implementation will form the speculative focus of the remainder of this chapter. To ground these abstractions, the following sections survey emerging implementations across three scales: local prototypes testing governance primitives, bioregional coalitions coordinating across watersheds, and planetary-scale architectures mediating global environmental commons.

THE LITTLE PICTURE: PROTOTYPES AND PERSONS

The exploration of novel ideas often begins in low-stakes domains with high technical and innovation demands at small scale. Like all technological development, these small-scale experiments aim to identify practical scalability and usability challenges early on, when security and compliance concerns are less critical than in financial or commercial applications. These use cases emphasize the role of

TABLE 4.2
Properties of Crypto-Institutions

Property	Discussion	Green Affordance
Open-source	Open-source principles enable better reliability, cost-effectiveness, and enhanced security (Raymond 2004).	Shared MRV standards; reusable verification infrastructure; protocol forking for bioregional adaptation
Shared immutable database	The public blockchain's immutable and shared computational substrate serves as a common infrastructure for the networked information economy. The costs of verification and integration of disparate institutional primitives across identification, voting, governance, rights management, collective ownership, and civic engagement are lowered by this common infrastructure. These primitives can be composably innovated, enabling more precise preference measurement (Dávila 2023, 226; Tan, Merk, and Hubbard 2024). Blockchains can make strong commitments about their future behavior—code persists as designed (Dixon 2024, 66).	Cross-jurisdictional carbon accounting; interoperable credit registries; tamper-proof permanence records
Transparency	Crypto-institutions offer systematically rich, granular, and longitudinal data without typical censoring or sampling issues (Tan, Merk, and Hubbard 2024). This contrasts with traditional verification where consultants may lack incentive to uncover evidence that credits failed to yield environmental gains (McAfee 2012).	Eliminates verifier conflicts of interest; enables public audit of credit claims; donor accountability for impact funding
Open liquidity environment	Institutional operations previously limited to banks and states—lending, collateralization, asset issuance—are now accessible to all market participants, driving down costs and removing centralized gatekeepers.	Bioregional financing without banking intermediaries; carbon credit collateralization; democratic access to environmental finance
Ability to model the future	Crypto-institutions can leverage "computer-aided design tools for governance" due to the transparency and immutability of their ledgers, enabling quantifiable governance through metrics like participation rates, decentralization indices, and voting-bloc entropy (Tan, Merk, and Hubbard 2024).	Predictive governance calibration; scenario modeling for policy interventions; automated triggers tied to ecological thresholds
Cultural diversity	Web3 working groups prioritize inclusivity and diverse perspectives, enabling global participation in DAO governance. Diverse teams consistently outperform homogeneous ones on complex problem-solving (McKinsey & Company 2020).	Global-local knowledge integration; indigenous data sovereignty protocols; multi-stakeholder governance across jurisdictions

Source: Table by the authors.

Note: These properties represent theoretical capabilities, not guaranteed outcomes. Implementation varies significantly across projects. Practitioners should evaluate whether specific crypto-institutions actually deliver on these properties through their technical architecture and governance design, rather than assuming them from blockchain use alone.

fine-grained, local subsystems and their corresponding feedback loops within higher-scale green institutions. As Nassim Taleb observes, "it is easier to gauge micro-performance than macro-performance"—there is a convexity to localism where stronger bonds form through repeated local interactions than through dispersed global ones (Taleb 2019, 10–11). Present examples include augmented forests, smart solar farms, and RFID-equipped wallets that facilitate decentralized interactions. Web3 projects like Arkreen operate at the appliance, household, and vehicle scales to unlock the "long-tail potential of micro green assets," whose "small-scale green behaviors" can be aggregated "into a significant collective market" (2077 Research 2024).

In 2016, Terra0 proposed a vision of a self-owning forest that would generate revenue through automated smart contract timber commodity sales. Though ambitious, the project encountered significant obstacles, including a lack of legal and institutional infrastructure. This absence of a framework for recognizing environmental or nonhuman entities within these systems ultimately led Terra0 to conclude that its foundational thesis—that smart contracts could define new forms of personhood—was flawed (Mohebbi and Heiman 2024, 192–200). Similarly, empirical evaluations suggest roughly half of self-identified ReFi initiatives achieve their stated implementation goals, with the remainder still navigating technical and institutional constraints (Bennett 2025).

Positive experiments demonstrate how local initiatives can scale. Consider the Traditional Dream Factory (TDF), which integrates the ideals of a "Regenerative Village" with advanced DAO tools, including crowdfunding platforms, land-based impact DAOs, and Web3 identity solutions (Bryant 2023). True to a regenerative ethos, TDF is designed around communal spaces, studios, coworking gardens, cafes, and sustainable food forests, alongside water-retention landscapes. By leveraging the full spectrum of crypto-institutional tooling, TDF embodies a new kind of cybernetically enhanced localism, blending technological and ecological ambitions to exceed the capabilities of traditional eco-villages. Furthermore, it forms part of a broader ecological conservation network called OASA and collaborates with the blockchain-based Open Forest Protocol to monitor and support forest growth and development (OASA 2025). This pan-regional collaboration illustrates the transition to meso-institutional design questions.

THE MESO-INSTITUTIONAL: LIVING LANDSCAPES

To scale, place-based crypto-institutions connect with physical neighbors and virtual allies, integrating their "techno-geographical milieu"—natural resources included—into networked coalitions (Hui 2020). Building on this, Michel Bauwens—founder of the P2P Foundation and a leading theorist of commons-based peer production—identifies how these relationships seek to tie "systems of provisioning... such as food, shelter, and energy" together, becoming "stronger as they interconnect with each other" (Bauwens, Kostakis, and Pazaitis 2019, 63). Bioregionalist thinkers Power and Seefeld use the term "Bioregional Financing Facilities" to describe the "semi-permeable membranes between institutions rooted in the status quo... [and] emerging bioregional economies... [of] different economic

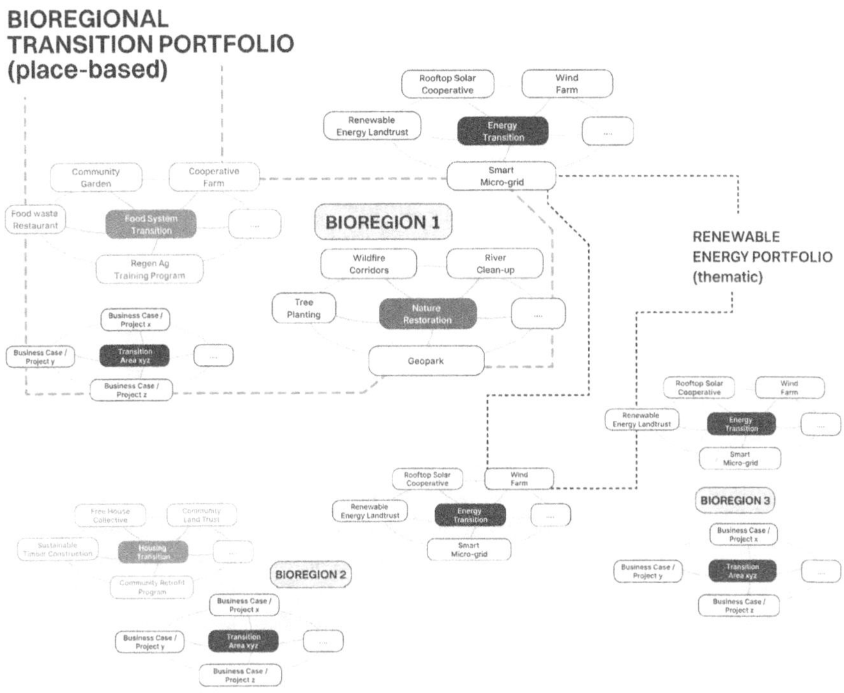

FIGURE 4.2 Bioregional Transition Portfolios link micro-scale institutions into regional networks for impactful change.

***Source*: Power and Seefeld, eds. Bioregional Financing Facilities. BioFi Project, August 2024, p. 104. https://de.scribd.com/document/744694621/Bioregional-Financing-Facilities-E-book**

and value systems" (Power and Seefeld 2024, 8). Figure 4.2 illustrates this networked topology: Indigenous entities, trusts, DAOs, Natural Asset Companies, commons groups, and cooperatives linked into regional portfolios. These concepts are moving from theory to practice: the BioFi Cultivator program is training cohorts who are implementing Bioregional Financing Facilities across multiple regions—systematizing the approach the Traditional Dream Factory embodies at micro-scale (Gitcoin 2025).

Two existing channels illustrate what crypto-institutions might augment—not exhaustively, but as illustrative case studies. First, the traditional climate finance pipeline: multilateral development institutions channel funds to national governments, who engage intermediaries, who finally reach project developers. According to the Climate Policy Initiative, 69% of public climate finance takes the form of debt—typically foreign debt—limiting accessibility for early-stage projects and creating dependency dynamics (Climate Policy Initiative 2023, 1). Crypto-institutional primitives offer concrete efficiencies: programmable disbursement, transparent tracking, reduced intermediary overhead, and mechanisms for endogenous debt origination. Second, cooperative provisioning systems: in Europe, agricultural cooperatives handle 60% of produce, while 4,000 cooperative banks serve 50 million members with a 20% market share (Manley, Webster, and Kuznetsova 2023). These institutions already solve coordination problems at regional scale. Crypto-institutional tooling—shared registries, tokenized membership, automated governance—can extend their capabilities rather than replace them.

Furthermore, crypto-institutional coalitions can compose the assets they produce into functional financial systems. OpenEarth proposed a model where ecological assets are originated by crypto-institutions in lieu of traditional green instruments issued by intermediaries (Wainstein, Constant, and Clippinger 2023). These assets can serve as collateral for spending currencies (i.e., stablecoins), scaffolding monetary systems backed by natural capital—Azos Finance, for instance, offers an over-collateralized stablecoin backed by tokenized carbon credits (Azos Finance n.d.). Emerging institutional theory conceptualizes such arrangements as "ecocapital"—bookable capital assets derived from ecological contributions that can compound investment (Potts, Rennie, and Landua 2025). Unlike natural capital accounting, which estimates value but cannot generate financial leverage, ecocapital creates fungible capital assets that function within existing financial logic.

Earlier in this chapter, we argued that institutions are increasingly moving toward cybernetic forms with high trust guarantees to solve coordination problems. This convergence is visible at the meso-institutional scale: traditional standards bodies and blockchain-based platforms need not remain separate institutional types. Monitoring, reporting, and verification (MRV) requirements—long a bottleneck for green asset legitimacy—increasingly benefit from blockchain infrastructure that can serve both. The World Bank has identified blockchain-based digital MRV as a promising path for evolving manual MRV practices (World Bank 2018). Ultimately, ecocapital formation requires these systems, as its minting and distribution depends on trust-minimized attribution registries that record and evaluate contributions to observed ecological regeneration. Chapter 5 examines these protocol primitives in detail and how they can be leveraged by sustainability practitioners.

Various prototypes illustrate what meso-institutional collaboration might look like. The Zazelenimo pilot in Split, Croatia demonstrated municipal-scale coordination concretely: a 3:1 matching model funded community-driven urban greening projects using Ethereum-aligned infrastructure (Baeva 2025). These prototypes draw on a rich taxonomy of meso-scale institutional forms that predate blockchain but share its coordination logic. Table 4.3 surveys these forms, each of which blockchain tooling may augment.

Innovation economists describe "Innovation Commons" as collaborative communities that serve as precursors to new business models—"private governance for discovery of public goods." Such innovation commons are systems of rules for cooperation that pool distributed knowledge under conditions of uncertainty, facilitating collective opportunity discovery that no individual entrepreneur could

TABLE 4.3
Meso-scale Institutional Forms

Institution	Description	Examples
Bioregional Governance	Regional systems adapting governance to local ecological and social conditions.	Bioregional Councils, Transition Towns
Landscape Enterprise Networks	Connects businesses, public bodies, and community groups for sustainable land management.	Regional Conservation Partnerships
Local Microgrids	Decentralized energy systems generating and distributing power locally.	Brooklyn Microgrid
Cooperatives	Member-owned organizations providing services to members rather than external shareholders.	Mondragon Corporation
Community Land Trusts	Non-profit entities holding land for community benefit.	Dudley Street Neighborhood Initiative
Watershed Councils	Collaborative bodies managing water resources at watershed level.	Willamette Partnership
Mutual Aid Networks	Networks organizing collective care and support among members.	Food Not Bombs

Source: Table by the authors.

Note: Specific examples include: Mondragon corporation, a federation of worker cooperatives in spain; community land trusts such as the dudley street neighborhood initiative; the willamette partnership for watershed governance; and food not bombs, a mutual aid network founded in 1980 (see butler and mchenry 1992). Jeremy rifkin's *the age of resilience* (2022) offers deeper discussion of many of these forms and their role in adaptive, place-based governance.

achieve alone. The green crypto ecosystem exhibits this pattern. What began as informal working groups has given rise to structured organizations: Greenpill Network supports local chapters advancing regenerative finance; ReFi DAO coordinates ecosystem-wide initiatives; and networks like Ma Earth, Bloom Network, and AgroforestDAO bring expertise in ecological regeneration. The Regen Coordination initiative weaves these networks together through shared work and collaborative funding rounds (Papenbrock, Ashley, and Schwendner 2022). For practitioners, the implication is strategic: participating in these networks during their formative phases offers both influence over their development and positioning for their eventual institutionalization.

AI AND THE PLANET SCALE

At a planetary scale, comprehensively understanding and managing a cybernetic network capable of addressing global challenges like the climate crisis exceeds the cognitive capacity of any single individual or institution. Climate-aware portfolio managers illustrate the problem: they increasingly struggle to integrate vast, heterogeneous datasets. Constructing optimal investment strategies requires evaluating "the full set of information to find the optimal portfolio that incorporates all external environmental, social and governance exposures and costs after evaluating diverse and conflicting data sources" (Papenbrock, Ashley, and Schwendner 2022). From a theoretical standpoint, their work requires solving a Bayes-optimal classification problem across an ensemble of models and objectives—a task that hinges on determining which datasets to connect and how to interpret their outputs, both of which remain unresolved coordination challenges (Papenbrock, Ashley, and Schwendner 2022). At planetary scale, the computational complexity renders manual analysis infeasible.

AI augmentation offers a path forward—not through abstraction, but through the aggregation of systems already demonstrating what augmented environmental governance looks like in practice. These systems align directly with the management of the MRV infrastructure surveyed in Chapter 2, and the predictive models of Chapter 3. WWF uses machine learning to process camera trap data, enabling rapid identification of over 150 species in Australia's post-bushfire recovery efforts. Forest Foresight achieves 80% accuracy in predicting deforestation up to six months out from satellite inputs (Forest Foresight 2024; WWF n.d.). Mercy Corps Ventures' 2023 pilot fused remote sensing, satellite imagery, cryptocurrencies, and AI-driven climate analytics to deliver rapid aid to disaster-struck African regions, demonstrating real-time adaptability (Mercy Corps Ventures 2025). These applications leverage anticipatory cybernetic regulation—sensors and AI—to detect environmental changes, respond with resource allocation, and mediate damage before it becomes irreversible.

These tools work. But they operate as siloed applications—a deforestation alert here, a species identification there. The challenge practitioners face is connecting these capabilities into coordinated institutional action across global boundaries. This is where AI augmentation becomes essential: it helps institutions co-create and adapt "a living model of the world" from their "asynchronous contributions" and "preferred outcomes," equipping them to speak "a common language through which these internalities can connect, converse, and coordinate" (Martinez-Diaz and McClamrock 2019; Zargham and Ben-Meir 2023). This common framework supports the creation of digital twins—virtual replicas of ecosystems that "pinpoint feedback loops, assess ecosystem health, and measure the impacts of species interactions and human interventions" (Peborgh 2024).

The coordination problems surveyed earlier in this chapter—free riding, information asymmetry, principal-agent conflicts—explain why institutions exist. The blockchain properties that follow—transparency, shared immutable databases, open liquidity—explain how crypto-institutions reduce the coordination costs of addressing these problems. But a residual challenge remains: even with transparent global ledgers and programmable governance, crypto-institutions face operational overhead in finding qualified partners, confirming work quality, ensuring contractual compliance, reaching agreement across jurisdictions, resolving disputes, and achieving consensus among distributed stakeholders. These are precisely the cognitive tasks that AI agent-to-agent (A2A) protocols can make cheap (Owocki, Stringer, and Ospina

2025). When AI handles partner discovery, due diligence, contract execution, and dispute arbitration, much of what organizations once internalized can be unbundled into open networks. For green crypto-institutions, this means bioregional coalitions can coordinate at scales previously requiring extensive intermediary infrastructure—AI agents operating on behalf of institutions negotiate resource allocations, execute cross-organizational trades, and manage portfolio rebalancing across watershed boundaries, while human governance retains authority over constitutional decisions (Owocki, Stringer, and Ospina 2025). Blockchain's "first billion users" may well be these AI agents, as evidenced by a "growing onchain economy" where they autonomously handle funds, engage with decentralized applications, and learn to operate with minimal human oversight (Selva 2024). Figure 4.3 illustrates the simplest version of this logic: an autonomous ecological institution that ingests data-oracle inputs and executes predefined actions when environmental thresholds change.

These agents and their "agentic protocols" are described as "self-developing" entities that aim "to have no human employees"; they generate cashflows by "licensing IP

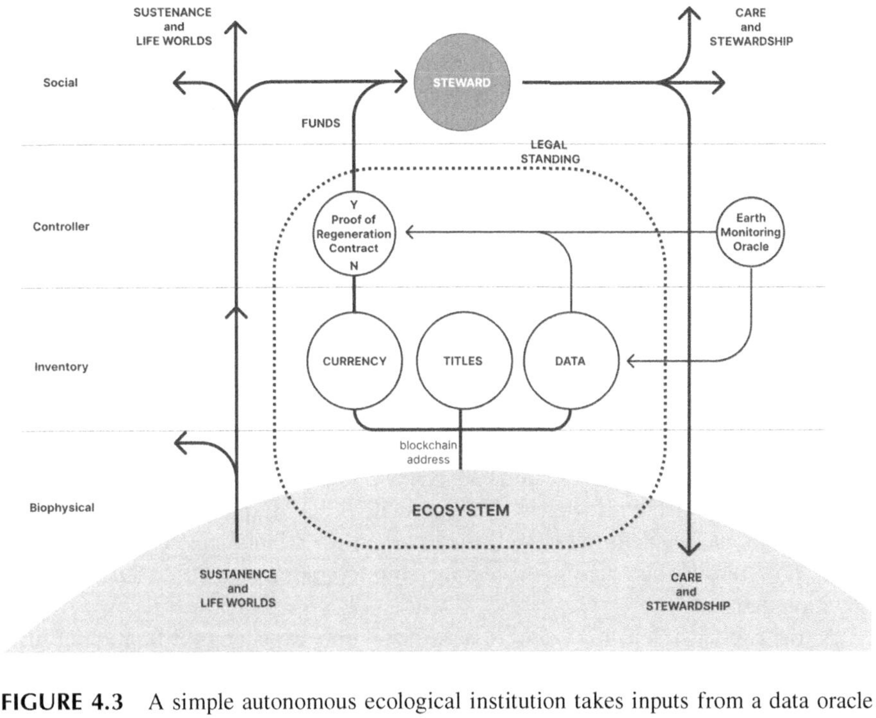

FIGURE 4.3 A simple autonomous ecological institution takes inputs from a data oracle and executes a finite set of actions based on whether environmental conditions are met. Autonomous ecological institutions are a kind of sovereign ecological actor whose interaction with legal, economic, or political systems is not reliant upon human governance except for its conception and configuration. They are essentially DAOs pegged to ecological features through legal means.

***Source*: Wade Smith (2025).**

or other technology products" as well as through market speculation (goodalexander 2024). They engage in both A2A and AI-to-human payments (Payman AI 2025). Furthermore, they have:

> [T]heir own native cryptocurrency token which (1) is the currency by which its products are sold or licensed which (2) allows human or AI users to participate in the upside of its financial activities (3) validates and pays for the opex of the system which is primarily compute, training and storage.
>
> **goodalexander (2024)**

The deployment of autonomous AI systems in environmental governance warrants careful evaluation. As the empirical research discussed earlier in this chapter demonstrates, regenerative alignment cannot be assumed from technological sophistication alone—practitioners should question whether AI deployment advances regenerative principles or merely automates extractive logics at greater scale and speed.

Through the aggregation of green-aligned agents and their embedding into crypto-institutions, a "Digital Earth" emerges where species other than humans can be incorporated into global governance—much like Isabelle Stengers' notion of "cosmopolitics," or Bruno Latour's vision of a "Parliament of Things." Imagine: a DAO in which whales—or at the very least, their digitized twins—can submit proposals to deviate shipping routes, or a DAO forest that incentivizes ecological restorers to recover from a wildfire, or a river with already existing legal form financing its own cleanup. The number of eco-jurisprudent cases and legal mechanisms is rapidly increasing since the early 2000s; when combined with these legal efforts, the introduction of crypto-institutions can harden and strengthen the capacities of these actors ("Eco-Jurisprudence Monitor" n.d.).

Nonhuman representation in governance is less far-fetched than it may appear, given the infrastructural advances in interspecies interfaces through AI and institutional advances in legal frameworks supporting this endeavor. The "Earth Species Project… is [already] harnessing AI to decode nonhuman communication" (Armstrong 2024, 89). CETI "aims to achieve bidirectional communication… to speak back and forth with whales" (Salguero 2024, 93). Experimentation with various institutional legal forms is well underway, with nonhumans exercising governance powers ranging from board membership to contracting ("Eco-Jurisprudence Monitor" n.d.).

As the twenty-first century progresses, the authors expect a proliferation of institutional interfaces enhancing the capacities of nonhuman actors. The question practitioners face is not whether AI will reshape green crypto-institutions, but whether that reshaping advances regenerative outcomes—a question that design choices made in the present will determine. As Wade Smith has argued, "The institutional forms of the future must reflect a more whole world, populated by more subjects than human beings, leading to the emergence of novel eco-social assemblages which redefine concepts like rights, ownership, identity, privacy, responsibility, and politics beyond solely the human realm" (Wade Smith 2025).

(Ø1) DESIGNING GREEN CRYPTO-INSTITUTIONAL GOVERNANCE SURFACES

BOX 4.1 MINIMUM VIABLE GOVERNANCE

Add complexity only as coordination problems emerge: If delegation becomes necessary, add it; if vote-buying appears, add quadratic voting; if participation drops, add reputation decay. Premature optimization kills daos faster than missing features.

START HERE: MINIMUM VIABLE GOVERNANCE

Most practitioners are overwhelmed by options. For most green crypto-institutions, three decisions come first:

Who can participate? (membership policy)—Open to all token holders? Curated by existing members? Tied to verified land stewardship?

What threshold triggers action? (quorum + majority)—Too high and proposals never pass. Too low and small groups capture the treasury.

What happens when things go wrong? (fallback mechanisms)—Pause functions, multi-sig overrides, time delays, emergency councils. Automation fails; practitioners should plan for it.

This section turns from theory to practice. As Box 4.1 suggests, practitioners should begin with minimum viable governance and layer in complexity only as coordination problems demand it. The preceding sections examined why crypto-institutions matter and at what scales they operate. Here, we focus on the specific design tensions sustainability practitioners face when configuring governance surfaces, the primitives and tools DAOs use, and the parameters they tune. This section is in part a foreword to Chapter 5, the Protocol Layer, which extends governance to the full suite of policy-making instruments. Echoing the overarching theme of this chapter, the Taskforce on Nature Markets notes that these "decentralised governing instruments" are key to effective nature market governance (Taskforce on Nature Markets and Finance for Biodiversity Initiative 2022, 9).

Good governance design should start simple, choosing to add complexity only when coordination problems demand it. Four high-level recurring tensions shape these design choices. Every governance surface parameter configuration resolves them differently; there are no right answers, only design trade-offs matched to context:

1. **Decentralization vs. Coordination.** More distributed governance resists capture but slows decisions. If a project requires rapid response to ecological

events—fire, drought, invasive species—build in emergency authority. If long-term stewardship matters more than speed, distribute power widely.

2. **Privacy vs. Transparency.** Open ledgers build trust but can expose sensitive data without privacy-by-design. Land steward locations, endangered species sites, and community financial information may require shielded approaches. On the other hand, hidden governance invites corruption.
3. **Incentives vs. Participation.** Token rewards and other forms of green financing may boost short-term engagement but attract extractive actors. Merit-based systems screen for commitment but can limit growth. Most green projects need both: green finance for liquidity, reputation for legitimacy.
4. **Embeddedness vs. Detachment.** Technical governance sophistication means nothing if the institution isn't embedded in the community it serves. Will Ruddick's Community of Practice framework—developed through his work building blockchain-based community currency networks in Kenya—maps institutions along *proximity* (shared daily life, embodied presence) and *accountability* (peer checks, open ledgers) (Ruddick 2025). The goal is close and accountable; distant-and-unaccountable is the failure mode. For green crypto-institutions, this framework suggests that governance parameters matter less than whether the institution is embedded in the community it serves. In general, issues of sustained participation from the third tension are resolved when Web3 practitioners have something practical and in proximity to govern. Place-based food systems, renewable energy cooperatives, watershed commons, community land trusts tend to sustain embedded engagement beyond speculative token cycles.

These four top-level design tensions play out differently across institutional forms. Before diving into specific parameters, consider how crypto-institutional and traditional governance designs differ. Table 4.4 compares Regen Network with Verra, the dominant traditional carbon registry. The comparison reveals how each approach navigates the tensions outlined above: different trade-offs between participation and expertise, transparency and efficiency, stakeholder breadth, and operational focus.

The restructured comparison maps each tension directly: Regen's token governance and multi-entity structure resolve the decentralization-coordination trade-off toward distributed participation; its onchain visibility and open forums maximize transparency; token staking creates incentive alignment while lowering participation barriers; and direct land steward relationships embed the network in its communities. Verra's choices optimize differently—centralized expertise enables consistent standards, controlled communication maintains institutional credibility, standardized requirements ensure verification quality, and third-party verification scales globally. Neither configuration is inherently superior; each reflects deliberate trade-offs. What both share is the underlying architecture: governance surfaces composed of configurable parameters that establish the rules for collective action.

All crypto-institutional governance surfaces ultimately establish rules for (a) the establishment of rules, understood as constitutional rules, or (b) other forms of conditional operations that require some sort of consensus-making process to be

TABLE 4.4
Comparison of Crypto-Institutional and Traditional Governance in the Carbon Sector

Aspect	Regen Network	Verra
Description	Blockchain-based platform facilitating ecosystem regeneration through transparent tracking and trading of ecosystem services.	Non-profit organization developing and managing standards for certification and verification of environmental and sustainability initiatives.
Decentralization vs. Coordination	Multiple entities: Regen Network Development, Inc. (for-profit software), Regen Foundation (501(c)(3) non-profit), and decentralized network governed by token holders. Anyone staking $REGEN can vote on and submit proposals for software upgrades, parameter changes, and community pool spending.	Monolithic non-profit governed by Board of Directors with technical committees and expert advisory groups responsible for standards development. Board-directed decision-making with public comment periods on methodology updates.
Privacy vs. Transparency	Discord, Telegram, bi-weekly community calls, X spaces, blogs. All governance proposals publicly visible onchain.	Press releases, newsletters, webinars. Internal deliberations not publicly accessible.
Incentives vs. Participation	Actively involving diverse landowners, farmers, project developers, and investors. Token staking aligns participation with network success.	Standardized requirements prioritize consistency and scalability, though can create barriers for smaller landholders.
Embeddedness vs. Detachment	Direct relationships with land stewards through Regen Registry; project developers as network participants.	Operates through accredited third-party verifiers; standards body detached from on-ground implementation.

Source: "Governance Basics," Regen Network Guidebook, https://guides.regen.network/guides/network-governance/governance-basics/about; "Overview," Verra, https://verra.org/about/overview/. Table by the authors.

initiated, such as defining a crypto-institution's membership via a registry or distributing funding to said registry. These rules are constrained by what we will call governance parameters, encodable via smart contract for DAOs (but may strategically not be, e.g., to avoid the "economic logics" that may diminish the "democratic politics" of decision-making). These governance parameters can be modularly applied, with many simultaneously exercised for certain types of decision-making. Each parameter implies the resolution of a governance design decision: take, for example, the parameter of Weighted vs. Unweighted voting; in the former, feedforward loops may accumulate wealth to the wealthiest by making their voice more powerful due to the existence of a fungible and transferable token-based voting system, while unweighted voting (e.g., one-person-one-vote) may undervalue their stake, highlighting trade-offs in influence and equity.

Table 4.5 catalogs the governance parameters practitioners must configure. Many already exist in traditional institutions; the table presents them with the assumption

TABLE 4.5
Governance Parameters for Green Crypto-Institutions

Parameter	Description and Trade-Offs	Green/Climate Application
Weighted vs. Unweighted	Token-weighted voting assigns influence proportional to stake; unweighted voting provides equality (one-person-one-vote). Hybrid approaches include quadratic voting (more weight to the long tail of smaller holders) and correlation discounting (reduces voting power when voters exhibit similar behavior, preventing bloc dominance). **Trade-offs:** Weighted systems concentrate power in large holders. Unweighted enables sybil attacks without identity verification.	Shares in a Natural Asset Company weight voting by ownership stake; cooperative land trusts use unweighted membership votes.
Single vs. Multi-preference	Single-preference voting forces a binary choice; multi-preference methods allow voters to express ranked or graded support across options, reducing strategic voting and surfacing broader consensus. Options include approval voting (support multiple candidates), ranked-choice (order preferences), and pairwise comparison (voters evaluate options in pairs, with algorithms aggregating results across all comparisons). **Trade-offs:** Single-preference wastes information and forces false binaries. Multi-preference increases complexity and can confuse unfamiliar participants.	A bioregional coalition could use ranked-choice voting to prioritize watershed restoration projects, allowing members to express nuanced preferences rather than forcing winner-take-all competition between proposals.
Delayed vs. Instant	Delayed execution enforces a waiting period between decision and action, enabling review and preventing hasty or malicious proposals from executing before community response. Zodiac's Delay module (Gnosis Guild 2024) implements configurable time-locks for DAO transactions. **Trade-offs:** Too-long delays frustrate urgent needs. Too-short allows governance attacks before community can mobilize.	Time-locks on treasury withdrawals allow review; delayed execution can prevent flash-loan governance attacks, where an attacker borrows tokens, votes, and repays within a single transaction block.
Quorum Threshold	Minimum participation required for valid decisions. Absolute majority requires majority of all possible votes; relative majority needs plurality once a participation threshold is met. Setting thresholds involves balancing legitimacy (high quorum) against operational efficiency (low quorum). **Trade-offs:** Low quorum enables small-group capture of governance. High quorum causes gridlock and proposal fatigue.	A conservation DAO might set higher quorum (e.g., 67%) for irreversible decisions like land sales, while routine grant disbursement could proceed with lower participation thresholds (e.g., 20%).

(Continued)

TABLE 4.5 ***(Continued)***
Governance Parameters for Green Crypto-Institutions

Parameter	Description and Trade-Offs	Green/Climate Application
Single vs. Multistage	Single-stage applies one vote to reach a decision; multistage processes use different methods at each phase with increasing formality. DAOstack's holographic consensus adjusted quorum thresholds based on economic stake committed to a proposal's outcome. **Trade-offs:** Single stage risks passing undervetted proposals. Too many stages exhaust participants and slow response.	Gitcoin Grants proceeds through multiple stages: informal temperature check via forum poll, detailed proposal development with community feedback, then formal onchain allocation vote (Gitcoin 2025).
Delegated vs. Direct	Liquid democracy allows token holders to delegate votes or vote weight to representatives while retaining the ability to vote directly on specific proposals. Delegation can be transitive (delegates can re-delegate) or non-transitive. **Trade-offs:** Without accountability mechanisms, delegates become a permanent oligarchy. Direct-only voting yields low turnout on technical matters. Research suggests most users don't delegate unless incentivized (Jennings and Kerr 2022).	Watershed councils could delegate to hydrology experts for technical assessments while members vote directly on land-use policy affecting their parcels.
Onchain vs. Offchain	Onchain governance executes decisions via smart contracts, providing trust-minimized enforcement where outcomes follow automatically from votes. Offchain governance preserves flexibility and reduces costs but requires trust in executors. Hybrid models bind legal entities to honor onchain votes. **Trade-offs:** Full onchain is expensive, slow, and rigid. Full offchain provides no trust-minimized enforcement and relies on social accountability.	SafeDAO's model binds an offchain Foundation to implement onchain token holder decisions.
Curated vs. Open	Membership curation determines who can participate in governance. Options range from fully open (anyone can purchase tokens) to sponsored (existing members vouch for new entrants) to merit-based (demonstrated contribution required). Protocol Guild uses peer sponsorship where existing contributors nominate and approve new members. Progressive ownership models (Jin and Walden 2023) weight governance toward active participants. **Trade-offs:** Curation can become exclusionary gatekeeping. Open membership attracts speculators who dilute mission focus.	Regen Network requires verified land stewardship for full governance participation.

(Continued)

TABLE 4.5 (*Continued*)
Governance Parameters for Green Crypto-Institutions

Parameter	Description and Trade-Offs	Green/Climate Application
Role Separation	Powers can be distributed equally across all members or separated into distinct roles with specific authorities. Hats Protocol represents roles as tokens with defined permissions. Separation enables specialization: Metamorpho separates Curators (market selection) from Guardians (emergency intervention). **Trade-offs:** Role proliferation creates bureaucracy. No separation means diffuse accountability when problems arise.	Stewardship DAOs can assign distinct roles: field monitors, verification auditors, and treasury guardians each hold different permissions.
Discrete vs. Continuous	Governance can operate through periodic votes (discrete) or ongoing signal aggregation (continuous). Conviction voting (e.g., 1Hive) weights decisions by both stake size and duration of commitment. Colony's reputation system continuously adjusts influence based on contribution history. **Trade-offs:** Discrete systems miss emerging consensus between voting periods. Continuous systems create attention overhead and favor always-online participants.	Superfluid enables continuous token streams; carbon credit payments could flow proportionally to ongoing sequestration rather than lump-sum disbursements.
Exit vs. Voice	Hirschman's framework: members can exit (withdraw resources) or exercise voice (attempt repair through participation). Zodiac Exit module (Gnosis Guild 2024) allows members to redeem governance tokens for a proportional share of treasury assets. Place-based institutions may require stronger voice mechanisms since physical exit means abandoning land. **Trade-offs:** Easy exit causes capital flight at first difficulty. No exit traps hostile or disengaged members.	Impact investors could use ragequit mechanisms to redeem tokens at net asset value if governance direction diverges from their thesis; land stewards with territorial commitments need robust dispute resolution and voice mechanisms instead.
Human vs. Algorithmic	Decisions can require human judgment or execute automatically based on data inputs. Decision markets aggregate predictions about which policy option will produce better outcomes, using economic incentives to surface distributed knowledge (Buterin 2024). Ecological oracles can trigger governance actions when sensor data crosses thresholds. DeepGov (Gitcoin 2025) uses AI agents to evaluate proposals against stated community values, scoring alignment before human review. **Trade-offs:** Oracles can fail silently or be manipulated. Algorithmic governance may execute inappropriate actions with no appeal process.	Automated payments could release when IoT sensors confirm water quality targets; human override available for edge cases.

(Continued)

TABLE 4.5 (*Continued*)
Governance Parameters for Green Crypto-Institutions

Parameter	Description and Trade-Offs	Green/Climate Application
Merit vs. Money	Governance power can derive from financial stake (token holdings) or demonstrated contribution (reputation, work history). Futarchy uses prediction markets to select policies: stakeholders bet on outcomes under different policy options, and the policy predicted to perform best is implemented. This separates "what do we want" (values) from "how do we get it" (predictions). **Trade-offs:** Merit systems can become insider credentials impossible for newcomers to achieve. Pure financial governance becomes plutocracy. "Governance tokens are often used for speculation rather than governance" (Tan, Merk, and Hubbard 2024).	Coinage Cooperative distributes patronage dividends to active NFT members based on participation. Regenerative asset cooperatives could weight governance by verified restoration work rather than token purchases.
Private vs. Public	Voting can be visible (public) or shielded (private) during deliberation. Public voting enables accountability but can cause herding toward early leaders. MACI (Minimal Anti-Collusion Infrastructure) enables shielded voting that reveals only aggregate results. BlockchainGov research notes that opaque influence "behind the scenes" undermines legitimacy (De Filippi et al. 2024). **Trade-offs:** Privacy enables hidden coordination and vote-buying. Full transparency exposes vulnerable community members to coercion.	A DAO could use shielded voting during active deliberation to prevent herding, reveal results publicly after the vote closes to enable accountability, and maintain transparent treasury flows to satisfy donor reporting requirements.

Source: Table by the authors.

that smart contract encoding is possible. For comprehensive treatment, the authors recommend BlockScience's *Governance Module Library* (Blockscience 2023), the *Mechanism Institute Library* (Mechanism Institute 2025), or the *Handbook of Computational Social Choice* (Brandt et al. 2016). The latter resource provides an apt history of the dilemmas and paradoxes inherent to any governance system and offers rigorous mathematical proofs with regard to many of the parameters discussed in Table 4.5.

A NOTE ON LEGAL

These governance parameters do not exist in a legal vacuum. The institutional protocol and the legal are mutually reinforcing: smart contract logic gains enforceability through legal recognition, while legal structures gain operational efficiency through automated execution. Practitioners must consider jurisdictional choices—examples include Wyoming DAO LLCs, Marshall Islands nonprofit LLCs, Swiss associations,

Cayman foundations, and others—that determine how onchain governance binds offchain obligations. The SafeDAO model demonstrates this integration: token governance controls a legal entity that can sign contracts, hold assets, and bear liability. For green crypto-institutions operating across jurisdictions, legal wrapper selection affects regulatory compliance for carbon credit issuance, liability for environmental claims, and the enforceability of cross-border agreements. The parameters above should be understood as technical constructs that operate within, and are strengthened by, appropriate legal scaffolding.

This chapter does not provide legal advice. Regulations governing DAOs, digital assets, and environmental markets shift rapidly across jurisdictions; fundraising requirements vary by entity type and investor base; and tax implications depend on domicile, activity, and token classification. Practitioners should research comparable projects in their target jurisdictions, consult qualified legal counsel, and monitor regulatory developments. Organizations like LexDAO, a16z's legal resources, and the Coalition of Automated Legal Applications (COALA) provide starting points, though no substitute for tailored advice (COALA n.d.; Jennings and Kerr 2022; LexDAO n.d.).

That said, legal and cybernetic integration is becoming increasingly sophisticated. The 2024 UNCITRAL Model Law on Automated Contracting (MLAC) exemplifies this trend, providing a framework for designing smart contracts that achieve legal recognition while preserving autonomy. Under MLAC, a contract cannot be denied legal effect solely because it was formed or performed by an automated system, provided it contains essential contract elements (UNCITRAL 2024). For green crypto-institutions, this suggests practical design requirements: hybrid contracts that supplement code with natural-language terms; fallback mechanisms enabling human intervention when automation misfires (time delays, pause functions, multi-signature approvals); and clear dispute resolution clauses specifying onchain or offchain processes. Smart contracts governing the green crypto-assets discussed in Chapter 6—tokenized carbon credits, biodiversity credits, renewable energy certificates—benefit from this hybrid approach, retaining automation's efficiency while ensuring legal recourse when real-world obligations (physical restoration work, delivery of ecosystem services) cannot be fully executed onchain.

For practitioners, the key questions when selecting legal structure include:

- What assets will the institution hold (land, carbon credits, tokens, intellectual property)?
- What liabilities might arise (environmental claims, investor disputes, regulatory enforcement)?
- What governance decisions require legal enforceability versus social consensus?
- How will the entity raise capital (grants, token sales, traditional investment)?
- What reporting and compliance obligations attach to each option?

The answers determine whether a Wyoming DAO LLC (favorable for US-based tokenized governance), a Swiss association (appropriate for member-based organizations with global reach), a Cayman foundation (common for protocols seeking regulatory distance), or another structure best fits the institution's needs.

PUTTING IT ALL TOGETHER: CONFIGURATION GUIDANCE

These parameters don't operate in isolation—effective governance design requires configuring them as an ensemble matched to institutional purpose. The following examples illustrate how practitioners might approach three green crypto-institutional patterns at ascending scales, walking through the reasoning at each decision point. Each pattern draws on specific DAO types cataloged in Appendix A (Table 4A.1), addresses coordination problems from Table 4.1, and leverages the crypto-institutional properties from Table 4.2.

RENEWABLE ENERGY COOPERATIVE

Consider a residential building or small neighborhood pooling resources to install rooftop solar panels and battery storage. This is governance at its most tangible: a shared physical asset, a defined membership, and recurring decisions about maintenance, upgrades, and energy allocation.

What makes a crypto-institutional approach worth considering at this intimate scale? The core affordance is *transparency* (Table 4.2) in resource accounting. Smart meters can feed production and consumption data directly to an onchain ledger, creating an auditable record that all members can verify. Energy credits accumulate automatically; allocations follow programmed rules rather than manual bookkeeping prone to error or dispute. For a cooperative of 20 households, this might seem like overkill—but it establishes habits and infrastructure that scale.

The coordination problems at this scale are familiar from Table 4.1. The *free rider problem* emerges when some residents consume more than their share or resist contributing to maintenance funds. *Information asymmetry* appears when the building manager knows more about system performance than individual unit owners. A *shared immutable database* addresses both: contributions and consumption are visible to all members, and no single party controls the records.

Governance parameters for a residential energy cooperative can remain minimal. Unweighted voting (one unit, one vote) suits the egalitarian structure. Direct participation works when membership is small enough for everyone to engage meaningfully—delegation becomes useful only as the cooperative grows or technical complexity increases. Single-stage voting suffices for routine decisions; reserve multistage processes for capital expenditures above a threshold. Open membership within the building, but curated if the cooperative expands to neighboring properties.

The temporal structure favors discrete governance. Energy production is continuous, but the decisions that matter—rate structures, maintenance schedules, equipment upgrades—occur periodically. Conviction voting or continuous signal aggregation would be excessive; quarterly or annual votes align with natural decision cycles.

Exit mechanisms matter even at this scale. If a unit owner sells their apartment, their cooperative share should transfer with the property—or be redeemable at fair value. Ragequit provisions, however simple, prevent lock-in that breeds resentment.

Legal structure at this scale typically involves a traditional cooperative or homeowners association with blockchain-based record-keeping layered on top. The legal wrapper handles property rights and liability; the crypto layer handles transparent accounting and participatory decision-making. This hybrid approach—familiar legal forms enhanced with crypto-institutional infrastructure—offers the lowest barrier to entry for communities testing these ideas.

Projects like Arkreen demonstrate how these micro-scale installations can aggregate into larger networks, with individual households contributing to collective pools that unlock wholesale energy markets or carbon credit certification. The governance skills developed at the building level—transparent accounting, participatory budgeting, equitable allocation—transfer directly to larger-scale coordination.

BIOREGIONAL FINANCING FACILITIES

Scaling up from individual buildings, consider a facility coordinating watershed restoration across multiple landholders—a Bioregional DAO as described in Appendix A. What makes a crypto-institutional approach worth the added complexity?

The core affordance is coordination across property and jurisdictional boundaries. Watersheds don't respect ownership lines or municipal borders, but traditional institutions struggle to pool resources and allocate benefits across independent actors operating under different legal regimes. A crypto-institution can hold shared funds in a transparent treasury, allocate grants through participatory mechanisms, and maintain an auditable record of both financial flows and restoration outcomes. The *shared immutable database* (Table 4.2) creates accountability without requiring trust in any single administrator—important when participants include land trusts, municipal governments, and individual smallholders who might otherwise lack standing or common legal frameworks.

This structure directly addresses several coordination problems from Table 4.1. The *free rider problem*—upstream landholders benefiting from downstream restoration without contributing—can be mitigated through transparent contribution tracking and governance weight tied to participation. *Information asymmetry* about restoration outcomes diminishes when all participants can verify the same onchain records and MRV data.

The temporal structure of watershed restoration shapes governance choices. These are multi-decade commitments: riparian buffers take years to establish, aquifer recharge happens over even longer timescales. This argues for Voice over Exit. Participants cannot meaningfully ragequit a watershed—their land remains hydrologically connected regardless of governance disputes. Strong dispute resolution and community mediation therefore matter more than redemption mechanisms. Reputation systems should decay for inactive participants, ensuring those doing ongoing stewardship work maintain governance weight.

Technical decisions about hydrology, species selection, and monitoring protocols benefit from expert judgment, suggesting delegation to qualified specialists. But land-use decisions affecting individual parcels should remain with direct stakeholders. Liquid delegation enables this split: members delegate technical questions to credentialed experts while retaining direct voice on matters affecting their property.

Membership curation matters because watershed governance requires ongoing physical presence. Open token-based membership would attract speculators with no connection to the landscape. Merit-based entry tied to demonstrated stewardship—documented restoration work, land ownership within the watershed, or verified volunteer hours—ensures participants have skin in the game beyond financial speculation.

A bioregional facility may encompass constituent entities with more demanding governance requirements—particularly when managing irreversible assets like old-growth forest, critical habitat, or species refugia. These conservation components function as Autonomous Ecological Institutions (Appendix A), where the crypto-institutional affordance is perpetuity: ensuring that protective commitments survive changes in personnel, funding, and political context.

Conservation confronts the *collective action problem* (Table 4.1) in its purest form: everyone benefits from preserved ecosystems, but concentrated interests profit from extraction. For these sub-entities, high quorum thresholds for disposition decisions—selling land, modifying easements, extracting resources—ensure that consequential choices require broad consensus. Role separation becomes essential: field monitors, verification auditors, and treasury guardians hold distinct permissions through systems like Hats Protocol. Strong fallback mechanisms—time-locks via Zodiac Delay, multi-signature requirements, emergency councils—enable human intervention when automated systems misfire.

The legal wrapper for conservation components should constrain the governance surface rather than simply execute its decisions. A perpetual conservation trust structured to prevent disposition regardless of token holder preferences protects irreversible assets from short-term incentives. The DAO governance layer handles operational decisions within these constraints; the legal structure ensures that even a captured DAO cannot sell the forest. This is governance bounded by law rather than law bounded by governance—an inversion that makes sense precisely because the assets at stake cannot be restored once lost.

For the broader bioregional facility, legal structure depends on both function and jurisdiction. A facility focused primarily on grant-making might use a charitable foundation or donor-advised fund structure; one that needs to hold and transfer land titles requires an entity with real property capacity; one pooling investment capital faces securities considerations that shape entity choice. Within those functional constraints, jurisdiction determines specific options: a blockchain-linked LLC (such as a Wyoming DAO LLC in the United States), an association (such as a Swiss Verein for European operations), or a purpose trust in common-law jurisdictions. Where the watershed spans multiple countries, a network of jurisdiction-specific legal entities can share a common governance layer onchain while maintaining local legal compliance.

TOKENIZED CARBON CREDIT MARKETS

At planetary scale, a tokenized carbon credit marketplace—a Protocol DAO or Capital Allocation DAO per Appendix A—faces different affordances and constraints. Here the crypto-institutional value proposition centers on disintermediation and *transparency* (Table 4.2). Traditional voluntary carbon markets suffer from opacity: buyers cannot verify credit quality, sellers face high intermediation costs, and the chain from project to retirement passes through multiple rent-extracting middlemen. Blockchain-based registries make the full lifecycle visible—from project certification through trading to retirement—reducing *information asymmetry* and transaction costs.

Carbon markets address the *negative externality* problem (Table 4.1) by pricing emissions, but traditional markets suffer from *moral hazard*—verifiers paid by project developers have weak incentives to find problems. The crypto-institutional *open liquidity environment* enables competitive verification markets where any qualified auditor can challenge claims, reducing conflicts of interest.

The temporal structure differs sharply from bioregional governance. Carbon credits represent discrete, verifiable events: a specific tonnage sequestered over a defined vintage period. This discreteness enables more algorithmic governance than ongoing land stewardship. Payments can release automatically when MRV sensors confirm sequestration thresholds, with human override available for edge cases. The hybrid approach—algorithmic triggers for routine verification, human judgment for disputes and novel situations—matches the asset's characteristics.

Voting weight should track verified sequestration contributions rather than token holdings. Those with actual carbon removal at stake have aligned incentives; pure financial speculators do not. Delayed execution with milestone-based vesting ensures that governance decisions affecting long-term permanence commitments cannot be rushed through before their implications become clear.

Legal structure for carbon markets requires careful attention to cross-border enforceability. An offshore foundation (Cayman, BVI) or purpose-built entity (Marshall Islands nonprofit LLC) provides flexibility for global operations while limiting liability exposure. The SafeDAO model, where a legal entity is bound to honor token holder decisions while bearing liability for credit issuance claims, offers a template for this hybrid approach.

CONCLUSION

This chapter has examined how crypto-institutions can structure governance for sustainability outcomes through the lens of cybernetics. The core insight is that DAOs offer a substrate for experimenting with institutional design in support of the biosphere—providing the transparency, programmability, and adaptive capacity that environmental governance requires at multiple scales.

The progression from local prototypes through meso-institutional coalitions to planetary-scale coordination reveals a consistent pattern: effective green crypto-institutions embed themselves in the material realities they seek to govern. Whether at the scale of a single building, a bioregional financing facility, or a global carbon market, legitimacy flows from demonstrated accountability to the communities and ecosystems affected by institutional decisions.

For sustainability practitioners, the governance parameters cataloged in this chapter represent a toolkit rather than a prescription. The specific configuration depends on what the institution governs, who it serves, and what failure modes it must prevent. Energy cooperatives demonstrate that even minimal governance surfaces require careful design. Bioregional facilities prioritize voice and embeddedness because their participants cannot exit the watershed. Carbon markets prioritize transparency and algorithmic execution because their assets are discrete and verifiable. Start with minimum viable governance and add parameters as coordination problems demand them.

The parameters cataloged in Table 4.5, the configuration reasoning illustrated, and the legal scaffolding options together form the practitioner's toolkit for building governance surfaces. Chapter 5 extends this discussion to the Protocol Layer, where the governance surfaces designed here are operationalized through specific mechanisms for registries, attestations, and smart contracts. The institutional forms explored in this chapter provide the governance scaffolding; protocols execute the operations that governance determines.

REFERENCES

2077 Research. 2024. "Arkreen: Net-Zero Decentralized Energy Data Network." In DePIN on Ethereum: Redefining Coordination Systems, December 11, 2024.

Armstrong, Kate. 2024. "Towards Interspecies Communication." In Interspecies Future: A Primer, p. 89. LAS Art Foundation.

Azos Finance. n.d. "Impact Backed Stablecoin." https://www.azos.finance/. Accessed March 2026.

Baeva, Svetla. 2025. "Reimagining Urban Finance: How Western Balkan Innovators Are Transforming Cities." UNDP Innovation Platform for Europe and Central Asia, May 8, 2025.

Bauwens, Michel, Vasilis Kostakis, and Alex Pazaitis. 2019. Peer to Peer: The Commons Manifesto. University of Westminster Press.

Bennett, Kate. 2025. "An Evaluation of the Regenerative Claims of Web3's ReFi Movement." Frontiers in Blockchain 8, June 2025. https://doi.org/10.3389/fbloc.2025.1564083. Accessed March 2026.

BlockScience. 2023. "Launching an Open Source Library for Governance Modules on Soroban." BlockScience (blog), November 29, 2023. https://blog.block.science/launching-an-open-source-library-for-governance-modules-on-soroban/. Accessed March 2026.

Brandt, Felix, Vincent Conitzer, Ulle Endriss, Jérôme Lang, and Ariel Procaccia. 2016. Handbook of Computational Social Choice. Cambridge University Press.

Bryant, Monty M. 2023. "ReFi Villages + How to Build One." ReFi DAO. January 15, 2023. https://blog.refidao.com/refi-villages-web3-enabled-communities-for-people-and-planet/. Accessed March 2026.

Buterin, Vitalik. 2024. "From Prediction Markets to Info Finance." Vitalik Buterin's Website, November 9, 2024.

Butler, C.T., and Keith McHenry. 1992. Food Not Bombs. New Society Publishers.

Climate Policy Initiative. 2023. Global Landscape of Climate Finance 2023. Climate Policy Initiative.

Coalition of Automated Legal Applications (COALA). n.d. "Model Law for Decentralized Autonomous Organizations (DAOs)." https://coala.global/wp-content/uploads/2022/03/DAO-Model-Law.pdf. Accessed March 2026.

Davidson, Sinclair, Primavera De Filippi, and Jason Potts. 2018. "Blockchains and the Economic Institutions of Capitalism." Journal of Institutional Economics 14, no. 4: 639–658. https://doi.org/10.1017/S1744137417000200.

Dávila, Joshua. 2023. Blockchain Radicals: How Capitalism Ruined Crypto and How to Fix It. Repeater Books.

De Filippi, Primavera, Sofia Cossar, Morshed Mannan, Kelsie Nabben, Tara Merk, and Jamilya Kamalova. 2024. "Report on Blockchain Governance Dynamics." Project Liberty Institute and BlockchainGov, May 2024.

De Filippi, Primavera, and Jessy Kate Schingler. 2023. "Coordi-nations: A New Institutional Structure for Global Cooperation." Medium, June 13, 2023.

De La Rouvière, Simon. 2024. "On Hardness and The Social Institutions of Crypto." https://sceneswithsimon.com/p/on-hardness-and-the-social-institutions. Accessed March 2026.

Delphi Labs. 2023. "Assimilating the BORG: A New Cryptolegal Framework for DAO-Adjacent Entities." Medium, April 20, 2023. https://delphilabs.medium.com/assimilating-the-borg. Accessed March 2026.

Dixon, Chris. 2024. Read Write Own: Building the Next Era of the Internet. Random House.

Eco-Jurisprudence Monitor. n.d. https://ecojurisprudence.org/?map-style=political. Accessed March 2026.

Esposito, Mark, Terence Tse, and Danny Goh. 2025. "Decentralising Governance: Exploring the Dynamics and Challenges of Digital Commons and DAOs." Frontiers in Blockchain 8: 1549568.

Forest Foresight. 2024. World Resources Institute. https://www.globalforestwatch.org/. Accessed March 2026.

Foucault, Michel. 1982. "The Subject and Power." Critical Inquiry 8, no. 4: 777–795.

Gitcoin. 2025. "Ethereum Localism x Regen Coordination: Gitcoin 3.0 Sensemaking Report." Gitcoin Governance Forum, July 2025. https://gov.gitcoin.co/t/ethereum-localism-x-regen-coordination-gitcoin-3-0-sensemaking-report/21940. Accessed March 2026.

Gnosis Guild. 2024. "GitHub - Gnosisguild/Zodiac: A Library for Composable Tooling for Onchain Entities." GitHub, September 19, 2024. https://github.com/gnosisguild/zodiac. Accessed March 2026.

goodalexander. 2024. "Agentic Protocols." Goodalexander.com, April 6, 2024. https://goodalexander.com/posts/agentic-protocols/. Accessed March 2026.

Hardin, Garrett. 1968. "The Tragedy of the Commons." Science 162, no. 3859: 1243–1248.

Hart, Sam, Laura Lotti, and Toby Shorin. 2024. "Crypto's Three-Body Problem." Other Internet, January 15, 2024.

Hui, Yuk. 2020. Fragmentar el futuro. Caja Negra.

Hui, Yuk. 2024. Cybernetics for the 21st Century. Vol. 1: Epistemological Reconstruction. University of Minnesota Press.

Jagoda, Patrick. 2016. Network Aesthetics. University of Chicago Press.

Jennings, Miles, and David Kerr. 2022. "DAO Entity Features & Entity Selection." Andreessen Horowitz. May 23, 2022. https://a16z.com/dao-entity-features-entity-selection/. Accessed March 2026.

Jin, Li, and Jesse Walden. 2023. "Progressive Ownership: A Model for Application Tokens." Variant, November 14, 2023.

LexDAO. n.d. "Legal Engineering Guild." https://lexdao.org/. Accessed June 2025.

Manley, Julian, Anthony Webster, and Olga Kuznetsova. 2023. "Introduction: European Co-Operativism in a Changing World." In Co-Operation and Co-Operatives in Twenty-First-Century Europe. Bristol University Press.

Martinez-Diaz, Lauren S., and Jack McClamrock. 2019. "Climate Disasters Are Getting Worse. Here's How Developing Countries Are Insuring Against Them." WRI. September 4, 2019. https://www.wri.org/insights/climate-disasters-are-getting-worse-heres-how-developing-countries-are-insuring-against. Accessed March 2026.

McAfee, Kathleen. 2012. "The Contradictory Logic of Global Ecosystem Services Markets." Development and Change 43, no. 1: 105–131.

McKinsey & Company. 2020. Diversity Wins: How Inclusion Matters. May 2020.

Mechanism Institute. 2025. "Mechanism Institute | Mechanism Library." https://mechanism.institute/. Accessed March 2026.

Mercy Corps Ventures. 2025. "Anticipatory Action Accelerator: Expanding the Innovation Frontier for Humanitarian Aid." Medium, January 15, 2025.

Mohebbi, Sohrab, and Talia Heiman. 2024. "A Tree; A Corporation; A Person." In Interspecies Future: A Primer, pp. 192–200. LAS Art Foundation.

Novak, Graham. 2024. "From DAOs to Network States: Mapping the Spectrum of Onchain Organizations." Onchain Organization Alliance, Paragraph, July 19, 2024. https://paragraph.com/@ooa/mapping-the-spectrum-of-onchain-organizations. Accessed March 2026.

OASA. 2025. "OASA Is a Web3 Powered Nature Conservancy." oasa.earth. Accessed March 2026.

Owocki, Kevin, Alejandro Stringer, and Pablo Ospina. 2025. "The Networked Firm: Capital Allocation in the Age of Blockchain and AI." Digital edition. https://www.allo.capital/resources/thenetworkedfirm. Accessed March 2026.

Papenbrock, Jochen, John Ashley, and Peter Schwendner. 2022. "Accelerated Data Science, AI and GeoAI for Sustainable Finance in Central Banking and Supervision." In Statistics for Sustainable Finance, IFC Bulletins 56. Bank for International Settlements.

Payman AI. 2025. "Payman." https://paymanai.com/. Accessed March 2026.

Peborgh, Ernesto van. 2024. "White Paper for Designing Nature Finance." Medium, July 2024. https://ernesto-87727.medium.com/white-paper-for-designing-nature-finance-a6f0ac5c7efb. Accessed March 2026.

Potts, Jason, Ellie Rennie, and Gregory Landua. 2025. "Making Ecocapital: Institutions for Aligning Economic and Ecological Systems." Working paper, April 2025. SSRN. https://ssrn.com/abstract=5199712

Power, Samantha, and Leon Seefeld. 2024. Bioregional Financing Facilities: Reimagining Finance to Regenerate Our Planet. BioFi Project, Dark Matter Labs Capital Systems, and Buckminster Fuller Institute.

Raymond, E.S. 2004. "Point - Up from Alchemy." IEEE Software 21, no. 1: 88–90.

Rifkin, Jeremy. 2022. The Age of Resilience: Reimagining Existence on a Rewilding Earth. St. Martin's Press.

Ruddick, Will. 2025. "Community of Practice." Journal of a Grassroots Economist (Substack). https://willruddick.substack.com/p/community-of-practice.

Salguero, Oscar. 2024. "Journal of the Association of Therolinguistics: Winter 2024 (50th Anniversary)." In Interspecies Future: A Primer, p. 93. LAS Art Foundation.

Selva, Jorge. 2024. "The Safe Case: How AI and Smart Accounts Will Revolutionize Crypto." Safe Blog, March 25, 2024. https://safefoundation.org/blog/the-safe-case-ai-smart-accounts-crypto. Accessed March 2026.

Taleb, Nassim N. 2019. Principia Politica. Third draft, July 2019.

Tan, Joshua Z., Tara Merk, Sarah Hubbard, et al. 2024. "Open Problems in DAOs." arXiv:2310.19201v2.

Taskforce on Nature Markets and Finance for Biodiversity Initiative. 2022. "The Future of Nature Markets."

UNCITRAL. 2024. Model Law on Automated Contracting. United Nations Commission on International Trade Law.

Wade Smith, Austin. 2025. "Ecological Institutions → Protocols to Grow Autonomous and Convivial Ecological Actors." Paragraph, Regen Foundation. https://paragraph.com/@austinwadesmith/ecological-institutions-protocols-to-grow-autonomous-and-convivial-ecological-actors. Accessed March 2026.

Wainstein, Martin, Axel Constant, and John Clippinger. 2023. "Nature-Based Currencies: Integrating Natural Capital in Advanced Monetary Systems." Open Earth Foundation. https://cdn.prod.website-files.com/62192ceb9199b3dd08431a6b/647d5895085b1d0a2c5ba6de_NatureBasedCurrencies_v2.pdf. Accessed March 2026.

Weiss, Yoav, Vitalik Buterin, and Marissa Posner. 2025. "The Trustless Manifesto." November 11, 2025. https://trustlessness.eth.limo/general/2025/11/11/the-trustless-manifesto.html. Accessed March 2026.

Whitten, Stuart, James Salzman, Dave Shelton, and Wendy Proctor. 2003. "Markets for Ecosystem Services: Applying the Concepts." 47th Australian Agricultural and Resource Economics Society (AARES) Conference, February 12–14, 2003, Fremantle, Australia.
World Bank. 2018. Blockchain and Emerging Digital Technologies for Enhancing Post-2020 Climate Markets. World Bank.
World Economic Forum. 2022. "Re-Envisioning Corporations: How DAOs and Blockchain Can Improve the Way We Organize." February 2022.
World Economic Forum. 2023. "DAOs for Impact." White Paper, June 2023.
World Wildlife Fund. n.d. "Artificial Intelligence and Conservation: Harnessing the Power of Technology to Protect Nature". https://www.worldwildlife.org/our-work/science/artificial-intelligence-and-conservation/. Accessed March 2026.
Zargham, Michael, and Ilan Ben-Meir. 2023. A Language for Knowledge Networks. BlockScience.
Zargham, Michael, and Kelsie Nabben. 2023. "Aligning 'Decentralized Autonomous Organization' to Precedents in Cybernetics." MIT Computational Law Report.

APPENDIX A: TYPES OF DAOS

This appendix categorizes DAOs relevant to green crypto-institutions, synthesizing multiple taxonomies including the World Economic Forum frameworks, and specialized ecological governance research.

TABLE 4A.1
Types of DAOs Relevant to Green Crypto-Institutions

Category	Sources	Definition	Examples
Protocol DAOs	World Economic Forum (WEF) 2022; Novak 2024	Govern parameters of networks and onchain primitives.	Regen Network, MakerDAO, AaveDAO
Capital Allocation	WEF 2022; Novak 2024	Pool resources for investment, grants, acquisition, or risk coverage.	Gitcoin Grants, KlimaDAO, Big Green DAO, NounsDAO, Nexus Mutual
Service DAOs	WEF 2022	Coordinate expertise, data, production, and contributor compensation.	dOrg, LexDAO, ReFi DAO, Data Trusts
Impact DAOs	WEF 2022, 2023; Esposito, Tse, and Goh 2025	Pursue mission-driven objectives across climate, community development, and UBI.	UkraineDAO, Kolektivo, GoodDollar, Endaoment
DePIN (Decentralized Physical Infrastructure Networks)	2077 Research 2024	Coordinate deployment and operation of physical infrastructure, including MRV sensor networks.	Arkreen, Helium, Glow

(Continued)

TABLE 4A.1 (*Continued*)
Types of DAOs Relevant to Green Crypto-Institutions

Category	Sources	Definition	Examples
Autonomous Ecological Institutions; Regenerative DAOs	Wade Smith 2025	Decentralized entities managing ecological assets through self-executing governance, blending digital commons with community-based resource management to foster environmental sustainability.	Smart Aquifers, Ecological Data Trusts, Self-monetizing Forests, Parametric Insurance Unions
Bioregional DAOs	Power and Seefeld 2024	Polycentrically networked crypto-institutions structured around bioregions, orchestrating funding for constituent land trusts, conservation areas, and regenerative enterprises. Operate under permaculture ethics and ecological accounting, with bioregions coordinating their constituent member organizations.	First Nations Territories, Biome Guardian Communities, Land Trusts, Watershed Conservation Areas, Bioregional Venture Studios
Community Currencies; Mutual Credit	Ruddick 2025	Local exchange systems enabling communities to coordinate economic activity through complementary currencies or mutual credit clearing.	Grassroots Economics, Circles UBI, community credit networks
Onchain Societies	De Filippi and Schingler 2023; Novak 2024	Non-territorial governance networks formed through voluntary association and shared values rather than geographic boundaries.	Network States, Coordinations, Popup Villages

Note: Any category may be structured as a BORG (Cybernetic Organization)—a traditional legal entity incorporating smart contract governance (Delphi Labs 2023).

Source: Table by the authors.

5 Protocol Layer
Design Methods for Green Crypto-Asset Production

As Vitalik Buterin observed, blockchains are fundamentally about "creating the freedom to create a new mechanism with a new ruleset extremely quickly and pushing it out" (Buterin 2015). The previous chapter examined how blockchain-enabled institutions support collective action through new forms of coordination and governance. Building on that foundation, this chapter turns to the technical mechanisms through which such crypto-institutions operate day-to-day. More specifically, it analyzes how blockchain-based institutional protocols structure both internal decision-making and interactions with external counterparts. For sustainability professionals—many of whom may be encountering these systems for the first time—the aim is to clarify how these protocols function as the "operational layer" that enables green crypto-institutions to implement environmental projects, manage digital assets, and coordinate autonomously at scale.

In the environmental finance stack presented throughout this book, the Protocol Layer serves as the bridge between institutional intent and technical execution. It is here that rules are encoded, parameters are set, and automated interactions with broader blockchain ecosystems occur. As seen in Figure 5.1, to make this layer legible, protocol operations are categorized into four broad types:

- **(Ø1) Changing Constitutional Rules:** These operations modify the fundamental governance rules that define how a crypto-institution changes its own procedures or authority structures. Because the design of governance surfaces was extensively discussed in the previous chapter, only a concise summary is provided here.
- **(Ø2) Legal and Social Declarations:** Crypto-institutions emit declarations that structure their social and legal relationships—such as membership criteria, contributor agreements, or contractual terms of use. While these artefacts are essential to institutional functioning, they remain only partially onchain. Their detailed legal analysis lies outside the scope of this chapter, though resources such as the European Crypto Initiative offer further guidance.
- **(Ø3) Adjusting Interior Parameters:** These operations involve modifying the configurable parameters that define how an institution's systems function—for example, altering the rules by which a green crypto-asset is minted or updated. This chapter devotes substantial attention to these parameterized "interiorities," as they represent a central mechanism through which sustainability-oriented blockchain projects encode environmental logic into digital form.

 DOI: 10.1201/9781003748472-5

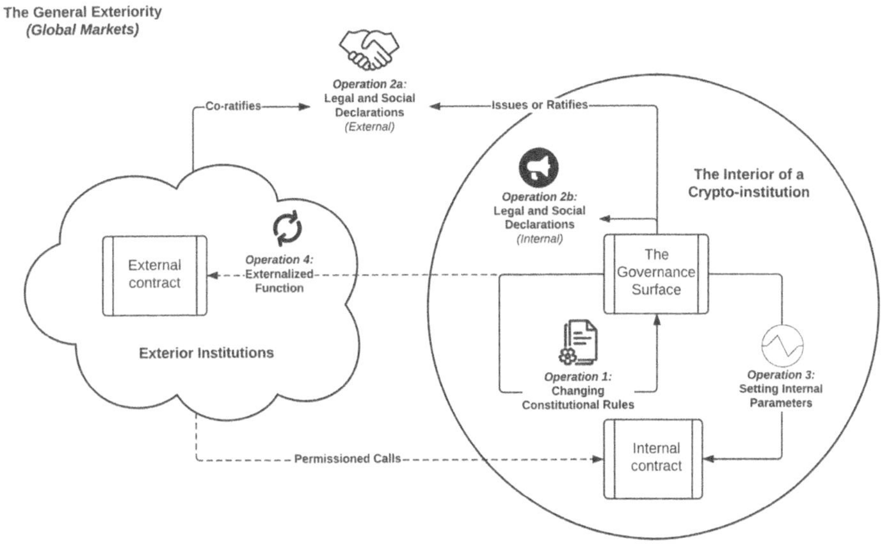

FIGURE 5.1 The four types of protocol operations.

***Source*: Diagram by the authors.**

- **(Ø4) Calling External Functions:** Finally, crypto-institutions routinely interact with smart contracts and protocols beyond their direct control. These operations can be simple—such as issuing funding—or complex, such as interfacing with decentralized finance (DeFi) systems to automate revenue distribution or liquidity management. Any protocol call to an external contract generally falls into this category.

The chapter proceeds from basic protocol primitives to more complex structures, illustrating how these technical components enable the production and management of green assets. It concludes with three case studies that demonstrate how green crypto-institutions apply protocol-layer operations in practice: two drawn from existing initiatives, and one a forward-looking design proposal.

($Ø_1$) CHANGING CONSTITUTIONAL RULES

The adjustment of the rules to change the rules, or the parameterization of an institution's constitutional-choice governance surface, was already discussed in the previous chapter. The authors nonetheless invite readers to mull over the $Ø_1$ protocols necessary to realize effective green crypto-institutions while reading this chapter.

($Ø_2$) LEGAL AND SOCIAL DECLARATIONS

In this framework, Ø2 refers to those institutional operations that rely on legal authority or social norms rather than on blockchain-based technical mechanisms such as smart contracts or consensus algorithms. These declarations operate through what jurists call the *force of law*—formal rules backed by state authority—or through *normative* social expectations within a community. Unlike blockchain-native protocols, which are enforced automatically by code, Ø2 mechanisms depend on established legal systems, administrative processes, and social institutions.

For conventional organizations, Ø2 processes constitute the primary means of formalizing and enforcing decisions. Consider that legal instruments can:

- **Modify constitutional rules**, such as amending a company's Articles of Association to change how it is governed.
- **Determine interior parameters**, for example, by issuing an official certification that validates the methodology of a carbon sequestration project.
- **Initiate external engagements**, such as drafting a binding contract with a project developer or service provider.

In short, law permeates every stage of green asset creation, from land tenure and permitting to monitoring, verification, and trading. Where legal frameworks are missing, incomplete, or overly restrictive, sustainability initiatives face significant barriers. This is evident in cases such as conservation projects that require rare or slow-moving state permits for species translocation (Jepson and Blythe 2020, 124–125); Indigenous communities whose ability to steward biodiversity hinges on secure land rights (Dimock 2022); or European conservation regimes where rigid statutory provisions "do not include clauses that allow for innovation," obliging administrators to "stick with existing rules and procedures" (Jepson and Blythe 2020, 135). These examples illustrate how gaps or bottlenecks in Ø2 processes can inhibit environmental innovation.

Developing legal foundations for novel digital green assets is equally resource-intensive. Emerging securities token standards have reportedly required substantial legal expenditure before any external fundraising could occur (Lorberg and Labetzsch 2021). Such cases underscore a central feature of Ø2: legal credibility enables innovation, but its creation and maintenance carry significant costs and can impose strong constraints. For sustainability professionals, understanding these dynamics is essential, as environmental and digital systems ultimately intersect at this legal–institutional layer.

($Ø_3$) SETTING PARAMETERS OF INTERIORITY

Ø3 refers to the set of technical operations through which a crypto-institution adjusts the internal rules that govern its functioning, including the parameters that define how environmental data is translated into digital assets, how those assets behave, and how they interact with broader ecological or economic systems. These choices are made within the institution's *governance surface*—the zone of authority in which an organization may autonomously change configurations encoded onchain.

For sustainability professionals, an accessible analogy is to think of Ø3 as the digital equivalent of adjusting the operating rules of an environmental program:

defining measurement protocols, specifying eligibility criteria, setting monitoring intervals, determining how units are created or retired, or modifying how benefits are distributed. In blockchain-based systems, however, these adjustments operate through programmable smart contracts, tend to be more transparent, and are often automatically enforced.

This section examines how interior parameters are designed and modified within green crypto-institutions, drawing both from established environmental institutions and from emerging Web3 practices. Understanding these forms of parameter-setting is essential because they directly determine the integrity, credibility, and ecological relevance of green crypto-assets. As this section demonstrates, interior parameters are not merely technical settings; they are governance decisions that must reconcile environmental realities, data constraints, legal frameworks, and market dynamics.

Primitive Surfaces

In cryptoeconomics, all object primitives—e.g., tokens, green assets—can be systematically categorized into four distinct classes, delineated along two fundamental axes: *reversibility* and *transferability*. Figure 5.2 demonstrates this four-quadrant object taxonomy. These axes confer upon the objects a permissioned or

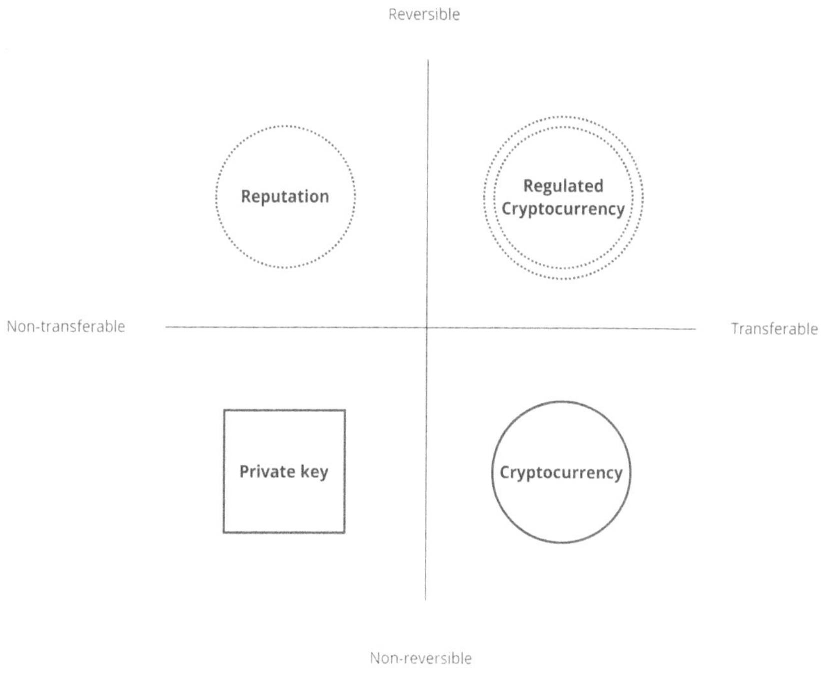

FIGURE 5.2 The four primitive surface classes of objects in cryptoeconomics.

***Source*: Diagram by the authors.**

permissionless character that either internalizes or externalizes their control vis-à-vis an institutional governance surface:

- **Reversibility** pertains to the capability of an institution, such as a DAO or a state entity, to assign or retract an object from some owner.
- **Transferability** hinges on an owner's ability to transfer the object.

Crypto-institutions leverage all four classes to define and exchange a wide spectrum of blockchain objects, from fungible tokens like ERC20s to tokenized treasuries. These classes are fluid: acts of governance, programmable triggers or broader social or technological shifts may transition an object from one class to another, such as a non-transferable token becoming transferable due to a DAO's governance vote.

Non-Transferable and Non-Reversible

Non-transferable and non-reversible objects are distinguished by their immutability and association with a specific address or identity, rendering them fundamental to the integrity and security of decentralized systems. These primitives are generally designed to remain perpetually tied to their original recipient or creator, without the ability to be revoked or altered by any institution. This permanence fortifies their trust and authenticity for some broader system.

A quintessential example of the class is the private key, an emblematic cryptographic primitive. The private key's sanctity lies in its resistance to external manipulation, safeguarding against unauthorized access unless compromised by clever exploits, the force-of-law, or brute force.

Non-Transferable and Reversible

Non-transferable and reversible assets are characterized by their inability to be transferred, yet are modifiable or revocable by an authoritative governance surface. Their restricted transferability enables a controlled and gradual engagement with external systems, rather than full exposure to traditional market dynamics. This category encompasses a range of assets that play pivotal roles in governance, identity, and reputation systems:

- **Smart contract wallets** represent a blend of non-transferability with reversible features controlled by the underlying contract logic. Imagine a recovery feature that selectively enables smart wallet reversibility if a user has not issued a transaction for a set period (implying that the user is deceased). To this end, recovery functions are being increasingly integrated by smart account providers to solve for unplanned loss of funds: a critical UX challenge that continues to hinder broader crypto adoption (Kesonpat 2023).
- **Reputation systems** are non-transferable yet fungible "points" that can be adjusted based on behavior, contributions, or other criteria set by a governing body. For example, platforms like SourceCred assign a "Cred" score to participants based on their contributions, which is then used later to distribute transferable token rewards (SourceCred 2025). As explained by the Apiary project, Web3 reputation systems generally "seek to enable trust,

incentivize participation, and foster community" and "often converge and diverge with the objectives of decentralized identity, membership systems, and governance" (Apiary 2023).

- **Badges and non-fungible soulbounds** demonstrate the use of non-transferable and reversible non-fungibles in applications where a governance surface wants to assign a specific credential, role, or certification. A university degree provides a good analogy here, as it can be revoked by the university after issuance, but it is not designed to be transferable. As of 2025, property-use licensing models are exploring non-transferable and reversible designs as a means of assigning stewardship or use rights over natural capital (Prewitt and Henderson 2024). This is of particular interest to green crypto-institutions that may not be able to assetize the ownership of the conservation property they steward, but still need to pursue monetization around its use rights.

Carbon emissions tokens (CETs) offer a useful illustration of token designs that deliberately incorporate non-transferability and reversibility. In such models, reversibility allows certain actions associated with the token to be delegated to an authorized third party, which may execute or modify token-related operations on behalf of the holder. Non-transferability, by contrast, prevents the holder from sending the token to external parties or accounts, thereby ensuring that the token remains confined within a defined organizational boundary and retains its intended governance properties.

Transferable and Reversible

Transferable and reversible objects illustrate an intricate interplay between control, regulation, and innovation in the digital economy. While they can be freely transferred between parties, they are not sovereign; these assets retain a layer of control or influence from an authoritative institution.

Staked ETHIX, as detailed by EthicHub, serves as an example of how transferable and reversible assets can be conditionally utilized to secure systems via collateralization and generate liquidity (EthicHub n.d.). Holders of ETHIX—a transferable ERC20—may stake their tokens to underwrite micro-loans for regenerative coffee farmers, in exchange for rewards and governance rights within EthixDAO. In case of default, the staked ETHIX is seized, demonstrating the asset's reversible nature while staked.

Transferable and Non-Reversible

Transferable and non-reversible assets are uniquely characterized by their fluidity in exchange and irrevocability. This dual nature not only underscores their robustness in value exchange but also their resilience against censorship and external manipulation. Cryptocurrencies such as Bitcoin and unstaked Ethereum fall into this category.

Numerous transferable and non-reversible green crypto-assets already exist. Fungible innovations like the Toucan Base Carbon Tonne (BCT) (Toucan Protocol 2025) establish a reliable and enduring record of environmental-related contributions that can be freely exchanged in an open liquidity environment (see Chapter 7). Additionally, non-fungible digital impact certificates offer new avenues for investors and philanthropists to support value-aligned holders by combining the flexibility

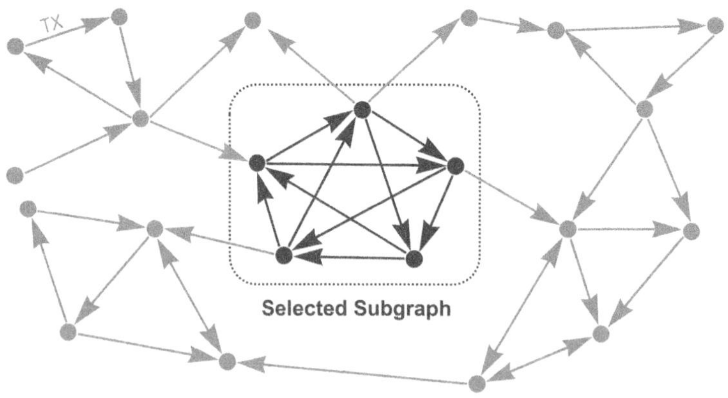

FIGURE 5.3 A subgraph of a larger financial transaction data network; a targeted segment of a transaction graph to which protocols can be applied. Key flow motifs of goods and services within a local institutional network can be filtered by topological parameters such as degrees of freedom or centrality.

***Source*: Diagram by the authors.**

of transferability with the certainty of non-reversibility—e.g., Hypercerts or OpSci (Hypercerts 2025; OpSci 2025).

Registries

A registry can be understood as an array of objects, addresses, or entities that are afforded or disafforded certain functionality within a network. Alternatively, registries can indicate that other actors now have extended powers vis-à-vis their content. Figure 5.3 illustrates a subgraph of a financial transaction network, a subset of the network's transaction registry.

While the Registries section covers different types of registries relevant to green finance, it is by no means exhaustive. Registries have a long history as legal instruments ranging from land to company registries and serve three main functions:

- **Access:** Registries determine which actors can or cannot view, read, or write crypto-institutional functions. KYC/AML is the most well-known access registry: when it fails, a user cannot create a bank account or may find their bank account frozen.
- **Attribution:** Object primitives, such as green crypto-assets, can be minted or assigned to registry members (e.g., an airdrop). More complex attributions are possible: imagine the assignment of assets to a polycentric network of crypto-institutions in some bioregion, which then governs their cascade distribution across a registry of reputation holders who have been attributed a non-transferable fungible point score based on their regenerative activities.
- **Selection:** As selectors, methodological or formulaic registries can extend properties, policies, and constraints to well-bounded and useful selections. This may be necessary for issuing targeted monetary, fiscal, and geospatial

policies to specific socioeconomic groups and geographies. These selections could be qualitative (what attributes does an object have?), quantitative (does a node possess more than X edges in a given network?), topological (is a node part of a local community structure?), or geometric (are nodes located within some geography?). Absent access or attribution assignment, selection can be merely conceptualized as a means of viewing potential opportunities. When Amazon was looking for a new HQ location, it compiled a registry of sites whose selection required a nearby major highway, population center, airport, and direct access to public transit; these conditions ultimately defined a registry of geographies as potential sites (Shekhar and Vold 2019, 128).

Identity Registries

An *identity registry* can be conceptualized as a database of identities where each entry points to specific attributes and information regarding an individual or organization. These registries can impose or lift restrictions and allocate or deny resources and privileges based on predefined criteria.

In Web3, identity registries play a fundamental role in facilitating trust, access, and participation in decentralized systems. In the context of DAOs, these types of registries are crucial for defining eligibility and access to services, serving as allow-lists for onchain accounts that benefit from provided services (Lotti, Houde, and Merk 2023).

Private proofs-of-identity are becoming more prevalent; using zero-knowledge proofs, members can prove their membership in a registry without disclosing their personal information. Although these techniques are not yet widely implemented, they are rapidly evolving to become industry standards as "passport"-branded identity products (Zupass 2025). Figure 5.4 depicts how decentralized identifiers function in proof-of-identity contexts.

Certification Registries

According to AgripolicyKit, "certification is a process used to provide evidence of compliance with certain quality requirements, in the form of binding or voluntary quality, environmental or social standards" (AgripolicyKit 2025a). *Certification registries* track assignments and serve as authoritative sources for certification.

As of 2025, existing environmental certification registries are adjusting standards and innovating, particularly in the carbon sector, as the durability of carbon reductions remains a major ongoing concern. So far, loosely defined carbon offset certifications have proven ineffective from a sustainability standpoint (Greenfield 2023). In response, new and stricter standards are filling this market gap by strengthening requirements for certification, emphasizing scientific rigor and transparency.

The EU's carbon removal certification framework is attempting to combat durability-related greenwashing by emphasizing removal over avoidance credits (see Chapter 6; Interreg Central Europe 2024). Overall, while these certifying innovations are useful and needed, they also lead to a high level of market fragmentation. Similarly, ESG has ballooned to "over 600 ESG reporting provisions globally" with "differing interpretations of sustainability." (EY and Oxford Analytica 2021) Addressing this fragmentation requires the use of protocological fungibility transformations, which we discuss later in this chapter.

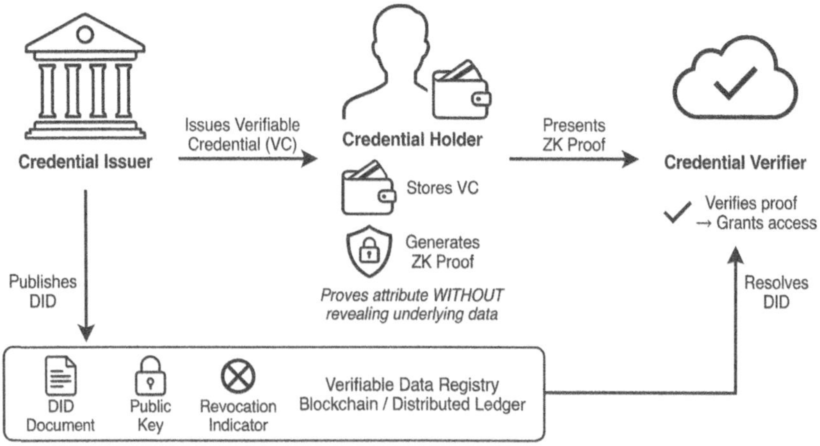

FIGURE 5.4 Decentralized identifiers (DID) are a type of verifiable credential for digital identification and authentication that operates in a decentralized manner. They are not controlled by a single, centralized institution but instead leverage Web3 to enable secure, private, and direct control over personal identity information by the individual to whom a credential belongs.

***Source*: Diagram by the authors.**

There are many ongoing Web3 advances in certification registry design:

- Meta-registry protocols, which aggregate existing registries for more flexible usage and standards setting, allowing impact projects to register claims and receive methodology certification (a.k.a. "stamps") from multiple evaluating bodies simultaneously. Claims and stamps can utilize the same interoperable data formatting to streamline this process (Nouroozi 2023).
- Fully digital blockchain-based monitoring, reporting, and verification (MRV) platforms are growing in popularity and usage (ReFiDAO 2024). These multi-stakeholder aggregation platforms connect projects, registry eligibility criteria, and financing (e.g., Open Forest Protocol 2023).
- Certified object primitive standards are trying to atomize certification in order to build liquid and inclusive impact marketplaces. Consider the Hypercert, an experimental non-fungible token standard that generalizes certification to "any impact vector" that can correspondingly be legitimized by a crypto-institutional "marketplace of impact evaluators" that retrospectively reward certificate minters or holders (Green et al. 2024a; Protocol Labs 2023).

Spatial Registries

Spatial registries play a crucial role in resolving collective action problems. They enrich protocol design by delimiting geospatial boundaries, geolocating economic factors of production, and spatializing transactions. Simply put, spatial registries enable geo-aware protocological operations, such as location-based incentives. Figure 5.5 illustrates the layers of a typical geographic information system (GIS)

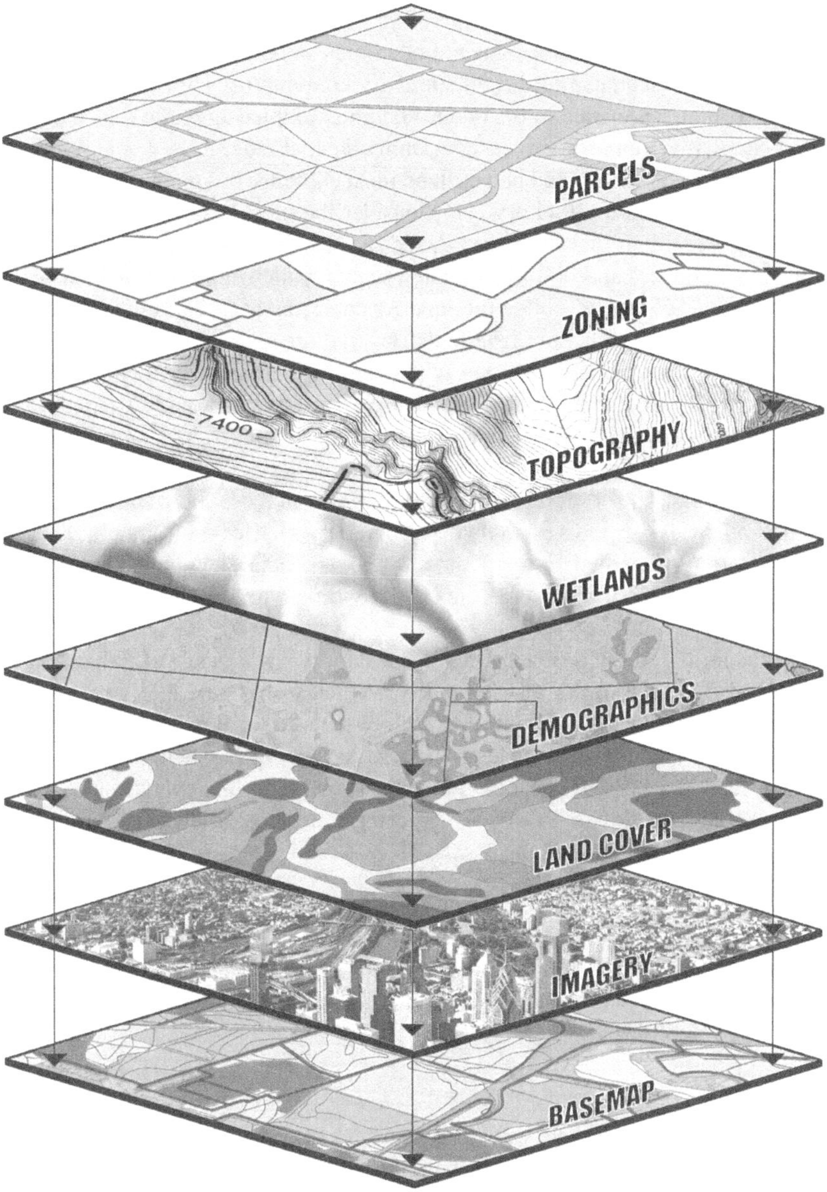

FIGURE 5.5 Deconstructed stack of a typical Geographic Information System (GIS), where vital spatial and environmental data is organized into layers. Some layers, like the Zoning layer, are primarily composed of vector data, formulating clear shape-based geometries. Others, like Demographics, are generally raster-based, displaying hotspots with pixelated grids. Collectively, these layers help delineate overlaps and points of collision between the underlying material reality (see Chapter 2) and human-designed institutional protocol.

***Source*: Ontario County NY and USGS. Public domain. https://geos.louisiana.edu/news-events/news/20230124/undergraduate-certificate-geographic-information-systems**

stack, which shows the real-world layers to which spatial registry operations can be applied. Clear spatial demarcations target and ground protocol in the real-world in order to better optimize socioecological outcomes. As of 2023, "on average" across countries, smarter land use could "double… economic returns or environmental outcomes… without a sacrifice in the other outcome," emphasizing the role spatial registries occupy in green protocol design (Damania et al. 2023).

Spatial registries have long been utilized in an Ø2 sense by spatializing the boundaries of many forms of regulatory law. Consider the most basic spatial mechanism: a land-registry system that demarcates land use, ownership, or zoning. This protocol primitive clarifies and delimits property rights while simultaneously serving the general state necessity "of collecting land revenue"; as of 2023, multiple states are experimenting with blockchain land registries to these ends (Bal 2017).

Spatial registries, when combined with certification registries, help delimit precise boundaries and distinguish between ecosystem service-providing (spatial zones generating ecosystem benefits), service-connecting (the corridors or pathways that transfer benefits), and service-receiving areas (their places of receipt and utilization; Wang et al. 2022). The observed ecological state within these sets of bounded or connected geometries—e.g., CO_2 levels or biodiversity metrics—ultimately determine the certifications they qualify for. This interplay is crucial in contexts where spatial ownership or stewardship must be transparently linked to ecological outcomes, e.g., reforestation.

Blockchain-based spatial registries unlock more than just certifiable zones of impact. Imagine "geo-aware transferability," which would only allow crypto-assets to be traded within some locale to the sole benefit of a local economy. More exotic use cases could include alert systems that create incentives when property-damaging wildlife exits a certain conservation area. If inverted, this exotic use case could incentivize the proper care of species entering a designated area, as described by various conservation banking proposals:

> [B]ankers [should] generate credits by following a specific species as it migrates, establishing habitat not just on one purchased piece of land but instead by identifying viable habitat the species may migrate to and working with private landowners through incentives… the accompanying sale of credits… [supports] an endangered species as they follow species migration…
>
> **Graybill (2024)**

It's important to note that while Ø3 spatial registries would allow for fine-tuned control over interspecies spatial access rights and incentivization schema, they do not replace present Ø2 realities. This highlights the importance to the Rights of Nature as a movement—legal advocacy that aims to increase nonhuman representation in legal systems. This being said, Ø3 spatial registries *can* establish additional monitoring guarantees through composability with other Ø4 primitives—such as blockchain-based arbitration. With them, the operational cost of disputing damages caused by migratory species can be automated and brought to a much higher efficiency. Figure 5.6 presents a high-level architecture for a blockchain-based proof-of-location system; multiple proofs, in aggregate or part, formulating a spatial registry:

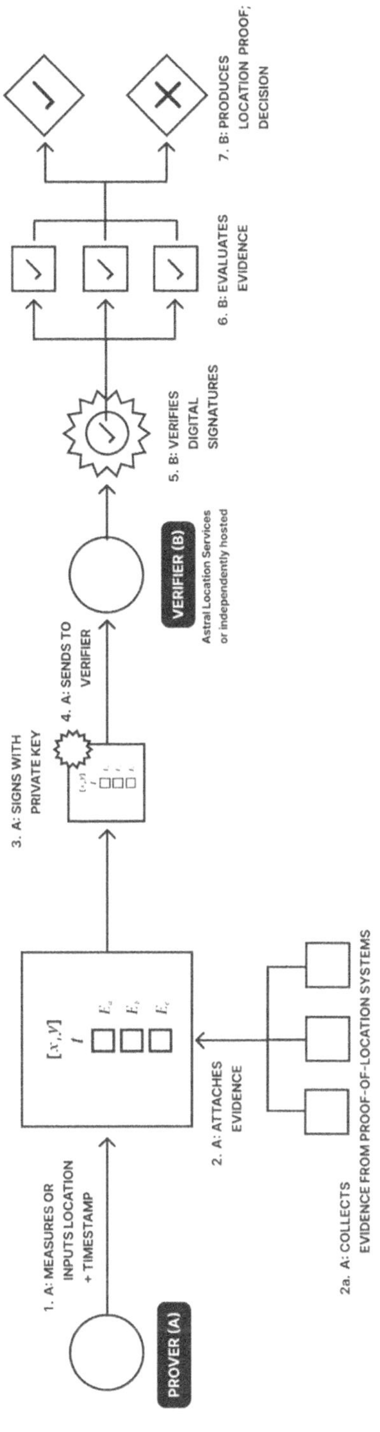

FIGURE 5.6 Process for producing proofs-of-location.

***Source:* Astral Protocol.**

Despite significant technological advances, Web3 spatial registries remain an underdeveloped primitive with no overarching industry standard (unlike, for instance, ERC20 for fungible tokens). Nonetheless, standards such as the Geospatial Non-fungible Token (GeoNFT) have been proposed to bridge this gap (Grimm et al. 2022). Other projects, such as zkMaps and zkLocus (Gerasymchuk 2023; zkMaps 2024) have worked on supporting infrastructure that allow for the verification of geographic locations without compromising privacy. This capability is vital for accurately assessing and trading natural assets while maintaining user privacy. Overall, however, these projects are still in their early stage and have not yet gained widespread acceptance or utilization.

Collateral Registries

Collateral registries enumerate and parameterize crypto-assets for collateral usability to back currency or debt issuance.

Several innovative concepts have been proposed to make currency more sustainable and less reliant on its high entropy petrodollar roots. Notably, the Silver Gun Hypothesis proposes the collateralization of carbon assets by Central Banks to create a green, carbon-backed currency (Chen 2018).

Within Web3, collateralized stablecoins such as Sky Protocol's Dollar (USDS) and Mento's Euro (EURM) are pegged to fiat currencies and backed by various crypto-assets. Their collateral registries tend to be community-governed by token holders: SKY token holders, for instance, can add or remove accepted collaterals backing USDS. Sky Protocol's founder, Rune Christensen, published a manifesto outlining "The Case for Clean Money," where he posited the potential for stablecoins to drive sustainable investment globally by backing themselves with reserves of green tokens (Dale 2021). His vision, however, has yet to come to fruition at any great scale; to this date, no major Web3 real-world implementation of "clean money" yet exists.

Fungibility Transformations

Fungibility refers to the characteristic of a good or asset that allows it to be exchanged with other identical items (Frankenfield 2020). This attribute is crucial in simplifying trading and exchange processes, as it ensures that each unit of an asset holds equivalent value to its counterparts.

Unlike traditional financial assets, crypto is uniquely differentiated by its capital fluidity: the capacity for an asset to transition across different fungible or non-fungible states. The fungibility of assets is often framed in this binary manner, but this perspective deserves a more nuanced understanding where fungibility is a set of possible states. Similar to the transferability or reversibility of tokens, conditional fungibility suggests that assets can exhibit varying degrees of interchangeability and transformation based on predetermined or imposed adjustments by an authoritative governance surface. Table 5.1 summarizes these fungibility transformations across traditional and Web3 frameworks. This gradation enables more tailored policy decisions that accommodate both complete or partial fungibility, enhancing market flexibility—particularly for environmental assets, where multi-dimensional attributes like permanence should affect asset properties (Grantham Research Institute 2024).

TABLE 5.1
Fungibility Transformations

Primitives or transformation	Traditional General Example	Traditional Specific Example	Web3 General Standard	Web3 Specific Example
Non-fungible object primitive	Legally designated conservation area	Yellowstone National Park	NFT	GeoNFT (Astral Protocol) (Astral Protocol 2024)
Fungible object primitive	Shares of a natural asset company (NAC) or community land trust.	Champlain Housing Trust (Champlain Housing Trust 2025)	ERC-20	Toucan Carbon Token (e.g., NCT, CHAR) (Toucan Protocol 2025)
Non-fungible to fungible process (fractionalization)	Conservation area incorporated as NAC and split into shares	Intrinsic Exchange Group and Costa Rican government NAC pilot. (Goulart 2021)	There are many standards for NFT fractionalization depending on use case.	Batch NFT split into TCO2 fractions (Toucan Protocol 2025)
Fungible to non-fungible process (reconstitution)	Company buyout; existing shares are merged and ownership transfers to the parent entity.	Acquisition of First Utility by Royal Dutch Shell in 2018 (Bousso and Twidale 2019)	Typically, a "buyout" mechanism. (Vohra 2023)	Retirement of offsets to upgrade an NFT, such as an EcoSapien (Ecosapiens 2025)

Source: Table by the authors.
Note: The methods and strategies that alter an asset's degree of fungibility. These transformations facilitate more dynamic market interactions as they allow for continuous adaptation as new data or technologies emerge.

A practical example of conditional fungibility in green crypto is Klima 2.0, which organizes carbon credits into semi-fungible "carbon classes" whose internal interchangeability can be dynamically adjusted via onchain voting. This mechanism allows participants to refine pricing and allocation in real time, reflecting both supply-demand dynamics and qualitative distinctions such as vintage, registry, or geography, thereby operationalizing fungibility transformations for environmental assets (Klima Protocol 2026).

Minting (x → 1)

Minting refers to the process of generating an asset and establishing its unit of account. For many green assets, minting is derived from a specific measurement or MRV methodology that captures the underlying material reality, such as an environmental index (see Chapter 2). These mint conditions vary widely across environmental asset classes. Biodiversity credits, for example, can be minted through numerous schemes depending on what is being measured. One recent classification identifies

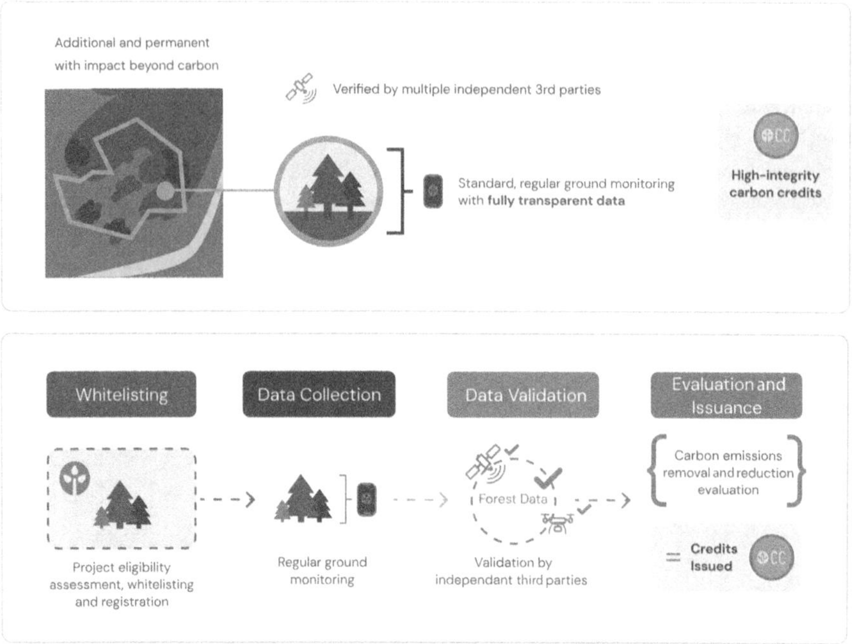

FIGURE 5.7 Minting flow for Open Forest Protocol Carbon Credits. The type and quantity of credits minted is largely determined by MRV processes.

***Source*: Open Forest Protocol. Afforestation, Reforestation, Revegetation (ARR) Carbon Whitepaper. Version 1.1, April 2024. Pages 6, 8. https://docsend.com/view/75zb4teqgzvvmyva**

four overarching categories—species, habitat, ecosystem, and miscellaneous—which together contain around sixteen distinct subcategories, each corresponding to a different type of ecological outcome and associated measurement approach (Gradeckas 2023). Figure 5.7 demonstrates how the Open Forest Protocol mints carbon credits.

Minting need not be limited to fungible tokens, and tokens may be minted in complementary fashion. Consider Coorest's NFTrees, which are digital representations of real-world trees. While the NFT representation of the trees is purely symbolic as a digital collectible, these NFTs mint in parallel fungible CO_2 tokens to their holders that correlate to the sequestration of their real-world arboreal counterparts (Coorest 2023).

Wrapping (1 → 1)

Wrapping typically refers to the transformation of a crypto-asset to render it "operable on another blockchain" or off-chain database while retaining "the exact same value" (note that "off-chain" in this context refers specifically to a non-blockchain database, not the broader material world; Musharraf 2023). A simple example of wrapping is the transformation from ETH → WETH (wrapped ETH), where ETH is rendered technically operable with a broader ecosystem of decentralized applications. Beyond this understanding, wrapping as a 1 → 1 transformation can take more complex forms:

- *Custodians* are entities responsible for the safekeeping and management of traditional assets when they are tokenized, i.e., "wrapped" into a token. Custodians generally hold liability for ensuring that tokenized asset representations accurately reflect their underlying traditional assets. Custodians are important for green crypto-assets: consider the case of Agrotoken, which specializes in the tokenization of agro-commodities. A producer deposits grains with an Agrotoken custodian that immobilizes them and issues tokens in equivalence. As the sole custodial entity, Agrotoken holds the Ø3 authority to adjust token supply to ensure system solvency: the equivalence of tons of grains and their tokenized counterparts (Agrotoken 2020).
- *Cross-chain transactions* can be considered a form of wrapping, where assets are transferred across blockchains. This process involves the conversion of assets from one blockchain's technical formatting to another. In this context, bridges play a pivotal role in the wrapping process. See Chapter 3 for a technical discussion of these types of bridges.
- *Restaking*, as seen with projects building in the Eigenlayer ecosystem, represents an advanced form of wrapping where cryptocurrencies like ETH are used to provide the same blockchain security consensus guarantees to multiple AVS, such as sidechains, data availability layers, new virtual machines, keeper networks, oracle networks, bridges, threshold cryptography schemes, and trusted execution environments. For more discussion on these data primitives as well, see Chapter 3.

Fractionalization (1 → n)

Fractionalization, or *sharding*, is a key fungibility transformation where a non-fungible asset is made fungible through a process of division. With this, the asset becomes more accessible for exchange in the market, e.g., trading a house vs. trading shares in a house.

Sharding helps price discovery by accommodating a larger pool of participants who can now trade fractional shares for partial ownership of an NFT at lower operational cost. Above all, it becomes easier to layer financial products and investment vehicles on top of fungible sharded assets—e.g., index funds, ETFs. In Web3, sharding can also be used to provoke more dynamic price discovery: consider the *progressive integration* method of shard issuance, where new shares for a given NFT are issued at a constant rate—for example, 1% per day, or 5% per month. These new shards are auctioned for ETH that is then issued to existing shard holders as staking rewards. This achieves two critical financial objectives simultaneously: supply reduction through staking, and more efficient price discovery through auctioned-shard sales (White, Robinson, and andy805 2021).

Sharding is highly relevant to ecosystem services (ES). In ES, one creates "mapping units" by splitting a large area (the "study area") into smaller, easier-to-manage spatial shards. These units can be defined by various criteria such as geographical features, administrative boundaries, or specific land uses. This approach allows for more precise measurement, attribution, and management of the ecosystem services provided by different parts of the landscape (Shen, Chen, and Wang 2021). Ultimately, this sharding method produces "a unit of reference" that can be "measured" and "translated into information" for green crypto-asset production and exchange (Tiqqun 2020, 72). As territories become increasingly tokenized and spatial and certification registries gain acceptance as Web3 primitives, one can expect them to increasingly explore the design space afforded by fractionalization.

Reconstitution (n → 1)

Reconstitution refers to the inverse process of sharding, where fractionalized tokens are aggregated back into a non-fungible whole, restoring the "original" asset. Reconstitution is not a one-size-fits-all process; it encompasses a diverse range of methods that can have strong effects on the governance surface for some non-fungible asset. The most popular method is a 51% takeover: once a single owner controls over half of the shares of an asset, or is willing to pay for more than half of the value of the asset's market capitalization, they can reconstitute the asset for themselves. With these types of mechanisms, the rights and responsibilities associated with fractionalized ownership require clear and equitable processes for reconstitution, such as ensuring that each fractional owner receives their fair share.

A pertinent design question arises: if a green asset cannot be reconstituted and sold on the market, does it hold any intrinsic value? Consider, for instance, a conservation area governed by an institution that has issued shares to assign and determine its ownership. If buying 51% of the shares cannot be used to gain the right to privatize and sell the conservation area, do the shares themselves have value? The answer to this question has profound implications for investors of natural capital, as assets whose reconstitution does not confer rights of sale may be less attractive or even devoid of exchange value.

Indexing (n → m)

Indexing ("pooling," "basketing," or "batching"; in some cases "redenomination") refers to the concept of crypto-asset pooling where multiple fungible assets (N) are basketed in a fungible index (M). Whereas liquidity pools in blockchain are typically pools of tokens locked in a smart contract to facilitate decentralized trading by crowdsourcing liquidity, *indexing* in environmental asset markets involves aggregating similar assets to create a more homogenized, tradeable asset. The authors' general preference for the term "indexing" over "pooling" arises from the need to distinguish this process from "liquidity pools," a common Web3 term; nonetheless, this section will use the two terms interchangeably.

Creating liquid assets is a common challenge in environmental asset markets. Notably, cumulative VCM issuances and retirements by project category can be understood as an attempt to aggregate fungible carbon credits (N) into composite groups (M) based on issuance and retirement volumes, project types, and vintage years (Forest Trends' Ecosystem Marketplace 2023). Indexing helps generate price signals and boost liquidity by batching green crypto-assets based on specific criteria or attributes and minting fungible tokens representing a share of the batched assets. For example, an index might amalgamate nature-based carbon credits from a certain year, with Ø3 parameterized smart contracts guaranteeing that only credits meeting the pool's criteria are included. The pioneering efforts of the Toucan Protocol with their Nature Carbon Tonne pool exemplifies this approach (Toucan Protocol 2025). Other notable examples include SolidWorld's CRISP-M token, a collateralized basket of Verra-certified mangrove forward contracts.

Retiring/Burning (n → 0)

Burning, in the Web3 lexicon, refers to the process of permanently removing a crypto-asset from circulation and thus from any further fungibility transformations. This is typically achieved by sending the token to an address from which it cannot be retrieved, effectively reducing the total supply and rendering the token unusable. It is for all protocol purposes the same process as *retirement*, a term specific to the context of carbon and other environmental assets. Retirement of a carbon asset denotes the act of permanently removing it from the market to ensure that the associated reduction or removal of greenhouse gasses is not double-counted or resold.

To illustrate, consider the retirement flow of a tokenized carbon asset. Once a carbon asset is tokenized, it becomes a digital representation of the removal or counterfactual avoidance of carbon emissions. The holder of this tokenized asset can then choose to "retire" it. This retirement is executed by sending the token to a designated address where it is effectively "burned" or permanently removed from circulation. When recorded on the blockchain, the carbon token's retirement provides a transparent and immutable record of its utilization. This ensures that the environmental benefit represented by the asset is accounted for and not reused, upholding the credibility and environmental integrity of its offsetting function.

For produced goods, Extended Producer Responsibility (EPR) is an emerging concept where a fee is automatically charged to producers to cover the cost of sustainably retiring a good in question. Simply put, the producer would take "the responsibility for managing the product's end-of-life," with the fee covering "downstream costs of waste management, in particular collection, transport, sorting and recycling/treatment" (Sachdeva, Araujo, and Hirschnitz-Garbers 2021). This policy could be extended to tokenized natural assets and commodities, where the final sale or consumption of a good simultaneously releases an Ø4 escrow contract claimable through a real-world proof-of-disposal (see Ø4 section).

Socioeconomic Interventions

Socioeconomic interventions represent a complex array of institutional strategies and policies that institutions typically employ to influence economic behavior and control the distribution of factors of production. Such measures include fiscal policy, dealing primarily with spending and tax policies, and monetary policy, conventionally implemented by central banks to control fiat money supply and interest rates. In this section, the authors separate out a third category of socioeconomic intervention: treasury/vault settings, representing the interior Ø3 parameterization of an "automated investment platform"—i.e., a smart contract that generates yield through investment—that can be engaged with by any onchain actor.

Socioeconomic interventions are of high protocological concern for green crypto-institutions. These policies, when based on unfounded or unscientific claims, can hinder effective climate action. Note that while fiscal and monetary policies in this chapter are generally discussed in the context of their application to crypto-assets, they could easily be substituted for policies dealing with the real exchange of goods or natural assets, e.g., a currency import quota that defines the maximum of a crypto-asset that can be deposited to a DAO's reserve vs. an import quota that defines "the maximum quantity of a product that can be imported based on factors such as weight" (AgripolicyKit 2025b). For a more generalized catalog of socioeconomic policies that transcend $Ø_3$ crypto-financial application, readers can visit the AgripolicyKit website (AgripolicyKit 2025c).

Fiscal Policy

Fiscal policy refers to a variety of mechanisms primarily designed to control the ownership and distribution of capital in society, using registries as targeting and attribution mechanisms. Solving distribution and attribution problems in "an equitable and credibly neutral way" is a "key aspect of ensuring financial stability" (Lotti, Houde, and Merk 2023). If a non-significant portion of an institution's constituents feels that fiscal policies are unfairly applied, it can lead to extreme shifts within an institution's governance surface, membership, or its very existence.

To understand how registries target fiscal policies, we use the real-world example of a state tax applied to a spatial registry. In Russia, authorities automate and levy taxes based on graph-based spatial data that measures a vehicle's journey from the point of highway entry to exit, taxing "the total distance taxpayers drove" (Shekhar and Vold 2019, 43). The taxpayer's trajectory, a line segment connecting topospatial entry and exit nodes, serves as the targeting mechanism for implementing the fiscal intervention—specifically, a tax. These types of "nudging" measures are critical to broader twenty-first century political agendas, where digital tools are now used to subtly influence or adjust citizen behaviors.

In cryptoeconomics, there is a much wider design space for fiscal policy. Crypto-institutional fiscal policy can extend beyond public sector budgeting, spending, and taxation toward greater cybernetic interactivity. Redistribution mechanisms can, for example, be tailored to the specific capital dynamics of a crypto-institutional topology, encouraging spending or more efficient circulation of capital within an interiority (or alternatively, preventing excessive capital accumulation). While evaluating each policy in Table 5.2, readers should keep in mind the dynamic and surgical capabilities of blockchain-based interventions:

Monetary Policy

Monetary policy traditionally refers to the task of governing a nation's currency and its properties, such as supply. Monetary policy is often orchestrated by a Central Bank or a similar financial authority; Figure 5.8 generalizes these Central Bank mechanics to the Protocol Layer. These policies encompass tools and strategies to control inflation, attenuate the flow/money velocity of a daily spending currency,

TABLE 5.2
Ø3 Fiscal Policies

Mechanism	Definition	Discussion
Token Offering	The sale of a token or another crypto-asset by a crypto-institution to raise funds in a different crypto-asset.	Crypto-institutions typically sell fungible tokens to raise funds, but an increasing number of green crypto-institutions are selling non-fungibles, such as a collectible digital tree. In the case of fungible tokens, offerings typically utilize capital controls to control secondary market inflation, e.g., vesting contracts. There are many ways to execute a token offering, but three of the most popular include: **Fixed Purchases:** Token X is purchased for Y at some fixed X/Y rate—the standard model. In the past few years, a resurgence of Initial Coin Offering (ICO)-style fundraising through Launchpads has been observed, where platforms like Echo, Legion and Coinbase facilitate initial token offerings that exchange stablecoins for project tokens at a fixed rate. These platforms aim to streamline access to a broader investor base. **Liquidity Bootstrapping Pools (LBP):** LBPs allow a project to generate liquidity through the variable weighting of crypto-assets. Funds are raised by setting up a two-token pool with a project and a collateral token. Weights are initially biased in favor of the project token, then adjust to favor the collateral token by the offering's end (Balancer 2025). This sort of price-finding mechanism ensures fair price discovery for any fungible token and bootstraps market liquidity. **Auctions:** Similarly to LBPs, auctions tend to be robust mechanisms that assist the initial price discovery process for new tokens. See the Mechanism Institute library for a comprehensive list of auction implementations (Mechanism Institute 2025a).
Redistribution (Taxation)	Reversible crypto-assets are redistributed from one cohort of crypto-institutional holders to another.	Redistribution can be discrete (single event), periodic (repeats every *t*), or continuous (streamed). In general, four types of redistribution are possible: **Regressive**: Members with low balances pay members of high balances. **Progressive**: Members of high balances pay members of low balances or a crypto-institutional treasury. **Proportional**: An equal tax is applied to all members. **Flat**: An equal tax is applied to all balances (e.g., a membership fee). Redistribution may be applied based on registry membership or parameters interior to a specific cryptoeconomy. Note that Ø3 redistribution has not been generally implemented by crypto-institutions, as they tend not to issue reversible crypto-assets, unlike bank money, which is reversible by default.

(Continued)

TABLE 5.2 (*Continued*)
Ø3 Fiscal Policies

Mechanism	Definition	Discussion
		There is a wide design space for taxation; e.g., *holding taxes* that automatically tax balances greater than some capital threshold, *demurrage* mechanisms that adjust user balances based on how long they've held a currency, or *inheritance taxes* that trigger on event of death. Redistribution can be structurally embedded in crypto-asset transactions, passed upstream to previous transactors of a unique currency unit. When combined with spatial registries, redistribution can be selectively applied in the form of tariffs; eco-tariffs such as the EU Carbon Border Adjustment Mechanism are increasingly playing a role in cross-border transactions. Bioregional tithing and Business Improvement Districts are voluntary forms of taxation that utilize spatial registries to pool funds and issue local investments (Power and Seefeld 2024, 124).
Insurance (Mutual Aid)	A crypto-institution collectivizes funds and governs a smart contract that redistributes these funds upon certain well-defined event(s) occurring.	Release mechanisms, and the quantity released, may be determined by an oracle, arbitrator, governance surface, assessor, or other decision-maker. Agricultural pension systems are a key example of how insurance protocols intersect with the management of natural capital (AgripolicyKit 2025d). Combining insurance with spatial and certification registries can introduce novel mechanics where a significant change in ecological state for some area automates restoration payouts.
Crypto-asset Seizure (Asset Forfeiture)	Some quantity of a user's reversible crypto-assets are frozen or seized by a crypto-institution.	Ø3 seizure has not been generally implemented by crypto-institutions, as they tend not to issue reversible crypto-assets. This being said, as crypto-assets become more regulated, large stablecoin issuers (e.g., Tether) and RWA providers are increasingly issuing reversible crypto-assets that can be frozen per the directive of a state institution.
Obligation-clearing (Invoice Clearing)	Debt network cycles between holders of a reversible crypto-asset are canceled out by a crypto-institution.	Obligation-clearing is a powerful tool of mutual credit and collaborative finance systems that enhances the liquidity efficiency of the network—especially in times of crisis (Fleischman, Dini, and Littera 2020). Note that obligation-clearing may occur through discrete, periodic, or continuous clearing for any period t. For a recent Web3 implementation, see Cycles (Buchman et al. 2024).

Source: Table by the authors.

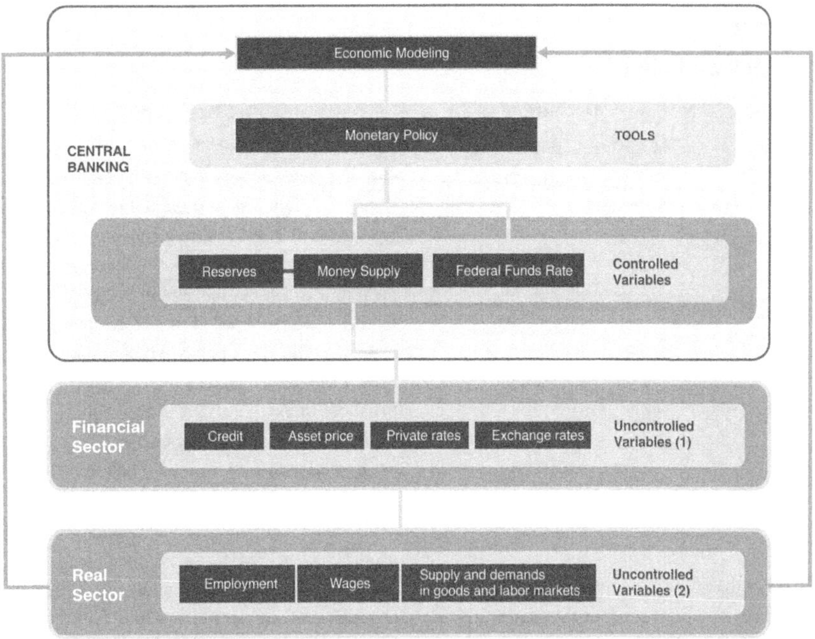

FIGURE 5.8 The mechanics of Central Banks can be generalized to the Protocol Layer, which refers to the "controlled variables" and "tools" that central banks use to produce assets that enter the "financial" and "real sector"—the Market Layer. "Economic modeling" in turn, takes place in the Data Layer.

***Source*: Open Earth Foundation. Nature Based Currencies: Integrating Natural Capital in Advanced Monetary Systems. Whitepaper Draft v1. "Design Iteration: Central Bank Perspective." https://uploads-ssl.webflow.com/62192ceb9199b3dd08431a6b/647d5895085b1d0a2c5ba6de_NatureBasedCurrencies_v2.pdf**

stabilize credit bubbles, and achieve sustainable economic growth. In the pursuit of harmonizing ecological sustainability with economic development, monetary policy can be tailored to incentivize practices that benefit the environment, such as structuring preferential interest rates for farmers who adopt nature-positive cultivation methods.

Most monetary policies refer to control of a daily spending currency rather than a store-of-value asset; instead, reserve assets are used as collateral to back daily use currencies. Leveraging assets in this way comes with inherent risks, necessitating capital controls to maintain economic equilibrium and prevent currency crises. Conservative policies tested through simulation and gradually relaxed as confidence in an economic interiority grows are crucial for stable spending currency expansion. With this in mind, readers should conceptualize the policies in Table 5.3 in relation to good stablecoin design, as stablecoins are the *de facto* spending currencies of Web3.

Table 5.3 outlines the monetary policy mechanisms available to crypto-institutions.

TABLE 5.3
Ø3 Monetary Policies

Mechanism	Definition	Discussion
Interest rates	The cost of collateralizing reserves to mint a spending currency.	Interest rates help control the flow of reserves by enticing yield farmers to deposit collateral. Similarly, higher interest earned from staking crypto-assets helps reduce circulating supply. Caps and floors can be set on floating interest rates to prevent their excess movement in a certain market direction. These types of limits are characteristic of US Central Bank policy which implements a "set of rate levels" across spatial registries (on- vs. off-shore rates). One notable advance in DeFi interest-rate setting is the transition to rate-setting by collateral depositors themselves, effectively decentralizing risk management, as implemented by the Liquity project (Pecek 2024).
Transaction Tax (or in some cases, Royalties)	A tax applied to transactions of some crypto-asset.	Transaction taxes can be dynamically weighted according to some period *t*, where a user pays a higher tax the longer they have held some reversible crypto-asset. A governance surface may opt to tax transactions higher or lower for certain users. NFT royalties are similar to transaction taxes in that a portion of an NFT's sale is diverted to its creator.
Negative Transaction Tax (Rebate)	A cash back subsidy applied to transactions of a reserve's spending currency.	A negative transaction tax is a type of "cash back scheme" that can be used to stimulate money velocity (Copic and Franke 2020). Cash back bonuses can be bound to a certain quantity of spending, or combined with fiscal policies—such as a holding tax or demurrage fee—for targeted money velocity management.
Mint Ceiling	A maximum ceiling of spending currency that can be minted against some collateral or set for some user.	Ceilings are set typically by stablecoin providers as a risk-mitigation mechanism. Generally, the less liquid a particular collateral, the lower the ceiling.
Time Delay	Receive redeemed collateral after period *t*.	As reserves tend to lend assets to earn income on yield, and RWAs become more and more important in the context of stablecoin collateralization, introducing a time delay is valuable for adjusting active positions in response to strong or unexpected capital flows.

(*Continued*)

TABLE 5.3 (*Continued*)
Ø3 Monetary Policies

Mechanism	Definition	Discussion
Rate Limit (Currency Import/Export Quota)	Up to a certain amount of currency can be redeemed for a certain collateral for some period t, or up to a certain amount of collateral can be deposited to issue currency over some period t.	Rate limits help control a reserve's exchange flow. This may be useful for responding to cryptocurrency market cycles. In bull markets, a reserve's crypto-assets will likely increase in fiat exchange value, and a higher redemption rate limit can be applied; in bear markets, a low rate may be favorable to maintain collateral stocks. A rate limit of zero implies economic autarky.
Tobin and Reverse Tobin Taxes (Entry and Exit Fees)	Receive the exchange value—e.g., the global spot price—when exchanging some crypto-asset against a crypto-institution's reserve, less some fee.	If a reserve's collateral falls below a certain threshold, a special transaction tax can be activated to build back reserve stocks.
Currency Import and Export Subsidies	A payment is issued for depositing or redeeming a certain crypto-asset to/from a crypto-institutional reserve.	Currency import subsidies are useful for building up highly liquid collateral stocks. With either import or export subsidies, a target portfolio composition can be crowdsourced by monetary managers. Note that export subsidies cannot be instantaneously triggered without some sort of time delay without introducing systemic flaws into a reserve.

Source: Table by the authors.

Treasury/Vault Strategies

DeFi vaults are automated investment platforms that seek out the most profitable lending, staking, trading, and arbitrage opportunities to grow deposits. As shown in Figure 5.9, they pool crypto-assets and then strategically allocate them based on their parameters. These vaults can be parameterized in an Ø3 manner by an authoritative crypto-institution to constrain the activities of their managers or set the vault's automated investment strategy. To the extent a distinction can be drawn between vault strategies and the collateralized monetary policies of the previous section, it would be the absence of the overarching objective of producing spending money through collateralization.

Treasuries and vaults themselves can be tokenized in either non-fungible or fungible manners; their tokenization represents a claim on an underlying pool of tokens that grows with fees being generated. Such tokenized vaults are a design frontier for socioeconomic policy tools, where claims on diversified and dynamically managed resources can be traded, leveraged, or used as collateral, reshaping the contours of asset management and ownership.

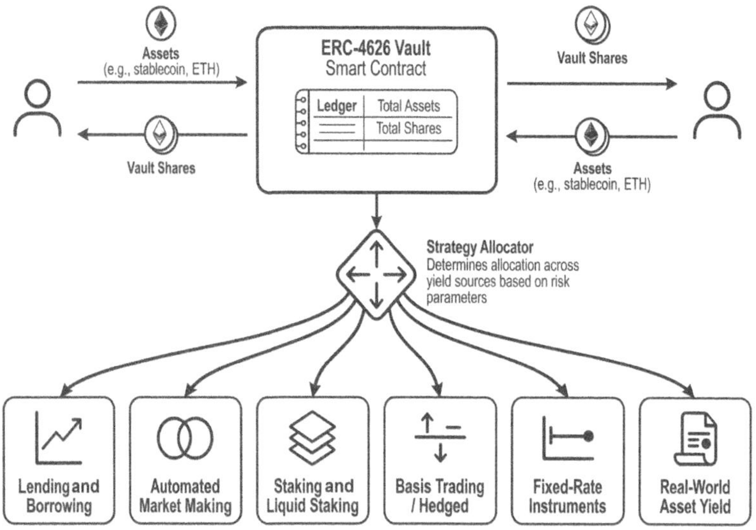

FIGURE 5.9 Architecture of an ERC-4626 tokenized vault. Depositors supply crypto-assets (e.g., stablecoins, ETH) to a smart contract that issues proportional vault shares. A strategy allocator routes pooled capital across yield sources—lending, automated market making, liquid staking, basis trading, fixed-rate instruments, and real-world asset yield—based on configurable risk parameters.

***Source*: Diagram by the authors.**

($Ø_4$) CALLING EXTERNAL FUNCTIONS

Ø4 operations orient a crypto-institution toward actors and systems outside its immediate governance control, or institutional interiority. At a basic level, an Ø4 action might involve a simple non-reversible payment, transferring tokens from a community-managed treasury to an individual wallet, thereby shifting control over these tokens from the institution's internal governance surface to an external party. The purpose of Ø4—and all inter-institutional commerce generally—is to extend the functional capabilities of a protocol beyond its internal boundaries, enabling the institution to participate in and shape larger environmental and socio-technical ecosystems.

These operations are not limited to simple transfers. Ø4 includes interactions such as integrating decentralized finance protocols to optimize resource allocation, coordinating technical processes jointly with other institutions, or engaging in blockchain-based arbitration and dispute resolution. In each case, the goal is to create new cooperative equilibria across institutional boundaries, fostering collaboration, transparency, and efficiency.

For sustainability practitioners, Ø4 is particularly significant because it allows for direct, automated, and verifiable interactions that bypass some of the inefficiencies of traditional legal and bureaucratic processes (Ø2). By doing so, Ø4 can help mitigate negative environmental externalities, improve equitable resource distribution, and accelerate the implementation of sustainable initiatives that might otherwise be constrained by rigid or slow-moving institutional frameworks.

Funding, Investment, and Subsidies

Funding in the context of this book is uniquely analyzed as Ø4, while in traditional bank finance it is typically Ø3. A distinction must be recognized between bank money, which is reversible and internal to the governance surface of financial and state institutions, and cash exchange, which bears Ø4 properties. Cryptocurrency transactions resemble cash more so than bank money in that they uniquely possess digital Ø4 sovereignty. It is their inherent non-reversibility that creates tension with existing institutions, who have trouble adjusting to financial technologies that naturally resist historical Ø3 permissioned financial transmission protocols.

Funding mechanisms can be roughly characterized by their breadth—how many nodes are funded—and depth—how equally each node is funded. In this characterization, the deepest funding operation would be a 1:1 P2P transaction, where one node funds another. Direct investments similarly emphasize a narrow funding verticality through targeted payment to some singular entity. Investment payments do not necessarily need to be made all-at-once, but can be continuously implemented and tapered according to some prefigured contract.

Broad funding protocols like UBI or consumer subsidies tend toward equalizing financial support over a network of nodes. This type of funding is prevalent in open-source crypto-institutional finance, where innovative computational social choice approaches like quadratic funding aim to optimize the allocative efficiency of a decentralized network (Weiss 2022). Retroactive funding—an ecosystem-wide funding method—aims to incentivize crypto-institutional ecosystems to grow in the present "based on the assurance that they [contributors] will be rewarded for it in the future." (Green et al. 2024b) For these social choice capital distributions, funded nodes are oftentimes defined by an Ø3 identity or certification registry, e.g., Protocol Guild's streaming of funds to Ethereum developers who meet "eligibility requirements outlined in Protocol Guild's documentation" (Lotti, Houde, and Merk 2023).

The infrastructure underpinning Web3 allows for innovative funding models that play with various weightings of breadth and depth. Gitcoin Grants Round #24 (GG24) illustrated how Web3 funding is evolving from single-mechanism allocations to multi-mechanism ecosystems. In GG24, domain operators deployed a variety of approaches—including quadratic funding, retroactive funding, and conditional funding markets—to aim to match funding mechanisms to the specific objectives of each funding domain (McCarthy 2025).

Among innovative funding primitives uniquely enabled by Web3, *token streams* facilitate a continuous transfer of value perfect for subscription services or salary disbursements (Mechanism Institute 2025b). Meanwhile, *token vesting* schemes incrementally release funds according to a specific schedule or performance, ensuring long-term alignment and commitment from institutional stakeholders (Mechanism Institute 2025c). *Payment splitters* automate the division of incoming payments, greatly reducing the operational cost of circulating capital across a lateral network of contributors (Mechanism Institute 2025d).

When combined with these primitives, and Web3's aforementioned registries, payments for ecosystem services (PES) can be spatially targeted or issued based on some certified performance. The operations costs and institutional inefficiencies associated with traditional PES become dramatically reduced: a splitter, for instance, can modulate streams to various PES recipients as measured by "a combination of (a) the extent to which the original goals of the PES scheme were met, and (b) the added value in terms of an overall improvement of the ecological, economic, and social conditions of the region" (Grima et al. 2016). This being said, Web3 is "no silver bullet to immediately improve the environmental outcome of all PES schemes" (Granados, Schlüter, and Lahl 2023).

Decentralized Finance and Yield Generation

DeFi has democratized the ability to earn passive yield on crypto-assets through yield farming and liquidity mining processes in a 24/7, globally spanning open liquidity environment. This phenomenon is a testament to the high global demand for dollar-denominated instruments, with stablecoins fetching interest rates that often surpass those offered by traditional banks (Bronstein and Felman 2020). Overall, DeFi's versatility enhances liquidity and funding opportunities without the constraints of traditional financial systems; DeFi's "innovative protocols, mechanisms, and methodologies" seamlessly "work together to make loans cheaper, more efficient, and more transparent for borrowers" (Defactor 2023). Below is a list of common DeFi mechanisms that illustrate this point:

- **Decentralized lending platforms** help eliminate or mitigate traditional financial intermediaries by enabling P2P digital lending, allowing users to earn interest directly on their crypto-assets through decentralized lending pools and protocols. Automated yield farming algorithms help users maximize returns by efficiently navigating the complex yield farming landscape. Innovation in DeFi lending is accelerating; examples include self-repaying loans (Alchemix 2023), the ability for borrowers to arbitrarily switch between fixed and variable yields (Shah et al. 2023), and flash loans—an extreme, DeFi-specific form of collateral-free lending where a loan operation is executed within a single block, usually lasting mere seconds. The "credit trilemma" is a noteworthy design problem for DeFi lending protocols that aim to be permissionless (anyone can borrow without intermediaries), composable (other protocols can engage in an $Ø_4$ manner), and undercollateralized (borrowing doesn't need to be backed fully by collateral deposits). Characteristic of Ø4, resolving the credit trilemma may "look somewhat like an archipelago… each protocol linked via mutual agreements between them… [an] inter-protocol "trade" enabled by reciprocal agreements to honor debt positions" (Baker 2022).
- **Vault managers** are delegated entities who, under specified governance constraints, set the risk tolerance and yield strategies of the funds in their vaults. Vault constraints determine how the managers of funds may engage with external contracts, such as approved yield sources or the utilization rate, "the proportion of the pool's funds currently in use as loans" (Defactor 2023). While the setting of vault parameters and constraints is Ø3, the delegated deposits of funds into vaults can be considered Ø4.
- **Decentralized Insurance** is another key DeFi mechanism in which anyone can participate as an underwriter for some insurance pool to earn a yield on their

collateral deposits. EthicHub uses such a decentralized insurance marketplace to underwrite microcredit to farmers in the global south (EthicHub n.d.). As the intersection of climate finance and crypto continues to develop, one should expect to see novel insurance schemes where the permanence of carbon assets and other ecosystem services are underwritten through similar mechanisms.

DAO-to-DAO: Collaborative Agreements

DAO-to-DAO (D2D) agreements enable crypto-institutions to collaborate through structured negotiations and iterative concessions. These agreements foster ecosystems where crypto-institutions coordinate and implement protocols at scale.

The limitations of circular economic designs when institutions operate in silos emphasize the need for D2D operations. For example, if every manufacturer in a sustainable value chain only focused on recovering, refurbishing, and reselling its own products, broader network-wide potential would be severely curtailed. This calls for a shift toward green Ø4 D2D protocols that transcend proprietary material flows and structure institutional relations across the entire value chain.

In principle, any Ø3 operation can be reformulated as a collaborative D2D agreement: Registries can be co-governed, token fungibility transformations can be mutually enacted, socioeconomic interventions can be collaboratively enforced. The token merger between Ocean Protocol, FetchAI, and SingularityNET is a recent example of an Indexing fungibility method (n $\rightarrow$ m) applied across three collaborating crypto-institutions, who in turn went through their respective Ø1 governance processes to ratify the token merger (Finst 2024). With this Ø3 $\rightarrow$ Ø4 principle in mind, Table 5.4 lists a collection of common D2D operations that tend to resemble Ø4 extensions of Ø3 socioeconomic interventions:

Blockchain-based Arbitration

Arbitration is a form of dispute resolution where a neutral third-party—the arbitrator—makes a decision to resolve a conflict between two or more parties. It is an alternative to litigation and is often chosen for its speed, confidentiality, and the specialized expertise arbitrators can provide. In institutional settings, arbitration can be a preferred mechanism for resolving disputes because it allows the institutions to specify the initial conditions for dispute resolution prior to engagement, such as the choice of arbitrator or the rules for the arbitration process. This process is usually legally binding, meaning the arbitrator's decision is final and enforceable, much like a court order, offering a definitive resolution that allows the parties to avoid the uncertainties and public nature of going to court.

Disputes over natural asset production—such as mining—are inevitable given their complex financing and geopolitical importance, inducing conflicts between international companies and host states or other supply chain participants. Blockchain-based arbitration, global by default, can augment the institutional sovereignty of the Global South by providing a decentralized and transparent mechanism for resolving disputes over natural assets, transparently recording and enforcing terms of contracts and agreements on credibly neutral public ledgers.

TABLE 5.4
DAO-to-DAO Collaborative Policies

Intervention	Definition	Discussion
Co-liquidity	A co-collateralized liquidity pool by collaborating crypto-institutions.	Collaborative liquidity pools can be either fixed or floating. Fixed pools allow the exchange of one crypto-asset for another at a certain pegged price—essentially, a fixed exchange rate. Floating pools use a bonding curve or other automated market making algorithm to calculate the exchange rate.
Collaborative Open Market Operations	Crypto-institutions collaborate through joint purchases, perhaps using an assurance contract to guarantee a certain fixed level of commitment.	Crypto-institutions co-purchase crypto-assets to benefit a broader network. A similar policy, the parity grid, may automate the stabilization of the price of two distinct crypto-assets vis-à-vis a given oracle-reported basket of goods. This policy was used by European states before the introduction of the Euro to stabilize their currencies relative to each other.
Co-insurance; Co-security; Mutual Aid; Profit Pooling (for blockchains: restaking)	A common fund is created that releases funds to cryptonetwork participants under certain conditions.	Mutual aid societies have historical precedent. Crypto-institutional co-insurance schemes should be considered for many ecosystem and social services, ranging from underwriting ecological state to providing smart contract coverage. Crypto-institutional co-insurance can help stimulate ecosystem services markets; service providers that "perceive technical assurance that their risk exposure is credibly covered by automatic additional payments" are more "likely to agree to long-term agreements that promote permanence." (Granados, Schlüter, and Lahl 2023, 38)
Token Swaps, Swap Lines	Two crypto-institutions agree to exchange crypto-assets. The exchange can be either permanent or lent.	Token swaps and lending may offer favorable rates across a registry of pre-approved partners to stabilize liquidity needs.
Co-governance	Crypto-institutions exchange governance rights to foster tighter relations.	For two crypto-institutions that have a close relationship, but no physical or economic proximity, this may be an effective means of granting voice to non-local actors.
Co-investment	Crypto-institutions co-fund a particular organization as a joint venture or collaborative initiative.	The narrow co-funding of a common effort can be achieved through a proposal inverter mechanism, which provides semi-automated payment flows through pre-negotiated contracts. Using it, a trusted group may be funded by multiple crypto-institutions for continuous services (Inverter Network 2025). The dominant assurance contract is another experimental Web3 primitive that aims to incentivize co-investment by layering incentives on top of a traditional assurance contract, e.g., if the contract reaches its investment target, the most invested party receives a bonus subsidy (Green et al. 2024c).

Co-subsidies	Crypto-institutions collaboratively finance wide distributions such as airdrops to each other's networks, or offer favorable rates to farmers of their respective liquidity pools.	Co-subsidies can virally grow a cryptoeconomic interiority or institutional neighborhood through the combination of non-transferable points or specific performance-based bonuses (e.g., referrals). Co-subsidies can be used to attract liquidity to shared services.
Co-sanctions	Crypto-institutions collaboratively maintain an identity registry of addresses that cannot interact with them or their reversible crypto-assets.	This mechanism may help mitigate regulatory concerns by tightening the boundary vis-à-vis problematic actors. Similar to sanctions, collaborative blocklists have been proposed as "a barrier against spam" for decentralized social platforms that need to "exclude undesirable content or accounts" without eschewing a "democratic and resilient approach to content moderation" (Nir.eth 2024).
Data Pooling	Collaborative crypto-institutional accessing, sharing, and licensing of data.	Data's context dependency complicates its monetization since it primarily holds value at either very large scales or within constrained actor interactions. With this, the distribution of benefits and bartering power for data producers is augmented through collaboration (Wiseman et al. 2019). Revealing, sharing, and licensing data between crypto-institutions is crucial for the production of green crypto-assets at bioregional scale. Interconnected data collection and aggregation is instrumental for training AI models. In this context, emerging tools like zkMaps are critical, as they can protect privacy and location information without compromising the utility of environmental data (zkMaps 2024).
Commitment Pooling	Collaborative aggregation of redeemable currencies usable for particular goods and services.	"[C]ommitments" in goods and service "can be effectively pooled to" enhance "efficacy of traditional mutual service practices" (Ruddick 2023). Doing so enhances trade velocity between participating nodes. When combined with primitives such as a Redeemable NFT—an NFT that can be used to purchase a good or service— (Boson Protocol 2025) commitment pooling suggests the ability to aggregate, trade, and leverage an entire crypto-institutional inventory.

Source: Table by the authors.

Below are some common arbitration types, moving from meatspace to digital formatting:

- **Alternative Dispute Resolution (ADR)** refers to any method used to resolve disputes outside of the courtroom. Common forms of ADR include *mediation*, where a neutral third party helps the disputing parties to reach a voluntary agreement; *arbitration*, where a neutral third party makes a decision that is often binding; and *negotiation*, where the parties themselves work toward a settlement.
- **Online Dispute Resolution (ODR)** uses digital technology for resolution. ODR is particularly useful in e-commerce, where it offers a fast, accessible, and cost-effective alternative to traditional legal proceedings, often utilizing tools like automated negotiation software, video conferencing, and digital case management systems to assist parties in reaching an agreement.
- **Blockchain dispute resolution (BDR)** innovates beyond the prior two Ø2 methods to use smart contracts for Ø4 dispute resolution automation. BDR utilizes a variety of untraditional yet effective adjudication methods, such as dispute resolution games that reward "honest jurors" and penalize "dishonest jurors" to create epistemological Schelling points (Mechanism Institute 2025e). BDR can be highly customized throughout a crypto-institution's governance process, e.g., a time delay period prior to the execution of a DAO proposal in which arbitration can be initiated. In this example, there would be a set time between the moment a decision has been submitted or finalized, and the moment that it is executed; in this pause the arbitrators for the decision would determine its validity. Overall, these automations enhance efficiency and cost-effectiveness by streamlining the inputs of intermediaries during the dispute resolution process (Kadioglu Kumtepe 2021). BDR cost-effectiveness may also be further augmented by ongoing productivity developments in AI-legal software (Choiet al. 2023), suggesting the future potential for autonomous agents to independently mediate cases onchain with maximum efficiency. It is worth noting that these types of decentralized justice systems are gaining institutional recognition and acceptance, such as in Mexico (Carrera 2022). Since 2017, one noteworthy BDR example is Kleros, whose system is based on selecting jurors for each case randomly from a large group, such that it is unlikely the jurors can coordinate, and then rewarding jurors if they select the winning side of the dispute (thus creating an epistemological Schelling point; Bergolla et al. 2022).

Green crypto-institutions have the capacity to utilize blockchain-based dispute resolution not only as a means for settling disputes but also as a strategic tool to ensure adherence to environmental standards and the effective stewardship of natural resources, thus reinforcing crypto-institutional commitments to the sustainable generation of natural capital. This is particularly pertinent in areas that require a deep understanding of local context and hands-on management—domains where centralized state institutions may not be as effective. A well-constructed arbitration system furthermore acts as a preventive measure, deterring individuals or institutions *ex ante* from exploiting or mismanaging environmental resources.

PROTOCOL CASE STUDIES

This chapter concludes with an examination of three institutional protocol case studies: the Sarafu-Credit by Grassroots Economics, an analysis of carbon market policies, and a conceptual sketch of a decentralized communal tenure system applied to a Spirulina farm. These studies help illustrate the breadth of protocol designs available to green crypto-institutions as they navigate and adapt to the ongoing climate crisis.

Collaborative Finance: The Sarafu-Credit

The Sarafu-Credit is a complementary currency system based in Kenya (also called social, alternative, or community currencies). As shown in Figure 5.10, the system aims to foster local trade by mobilizing underutilized resources, helping residents satisfy basic needs, and enabling financial transactions despite the scarcity of state-issued fiat. It initially took the form of paper notes, circulating alongside the Kenyan Shilling in several informal settlements and slums as an alternative means of exchange for local businesses and schools, but has since then been increasingly digitized. The system works approximately as follows:

1. Local goods and service providers are organized into a network which is legally registered as a community-based organization or cooperative.
2. This network develops or acquires shared businesses, such as factories, wholesale shops, or transportation services.
3. The inventory and profits from network businesses serve as collateral for a voucher, which functions as the complementary currency. The currency can be used for social services like afforestation, road maintenance, and employing youth for waste collection.
4. Network business owners trade in both Kenyan Shillings and Sarafu-Credit. The complementary currency particularly assists those with limited access to the national currency.
5. Sarafu-Credit holders generally use any accumulated excess to purchase cooperative business inventory (Sarafu Credit 2025).

Substantial empirical research showcases the efficiency gains and overall success of the Sarafu-Credit system. In one study, its adoption supported a 22% average increase in the incomes of participating businesses, and up to 10% of local food purchases were conducted in it by its constituent communities (Ruddick 2011). Sales within communities adopting the system grow, monthly incomes increase (one study showed a 22% increase; Zeller 2020) and community trust between currency-using community members strengthened. Overall, the complementary currency system manifests greater triple bottom line outcomes compared to conventional development efforts (Zeller 2020, 271).

The Sarafu-Credit leverages rules and incentives to guide and weave its distribution into local circuits of production to coordinate user behaviors toward common

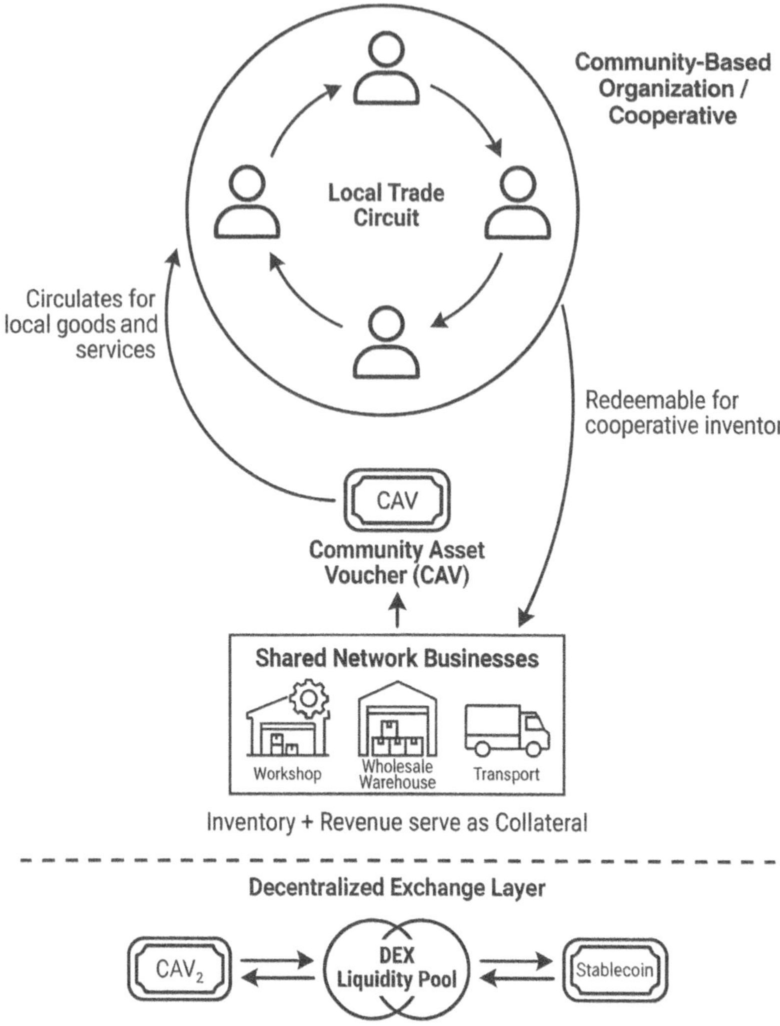

FIGURE 5.10 Community Asset Voucher (CAV) circulation model. A community-based organization issues vouchers backed by the inventory and revenue of shared network businesses (workshops, warehouses, transport). CAVs circulate within a local trade circuit for goods and services and are redeemable against cooperative inventory. A decentralized exchange layer enables cross-community trade by pooling CAVs from different networks alongside stablecoins.

***Source*: Diagram by the authors.**

communitarian network objectives. Each community issues a collection of intertwined sociotechnical Ø2–3 policies, and since the launch of the Sarafu Network, may Ø4 trade with other neighboring communities. A handful of these protocols are contextualized in Table 5.5.

TABLE 5.5
Case Study: The Sarafu Credit

Specific Rule or Action	Protocol Operation (Ø)
Minting of currency.	Ø3 Minting (x → 1)
New users receive a currency bonus for signing up or filling out a portfolio. If they make a transaction and were referred by an existing user, the referrer receives a bonus.	Ø4 Funding: Consumer Subsidy (if the currency is reversible, these are Ø3 operations)
Weekly currency bonus for high exchange activity.	Ø4 Funding: Consumer Subsidy
Other Kenyan currencies are deposited to a credit currency reserve; the depositors receive in return the fiat value of their principal *and* bonus credit currency.	Ø3 Monetary Policy: Currency Import Subsidy
If there is no trading activity, then currency is deducted from a specific user account and added to the reserve.	Ø3 Fiscal Policy: Asset Forfeiture
Currency-using shops act as backers of last resort, offering goods and services that can be purchased with the currency. It is correspondingly sponsored by the community treasury.	Ø3 Fiscal Policy: Redistribution
Shop profits are reinvested in community services.	Ø3 Fiscal Policy: Taxation Ø4 Funding: Investment
Two separate currencies decide to deepen their exchange and inter-credit liquidity, e.g., the BARAKA/MUMO pair of the *Kenya ROLA Pool* of the Sarafu Network (Sarafu Network 2025).	Ø4 D2D: Co-liquidity Pool

Source: Table by the authors.

Climate Finance: Carbon Dioxide Removal Policies

Carbon market policies aim to remove or avoid the production of carbon emissions. While certain regions such as the EU, UK, and US have started to engage in deliberate carbon dioxide removal (CDR) policymaking to grow the removal side of the sector, other states have been slower. Although over 100 countries have established net-zero emission goals, only a handful have produced detailed CDR plans for their long-term low-emission development strategies (UNEP 2023).

Balancing development with CDR is a difficult task. Key CDR policy challenges include accurately measuring carbon stocks and changes, increasing carbon stocks beyond usual practices, ensuring durable carbon storage, and controlling or reducing emissions of other greenhouse gasses that may arise with practices that boost carbon stocks. Furthermore, leakage must be addressed by measuring and mitigating unintended, displaced increases in GHG emissions outside a target geography (Ogle et al. 2023). To accomplish this range of objectives, CDR plans propose a diverse range of active and future policy levers, including:

- Direct regulations mandating the adoption of climate-friendly practices; Ø2 rules that require institutions to implement sustainable methods and technologies.
- Subsidies to drive adoption of the above.

- Tax programs that charge according to the GHG emissions emitted.
- The formation of cap-and-trade compliance markets that trade "carbon issuances," a.k.a. purchasable rights for emissions entities are mandated to buy to meet regulatory Ø2 limits set on greenhouse gas outputs.
- Policy bundles that together address the needs of specific CDR methods, such as carbon capture and storage. "CDR with carbon storage of ten thousand years or more" may need "fewer accompanying measures" as "less permanent methods are associated with a higher administrative burden" (Burke and Schenuit 2023).
- Innovative policies such as *carbon dividends*. Supported by economists like Larry Summers and Janet Yellen, carbon dividends are seen as a politically viable solution that issues a UBI funded by carbon emitters. In practice, Canada's carbon rebate program has tested this approach by returning the majority of carbon tax revenues directly to its citizens, effectively treating them as shareholders in public wealth. An open letter advocating for universal carbon dividends to be distributed to every citizen has been signed by many significant economists (Climate Leadership Council n.d.).

Table 5.6 reflects how those carbon market policy examples can be categorized as expressions of crypto-institutional protocol.

Cooperative Finance: The Spirulina Communal Tenure DAO

Spirulina is a type of blue-green algae that grows in both fresh and salt water and is renowned for its nutritional value. It is commonly consumed as a dietary supplement due to its high protein content, as well as its rich concentration of vitamins, minerals, and antioxidants.

Maintaining a spirulina farm requires consistent and careful attention. The amount of work and the number of people needed can vary based on the size of the farm, the farming methods used, and the level of automation. An SME may need two to five people working full-time, but larger farms or those with less automation may require more staff. The work on a spirulina farm can be labor-intensive, especially in terms of harvesting and cleaning.

The key difference between the SpirulinaDAO and a traditional spirulina cooperative is that its collective rules and protocols now have a technical means-of-enforcement and new revenue models enabled by the computational and financial affordances of Web3. With this context, the authors protocolize a design sketch of a "SpirulinaDAO," an original platform cooperative collectively owned and controlled by its workers. Its protocol architecture is diagrammed in Figure 5.11.

Foremost, the first farm is tokenized as a GeoNFT and appended to a spatial registry for SpirulinaDAO farms. This creates a scalable template for future expansion. Imagine a map interface of tokenized SpirulinaDAO farms with associated phygical inventories they can trade with each other via D2D operations.

Sharded from each GeoNFT are *Spirulina State Tokens (SST)*; access rights tokens that grant read access to a comprehensive database of the farm's ecological

TABLE 5.6
Case Study: Carbon Dioxide Removal Policies

Carbon Policy or Action Example	Definition	Real-World Example	Protocol Operation Type
Direct Regulations	Mandating the adoption of climate-smart practices through enforced rules	The EU's Renewable Energy Directive mandates that EU member states increase their share of renewable energies in their overall energy consumption by 2030	Ø2 Legal and Social Declarations
Subsidies	Financial incentives to encourage adoption of climate-smart practices	In the US, the federal government offers the Investment Tax Credit, which provides a tax credit for investments in solar photovoltaic systems	Ø4 Funding: Investment
Taxes	Imposing charges related to the GHG emissions to internalize environmental impacts	Sweden's carbon tax, first implemented in 1991, charges a fee on fossil fuels based on their carbon content	Ø3 Fiscal Policy: Redistribution
Cap-and-Trade	A system limiting the total greenhouse gas emissions but allowing exchange of allowances.	The California Cap-and-Trade Program, established by the California Air Resources Board, limits the total amount of greenhouse gasses that regulated entities can emit while allowing these entities to buy and sell emissions permits to comply with the cap	Ø2 Legal and Social Declarations—market demand is artificially structured through law.
Policy Bundles	Tailored combinations of policies for different CDR methods based on their permanence needs	Germany's *Energiewende* (Energy Transition) policy bundle combines subsidies for renewable energy, energy efficiency targets, and phasing out nuclear power	Variable, but Ø3 Certification Registries play a strong role
Carbon Dividends	Distributing revenues from carbon pricing directly back to citizens as a form of universal basic income	In Canada, the federal carbon pricing backstop policy redistributes the revenues collected from carbon taxes directly to households through a rebate system	Ø3 Fiscal Policy: Redistribution that converts to Ø4 Funding: Consumer Subsidy (assuming the UBI issued is reversible)

Source: Table by the authors.

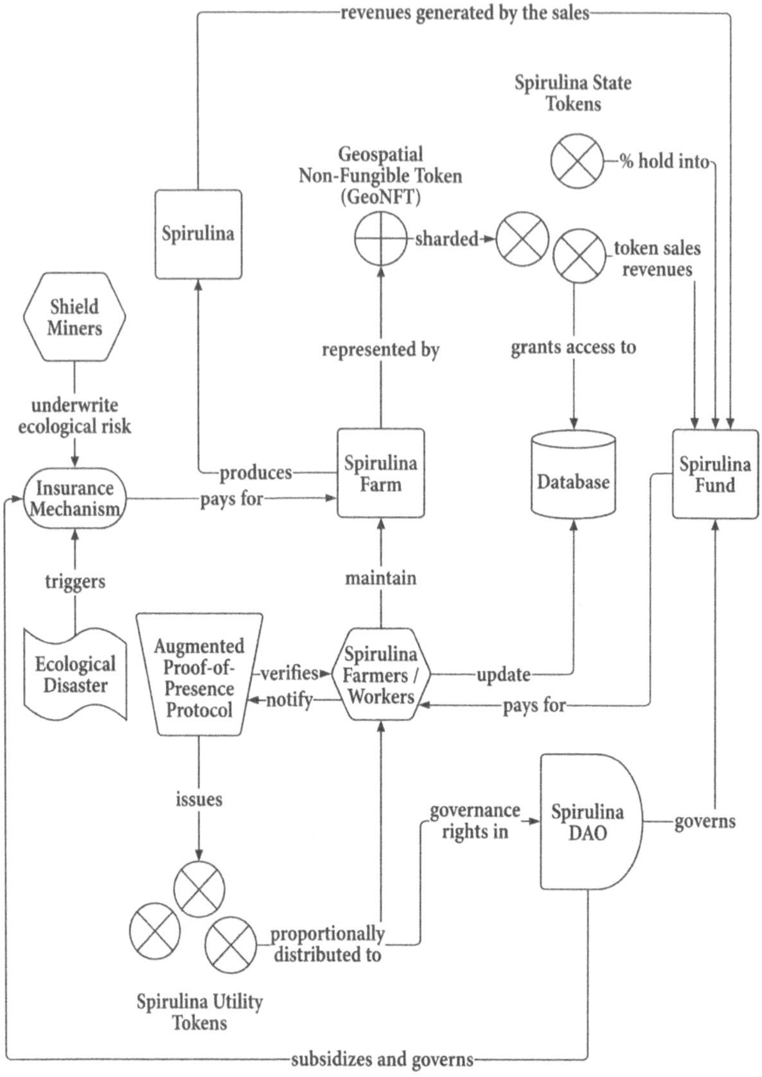

FIGURE 5.11 Design sketch of a communal tenure Spirulina farm, co-owned by the SpirulinaDAO.

***Source*: Diagram by the authors.**

state history, verifiable logs of worker actions attributed to changes in ecological state, as well as inventory and bookkeeping data. The sharding mechanism is pegged or tied in some way to the aggregate Spirulina farm cultivation area, binding its supply to the underlying material reality (e.g., 1 million SSTs are minted for every 100 m^2 of cultivated basin). In light of Spirulina's documented role in CO_2 sequestration, this ecological data holds value for a diverse array of stakeholders, such as scientists, other spirulina farmers, and environmental analysts (Zhu et al. 2020).

The sale of SST by the DAO's treasury generates revenue, which is channeled into a *Spirulina Fund*, managed by the SpirulinaDAO. Moreover, SSTs could offer holders various utilities, such as discounted access to farm produce or access to community events. On top of revenues derived from SST sales, the Spirulina Fund also collectivizes harvest profits to fairly compensate a local workforce of highly skilled, year-round employees. These loci of local knowledge are pivotal to successfully collaborating with a wider contractual and seasonal workforce, as is standard in the agricultural sector due to its harvest rhythm.

A simple *Proof of Presence* protocol tracks contributions while simultaneously enabling a system of communal tenure governance (Traditional Dream Factory 2022). Contributors receive *Spirulina Governance Tokens* for each day they work on the farm, a non-transferable reversible point score.

Lastly, the farm's operational stability is underwritten by a parametric insurance system. Governed by the SpirulinaDAO, this insurance system is supported by a staking contract that allows a network of so-called "shield miners" to underwrite ecological risks in exchange for rewards. For instance, following disastrous weather conditions, the contract automatically releases staked funds to finance necessary repairs and ensure the continuous operation and resilience of the farm network. In accordance with the SpirulinaDAO's governance, these rewards could be denominated in any object primitive interior to its surface: fiat-denominated stablecoins, governance tokens (a.k.a. points), SSTs...

Table 5.7 summarizes the previous description of the SpirulinaDAO system within the context of the chapter's terminology.

TABLE 5.7
Case Study: Spirulina Communal Tenure DAO

Action of the SpirulinaDAO System	Protocol Operation (Ø)
Minting of a Spirulina GeoNFT	Ø3 Fungibility Transformation: Minting (x → 1)
Registering a Spirulina GeoNFT on the SpirulinaDAO map	Ø3 Registries: Spatial Registry
Sharding a Spirulina GeoNFT into SSTs	Ø3 Fungibility Transformation: Fractionalization (1 → n)
Hiring a new worker in the Spirulina farm	Ø3 Registries: Identity Registry
DAO vote to change constitutional rules of SpirulinaDAO	Ø1 Changing Constitutional Rules
Augmented Proof-of-Presence Protocol	Ø3 Registries: Spatial Registry Ø3 Registries: Identity Registry Ø3 Primitive Surfaces: Non-Transferable and Reversible
Parametric insurance mechanism	Ø3 Fiscal Policy: Insurance (insurance contract parameters) Ø4 DeFi and Yield Generation (its shield miners)
Payment of farmers' salary	Ø4 Funding and Subsidies
Exchange of SSTs or other tokens between two SpirulinaDAO farms	Ø4 DAO-to-DAO: Token Swap

Source: Table by the authors.

REFERENCES

AgripolicyKit. 2025a. "Certification." https://agripolicykit.net/en/instruments/certification. Accessed March 2026.

AgripolicyKit. 2025b. "Import Quotas." https://agripolicykit.net/en/instruments/import-quotas. Accessed March 2026.

AgripolicyKit. 2025c. "Objectives by Policy Dimensions." https://agripolicykit.net/en/dimensions. Accessed March 2026.

AgripolicyKit. 2025d. "Pension Insurance Scheme." https://agripolicykit.net/en/instruments/statutory-agricultural-pension-insurance-scheme. Accessed March 2026.

Agrotoken. 2020. "Agrotoken Whitepaper."

Alchemix. 2023. "Getting Started." Alchemix Gitbook. https://v2-docs.alchemix.fi/. Accessed March 2026.

Apiary. 2023. "Motivations and Reputations: Mapping Reputation (Eco)Systems in Web3." Medium, July 21, 2023. https://apiary.xyz/articles/motivations-reputations-mapping-reputation-ecosystems-in-web3/. Accessed March 2026.

Astral Protocol. 2024. "GeoNFT." Astral Protocol. https://astral.global. Accessed March 2026.

Baker, Lucas. 2022. "Paradigms for On-Chain Credit." Jump Crypto, August 22, 2022.

Bal, Meghna. 2017. "Securing Property Rights in India through Distributed Ledger Technology." Observer Research Foundation, January 5, 2017.

Balancer. 2025. "Liquidity Bootstrapping Pools." Balancer Docs. https://docs.balancer.fi/concepts/pools/liquidity-bootstrapping.html. Accessed March 2026.

Bergolla, Luis, Karen Seif, and Can Eken. 2022. "Kleros: A Socio-Legal Case Study of Decentralized Justice & Blockchain Arbitration." Ohio State Journal on Dispute Resolution 37, no. 1: 55–98.

Boson Protocol. 2025. "Redeemable NFTs." Boson Protocol Docs. https://docs.bosonprotocol.io. Accessed March 2026.

Bousso, Ron, and Susanna Twidale. 2019. "Shell Goes Green as It Rebrands UK Household Power Supplier." Reuters, March 25, 2019. https://www.reuters.com/article/sustainability/shell-goes-green-as-it-rebrands-uk-household-power-supplier-idUSKCN1R50OM/. Accessed March 2026.

Bronstein, Max, and Avi Felman. 2020. "Crypto Dollars and the Evolution of Eurodollar Banking." April 7, 2020.

Buchman, Ethan, Paolo Dini, Shoaib Ahmed, Andrew Miller, and Tomaz Fleischman. 2024. "Cycles Protocol: A Peer-to-Peer Electronic Clearing System." v0.5, November 2024.

Burke, Josh, and Felix Schenuit. 2023. "Not All Carbon Removals Are Created Equally." CO2RE, November 30, 2023.

Buterin, Vitalik. 2015. "Visions Part I: The Value of Blockchain Technology." Ethereum Blog, April 13, 2015. https://blog.ethereum.org/2015/04/13/visions-part-1-the-value-of-blockchain-technology. Accessed March 2026.

Carrera, Mauricio Virues. 2022. "Acomodando a Kleros como una herramienta de resolución de disputas descentralizada para sistemas de justicia civil: modelo teórico y caso de aplicación." Kleros.

Champlain Housing Trust. 2025. "Champlain Housing Trust." https://www.champlainhousingtrust.org/. Accessed March 2026.

Chen, Delton. 2018. "The Silver Gun Hypothesis." MAHB, June 12, 2018.

Choi, Jonathan H., Kristin E. Hickman, Amy B. Monahan, and Daniel Schwarcz. 2023. "ChatGPT Goes to Law School." 71 Journal of Legal Education 387. https://papers.ssrn.com/sol3/papers.cfm?abstract_id=4335905. Accessed March 2026.

Climate Leadership Council. n.d. Economists' Statement on Carbon Dividends.

Coorest. 2023. "Coorest Whitepaper 3.0." Coorest Gitbook. https://coorest.gitbook.io/coorest-whitepaper-3.0/coorest-nftree. Accessed March 2026.

Copic, Ezechiel, and Markus Franke. 2020. "Influencing the Velocity of Central Bank Digital Currencies." SSRN Electronic Journal. https://papers.ssrn.com/sol3/papers.cfm?abstract_id=3518736

Dale, Brady. 2021. "Rune Christensen Makes Rallying Cry for MakerDAO to Help Fix Climate Change." The Defiant, October 4, 2021. https://thedefiant.io/news/defi/makerdao-climate-change. Accessed March 2026.

Damania, Richard et al. 2023. Achieving Sustainability, Efficiency, and Prosperity with Natural Capital. World Bank Group.

Defactor. 2023. "Lending Pools Unpacked – Unlocking Liquidity with DeFi Loans." https://assets-global.website-files.com/64555cbab4849ce1dcc3ff3d/652e5e55c09b1281c8ec8e7c_Ebook-Liquidity-Pools-Unpacked-compressed.pdf. Accessed March 2026.

Dimock, Wai Chee. 2022. "AI Can Help Indigenous People Protect Biodiversity." *Scientific American*, August 17, 2022. https://www.scientificamerican.com/article/ai-can-help-indigenous-people-protect-biodiversity/. Accessed March 2026.

Ecosapiens. 2025. "Ecosapiens." https://www.ecosapiens.xyz/. Accessed March 2026.

EthicHub. n.d. "Ethix". EthicHub Docs. https://www.ethichub.com/en/docs/financing-and-guarantee-mechanisms/ethix. Accessed March 2026.

EY and Oxford Analytica. 2021. "The Future of Sustainability Reporting Standards." June 2021.

Finst. 2024. "Fetch.ai, Ocean Protocol and SingularityNET Merge to Create Artificial Superintelligence Alliance." June 6, 2024. https://finst.com/en/blog/articles/fetch-ai-ocean-protocol-merger. Accessed March 2026.

Fleischman, Tomaz, Paolo Dini, and Giuseppe Littera. 2020. "Liquidity-Saving Through Obligation-Clearing and Mutual Credit: An Effective Monetary Innovation for SMEs in Times of Crisis." Journal of Risk and Financial Management 13, no. 12: 295. https://doi.org/10.3390/jrfm13120295

Forest Trends' Ecosystem Marketplace. 2023. Paying for Quality: State of the Voluntary Carbon Markets 2023. Forest Trends.

Frankenfield, Jake. 2020. "Fungibility: What It Means and Why It Matters" Investopedia. https://www.investopedia.com/terms/f/fungibility.asp. Accessed March 2026.

Gerasymchuk, Illya. 2023. "ZkLocus: Authenticated Private Geolocation Off and On-Chain." December 1, 2023.

Goulart, Janaina Borges De Padua. 2021. NYSE and Intrinsic Exchange Group Announce a New Asset Class. Inter-American Development Bank.

Gradeckas, Simas. 2023. "Biodiversity Credit Calculation Overview." Bloom Labs, October 10, 2023.

Granados, Julian, Achim Schlüter, and Rebecca Lahl. 2023. Policy Brief 2023/2: Implementing Blockchain Technologies in PES Schemes. Leibniz Centre for Tropical Marine Research.

Grantham Research Institute. 2024. "Trading Carbon Removals: Establishing the Rules of the Game." January 4, 2024. https://www.lse.ac.uk/granthaminstitute/news/trading-carbon-removals-establishing-the-rules-of-the-game/. Accessed March 2026.

Graybill, Bryan. 2024. Species on the Move: Considering the Future of Conservation Banking. Environmental Policy Innovation Center.

Green, Griff, Carl Lare, Cristina Suga, Kevin Owocki, and Octavian. 2024a. "Hypercerts." Gitcoin.

Green, Griff, Carl Lare, Cristina Suga, Kevin Owocki, and Octavian. 2024b. "Retroactive Public Goods Funding." Gitcoin.

Green, Griff, Carl Lare, Cristina Suga, Kevin Owocki, and Octavian. 2024c. "Dominant Assurance Contracts." Gitcoin.

Greenfield, Patrick. 2023. "Revealed: More than 90% of Rainforest Carbon Offsets by Biggest Provider Are Worthless, Analysis Shows." The Guardian, January 18, 2023. https://www.theguardian.com/environment/2023/jan/18/revealed-forest-carbon-offsets-biggest-provider-worthless-verra-aoe. Accessed March 2026.

Grima, Nelson, Simron J. Singh, Barbara Smetschka, and Lisa Ringhofer. 2016. "Payment for Ecosystem Services (PES) in Latin America." Ecosystem Services 17: 24–32.

Grimm, Holly, Daniel Serrano, Louise Tsondru, Pat Borreani, John Rawson, and Hoopes. 2022. "Regeneration Needs Location." Medium, Kolektivo. https://medium.com/kolektivo-co/regeneration-needs-location-b538cae97ff7. Accessed March 2026.

Hypercerts. 2025. "Hypercerts." https://www.hypercerts.org/. Accessed March 2026.

Interreg Central Europe. 2024. "Strategy for Mainstreaming Carbon Farming in Central Europe." September 2024.

Inverter Network. 2025. "Inverter Network." https://inverter.network/. Accessed March 2026.

Jepson, Paul, and Cain Blythe. 2020. Rewilding: The Radical New Science of Ecological Recovery. Icon Books.

Kadioglu Kumtepe, Cemre Ç. 2021. "A Brief Introduction to Blockchain Dispute Resolution." John Marshall Law Journal 14, no. 2: 137–157.

Kesonpat, Nichanan. 2023. "Wallet Infrastructure: Empowering the Next Generation of Dapps." Mirror, December 12, 2023. https://mirror.xyz/1kx.eth/vrFC1TS9JwksV7_4h1ElObXnJER6Oz3xd0y3YWzDL7Q. Accessed March 2026.

Klima Protocol. 2026. "Open Infrastructure for Carbon Markets." https://www.klimaprotocol.com/. Accessed March 2026.

Lorberg, Kai, and Christian Labetzsch. 2021. "Security Tokens — An ERC-Standards Comparison." micobo GmbH. https://micobo.com/security-tokens-an-erc-standards-comparison-2/. Accessed March 2026.

Lotti, Laura, Nick Houde, and Tara Merk. 2023. Social Security for Web3 Work. Social Science Research Network.

McCarthy, Sam. 2025. "Towards an Impact Taxonomy for Web3 Capital Allocation." DAOStar.

Mechanism Institute. 2025a. "Auction." https://mechanism.institute/library/?search=auction. Accessed March 2026.

Mechanism Institute. 2025b. "Token Stream." https://mechanism.institute/library/token-stream/. Accessed March 2026.

Mechanism Institute. 2025c. "Vesting." https://mechanism.institute/library/vesting/. Accessed March 2026.

Mechanism Institute. 2025d. "Splitter." https://mechanism.institute/library/splitter/. Accessed March 2026.

Mechanism Institute. 2025e. "Schelling Game." https://mechanism.institute/library/schelling-game/. Accessed March 2026.

Musharraf, Mohammad. 2023. "What Is Wrapped Crypto?" Ledger Academy, February 16, 2023. https://www.ledger.com/academy/what-is-wrapped-crypto. Accessed March 2026.

Nir.eth. 2024. "Blocklists: Decentralized Solutions to Combat Spam." Mirror, January 4, 2024.

Nouroozi, Cyrus. 2023. "A Meta Registry." GitHub, July 2023. https://gist.github.com/CyrusOfEden/ea1121fcc6bd178e952ecbbea9d0c3b5. Accessed July 2023.

Ogle, Stephen M. et al. 2023. "Policy Challenges to Enhance Soil Carbon Sinks." Frontiers in Climate.

Open Forest Protocol. 2023. "Afforestation/Reforestation/Revegetation (ARR) Whitepaper." October 2023. https://docsend.com/view/75zb4teqgzvvmyva. Accessed March 2026.

OpSci. 2025. "OpSci." https://www.opsci.io/. Accessed March 2026.

Pecek, Bojan. 2024. "Liquity V2: Enhancing the Borrowing Experience." Liquity Blog, April 3, 2024.

Power, Samantha, and Leon Seefeld. 2024. Bioregional Financing Facilities: Reimagining Finance to Regenerate Our Planet. The Biofi Project.

Prewitt, Matt, and Jack Henderson. 2024. "PCO: A New Model of Ownership." RadicalxChange, February 20, 2024. https://www.radicalxchange.org/media/blog/pco-a-new-model-of-ownership/. Accessed March 2026.
Protocol Labs. 2023. "Generalized Impact Evaluators." Protocol Labs Research, January 10, 2023.
ReFiDAO. 2024. "MRV Museum." Miro. https://miro.com/app/board/uXjVOwpH8wM=/. Accessed March 2026.
Ruddick, Will. 2023. "Commitment Pooling." International Journal of Community Currency Research 27: 54–79.
Ruddick, Will. 2011. "Eco-Pesa: An Evaluation of a Complementary Currency Programme in Kenya's Informal Settlements." International Journal of Community Currency Research 15, no. A: 1–12.
Sachdeva, Anurodh, Ariel Araujo, and Martin Hirschnitz-Garbers. 2021. Extended Producer Responsibility and Ecomodulation of Fees. Ecologic Institute.
Sarafu Credit. 2025. "Sarafu Credit." Grassroots Economics. https://grassecon.org/. Accessed March 2026.
Sarafu Network. 2025. "Kenya ROLA Pool." Grassroots Economics. https://sarafu.network/pools/0x48a953cA5cf5298bc6f6Af3C608351f537AAcb9e. Accessed March 2026.
Shah, Kaushal et al. 2023. "A Systematic Review of Decentralized Finance Protocols." International Journal of Intelligent Networks 4: 171–181.
Shekhar, Shashi, and Pamela Vold. 2019. Spatial Computing. MIT Press.
Shen, Jiake, Chundi Chen, and Yuncai Wang. 2021. "What Are the Appropriate Mapping Units for Ecosystem Service Assessments?" Ecosystem Health and Sustainability 7, no. 1: 1888655.
SourceCred. 2025. "How Cred Works." SourceCred Beta Docs. https://sourcecred.io/docs/beta/cred/. Accessed March 2026.
Tiqqun. 2020. The Cybernetic Hypothesis. Semiotext(e).
Toucan Protocol. 2025. "Overview on Your Carbon Assets." https://app.toucan.earth/. Accessed March 2026.
Traditional Dream Factory. 2022. "Proof of Presence." Mirror, April 1, 2022. https://mirror.xyz/traditionaldreamfactory.eth/hv5LRKDCWnBIMLR32MFGFd2f93K2FeJz4AEGJzH1HBE. Accessed March 2026.
UNEP. 2023. "Emissions Gap Report 2023: Broken Record." November 2023.
Vohra, Arnav. 2023. "Exploring the Buyout Mechanism in NFT Editionization." Medium, Nibbl, March 16, 2023.
Wang, Lijuan et al. 2022. "Systematic Review of Ecosystem Services Flow Measurement." Ecosystem Services 58: 101479.
Weiss, Kyle. 2022. "Gitcoin Grants – Quadratic Funding for the World." Gitcoin, August 29, 2022. https://www.gitcoin.co/blog/gitcoin-grants-quadratic-funding-for-the-world. Accessed March 2026.
White, Dave, Dan Robinson, and andy805. 2021. "RICKS." Paradigm, October 6, 2021.
Wiseman, Leanne et al. 2019. "Farmers and Their Data." NJAS – Wageningen Journal of Life Sciences 90–91, Article 100301.
Zeller, Sarah. 2020. "Economic Advantages of Community Currencies." Journal of Risk and Financial Management 13, no. 11: 271.
Zhu, Baohua, Yuanmei Meng, Fengjie Zheng, Yifan Yin, Qingshan Huang, and Libing Jiang. 2020. "Large-Scale Cultivation of Spirulina for Biological CO2 Mitigation in Open Raceway Ponds Using Purified CO2 From a Coal Chemical Flue Gas." Frontiers in Bioengineering and Biotechnology 7: 441. https://doi.org/10.3389/fbioe.2019.00441
zkMaps. 2024. "zkMaps." GitHub. https://github.com/zkMaps/zkMaps. Accessed March 2026.
Zupass. 2025. "Zupass." https://zupass.org/#/login. Accessed March 2026.

6 Asset Layer

Properties, Functions, and Types of Green Digital Assets

Assets are the oxygen of markets. This chapter surveys green digital assets, or crypto-assets—transferable financial instruments designed to generate economic value while contributing positively to underlying ecological systems. Unlike conventional financial assets, green assets are explicitly linked to environmental outcomes in the material world, such as carbon sequestration, biodiversity protection, or renewable energy generation.

Within the environmental finance stack developed in this book, green digital assets are issued by blockchain-using institutions that encode environmental objectives into programmable protocols. These institutions define the governance rules, technical parameters, and (within certain limits) the distribution mechanisms of the assets they issue. Once created on public blockchains, these assets circulate and are exchanged in the Market Layer examined in the subsequent chapter.

The chapter establishes a cohesive mapping of current and emerging green crypto-asset types. For each asset category and subtype, it identifies defining characteristics and situates them within ongoing technical, legal, and market developments.

Given the rapid evolution of blockchain systems, this mapping is not intended as a fixed taxonomy. Instead, it highlights the design principles that distinguish green crypto-assets from traditional environmental finance instruments—most notably their programmable, hybrid, and materially modular nature. Understanding these principles enables sustainability professionals across public and private sectors to assess how green digital assets can be designed to align more closely with ecological realities and policy objectives.

Three properties are particularly salient:

- **Composability.** A single digital asset can perform multiple functions across different institutional and technical contexts. For example, assets representing renewable energy claims may be used not only for investment but also as collateral within other financial arrangements. This composability enables the creation of novel systems, such as local exchange currencies backed by clean energy production.
- **Adaptability** (or evolutionary design). Digital assets can change their properties and functions over time, including their economic rights and regulatory characteristics. This is evident in tokenized securities, which range from purely synthetic instruments providing price exposure to fully onchain assets conferring ownership, governance, and transfer rights (Levin 2025).

DOI: 10.1201/9781003748472-6

In environmental markets, such evolution has already occurred, for instance when centralized carbon credits were transformed into fungible, onchain representations (Toucan Protocol 2021).

- **Material modularity.** Green crypto-assets can be designed to represent distinct yet complementary aspects of a single ecological system. Within a given territory, separate assets may correspond to carbon storage, biodiversity outcomes, or renewable energy infrastructure, allowing conservation and restoration strategies to be tailored and combined in flexible ways.

As international institutions have noted, programmable tokens can simultaneously perform multiple financial and non-financial functions, blurring traditional asset classifications (Garrido 2023). This increased complexity expands the design space available to sustainability-oriented finance, enabling experimentation with economic models that were previously infeasible. The implications of these new asset forms for market organization and capital allocation are explored in the final chapter.

GREEN CRYPTO-ASSET MAPPING

Table 6.1 provides the overview of green crypto-assets. Each will be discussed in turn in this chapter.

TYPE AND SUBTYPE

"Type" refers to the overarching categorization that a green crypto-asset belongs to, defined by its shared fundamental characteristics or a unified regulatory or framework alignment. Conversely, "subtype" describes further subdivisions within a primary type, characterized by distinctions in functionality, utility, or alignment with specific environmental initiatives. This demarcation between types and subtypes does not adhere to strictly delineated boundaries. For example, various subtypes of environmental process tokens could potentially be consolidated into a singular type. However, each subtype's distinct and respective impacts on the underlying material reality (see Chapter 2) advocate for separate and sequential discussion.

LEGAL DEPENDENCY

This column denotes the degree to which such an asset can effectively function and confer its intended economic or environmental advantages without substantial reliance on formal legal frameworks, including regulation, arbitration, or enforcement as exercised by state authorities. Low legal dependency means these green crypto-assets can ostensibly operate with relative autonomy, employing intrinsic, often automated, mechanisms to institute transparency and trust, mitigating the need for an external legal or regulatory party to ensure functionality and the realization of intended benefit. In short, legal dependency identifies the asset's inherent capability to self-regulate through crypto-institutional protocol and manage potential disputes or disruptions while still aligning with broader legal and ethical standards.

TABLE 6.1
Green Crypto-Asset Mapping

Asset Type	Asset Subtype	Definition	Example	Legal Dependency	Materiality	Novelty
Ownership	Green Real Assets	Fractional ownership of a commodity, usually land	LandX xTokens, Agrotoken	Yes	Strong	Rebirth
	Green Equities	Equity in enterprises: stocks, notes, warrants	"Green" xStock Tokens	Yes	Weak	Rebirth
	Renewable Real-World Assets	Investment in renewable energy infrastructure	Helios	Yes	Strong	Rebirth
	Green Digital Collectibles	Digital assets linked to material reality; can serve as wallets, used in "impact-to-earn" games	Ecosapiens, Play-to-Conserve, Plastiks	No	App-dependent	Birth
	Green Digiphysical Goods	Physical goods with cryptographic onchain records (NFTs, registry entries, signed IDs)	Save Pakistan NFTs, electric vehicles	Use-case dependent	Strong	Rebirth
	Ecological Data Rights & IP	Ownership of data/IP, sometimes collective	SimplexDNA, IP NFTs	Yes if enforceable	Depends on system & application	Birth
Nonpossessory Rights	Natural Asset Company & Stewardship Rights	Tokenized share in entity managing natural capital; no liquidation rights	Nature's Vault Natures Gold Token, INHABIT	Generally yes	Weak	Rebirth
	Output Rights (Profit-à-prendre)	Access to material/financial outputs or revenues from natural assets	Coorest NFTrees, Glow Production Credits	Generally yes	Strong for commodities; app-dependent for financial outputs	Rebirth (commodities) / Birth (staking/novel)
	Memberships & Use Rights	Non-equity access rights	Tekkon Manhole tokens, Traditional Dream Factory	Use-case dependent	Implementation-dependent	Birth/Rebirth
	Governance Tokens	Influence DAO decision-making without ownership	Kokonut DAO	Use-case dependent	Implementation-dependent	Birth

Environmental Process Tokens	Carbon Removal Credits	Tokens representing actual GHG removal	Regen Network GHG & Co-Benefits v1.0	No	Method-dependent	Rebirth
	Carbon Avoidance Credits	Tokens for avoided GHG emissions	Moss Amazon NFT	No	Method-dependent	Rebirth
	Carbon Issuances	Tradable instrument representing emission ceiling	Maseer Finance $CANA	Yes	Method-dependent	Rebirth
	Ecotokens	Units of environmental action: biodiversity, plastic removal, water purification	Open Earth Marine Ecosystem Credits, ERA Keystone Species, Rebalance Earth Nature Credits	No	Method-dependent	Birth/Rebirth
	Renewable Energy Certificates (RECs)	Certify 1 MWh electricity from renewable sources	Energy Web Origin, Arkreen AREC	No	Strong	Rebirth
	Impact-to-Earn	Tokens rewarding validated green tasks	VeBetterDAO	No	Method-dependent	Birth
Debt	Green, Blue, Sustainability-Linked and Impact Bonds	Bonds financing sustainable investments; blue bonds for marine/ocean projects	Frigg.eco tokenized green bonds, LandX perpetual agri-commodity bonds	Yes (state intervention if default)	Weak	Rebirth
	Green Real-world Asset Debt Finance	Socioecological lending, collateralized or not	Almavest Basket #7: Fintech and Carbon Reduction Basket	Yes (state intervention if default)	Weak	Rebirth
Derivatives	Environmental Process Derivatives	Forwards, futures, options, swaps on eco-assets	Carbon Futures (GreenTrade), Carbon Forwards (SolidWorld), Tokenized biodiversity derivative	No	Weak	Rebirth
	Commodity Derivatives	Derivatives of tangible goods (agriculture, metals, energy)	Tokenized coffee futures	No	Weak	Rebirth
	Power Purchasing Agreements (PPAs)	Long-term electricity forward contracts	WePower	Yes	Weak	Rebirth

(*Continued*)

TABLE 6.1 (*Continued*)
Green Crypto-Asset Mapping

Asset Type	Asset Subtype	Definition	Example	Legal Dependency	Materiality	Novelty
	"Green" Liquidity Provider Tokens (LP Tokens)	Share of DEX/AMM fees, akin to dynamic put options	KLIMA/MCO2 QuickSwap LP tokens	No	Asset-dependent	Birth
	"Green" Yield Tokens	Tokenized yield from green assets (debt, forwards, staked tokens)	Yield-bearing green tokens	No	Asset-dependent, likely weak	Birth
Insurance	Parametric Insurance	Underwrites natural asset condition based on event	Shamba Network/DIVA/ FortuneConnect, Quintana Roo Reef	No	Trigger-dependent	Rebirth
	Reinsurance	Insurance for climate/environmental insurers	Arbol	No	Weak	Rebirth
	Crypto-staking Insurance	Events underwritten by staked tokens; yield for staking	EthicHub	No	Trigger-dependent	Birth
Currency	Green Money or Nature-backed Currencies	Fiat-pegged currency backed by green assets	Celo-Mento stablecoins	Collateral-dependent	Peg/ collateral-dependent	Birth
	Green Reserve-backed Currencies	Currency backed by green assets, no fiat peg	SolarpunkDAO's EARTH Token	Collateral-dependent	Peg/ collateral-dependent	Birth
	Green Arcade Tokens	Stable in specific green apps/ ecosystems	Open for innovation	No	Weak	Birth
	Green Tracercoins	AI-driven stablecoins pegged to non-financial indices	Cogito Protocol GCOIN	No	Peg/ collateral-dependent	Birth
Indices, ETFs, and Portfolio Funds	N/A	Tokenized baskets of green/climate-aligned assets; dynamically rebalanced	Ondo Finance ETFs (OUSG)	No	Medium	Rebirth

Source: Table by the authors.

Certain primary types require a high degree of state involvement, namely, *Ownership*, which requires the enforcement of private property rights, and *Debt*, which may require the ability to claim and liquidate pledged real-world collateral. While many types can operate without extensive state intervention (such as environmental process tokens), regulatory oversight can provide a level of protection for buyers who expect institutional assurances regarding asset quality or vintage. In general, for tokens of high legal dependency, the law can benefit users by setting rules on reversibility (see Chapter 5), insolvency, and how to resolve jurisdictional conflicts of law.

MATERIALITY

The degree to which the intrinsic and extrinsic characteristics of an asset are interconnected with its tangible reality; its level of abstraction. This concept not only encompasses the physical and measurable aspects of the asset but also intricately links its qualitative and quantitative properties to the palpable, material world.

The complexity of assessing the degree to which the properties of green crypto-assets are coupled to material reality often results in the common ambiguous observation that "it depends." This ambiguity stems from the interaction between factors such as the asset's underlying technology, regulatory environment, economic conditions, and the specific purpose it serves within broader asset ecosystems and markets.

In designing green assets, there are several key principles that help guide their effectiveness and alignment with any intended materiality. While the field is evolving, fundamental principles of good green asset design tend to relate to the previous layers discussed in this document, such as the content of the asset's material backing, the method and transparency of its data collection, availability, and storage infrastructure, and the robustness of the issuing institution as understood by the character of its governance.

As of late 2025, audit checklists that comprehensively assess the viability and effectiveness of a token's economics are being standardized, and are highly applicable to the complex diagnostics materiality evokes (Kampakis and Stankevičius 2023). While certain types such as *carbon removal tokens* have a clear and methodological approach to materiality—e.g., one carbon removal credit token equals one ton of carbon sequestered—subtypes such as the *green equities* require greater due diligence that leverage advanced certification frameworks (e.g., Environmental, Social, and Governance; ESG). Tokenomic checklists serve as valuable tools to evaluate the strength and viability of more ambiguous assets within the broader financial ecosystem, and when extended to green crypto-assets, could include questions like:

- **Business-Token Interaction:** How well does the token's design align with the business goals and environmental objectives of the project?
- **Structural Analysis:** The token's technical architecture, including its scalability, security, and environmental compatibility with its underlying blockchain or platform.
- **Allocation and Distribution:** How tokens are allocated and distributed, ensuring fairness, addressing concentration of ownership, and considering

long-term institutional sustainability. As discussed in Chapter 4, commons-based governance of natural assets has had relatively equal distribution of control. Yochai Benkler, popular author of the *Wealth of Networks*, emphasizes how open-source software development and collaborative online communities can foster more equal participation and control over digital resources; these communitarian ideals extend to green crypto-institutions that manage natural assets (Benkler 2007).

- **Stability and Stress Tests:** Tests the token's economic model under various scenarios, including stress tests, to assess its resilience and ability to maintain stability while simultaneously maintaining its materiality.

NOVELTY

Novelty identifies the origin and uniqueness of an asset, determining whether it is an original creation (birth) within Web3, or a tokenization (rebirth) of pre-existing markets. An asset is deemed "novel" if it manifests intrinsically within the Web3 space, demonstrating unique onchain properties or utilities distinct from assets in conventional markets. Conversely, an asset experiences a "rebirth" when it represents a tokenized adaptation of a pre-existing, traditionally traded reference asset, transposed into Web3 to exploit public blockchain-based advantages while maintaining linkage to established market entities.

Some of the assets presented in the taxonomy are "birth" assets and would be novel entries to any green asset taxonomy. But many taxonomy assets are *real-world assets* (RWA), or tokenized, pre-existing green assets. Tokenized RWAs require a handful of critical features:

> [T]okenization involves five design features: 1) a blockchain, 2) a reference asset, 3) a mechanism to assess the value of the reference asset, 4) a means to store and/or provide custody for the reference asset, and 5) a mechanism to facilitate redemptions of the token and/or the reference asset.
>
> **Carapella et al. (2023)**

Of note is that certain organizations present a more complex reading grid than the "Birth-Rebirth" dichotomy employed in this chapter. The Bank of America Institute proposes a "three bridge thesis" where "tokenized pre-existing traditional assets … continues to exist off-chain in the 'real-world' but also exists within the digital asset ecosystem"—as compared to "tokenized traditional assets" where "at no point was token ownership recorded on a ledger" (see Carapella et al. 2023). Figure 6.1 illustrates a five-model framework of tokenization that has been proposed to examine how varying configurations of ownership rights and value-transfer mechanisms shape the efficiency gains associated with tokenized instruments. Within this framework, higher-order models, those approaching full onchain ownership and native settlement, generate the greatest operational and transactional cost advantages for market participants, including issuers and financial intermediaries such as banks and brokers.

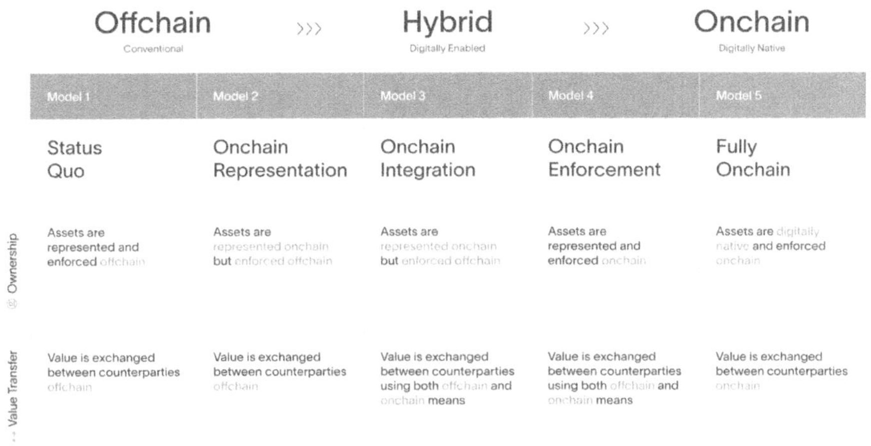

FIGURE 6.1 Tokenized assets take on a variety of forms depending on whether or not they are natively issued with their rights enforced onchain or simply onchain representations of assets whose rights are enforced offchain. Over time, more and more assets are expected to become fully onchain as trust-minimized protocols for dispute resolution progress.

***Source*: Erickson, Collin, Mac Naggar, and Jack Chong. "The Spectrum of Tokenization Report." RWA.xyz, Fall 2023. www.rwa.xyz/blog/the-spectrum-of-tokenization-report**

BREAKDOWN BY TYPE

Ownership

The primary ownership type can be understood as the act, state, or right of direct possession of green crypto-assets. In traditional markets, the natural assets most commonly owned include property or commodities like precious metals or agricultural products. With Web3, new and evolving objects of ownership are being introduced, such as virtual goods. Table 6.2 summarizes the different ownership types.

Green Real Assets

Tokenized "green real assets" are the most straightforward case of ownership. Green real assets could include sustainably produced commodities, fractional or whole ownership of land or real estate, or ownership of natural capital, such as natural assets. For example, LandX tokenized a property called Winnie Mandela, fractionally owned by xCorn token holders: if a single wallet accumulates enough xCorn tokens, they can claim private ownership of the farmland through a buyout and reconstitution mechanism (LandX 2025).

While many ongoing experiments are pioneering shared crypto-ownership, especially in real estate, few have tapped into shared ownership as a means of establishing privately held conserved territories, eco-villages, or other regenerative place-based designs. This is explainable in the inherent tension of ownership vs. stewardship:

TABLE 6.2
Ownership Type

Subtype	Green Real Assets	Green Equities	Renewable Real-World Assets	Green Digital Collectibles	Green Digiphysical Goods	Ecological Data Rights and IP
Definition	Fractional ownership of a commodity, usually land	Equity in enterprises: stocks, notes, warrants	Investment in renewable energy infrastructure	Digital assets linked to material reality; can serve as wallets, used in "impact-to-earn" games	Physical goods with cryptographic onchain records (NFTs, registry entries, signed IDs)	Ownership of data/IP, sometimes collective
Examples	LandX xTokens, Agrotoken	"Green" xStock Tokens	Helios	Ecosapiens, Play-to-Conserve, Plastiks	Save Pakistan NFTs, electric vehicles	SimplexDNA, IP NFTs
Legal Dependency	Yes	Yes	Yes	No	Use-case dependent	Yes if enforceable
Materiality	Strong	Weak	Strong	App-dependent	Strong	Depends on system and application
Novelty	Rebirth	Rebirth	Rebirth	Birth	Rebirth	Birth

Source: Table by the authors.

properties possessed as private goods tend to, on a long enough timeline, be eventually realized for profit (and by extension, environmentally degraded); properties of a commons-like nature tend to be well maintained in the long term due to the fact they are not realizable for profit in the first place. A secondary consideration regarding their lack of adoption is the security-like nature of ownership tokens: regulation is constantly changing and is jurisdictionally varied.

Excluding gold, tokenized commodities have yet to scale. The few projects that do exist, such as Agrotoken, are building custodial stockpile models that utilize transparent data oracles to provide verification of stocks, e.g., "Proof of grain reserves" (Agrotoken 2020). In general, the tokenization of natural assets challenges current price discovery methods: green coffee, for instance, is mostly priced by centralized futures exchanges in the USA and the UK (Genuine Origin 2021). While on one hand this practice reduces risk across the supply chain by standardizing financial instruments, on the other hand, it introduces a high level of financialization prone to manipulation (Flood and Blas 2007) that risks mispricing assets and centralizing revenues (Utrilla-Catalán et al. 2022). With coffee and other commodities, Web3's inherent P2P markets (DeFi) may end up being more efficient than existing market infrastructure once a network of secure and reliable private sector custodians is established.

Green Equities

Tokenized green equities represent ownership in public and private companies in nature tech, climate tech, clean tech, and other green or sustainable infrastructure. These RWAs are growing in popularity as new protocols emerge that navigate the tension between regulatory compliance and crypto's open markets. These types of tokenized instruments can take on a variety of forms, and introduce complexity that onchain cap tables strive to capture. The Open Cap Table Protocol (OCP)—an onchain standard for programmable, compliant, and composable equity management designed by an advanced legal and regulatory coalition—supports four broad categories of equity-based compensation (Favre et al. 2025):

- **Stocks:** Ownership shares; the basic equity building block. Multiple stock classes can exist with specific rights and restrictions. OCP enforces share issuance limits and distribution.
- **Convertible equity securities:** Debt notes that can be converted into equity under specific conditions. In OCP, these securities track investment amounts rather than share quantities, implement conversion terms, and maintain seniority relationships among investors. Upon conversion, OCP automatically creates new stock positions while preserving a complete transaction history. Convertible notes are an increasingly popular method for crypto to access traditional market liquidity, with multiple publicly traded US firms issuing them with the intent to build crypto-denominated treasuries, such as BTCS Inc.'s $57.8m convertible note raise earmarked for purchasing and staking ETH (BTCS Inc. 2025).
- **Equity-based compensation:** Encompasses options, restricted stock units, phantom shares, and restricted stock awards. *Options* give the holder the right, but not the obligation, to buy or sell an underlying equity asset.

Restricted Stock Units grant the right to receive equity shares after meeting certain conditions, such as a vesting period or performance milestones. *Phantom shares* pay out a bonus equal to the appreciation or value of a specified number of shares at a future date, typically used to reward stakeholders without issuing actual equity. *Restricted Stock Awards* are grants of actual shares subject to vesting conditions (e.g., time or performance), allowing recipients to hold and potentially benefit from ownership (e.g., dividends) before restrictions lapse. OCP integrates these incentive mechanisms to track exercise prices, vesting schedules, and grant-specific terms. OCP's smart contracts automatically validate conditions (e.g., vesting milestones) and create resulting stock positions. This approach allows tokenized compensation to be traded or leveraged in DeFi applications (e.g., as collateral).

- **Warrants:** A specialized equity derivative that grants holders the right to purchase stock at a predetermined price under specific exercise conditions. OCP's event-driven model allows for future extensions in warrant design, e.g., transferable NFT-based certificates of warrant ownership.

Assessing the materiality of green equities remains a significant challenge due to the lack of standardized metrics and the inherent complexity of measuring environmental impact alongside financial performance. The absence of uniform data collection methods and the variability in how "green" is defined across industries make it difficult to quantify the long-term value or risks associated with these assets. ESG frameworks are actively working to develop certifications and standardize criteria for assessing materiality, with the Task Force on Climate-related Financial Disclosures or its counterpart, the Task Force on Nature-related Financial Disclosures, working to create a common language to evaluate materiality (ImpactLabs 4 Earth and Nature Tech Collective 2024).

Renewable Real-World Assets

Blockchain's programmable accountability, interoperability, immutability, and transparency by default can help address key challenges inhibiting investment in renewable energy, such as solar power. In general, renewables are characterized by diverse regulatory frameworks, non-standardized contracts, and pervasive principal-agent due diligence dilemmas (World Economic Forum 2016). These investment obstacles mirror the structural advantages blockchain brings: for instance, distributed solar energy deployment is constrained by the absence of a unified platform for communication and information exchange (interoperability), incomplete data availability (transparency), deficient record-keeping practices (immutability), and limited information security (accountability) (Solar Power Europe 2025). With this in mind, blockchain is well suited to be the solar industry's decentralized trust layer (Gunarathna et al. 2022).

Helios is one protocol that exemplifies investment ownership in renewable energy infrastructure. Users invest in "Solar Pools" by depositing capital, which Helios channels toward financing, constructing, and ownership of solar installations developed via a worldwide network of solar developers. These installations sell clean energy under long-term contracts (typically spanning 20 years) to commercial customers actively engaged in climate mitigation efforts. The returns generated from the sale of this clean energy constitute 100% of the yield distributed to pool investors (Helios 2025).

Green Digital Collectibles

The term *digital collectible* inadequately captures the increasingly complex virtual economies emerging in Web3. In this book, the term is retained as shorthand for a wide spectrum of tokenized inventories within blockchain-native gaming and metaversal ecosystems. These inventories, in many cases, are not merely static NFTs but programmable, composable assets that may operate as economic agents in their own right. As we explore in later sections, such crypto-assets can function as autonomous AI agents in decentralized supply chains, driven by economic incentives.

Unlike traditional in-game purchases, which are siloed and locked within proprietary ecosystems, blockchain-native game economies (commonly referred to as GameFi) grant players durable ownership rights, composability across platforms, and embedded financial incentives. Any NFT or token created in one game can be recognized and utilized in others, enabling assets to accrue rich, cross-platform histories and metadata of use and transformation. The shift from passive consumption to active economic participation transforms users from mere players into co-creators and stakeholders in decentralized autonomous worlds (AWs, see definition below).

Environmental applications for digital collectibles take on new dimensions when the assets in question are designed with materiality in mind. A pioneering example is the *Ecosapiens* NFT series, which ties collectibles to carbon retirement actions (Ecosapiens 2025). Similarly, Greenpill's dynamic NFTs introduced a gameplay loop centered on environmental transformation: users mint a "Red Pill" NFT for a nominal fee and, through interaction with a suite of dApps, perform verifiable impact actions that incrementally evolve the NFT through red, orange, and ultimately green states (Atlantis Labs 2025). These transformations unlock both tangible impact metrics (e.g., "Impact Points") and exclusive digital rewards. The gamified mechanism encourages positive environmental behavior while reinforcing long-term asset engagement, blending digital prestige with ecological contribution.

These experiments illustrate the potential of *Autonomous Worlds* (1kx 2023a)—persistent, blockchain-native virtual environments governed by onchain logic. In such worlds, digital objects and characters are economic agents with property rights, privacy guarantees, and decision-making autonomy. Blockchains are essential to AWs because they provide the legal-informational substrate required for ownership, interoperability, and reputation-building. With AI agents, AWs evolve from static simulations into dynamic socioeconomic systems where AI-driven avatars can interact, transact, and co-govern.

The convergence of AI agents and autonomous worlds opens new pathways for green crypto-asset design. Smart collectibles could not only reflect external environmental data (e.g., biodiversity updates, carbon prices) but act on it—modifying their attributes, unlocking quests, or generating content. The completed Sovereign Nature Initiative (NB: project defunct)—an early pilot program for these types of green collectibles—notes that:

> [I]n-game items and cosmetics... gain wild abilities and attributes while saving real animals from extinction... Each time a conservation organization uploads new data from their field work, in-game avatars as well as item sets and accessories reflect the update.
>
> **Sovereign Nature Initiative (2025)**

These dynamics enhance the status-signaling nature of NFTs as *Veblen goods*. As luxury economics suggests, Veblen goods gain desirability as their price increases, functioning as positional markers in competitive social spaces. This speculative character is double-edged: while it draws capital and attention, it also risks detaching perceived value from material outcomes. NFTs, especially those tied to impact narratives or scarce environmental provenance, can counteract these tendencies as they transcend mere speculative, social-signaling dynamics to become green badges of merit. As the market for in-game purchases surpasses hundreds of billions of USD globally (Statista 2025), green crypto stands to benefit from directing even a fraction of these flows toward real-world outcomes.

Green Digiphysical Goods

Digiphysical (alternatively: phygital) goods typically refer to "goods that exist in physical form, and maintain a cryptographic link to its digital (onchain) record via NFC [near-field communication] technology" (1kx 2023b). In contrast to digital collectibles, the virtual half of a cryptonative digiphysical is bound one-to-one with an associated material asset; in effect, digiphysicals, when tightly coupled, are two simultaneous halves of a digital-physical whole.

Their key value proposition resides in their unique enjoyment of virtual and physical attributes, where when tightly coupled the NFT representing the physical asset cannot be transferred without the physical asset in question also being transferred. Looser couplings are also possible, such as Plastiks' endangered wildlife NFTs, which enter the charitable donor into a lottery for an autographed FC Barcelona T-shirt—an *opportunity to redeem* the NFT against the good in question (but not the good itself) (Plastiks 2025). Other loose couplings include *burn-and-redeem*, *redeem-and-replace*, or *access* functionalities, where an NFT is destroyed, exchanged, or presented in return for a physical good (1kx 2023b).

Digiphysicalism can improve the environmental quality of goods and services. In the case of goods, the field of green logistics is of particular interest. Green logistics refers to an approach to logistics and supply-chain management that systematically evaluates and seeks to reduce the sustainability footprint associated with transportation, warehousing, and distribution activities. Digiphysicals can help standardize the measurement of negative supply chain externalities, such as energy costs. Web3's true innovation is the global liquidity environment every blockchain "smart object" can participate in as its own market agent.

Recall from the digital collectibles section prior that blockchain-based smart objects can manage their own funds as autonomous agents using AI. Knowing this, it's possible to imagine public blockchain supply chains full of autonomous agents-as-objects that are capable of neutralizing the environmental impact of their production, travel, and consumption. The automatization of supply chain process management by smart objects has been posited—typically under the "Industry 4.0," "Logistic 4.0," or "Cyber Physical Systems" banners (Witthaut et al. 2017)—since 2011 (Xu et al. 2021). Witthaut et al. (2017) illustrate the unique functionalities these agents can perform through a standard shipping container:

> The container 'itself' detects that it will not reach the port on time, it 'picks' a suitable transportation alternative and 'chooses' a local carrier from a marketplace to conduct the transport. The container *'pays upon collection'* [emph] and reaches the destination punctually, while the financial transaction is being completed at the same time.
>
> **Witthaut et al. (2017)**

Extending this functionality to green logistics invites speculation on the creation of unique, environmentally friendly processes that *can only exist* on public blockchains. For example: a cryptonative digiphysical good internationally shipped can self-offset its carbon cost of transport between its point of origin and point of sale, so long as it can reference its transport distance and mode(s) of transport (as, for example, provided by an oracle). To do so, it would calculate its cost of carbon of transport at point of sale, then utilize a public decentralized exchange such as Uniswap to purchase and retire an equivalent amount of tokenized carbon assets. The cost itself could be borne by either the producer, consumer, or the smart object itself (if it has funds) in order for the sale to be processed. Figure 6.2 visualizes this self-offsetization process.

Beyond retirement, blockchain-native supply networks could also be subject to institutional economic interventions by higher-level governance bodies. Imagine a

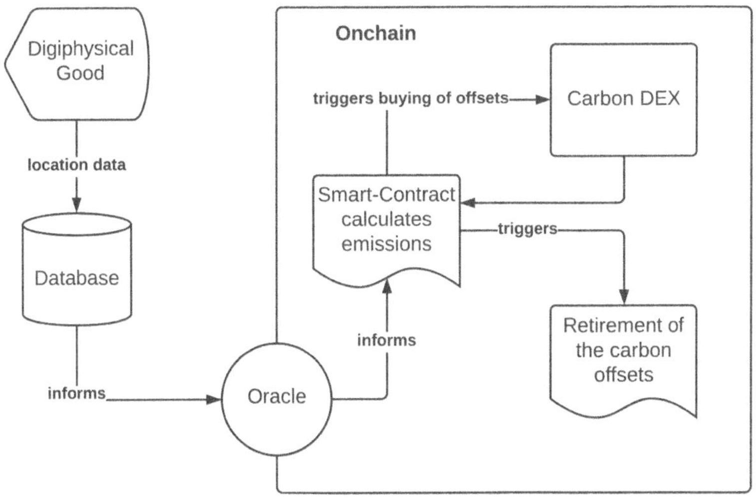

FIGURE 6.2 Visualization of the self-offsetization of carbon produced by transport of digiphysical goods.

***Source*: Diagram by the authors.**

DAO-token issuance policy where consumers mint tokens from purchasing locally produced goods. This is simply impossible today, as these automations are constrained by fragmented market liquidity and lack of technical interoperability. To summarize: entirely new green crypto-assets, subject to new forms of institutional climate-friendly interventions, are possible once cryptonative digiphysicals become the default means for addressing and managing smart objects in supply chains.

In conjunction with the prospective internalization of environmental costs at the nexus of supply networks, the capacity for commodities to manifest their own environmental interactions and histories introduces a novel dimension to their potential impact. Digiphysical entities can embody functionalities reminiscent of a "festival wristband" employed by attendees to facilitate entry, execute transactions with vendors, and redeem rewards (1kx 2023b). Extrapolating this to an environmental context, one might envision "wristbands" designed to regulate access and facilitate ecosystem services within conservation territories, accruing reward tokens in recognition of participation and verifiable, impactful activities. At its most extreme, we can imagine mechanisms for donation or trade with encountered species utilizing their own "interspecies" currencies (Ledgard 2022). Such a wristband, steered by the monetary policy of a territorially governing socioecological institution, emerges as a potent ecocybernetic instrument to incentivize and steer both human and nonhuman entities toward the co-construction of regenerative communities, characterized by impactful collaboration and trade.

Ecological Data Rights and intellectual property (IP)

Data tokenization is the process of converting data or intellectual property (IP) of any sort into tokens that can be securely transferred without revealing the original content. This process enhances "data security, privacy, and compliance while preventing unauthorized access and misuse" (Binance Academy 2023). Datatokens are a new Web3-native asset class, finding no equivalent in the traditional world where the technical access conditions of IP are embedded into its asset form. All forms of IP, from "patents, datasets, or contractual agreements" are being wrapped inside tokens like IP-NFTS, "enabling easy transfer and collective ownership over such assets" (Ortlepp 2022). IP-NFTs are an increasingly popular token model implemented in the decentralized science community (Nature Biotechnology 2023), having already proven their usefulness as investment instruments in the biotechnology and longevity sectors (Molecule Protocol 2025; VitaDAO 2025).

Data tokenization emerges as a potential data availability solution to the serious challenges faced by AI developers, particularly for small- and medium-sized enterprises (SMEs) and regions like the EU that are (as of late 2025) at a comparative data disadvantage (Verbeek and Lundqvist 2021). Growing the stock and quality of global environmental data is imperative when recognizing its indispensable role in refining and training AI, which is rapidly evolving from mere pattern recognition to advanced environmental forecasting and autonomous action.

In environmental decentralized science, interest is growing around use cases covering biodiversity DNA sequencing data. Projects such as the Earth Bank of Code propose IP tokens to access sequencing DNA data (Schiller 2018). SimplexDNA is developing the Franklin token as a "digital eDNA token" (SimplexDNA 2023) and the New Atlantis DAO aims to create an "open marine metagenomics biodiversity analytics platform" (Gould 2022). Space Time Labs, an environmental science and technology venture studio, purports that genetic sequencing data of the natural world holds "the potential for economic gain… [answering] the age-old question for the biodiversity community of how do we make sure a sustaining natural habitat is worth more than cutting it down" (Schiller 2018)?

Ecological datatokens can be considered "green" in the sense that their possession, staking, or exchange on markets generates financial flows that incentivize a growing observational awareness and understanding of complex ecosystems. They prime institutions for effective material interventions. As mentioned in previous chapters, the observation of the biosphere and its constituent ecosystems is the first critical step towards effective intervention. Ecological data informing an ecosystem's state is important for ongoing management of the environment, used in ecological simulations and model development, climate models, verification of research results, meta-analysis, natural resource management, and education (among other use cases).

The market for ecological state data has grown significantly over the years, and many applications requiring high-quality ecological data are being developed. New financial branches such as Spatial Finance that integrate geospatial data with financial analysis and decision-making and innovative AI algorithms/applications which have the direct aim of conserving or regenerating natural ecosystems are emerging. Example Web3 projects gathering environmental data include dClimate (2025) and the Open Climate database from Open Earth (Open Earth Foundation 2025). The global environmental monitoring data sector reached several billion USD in 2020, and is expected to double by 2030.

Despite the overall appetite for ecological state data of various types (agricultural, environmental monitoring, weather, and climate) available datasets remain limited and siloed across actors, territories, and industries. Web3 offers the possibility to collectivize large data sets to form so-called "data trust DAO[s]," strengthening the control and market power that data producers have. With this in mind, DAOs hold the potential to democratize the vast wealth afforded by biodiversity and other environmental scientific IP, further incentivizing adequate data collection. Other projects, such as Ambios Network—a decentralized environmental monitoring infrastructure on Solana, operating over 8,000 sensors across 20 countries to provide environmental data—propose rewards-based participation models to align incentives for large-scale ecological data production (Ambios Network 2025).

NONPOSSESSORY RIGHTS

Nonpossessory rights cover green crypto-assets that give access to certain features, data, or use related to natural assets, yet exclude direct ownership of the asset in question. Table 6.3 outlines the nonpossessory rights subtypes.

Natural Asset Company (NAC) and Stewardship Rights

Natural Asset Company (NAC) and stewardship rights refer to governance and control claims over natural capital that explicitly excludes the right to privatize or liquidate it. Instead of extractive ownership, these rights are configured to protect,

TABLE 6.3
Nonpossessory Rights Type

Subtype	NAC and Stewardship Rights	Output Rights	Memberships and Use Rights	Governance Tokens
Definition	Tokenized share in entity managing natural capital; no liquidation rights	Access to material/ financial outputs or revenues from natural assets	Non-equity access rights	Influence DAO decision-making without ownership
Examples	Nature's Vault Natures Gold Token, INHABIT	Coorest NFTrees, Glow Production Credits	Tekkon Manhole tokens, Traditional Dream Factory	Kokonut DAO
Legal Dependency	Generally yes	Generally yes	Use-case dependent	Use-case dependent
Materiality	Weak	Strong for commodities; app-dependent for financial outputs	Implementation-dependent	Implementation-dependent
Novelty	Rebirth	Rebirth (commodities)/Birth (staking/novel)	Birth/Rebirth	Birth

Source: Table by the authors.

restore, and steward ecological assets in perpetuity. NACs are specially chartered legal entities whose purpose is to manage and regenerate natural capital while legally excluding activities that would degrade or exploit the asset (Holland & Knight 2021). In the Web3 context, NACs would be tethered to decentralized autonomous organizations (DAOs) through hybrid legal wrappers. These arrangements enable DAOs to delegate authority to fiduciary boards bound by community-aligned mandates—an essential legal workaround, as DAOs themselves cannot directly own land or ecological assets in most jurisdictions (Paradigm 2025).

Tokenized shares in NACs, or other similar governance instruments, represent fractionalized stewardship over a commons—akin to equity but with non-extractive aims (Busch and Ferretti-Gallon 2017). These tokens function as control-bearing rights tied to ecologically mandated enterprises, granting holders decision-making influence over governance without enabling dispossession or commodification of the underlying natural asset. The Nepalese forest management reform of 1993, which authorized community forest groups to co-manage national forests, is a real-world analog to this logic. It successfully doubled forest cover under such a collective governance scheme (Cassidy n.d.).

Alternative models to NACs include institutional forms such as Benefit Corporations and steward-ownership, where profit is subordinate to mission and enterprise ethics. For example, Patagonia's legal structure ensures perpetual mission alignment over shareholder primacy (Purpose 2022). Tokens modeled on these principles—such as the Nature's Vault Gold Token, which governs gold that will never be mined—extend fiduciary logic to digital commons by granting holders influence over decisions like conservation project funding and mine acquisitions, without granting mineral extraction rights (Natures Vault 2025). Similarly, INHABIT's Stewardship NFTs represent plots of land within biodiversity hubs, granting lifelong stewardship rights linked to active participation in conservation, funding restoration efforts (Inhabit 2025). The innovation lies in embedding ecological responsibility directly into access and use rights—forming a new model of digitally mediated land tenure that incentivizes care and regeneration over extraction.

Looking forward, some stewardship frameworks envision AI-augmented governance structures in which generative agents help coordinate ecological management. Early experiments in resource distribution by generative agents, such as Google's "Democratic AI," suggest such systems can reflect and optimize human preferences around fairness and sustainability (Rose 2022). In this speculative frontier, stewardship rights could extend to nonhuman agents acting in service of planetary health.

Output Rights

In exchange for engaging in staking activities or retaining possession of a token, the user is endowed with the privilege to access various types of commodities, such as material yields (e.g., coffee), financial products (e.g., carbon credits), or royalties (financial revenues) derived from the outputs of a designated natural asset (e.g., a property). This concept diverges fundamentally from traditional notions of ownership, as it exclusively pertains to the entitlement to access and benefit of its *outputs*. Figure 6.3 highlights the diversity and modularity of output rights.

These types of leases are not alien to the world of traditional finance; *profit-à-prendre* contracts enable a person to take part of the soil or produce of land that someone else owns, as in the mining of minerals. However, with Web3, one deals with innovative crypto-asset utilities, such as staking to earn output rights—a concept with no traditional financial equivalent. Notably, the character of output rights assets assumes a *green* character when the source of the outputs in question stem from regenerative natural resources. For example, holders of Coorest's fruit-bearing NFTrees (NB: project defunct) used to receive a revenue share from sale of the fruits of "roughly 12 USDC per year," yet did not own the fruit, the land, or the trees themselves (Coorest 2025).

A compelling example of output rights is to be found within the Glow Protocol, a solar energy decentralized physical infrastructure network (DePIN), with the introduction of Glow Production Credits (Glow 2023). While Glow's carbon credits were originally sold in a Dutch auction format, an update proposed in early 2025 rendered them non-transferable. With this update, the only way to obtain Glow carbon credits is through ownership of *Production Credits*, a new type of perpetual forward-looking asset that assigns the right to direct the allocation of

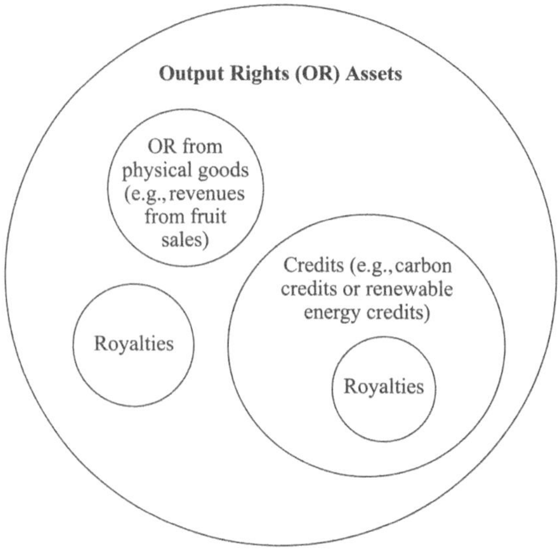

FIGURE 6.3 Graphic highlighting the diversity and modularity of output rights. Output rights assets may signify rights to commodity outputs (e.g., fruit), commodity output royalties (e.g., revenues from the sale of fruit), financial outputs (e.g., carbon credits produced through a certain methodology for some territory) or financial output royalties (e.g., revenues from the sale of carbon credits produced through a certain methodology for some territory).

***Source*: Diagram by the authors.**

GLW token emissions toward specific solar production zones. Unlike traditional carbon credits, whose one-time purchase retroactively finances a past emissions reduction, Production Credits perpetually finance carbon avoidance through their rights to claim carbon additionality. By holding and delegating Production Credits to a solar farm, users, called emissaries, decide where Glow's token rewards go, ensuring that funding supports the most effective projects, as these users, in principle, want to make the largest emission avoidance claims (Borreani and Rawson 2025). These Production Credits embody output rights by granting holders the privilege to direct and benefit from the carbon avoidance outputs of specific solar farms without owning the underlying solar farms.

Memberships and Use Rights

Membership and use rights are non-equity claims that grant privileged access to ecological services, land-based infrastructures, or data-producing platforms without conferring asset ownership. These tokens embody a logic of participation and utility rather than control or capital gain. They often resemble dynamic access passes, entitling holders to engage with green infrastructure or receive benefits tied to the performance of ecologically motivated DAOs. We offer three examples to highlight the diversity of this subtype:

- Located in Portugal, the Traditional Dream Factory (TDF) combines reforestation, agroecology, and Web3 tools through a legal structure in which the land is held by OASA, a form of Land Trust (Traditional Dream Factory 2025). Members hold tokens that enable use of TDF's facilities, glamping accommodations, food forests, biochar production sites, while obligating them to care for the land. This model establishes a hybrid form of usufructuary governance, where rights are granted not in ownership but in reciprocity. The collaboration between $EARTH and TDF expands the model by allowing $EARTH token holders to access TDF's regenerative infrastructure, as $EARTH is a reserve-backed currency (see below Currency section) backed by a portion of $TDF tokens. This demonstrates how tokenized use rights can support and extend the utilities of another currency, thereby broadening access to use rights across multiple user communities.
- The Japanese NGO Whole Earth Foundation launched a pilot for "manhole tokens," where in exchange for submitting a photo of a designated manhole, players of their crowdsourced data collection game received a token to cash out on Line Pay (Steger 2023). The token worked to incentivize a certain level of urban ecological data collection—a citywide fetch quest. It was a success, enabling the documentation of 10,500 manholes in three days when tested in Shibuya. Completing the same task would have required city engineers several years. This urban state monitoring is useful to municipal authorities, as a growing cohort of climate-change aware lawmakers aim to improve the territorial-level resilience of urban zones and their surroundings (Echave 2022). Monitoring helps them understand and respond to the infrastructural needs of their constituents, such as increased disaster readiness. Consequently, the manhole tokens prepared the city for inclement weather by lowering the possibility of "damaged manholes" at risk of backing up the water system (Steger 2023). Similar projects exist in the emerging DePIN sector, where network users are rewarded with tokens of various utilities for everything from environmental monitoring to weather station management (Nystrom 2023).
- Tokens could represent the right to utilize or govern certain green or clean infrastructure, such as electric vehicle fleets, without representing ownership in the underlying assets. It's not unusual for many services, as of late 2025, to sell access-based memberships, and following the example of electric fleet membership tokens, Uber has already experimented with membership subscription products. Translated to Web3, Uber memberships are dynamic NFTs that periodically transfer funds to a corporate entity and expire if no funds are available. This business model can be easily recreated with an environmental bias, and as of 2025, certain DePIN projects like DIMO are building this type of Web3 rideshare infrastructure (Polygon 2024).

Governance Tokens

Governance tokens represent a subtype that grants holders the ability to influence decision-making processes in DAOs without owning the underlying assets or holding a claim against a DAO's treasury. These tokens empower users to propose and vote on initiatives, directing the allocation of resources toward projects that align with a DAO's mission. The utility of governance tokens is typically modular, combined with other subtypes to create a more robust asset.

Governance tokens in green crypto take on an environmental dimension when their mandate prioritizes improving material reality through sustainable practices. A prime example is the Kokonut Network, a DAO operating on Gnosis Chain, where Kokonut DAO Voting tokens (vKKN) enable holders to govern a coconut-based agroforestry project in the Dominican Republic (Kokonut Network 2025). Each token, backed 1:1 by a real coconut plant, allows members to vote on proposals that fund regenerative farming, optimize production cycles, and replace aging plants to ensure long-term carbon sequestration and ecological benefits. By directing stablecoin tributes to enhance coconut yields and transparency via blockchain, vKKNs exemplify "green" governance tokens providing influence over sustainable outputs without owning them (Kokonut Network 2025).

ENVIRONMENTAL PROCESS TOKENS

Environmental process tokens are the green crypto-asset *par excellence*—flag-bearing assets that aim to represent proof of a specific environmental process, such as carbon sequestration or biodiversity. To ensure fair representation of these environmental processes, their production is institutionally constrained by methodologies defining Monitoring, Reporting, and Verification (MRV) standards (Curve Labs and Kolektivo 2023). As a rule of thumb, the stricter the methodology, the fairer its representation of the underlying material reality (see Chapter 2). Traditionally, centralized registries have developed, certified, and governed these methodologies through institutions, whose issued assets are exchanged on voluntary or regulated compliance markets. Table 6.4 categorizes environmental process token types.

For the past few years, environmental process assets have been tokenized due to the value-added benefits of improved market access, transparency, provenance, automation of payments, and streamlined integration with emerging digital MRV technologies (Sahay, Hughes, and Henretig 2022). Environmental process tokens generally fall into two separate categories: (1) bridged to the blockchain from the traditional world, or (2) natively issued as onchain assets—meaning that the asset was issued directly onto a blockchain as a token, rather than a prior centralized database controlled by a traditional institutional actor such as Verra. As of 2024, examples of natively-issued Web3 assets include Open Forest Protocol (2025), Nat5 (Nat5 2025), International Carbon Registry (2025), Inuk (2025), and Regen Network (Regen Registry 2025)—either using open-source standards such as the UN's CDM methodologies (Clean Development Mechanism 2025) or their own custom methodologies (Open Forest Protocol 2024a; Regen Market 2025). Generally, carbon

TABLE 6.4
Environmental Process Token Type

Subtype	Carbon Removal Credits	Carbon Avoidance Credits	Carbon Issuances	Ecotokens	Renewable Energy Certificates	Impact-to-Earn
Definition	Tokens representing actual GHG removal	Tokens for avoided GHG emissions	Tradable instrument representing emission ceiling	Units of environmental action: biodiversity, plastic removal, water purification	Certify 1 MWh electricity from renewable sources	Tokens rewarding validated green tasks
Examples	Regen Network GHG & Co-Benefits v1.0	Moss Amazon NFT	Maseer Finance $CANA	Open Earth Marine Ecosystem Credits, ERA Keystone Species, Rebalance Earth Nature Credits	Energy Web Origin, Arkreen AREC	VeBetterDAO
Legal Dependency	No	No	Yes	No	No	No
Materiality	Method-dependent	Method-dependent	Method-dependent	Method-dependent	Strong	Method-dependent
Novelty	Rebirth	Rebirth	Rebirth	Birth/Rebirth	Rebirth	Birth

Source: Table by the authors.

credit tokenization follows one of several models: bridging existing registry credits onchain, natively issuing credits through onchain registries, or creating derivative tokens from pooled credits (Khodai 2022).

Environmental process tokens began to be tokenized in 2020 (PRNewswire 2020) and their number grew steadily. As of August 2023, over 20m carbon credits have been tokenized through the Toucan Protocol, a notable voluntary carbon credit tokenizer (Toucan Protocol n.d.). Institutional infrastructure for tokenization keeps improving, and Web3 companies such as Thallo have built two-way bridges in collaboration with other registries to move assets bidirectionally between traditional closed markets and Web3's open market infrastructure (Thallo 2025). Some projects such as BetaCarbon are tokenizing carbon credits produced by state entities and not just the private sector—in this case, Australian Carbon Credit Units, issued by Australia's Clean Energy Regulator (BetaCarbon 2025).

As highlighted by an article published by Toucan Protocol, there are significant advantages for natively issuing carbon (and by extension, all environmental process assets) as tokens (Khodai 2022). Those advantages range from increased efficiency through disintermediation, better liquidity, more accurate price discovery, and mitigation of double-counting. Beyond general Voluntary Carbon Market (VCM) improvements, tokenization also constitutes new functionalities for native Web3 applications inconceivable prior, such as automated royalties for project developers, where a portion of the asset's profit is directly transferred to the project developer each time that the asset is traded (Khodai 2022). Similarly, protocols like token demurrage can automate the retirement of tokenized assets relying on outdated methodologies (Marcus.limo 2023).

Carbon Removal Credits

Carbon removal credits (sometimes known as "negative carbon credits") refer to tradable representations of CO_2 that have been removed from the Earth's atmosphere over a long or permanent timeframe. According to one analysis, these credits will likely represent 35% of carbon credits by 2030 (Porsborg-Smith et al. 2023). Methods to remove carbon are generally classified as either nature-based, such as tree planting, or technology-based, such as Carbon Capture & Storage or Direct Air Capture. A full overview of the technologies used to sequester carbon and their materiality is available via multiple academic and scientific reviews and is not the subject of this book (Kazemifar 2022). To see an example of crypto-native carbon removal credit, see the ReverdeC credits issued by Open Forest Protocol (2024b).

As compared to carbon issuances (see Carbon Issuance section below) that are typically exchanged via a state-regulated cap-and-trade system, carbon credits (removal or avoidance) tend to be traded via the VCM. The size of this market is somewhere between US$1-2b, but is growing fast and projected to surpass $500b by 2050 according to Bloomberg (BloombergNEF 2022). Demand factors for carbon credits include reaching national emission targets, compliance with carbon tax obligations (e.g., for countries such as South Africa or Singapore), or adoption of global market-based mechanisms such as the Carbon Offsetting and Reduction Scheme for International Aviation (CORSIA) (Curmi et al. 2023).

According to the World Bank, as of 2024, global carbon pricing instruments are expanding slowly, with 75 instruments in place and growing uptake in middle-income countries like Brazil, India, and Türkiye. Although carbon pricing revenues surpassed $10b in 2023 and new policy designs are emerging, coverage remains limited—only about 24% of global emissions are priced. Of note is that while "prices [have] declined across most project categories," it did not for carbon removal projects, signaling a heightened buyer interest in this category (World Bank Group 2024).

Carbon Avoidance Credits

Carbon avoidance credits (sometimes known as "counterfactual credits") refer to avoided CO_2 emissions, that is, CO_2 which would have been released in the Earth's atmosphere without the existence of the project financed by the asset. According to an analysis by the Boston Consulting Group avoidance credits currently represent about 80% of carbon credit supply (Porsborg-Smith et al. 2023).

Oxford University employs an even finer categorization, distinguishing between two primary carbon credit categories: avoided emissions or emission reduction without carbon storage, which encompasses activities such as renewable energy projects, clean cookstoves, and methane abatement, as well as avoided emissions or emission reductions accompanied by short-lived and long-lived carbon storage (Curmi et al. 2023). The temporality of counterfactual credits is important, as longer storage periods are generally recognized to be of higher quality.

Carbon Issuances

A carbon issuance as used in this book is a transferable financial instrument typically certified by state authorities to represent a right to emit carbon in a limited market in which exists an emissions ceiling, commonly referred to as emission trading schemes (ETS) or cap-and-trade systems. ETS carbon issuances represent "the right" to emit CO_2, and have value due to the supply-side scarcity of their issuance and demand-side requirements set by a state regulating authority. Like the VCM, ETS' encounter issues with over-crediting, unclear life-cycle of issued credits and double-spending due to the lack of transparency and inter-regional communications.

These systems exemplify the enforcement of artificial scarcity to yield positive externalities. They transform non-rivalrous, non-excludable goods into rivalrous, excludable ones, thereby increasing asset value and adhering to strong market design principles. Due to this, issuance prices may be as much as 300 times higher than voluntary credits. Markets like the EU Emissions Trading Scheme set limits on emissions and allow trading rights under the cap, advancing and incentivizing decarbonization by reducing total emissions (the cap) annually. Market pricing within these systems reflects the nature of scarcity and the specific environmental goals institutions aim to achieve. A 2019 analysis by Semarnat and GIZ outlined the case for onchain carbon issuance systems, highlighting potential benefits including enhanced transparency, reduced transaction costs, and improved market access for smaller participants.

The first global state managed carbon system, the Clean Development Mechanism, was created 30 years ago under the Kyoto Protocol (UNFCCC 2025). As of 2025, many fragmented markets exist, such as the European Emission Trading Scheme (EU ETS), New Zealand Emissions Trading Scheme (NZ ETS), the Midwestern Greenhouse Gas Accord (MGA), as well as California's cap-and-trade program. Given state-imposed market fragmentation, ETS tend to produce illiquid carbon assets with high market transaction costs. Helping mitigate these issues, some ETS legally permit the use of voluntary market carbon credits for entities to meet their compliance obligations. Nevertheless, compliance markets often command higher prices than voluntary markets due to the enforced scarcity and regulatory requirements they impose (CarbonCredits.com 2025).

In 2025, Maseer Finance was one of the first functional implementations of tokenized carbon issuances: their token $CANA provides DeFi users with exposure to California carbon issuances (Maseer Finance 2025). Of note is that $CANA is used as collateral to back the green stablecoin proposed by Azos (see Currency section). It remains uncertain whether ETS-style markets will fully transition onchain, as many state authorities are likely hesitant to adopt public blockchain infrastructures despite their transparency and efficiency benefits. Nevertheless, recent hybrid approaches are also emerging: carbon arbitrage models allow institutions to purchase carbon credits from cap-and-trade compliance markets and convert them into tokenized credits, as exemplified by projects like Climate Vault (2025).

Ecotokens

Ecotokens in this book refer to a catch-all subtype that consists of other environmental process assets that are not carbon-related. The most prominent of ecotokens are *biodiversity credits*, representing biodiversity units protected or restored (Waterford, FitzSimons, and Back 2023). Biodiversity credits are championed as a financial mechanism to integrate nature into economic systems, potentially enabling systemic monetization of conservation outcomes, improving impact integrity, and attracting private finance through standardized, scientifically grounded, performance-based tools. They aim to accelerate conservation funding by offering faster, more predictable, and innovative financial models. Yet, critics question their efficacy and realism, warning of risks such as greenwashing, speculation, and oversimplified ecosystem valuations. Measuring biodiversity units is extremely complex, as understanding and classifying indicators, metrics, and biodiversity "units" is challenging. It is commonly argued that without strong public governance, regulation, and fiscal measures, biodiversity credits risk delaying or displacing necessary structural reforms to halt biodiversity loss (Gradeckas 2024).

Despite those critics, evidence exists that biodiversity assets are gaining institutional legitimacy. In 2023, one Swedish bank purchased a batch of biodiversity credits from the Orsa Besparingsskog forest (Reklev 2023b). Recently, Verra opened the SD VISta Nature Framework for public consultation, which "outlines how projects can generate Nature Credits, which represent one quality hectare equivalent of biodiversity uplift from a baseline as a result of the project intervention" (Verra 2023). CarbonPulse, a climate news platform, forecasts the biodiversity credit market to be worth $18–43b by mid-century (Reklev 2023a).

Beyond biodiversity, other ecotokens include plastic removal, water purification, and sustainable development credits. Registries like Verra have methodologies which aim to produce "enhanced carbon credits" that gain in value through additional certifications—e.g., the Climate, Community, and Biodiversity Standard applied to Verra Verified Carbon Standard (Verra 2017). This is also the case on the Regen Marketplace (a marketplace for environmental process tokens), where ecocredits are designated with their "co-benefits" in addition to carbon sequestration (Regen Market 2025). Initially absent from Regen's early documentation, "ecocredit" is a term that gained prominence in 2020 as the network transitioned to a credit-based model. The concept now anchors a flexible and modular framework for ecological contracting, extending well beyond conventional offsetting to include asset- and value-based ecological accounting, performance-based payments, and ecosystem service provisioning. "Ecocredits" are thus positioned not only as units of ecological improvement but also as governance instruments within a commons-oriented

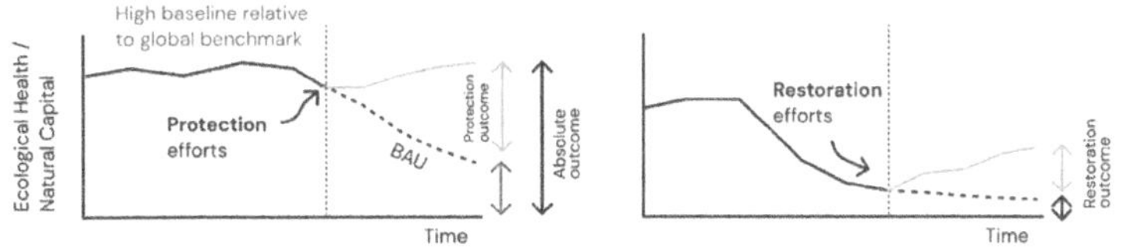

		Protection	Restoration
Payment Scheme	Effort-based Scheme	Rewards conservation efforts and costs involved, e.g., payments to surveil and enforce a marine protected area	Rewards the direct restoration efforts and interventions, e.g., payments per unit or area of kelp re-planted
	Outcome-based Scheme	Rewards the maintenance of ecological health and biodiversity compared to global indices, e.g., credits to a marine park for avoiding degradation from imminent illegal fishing threat and maintaining endemism	Rewards incremental outcomes from restoration efforts, e.g., 10% increase in biodiversity and water quality after kelp reforestation
Credit Type Examples	Biodiversity Credit	Protection of habitats with high biodiversity indices and endemism, e.g., Cocos Island Marine National Park	Re-insertion of species (e.g., coral or kelp) that help increase habitat biodiversity, e.g., Bull kelp reforestation in Puget Sound, USA
	Eutrophication Credit	Programs that pass and enforce regional or multilateral laws and agreements around nutrient runoff	Bivalve aquaculture projects that reduce nutrient and improves water health
	Plastics Credit	Not applicable	Project that remove Tons of plastics from marine circulation
	Carbon Credit	Projects that protect areas with high and healthy levels of primary productivity with effective sinks, and are faced with imminent threats	Projects that prove a sustainable increase in CO2 uptake by marine ecosystems through direct interventions, e.g., through seaweed

FIGURE 6.4 A handful of non-carbon credit types as identified by the Open Earth Foundation. These credits may be awarded for services rendered, as in effort-based schemes, or outcomes achieved.

***Source*: Open Earth Foundation (2022). Licensed under Creative Commons. https://uploads-ssl.webflow.com/62192ceb9199b3dd08431a6b/6371df5b39109b348b188447_whitepaper.pdf**

infrastructure co-developed by scientists, land stewards, and local communities (Landua 2024). Figure 6.4 shows a selection of non-carbon credit types.

The emerging ecotoken market requires non-carbon data. As posited by Ford et al. (2024), this data needs to meet so-called "SAGED" criteria: Scalable, Accessible, Granular, Evidenceable, and Directly measured. Traditional biodiversity monitoring is costly and expert-dependent, limiting scalability. This is where new technologies such as environmental DNA metabarcoding, passive acoustic monitoring, and remote sensing (as described in Chapter 2) play a significant role. Although these methods face challenges in resolution and standardization, combining them with ground validation and leveraging advances in automation and machine learning is critical for building credible and scalable credit systems beyond carbon (Ford et al. 2024). One key benefit from bringing these new types of assets onchain is the improved integration with MRV technologies situated in the Underlying Material Reality layer (see Chapter 2). As stated prior, Web3 technologies can help efficiently structure data from different sources, and pass data between different models, formats and technologies.

In addition, asset programmability affords the design of new types of modular stackable credits, such as the Marine Biodiversity Credits (MBCs) proposed by the

Open Earth Foundation (Open Earth Foundation 2022), which seeks to monetize marine ecological value using a standardized and transparent methodology grounded in natural capital accounting. Built around *Biodiversity Units*—defined spatial-temporal ecological reference areas—MBCs use a system of *Modulating Factors* to assess each unit's ecological and social value, resulting in a Marine Biodiversity Unit score. Unlike traditional crediting systems that rely on speculative counterfactuals, the MBC methodology rewards areas with high baseline biodiversity, thereby aligning incentives with conservation rather than degradation. This framework is adaptable to policy and financial applications alike, ranging from conservation guarantees and biodiversity-backed securities to nature-debt swaps (Ando et al. 2023).

Renewable Energy Certificates

Renewable Energy Certificates (RECs) authenticate the production of one megawatt-hour (MWh) of electricity via renewable energy sources for a given year. They are a type of Energy Attribute Certificate (EAC), functioning as a transferable record that documents or guarantees the quantity of energy or material resources used by an energy conversion device, typically in an industrial production context. RECs seek to decarbonize electricity consumption by verifying renewable electricity origin, e.g., wind, hydropower, solar, geothermal, or repurposed waste material.

Blockchain streamlines REC management, trading, and compliance processes, reducing administrative overhead and fortifying REC market integrity. REC tokenization enables each certificate to be uniquely identified, traded, and tracked throughout its lifecycle—critical for a growing market whose participants include many distributed small-scale producers, consumers, and prosumers. According to the EU Blockchain Observatory and Forum, blockchain enhances EAC markets by precisely and reliably tracking each unit of energy throughout its entire life cycle, as well as the issuance and transfer of EACs in real-time as electricity is generated—a leap in efficiency from prevailing monthly issuance practices (European Union Blockchain Observatory and Forum 2022).

Onchain REC projects are plentiful, and include Arkreen Network and Reneum. The former developed the AREC Bridge Protocol, which converts conventional RECs into tokenized assets on Celo (Garba and Lu 2023), while Reneum developed a marketplace selling RECs from ten existing renewable energy projects (Reneum 2025). The Energy Web Foundation is a non-profit entity who has developed the open-source Energy Web Origin (EW Origin) toolset, which intends to streamline and enhance renewable energy procurement in adherence to current standards and regulatory frameworks (Energy Web Foundation 2025). EW Origin has been used by various stakeholders within the energy sector to create decentralized exchanges for green EACs (Social Alpha Foundation 2021).

Impact-to-Earn

Impact-to-Earn (I2E) systems are blockchain-based incentive protocols that issue tokens to individuals or groups upon completion and validation of a predefined task. These tasks can range from species monitoring, invasive species removal, plastic collection, tree planting, and biodiversity data collection, among others. Central to this model is the bounty mechanism: a predefined token reward is placed in escrow and is only released upon successful verification of the task outcome. This framework relies on three core roles:

1. **Bounty Creators:** Typically DAOs, NGOs, institutions, or protocols that define the task, set parameters, and provide funding.
2. **Bounty Hunters:** Individuals or groups who execute the task, often using fieldwork, sensor technology, or digital labor.
3. **Verifiers:** entities or algorithms responsible for validating whether the task has been completed to the required standard—this can involve satellite imagery, environmental DNA (eDNA) data, AI-assisted verification, or committee-based human judgment. Smart contracts automate escrow management, disburse payments upon verification, and may include additional features such as tiered rewards for quality, penalties for fraud, or time-based bonuses to incentivize rapid completion.

VeBetterDAO is an Impact-to-Earn ecosystem targeting everyday sustainable behaviors. Users complete environmentally positive micro-actions, such as using public transportation, recycling, or buying certified eco-products, and are rewarded with tokenized incentives after verification. The protocol combines digital proof (e.g., mobile app data, QR codes) with verifier roles (sometimes community-based or institutionally governed) to validate impact (VeBetterDAO 2025). Users gain governance influence as well as B3TR tokens for participating. The initiative aims to gamify sustainability at scale, bridging consumer behavior with decentralized incentives.

DEBT

Stakeholders use *debt* to raise capital or generate investment income for environmental purposes (see Mac Naggar 2023). Debt, while ubiquitously recognized as a catalyst for attracting capital inflows, engenders a spectrum of tradeoffs. The leverage that debt introduces to institutional balance sheets amplifies fiscal vulnerability, particularly by magnifying exposure to interest rate volatilities and the imposition of stringent repayment schedules. While debt can accelerate critical investments in environmental initiatives, the obligatory nature of debt servicing can, paradoxically, divert financial resources away from other pressing socioecological imperatives, instigating a precarious balancing act between immediate obligations and long-term sustainability. Table 6.5 presents debt instrument types.

Green, Blue, Sustainability-Linked and Impact Bonds

Green, blue, sustainability-linked and impact bonds can be broadly understood as debt instruments that are earmarked to raise money for climate and environmental projects. These bonds are originated by both private and public institutions. "Blue" bonds are typically tied to marine environmental projects, and impact bonds to any

TABLE 6.5
Debt Type

Subtype	Green, Blue, Sustainability-Linked and Impact Bonds	Green Real-World Asset Debt Finance
Definition	Bonds financing sustainable investments; blue bonds for marine/ocean projects	Socioecological lending, collateralized or not
Examples	Frigg.eco tokenized green bonds, LandX perpetual agri-commodity bonds	Almavest Basket #7: Fintech & Carbon Reduction
Legal Dependency	Yes (state intervention if default)	Yes (state intervention if default)
Materiality	Weak	Weak
Novelty	Rebirth	Rebirth

Source: Table by the authors.

well-meaning cultural or environmental initiative with a positive social or ecological outcome. Traditionally, bonds are certified "green" by independent institutions such as the Climate Bonds Initiative, involving external verification and adherence to their Climate Bond Standard and Taxonomy (Climate Bonds Initiative 2021). Like carbon markets, these types of certifications are meant to legitimize issuer reputation and gain investor trust by demonstrating adherence to standards for transparent, ethical investment. In October 2023, EU legislators endorsed novel criteria for corporations engaged in the issuance of green bonds (Reuters 2023). This regulatory development aims to mitigate greenwashing and combat deceptive assertions of seemingly climate-friendly initiatives. Figure 6.5 displays global sustainable debt annual issuance trends.

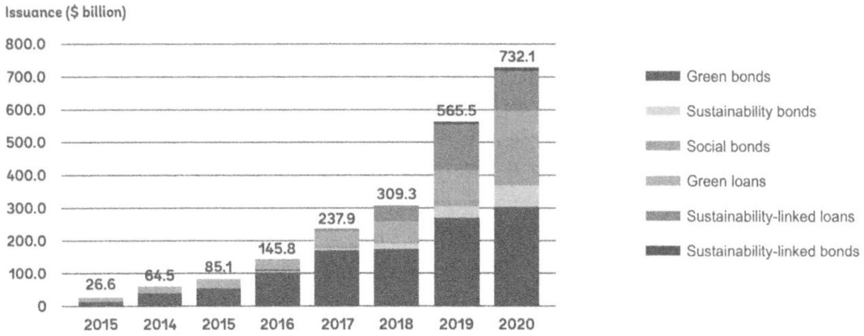

FIGURE 6.5 Global sustainable debt annual issuance, 2013–2020.

Source: **Dalhuijsen, Emma, Martijn Regelink, Rachel Mok, Fiona Stewart, and Henk Jan Reinders. "Toolkits for Policymakers to Green the Financial System." World Bank, 2021. https://documents1.worldbank.org/curated/en/374051622653965991/pdf/Toolkits-for-Policymakers-to-Green-the-Financial-System.pdf**

Blockchain offers the same general benefits to green bonds as it does other types of tokenized environmental assets, i.e., the improved validation, transparency, and auditability of data, scalability, open markets, and payout automation (Misra et al. 2023). The Hong Kong Monetary Authority tokenized its first green bond in early 2023, though failed to realize many of these benefits due to their use of a permissioned ledger system (Handagama 2023). Similarly, Crédit Agricole CIB and SEB are developing their own permissioned green bond networks (Crédit Agricole 2023).

While bonds are useful for centralized institutions to finance large infrastructure projects, it remains to be seen whether or not they can be meaningfully leveraged by more localized institutions. The bond market is heavily regulated by states, optimized to ensure repayment to investors (LCX Team 2023). As such, bonds are heavily reliant on state intervention for issuance and enforcement. Frigg, a green bond issuance and tokenization platform, developed a 15-point list of issuance requirements (Frigg.eco 2023), reaffirming that the fixed operations costs for issuing bonds are still high and unwieldy for small issuers.

While green bonds have an environmental outcome to determine payout, they may also be green in their denominated currency. Imagine: a clean infrastructure project issues tokenized bonds that are only repayable in green stablecoins (see below Currency section). These types of asset relationships may help reduce the negative externalities generated by the production of state money, whose debt markets are utilized to finance many environmentally harmful activities, such as the $1t in fossil fuel subsidies issued by states in 2022 (IEA 2023).

Green Real-World Asset Debt Finance

Outside bond markets, there exist various debt finance mechanisms that can be tokenized. In principle, any existing debt instrument can be tokenized, with the tokens representing a claim on the loan:

- **Collateralized lending** are asset-backed loans where the collateral is placed inside a vault or secured in a manner that can be claimed if the borrower defaults.
- **Tokenized invoice and supply chain financing** provides loans by tokenizing invoices or purchase orders. These tokenized receivables serve as the basis for short-term lending, helping to smooth cash flow for small projects, such as a clean energy developer.
- **Crowdlending** is a form of uncollateralized lending where lenders pool assets to issue the loan. ALMA, an investment management company focused on the sustainability sector, launched a $13m debt pool (a crowdlending mechanism) on Goldfinch, an institutional Web3-lending protocol. The pool uses debt to finance "carbon reduction project developers" in developing markets, and goes as far to claim that the pool itself is a "carbon neutral DeFi pool" (GoldFinch Finance 2025).

DERIVATIVES

Derivatives are financial instruments that derive their value from an underlying green crypto-asset, exhibiting value fluctuations in correspondence with it. Derivatives tend to be settled in the future, and serve various purposes from hedging risk to speculating on future prices. Green derivatives serve as financial instruments that directly tie to environmentally sustainable goals, facilitating investments and hedges in environmental markets through products such as futures, options, or swap contracts. For example, these instruments allow investors to bet on or hedge against the price of carbon emissions credits or contracts linked to the performance of renewable energy projects. Table 6.6 lists derivative types.

The European Capital Markets Institute (an independent think tank) believes that green derivatives have a key role to play in EU sustainable financing, arguing that they help channel capital towards green investments, hedge risk, improve market efficiency and price discovery, and contribute to long-termism (Lannoo and Thomadakis 2020). Despite these potentials, the authors advise skepticism towards green derivatives: given their intrinsic complexity and high level of financial abstraction, it remains to be seen if they have a high level of material impact.

TABLE 6.6
Derivative Type

Subtype	Environmental Process Derivatives	Commodity Derivatives	Power Purchasing Agreements	Green Liquidity Provider Tokens	Green Yield Tokens
Definition	Forwards, futures, options, swaps on eco-assets	Derivatives of tangible goods (agriculture, metals, energy)	Long-term electricity forward contracts	Share of DEX/AMM fees, akin to dynamic put options	Tokenized yield from green assets (debt, forwards, staked tokens)
Examples	Carbon Futures (GreenTrade), Carbon Forwards (SolidWorld), Tokenized biodiversity derivative	Tokenized coffee futures	WePower	KLIMA/MCO2 QuickSwap LP tokens	Yield-bearing green tokens
Legal Dependency	No	No	Yes	No	No
Materiality	Weak	Weak	Weak	Asset-dependent	Asset-dependent, likely weak
Novelty	Rebirth	Rebirth	Rebirth	Birth	Birth

Source: Table by the authors.

Decentralized derivatives have their own set of institutional challenges, such as regulatory compliance. Certain regulatory bodies like the Commodity Futures Trading Commission (CFTC) and the Securities and Exchange Commission (SEC) play central roles in governing US derivatives trading with the mission of safeguarding market integrity and protecting investors. Globally-spanning Web3 decentralized platforms exploring commodity derivatives (e.g., coffee futures) or other types, may need to diligently navigate a complex system of national regulatory frameworks to ensure compliance with existing laws and avoid punitive actions.

Environmental Process Derivatives

Many types of environmental process derivatives are being designed, such as biodiversity derivatives, which refer to the financialization of biodiversity metrics such as species conservation, ecosystem services, or biological resources. They are often formulated to fund biodiversity conservation projects, such as habitat formation or endangered species protection. Risks can emanate from failed conservation efforts, and these derivatives serve as a hedge against unfavorable outcomes, enabling investors and stakeholders to manage their financial exposure in biodiversity conservation projects. Thomas Hahn et al. (2015) explains that:

> The government might buy a ten-year biodiversity derivative for a species of concern wherein a predefined amount of funds would be released by the seller if a species' population falls below a threshold. Basically, the seller (issuer or writer of the derivative) is making the bet that the species population will not fall below the threshold, or that it can take measures to prevent such an occurrence whose costs are within the range wherein they can make a profit given their proceeds from issuing the derivative.
>
> **Hahn et al. (2015)**

As early as 2009, scholars have proposed "modified derivative contracts to sell species' extinction risk to market investors and stakeholders." As an example, Mandel, Donlan, and Armstrong (2009) proposed a biodiversity derivatives program using the endangered red-cockaded woodpecker in the US, proving that such a financial instrument "could proactively generate new funding, result in more cost-effective conservation, align stakeholders' interests, and create incentives for private conservation efforts" (Mandel, Donlan, and Armstrong 2009).

Some green environmental process derivatives have undergone varying degrees of implementation and experimentation in Web3:

- **Forwards** are agreements between two parties to deliver a specified asset quantity at a predetermined price in the future, such as a carbon or biodiversity forward. In climate finance, these contracts are typically over-the-counter (OTC), and are customized to suit the specific needs and requirements of both parties. Platforms like SolidWorld have previously attempted to tokenize carbon forwards, tied on a 1:1 basis with premium prepaid forward carbon credit (SolidWorld 2025). Certain risks pervade these derivatives, such as issuance-based risks where prefinanced assets may not materialize and market-based risks where the assets may not generate sufficient revenue to cover their prefinancing. Timing also poses a risk if the provision of assets or revenue collection fails to align with repayment schedules.

- **Futures**, unlike typically bespoke forwards, are standardized derivatives that also represent an agreement to buy or sell an underlying environmental process asset at a set price on a specific future date. They help mitigate counterparty risk and bring additional liquidity to the market. Carbon futures have long been used in traditional finance to speculate or hedge against the future prices of carbon allowances. For instance, a deal between Boston Consulting Group (BCG) and CarbonCapture procured 40,000 tons of atmospheric carbon dioxide removal services over five years (Boston Consulting Group 2023).
- **Perpetual futures contracts (perps)** are crypto-native derivatives distinguished by their absence of an expiry date, providing traders the convenience to hold positions indefinitely. This contrasts with traditional futures, which necessitate the settling of accounts at a pre-specified expiration date. Perps derive their value from an underlying cryptocurrency asset and have evolved into a predominant trading product in cryptocurrency markets, dating back to 2016 (Sergeenkov 2021). Perp mechanics involve an embedded funding rate mechanism that ensures that the contract price is tethered to the spot price of the underlying asset. Thus, traders pay or receive funding periodically, ensuring that perps remain closely pegged to the actual value of the underlying cryptocurrency. Perps open up opportunities for traders to capitalize on the price fluctuations of cryptocurrencies in a leveraged manner, often with the potential to take on positions that are many times a trader's collateral. A green perps contract would derive its value from an asset that is categorically green, e.g., carbon assets, RECs, or green bonds.
- **Options** grant the holder the right, but not the obligation, to buy (call option) or sell (put option) an underlying asset at a specified price before or at expiration, commonly used for hedging or speculation. Swaps are agreements between two parties to exchange cash flows or financial instruments over time, such as swapping fixed interest rate payments for floating ones, typically used to manage risks like interest rate or currency fluctuations. Neither options nor swaps have been experimented with in a green environmental process blockchain context.

Recent research argues that perpetual futures structurally disadvantage most traders due to funding-rate reflexivity and liquidation dynamics that systematically favor exchanges and liquidity providers. By contrast, options are said to align more closely with trader behavior by offering predefined risk, temporal flexibility, and exposure without forced liquidation, making them a structurally fairer leverage instrument. As cryptomarkets mature and move toward regulated, retail-facing environments, this literature suggests that options (rather than perps) are likely to become the dominant format, a trajectory that has direct implications for how green assets are productized onchain.

Commodity Derivatives

Commodity derivatives are derived from commodities, such as agricultural products (e.g., wheat, corn, soybeans), metals (e.g., gold, silver), and energy resources (e.g., crude oil). Their price dynamics are influenced by various factors, including industrial supply and demand, geopolitical events, investor speculation, and climatic conditions.

DeFi's market structure presents an opportunity to enhance inclusivity in the trading and management of tokenized commodity derivatives. With them, farmers could directly lock prices in advance without centralized intermediaries, mitigating information asymmetry while expanding market access. Alternatively, multiple prices could be established based off of new crypto futures products as determined by vintage certification, ensuring that farmers are rewarded with higher prices for producing high-quality commodities or managing their landholdings in sustainable ways.

Power Purchasing Agreements (PPAs)

Power Purchasing Agreements (PPAs) essentially act as long-term electricity forward contracts, helping hedge against the price volatility inherent to energy markets. The buyer, often an electricity supplier or a large-scale electricity consumer, agrees to purchase a specified amount of electricity at a predetermined price, effectively securing a stable and likely competitively priced energy supply. Such agreements enable consumers ranging from large-scale industries to smaller commercial businesses to procure electricity directly from the producer. This ensures energy security and price stability over the term of the contract, which usually ranges from 8 to 25 years.

Academic discourse surrounding PPAs often stresses their role in mitigating price volatility risk and making renewable energy projects viable by guaranteeing steady revenues. PPAs frequently correlate with renewable energy projects, which fosters symbiotic relationships between sustainable energy production and conscientious energy procurement.

Blockchain's foray into tokenized PPAs is still relatively young. PPA tokenization has been previously attempted by WePower (2018), which attempted to build a marketplace to buy, sell and trade long-term PPAs.

Green Liquidity Provider Tokens

In principle, any liquidity provider token (LP token) that contains at least one green crypto-asset is in part green. LP tokens are produced by adding liquidity to constant function market maker decentralized exchange protocols, such as Uniswap pools. LP tokens are similar to dynamically hedging options contracts (Bardoscia and Nodari 2023). Uniswap's algorithm effectively mimics the risk profile of holding short positions on the assets in its reserves by dynamically adjusting holdings and using market incentives to encourage external traders to rebalance reserves based on price differences with other exchanges. Alternatively, liquidity provider (LP) tokens can be interpreted as instruments that continuously expose holders to both upside and downside price movements, while generating an ongoing stream of income from trading fees. Holding LP tokens that market make green assets is therefore a green derivative unique to blockchain.

Green Yield Tokens

Yield refers to the return on an investment (rate payment), expressed as a percentage—i.e., the income generated from that investment over a specified period. Yields can take various forms, such as debt yield (income from lending) or staking yield (income from validating blocks or deposits). When packaged as a transferable unit, yields become assets. For example, yield derivatives, such as future yield contracts, are financial contracts whose value is derived from the expected future yield of an underlying asset or financial instrument. Another illustration are interest rate swaps (IRS): Instruments enabling the exchange of two yields (typically a fixed rate payment against a floating rate payment).

The difference between yield and output rights is subtle. Output rights relate to the rights on the product of an asset—e.g., rights on the revenues of fruits produced by the natural asset *tree*. Interest, on the contrary, is a utility of an asset. Put differently, yield is not what an asset produces, it is what an asset *earns*. For debt, yield is a payment for underwriting risk; for staking, yield is a payment for validating blocks.

In traditional finance, participants have used future yield contracts with a notional value exceeding $400 trillion as hedging mechanisms. Those financial instruments may bear a conditional green aspect. Crédit Agricole CIB introduced a green IRS in Asia-Pacific capital markets, where a "green feature" was introduced to "the hedge wherein the preferential fixed rate paid by the borrower was linked to the underlying facility's green classification… [which] steps up to non-preferential if the Green Condition fails" (Blanchard and Duval 2020).

Within the growing DeFi ecosystem, projects like Pendle Finance aim to integrate the yield derivatives market (Obasi 2023). Pendle Finance enables users to tokenize and trade future yields from diverse DeFi protocols. Pendle Finance's innovation centers on creating a market for standardized yield tokens divided into principal and yield components, facilitating their exchange on a dedicated automated market maker.

In this context, *green* yield tokens emerge as a novel innovation combining yield instruments with environmental sustainability. Green yield tokens provide an opportunity for portfolio diversification by batching assets with potentially different risk-return profiles. Concrete applications of green yield tokens may include the tokenization of interests earned from debt assets, other derivatives such as carbon forwards, or green crypto-assets with some sort of staking utility.

INSURANCE

Insurance is a mechanism to transfer or mitigate risk, traditionally by pooling resources to provide compensation when predefined adverse events occur. For natural and ecological assets, it enhances resilience to environmental shocks, incentivizes sustainable practices, and protects ecosystem services. As an asset, insurance represents a claim on future contingent value: holding an insurance contract or token gives its owner the right to a payout if specified conditions occur, making it a tradable, securitized form of risk coverage that can be integrated into broader portfolios of environmental and financial assets. Table 6.7 summarizes the insurance types.

TABLE 6.7
Insurance Type

Subtype	Parametric Insurance	Reinsurance	Crypto-staking Insurance
Definition	Underwrites natural asset condition based on event	Insurance for climate/ environmental insurers	Events underwritten by staked tokens; yield for staking
Examples	Shamba Network/DIVA/ FortuneConnect, Quintana Roo Reef	Arbol	EthicHub
Legal Dependency	No	No	No
Materiality	Trigger-dependent	Weak	Trigger-dependent
Novelty	Rebirth	Rebirth	Birth

Source: Table by the authors.

Parametric Insurance

Parametric insurance differs significantly from traditional insurance in its structure, pricing, and claims processes. Traditional models rely heavily on historical data and detailed underwriting to assess perceived risk and set premiums. In contrast, parametric systems use real-time and historical environmental data, often enhanced by climate models and machine learning, to generate predictive insights and define risk parameters in advance. When a loss occurs, the claims process under traditional insurance typically involves a lengthy series of evaluations, documentation requirements, and damage assessments by adjusters, which can result in delays and disputes. Parametric insurance streamlines this process: payouts are triggered automatically when predefined conditions (such as rainfall thresholds or wind speeds) are met. This removes the need for subjective claims assessments and minimizes administrative burdens.

In 2018, a parametric insurance safeguarding the ecological state of a natural ecosystem (i.e., coral reefs) was used for the first time (Green Finance Institute 2025). The insurance activated a claims payment when hurricane wind speeds crossed a defined threshold, enabling stakeholders to swiftly restore the coral reef in the affected region, preserving both the reef and its dependent local community.

To scale, parametric solutions require meticulous risk score calculation. Risk scores are formulated by harnessing a wide array of data to build risk score maps. Fathom, an example software tool for mapping risk, can calculate flood risk metrics for any location for an expansive spectrum of climate scenarios. Fathom provides a visual and quantitative representation of risk across different geographies and climates, which are assimilated downstream into insurance models and pools (Fathom 2025). Essentially, assets within an insurance pool are weighted according to their respective risk scores, ensuring that the collective risk is appropriately balanced and mitigated across the entire asset pool. They enable insurers to architect asset pools with tailored risk profiles, permitting the creation of structured insurance products that are inherently customizable for different types of coverage—whether it be for natural ecosystems, infrastructure, or local communities. For instance, during the March 2019 Nebraska floods, Fathom employed the Normalized Difference Water Index (NDWI) on satellite imagery to quantify event magnitudes for each river catchment, demonstrating how geospatial analysis can fine-tune the automation of parametric insurance triggers.

Despite its open markets and high potential to scale P2P insurance, Web3 parametric insurance remains relatively unexplored. Currently, some Web3 parametric insurance models are being tested, such as the one produced by the collaboration between Shamba Network, DIVA Protocol, and FortuneConnect (Mercy Corps Ventures 2024). In 2023, Mercy Corps Ventures worked with DIVA "to test anticipatory cash transfers to communities ahead of climate shocks leveraging blockchain technology," using the average "Normalized Difference Vegetation Index (NDVI) as a drought measure" to "trigger the donation release" (Walodja1987, 2023).

One unorthodox way parametric insurance could be implemented in Web3 is through the use of conditional tokens or prediction markets, where tokens are created for specific events or conditions, with each token corresponding to a possible outcome. Upon the occurrence of a climate-negative event, an oracle would allow users to redeem their conditional tokens for a payout. Note that, as of late 2025, it is becoming increasingly common in Web3 circles to hear proposals for using prediction markets as insurance primitives.

Reinsurance

Reinsurance, or "insurance for insurance companies," involves a reinsurer assuming a portion of an insurer's risk in exchange for a share of the premiums, thereby enabling insurers to underwrite more policies and manage their exposure to large-scale losses to climate risk or natural disasters. Reinsurance spreads risks and enhances sectoral capital efficiency.

Reinsurance comes in several forms, each offering distinct mechanisms for distributing risk. *Treaty reinsurance* involves a contractual agreement in which the reinsurer accepts a predetermined percentage of an insurer's policies within a defined class of risk over a set period. *Facultative reinsurance*, by contrast, is applied on a case-by-case basis, allowing the reinsurer to assess and decide whether to cover specific individual risks. Finally, *excess-of-loss reinsurance* provides protection against severe losses by requiring the reinsurer to cover any losses that exceed a specified financial threshold (Arbol 2023). These structures are foundational to risk transfer in traditional insurance markets and may offer parallels for emerging ecological or parametric risk systems in tokenized environments.

In Web3, smart contracts and decentralized platforms allow for automated, trustless risk transfer agreements, reducing administrative overhead and enabling real-time data validation. By reinsuring green insurance providers—those offering coverage for climate-resilient agriculture, renewable energy installations, or coastal community protection—reinsurance can itself take on the character of a green asset.

Crypto-staking Insurance

In the past, the authors of this book have proposed a design for an ecosystem-specific, crypto-staking insurance (Curve Labs and Kolektivo Labs 2022). The design focuses on safeguarding environmental assets within a designated local economy. Risk is underwritten by "shield miners" participating in a shared insurance staking contract. Governance of the contract and the associated claims processes would be tailored to each local economy, with underwriter capital attracted via global cryptocurrency markets. Notably, the staked insurance contract tokens would grant shield miners periodic prorated rewards, and insurance tokens (received by stakers) could be freely traded on secondary insurance markets. In this sense, those tokens inherently represent *green* assets given that they underwrite a desirable state for a particular environmental system—a potent means of conservation and when activated, restoration. Figure 6.6 presents the schematic of the proposed cryptoeconomic system for maritime regeneration.

Web3 projects like EthicHub are changing the structure of crowdlending by underwriting loans to small, typically organic farmers through staked crypto-insurance tokens. The staked "crowd-collateral secures the platform's loans, creating a de-risking system to reduce the perception of risk when investing in smallholder farmers in emerging economies." The staked tokens as crowd collateral is a crypto-native use case that decentralizes the underwriting process (EthicHub 2025).

CURRENCY

Currency refers to a system of money that, as a unit of account, has the potential to be used as a network means of exchange for payments or a store of value. Payments are the first and foremost utility of traditional assets that crypto-assets aim to replace. Currencies have a special type of network effect derived utility, as they are backed by the set of goods and services they can purchase. The economic strength of a currency is proportional to what it can buy (as a medium of exchange) and how much its users are willing to hold (as a store of value). With most fiat currencies, for most *users* of a currency, there is no special utility beyond this network effect. For *minters* of a currency, there is a particular utility afforded by a currency, and that resides in the protocological powers afforded the institution that mints the currency, such as the ability to control its scarcity and what collateral ultimately backs it. Table 6.8 presents the currency types.

The fundamental market innovation introduced by cryptocurrencies is that they rely on voluntary adoption rather than legal compulsion. In doing so, they realize a form of competing private currencies, akin to the vision proposed by F. A. Hayek, but in a more decentralized manner, offering unprecedented freedom to currency users worldwide. This has real sustainability implications. Historically, a business would find it very limiting to hold any currency other than fiat currency, even if fiat

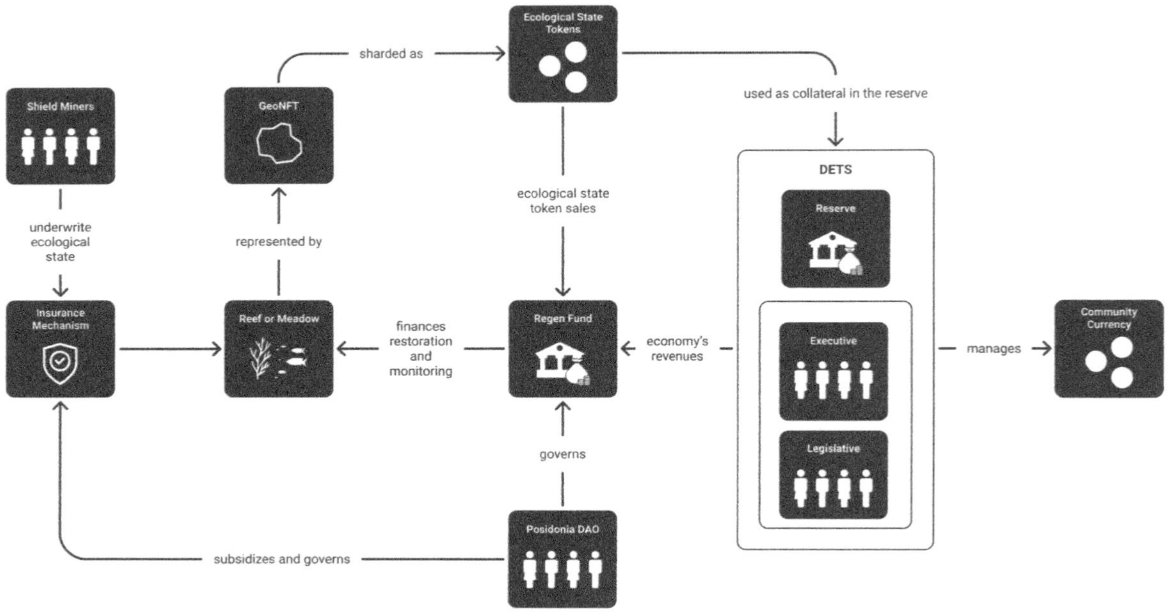

FIGURE 6.6 Schematic of a proposed cryptoeconomic system for maritime regeneration. Posidonia tokens would grant governance rights over a treasury (The Regen Fund) whose mission is to fund the protection and restoration of seagrass meadows and reefs in the Mediterranean Sea. In this context, the tokens enable control and effective environmental governance of rare and crucial natural assets. Highlighting Web3's composability, the tokens could be used as collateral to power a seagrass-backed currency governed by a larger bioregional body—a decentralized exchange trading system (DETS). Alternatively, the Posidonia tokens could be staked to underwrite an insurance mechanism that rewards underwriters (shield miners) by streaming Posidonia tokens. The smart control parameters for the insurance, such as the reward issuance rate, could be set by token holders, or a delegate on their behalf.

***Source*: Louise Borreani, "The Cryptoeconomic Neptune," Curve Labs Blog, January 8, 2022, https://blog.curvelabs.eu/the-cryptoeconomic-neptune-a96e3d7d9ff3**

TABLE 6.8
Currency Type

Subtype	Green Stablecoins	Green Reserve-Backed Currencies	Green Arcade Tokens	Green Tracercoins
Definition	Fiat-pegged currency backed by green assets	Currency backed by green assets, no fiat peg	Stable in specific green apps/ ecosystems	AI-driven stablecoins pegged to non-financial indices
Examples	Celo-Mento stablecoins	SolarpunkDAO EARTH Token	Open for innovation	Cogito Protocol GCOIN
Legal Dependency	Collateral-dependent	Collateral-dependent	No	No
Materiality	Peg/collateral-dependent	Peg/collateral-dependent	Weak	Peg/collateral-dependent
Novelty	Birth	Birth	Birth	Birth

Source: Table by the authors.

currency was primarily used for ethically distasteful or environmentally damaging activities by its institutional minters, such as petrodollars have been for the past decades. As green crypto becomes more adopted, any business anywhere can choose to hold cryptocurrency that matches its sustainability profile.

Green Stablecoins

Green stablecoins (alternatively: "nature-backed currency" or "clean money") refer to fiat-pegged cryptocurrencies that are minted by leveraging green crypto-assets in a reserve (a.k.a. "vault"). Collateralized tokens are well-established, with prominent examples including dollar-denominated stablecoins such as MakerDAO's DAI, and Euro-denominated alternatives such as Mento Euro (cEUR). The call for green money has gained traction within Web3, exemplified by the "The Case for Clean Money" manifesto by MakerDAO's founder outlining how DAI stablecoin issuance could catalyze global sustainable investment (Christensen 2021). As of 2025, the Azos project is trying to produce a USD stablecoin backed by regenerative crypto-assets where "every exchange supports and sustains an economy that cares for the earth and its people" (Azos 2025).

Convertible Deposits, a concept proposed by OlympusDAO, turn stablecoins into strategic positions by giving holders a receipt token plus a Conversion Right to acquire protocol tokens at a future price, while keeping liquidity flexible (OlympusDAO 2025). In a green crypto context, such deposits could let holders of nature-backed stablecoins lock their tokens to earn ecological or protocol-based rewards, support regenerative project treasuries, and maintain optional access to liquidity or upside from tokenized environmental assets.

Green Reserve-Backed Currencies

The stability of low volatility (i.e., stable) crypto-assets hinges on the quality of their collateral. To this end, Mento and MakerDAO's fiat-pegged stablecoins are backed by diversified crypto reserves. The "fiat" aspect of their peg reference introduces risk, however: the governance power to set USD properties, such as supply or interest rates, rests entirely with existing centralized institutions (i.e., the Fed). Unlike green stablecoins, green reserve-backed currencies do not require a peg, but freely float with their valuation often contingent on the quality and the value of the green crypto-assets in their reserve. The EARTH token is the foremost example: a green reserve-backed token backed by various green crypto-assets such as renewable real-world asset ownership tokens (SolarpunkDAO 2025).

Flatcoins are a special type of reserve-backed token proposed by Coinbase that primarily aim to: (1) preserve purchasing power and (2) hedge against traditional financial system risks (Base 2023). Flatcoins represent an emerging currency subtype where the value of the token, serving as a store of value, adjusts over time to mirror shifts in inflation. The fictional "i-DAI" (Inflation Corrected DAI) proposed by the cryptoeconomic design firm BlockScience illustrates this crypto-asset concept: i-DAI's value would be tethered to a reference time, and its price would dynamically adjust in response to inflation variations, maintaining the purchasing power for i-DAI holders (BlockScience 2023).

To the authors' knowledge, the possibility of flatcoins pegged to environmental indicators remains relatively unexplored. A natural asset-backed flatcoin could, in principle, mitigate inflation concerns by being tethered to a resource whose real-world utility and value is less susceptible to inflation. Beyond inflation-adjustment, green flatcoins could aspire to dynamically adjust their value based on environmental state for some bounded territory. Whether or not these types of green crypto-assets will emerge depends on their overall viability and their resilience to economic shocks, and at this stage in the industry, more research is required.

Green Arcade Tokens

Green arcade tokens are digital tokens that exist within specific green-focused applications or ecosystems. Unlike stablecoins or reserve-backed currencies, their value doesn't derive from collateral assets, but instead from their utility within the ecosystem: they can be spent to access services, earn rewards, or participate in the internal economy of a platform. These tokens are deliberately non-investible, meaning they are not designed to provide financial returns; their purpose is to facilitate transactions, incentivize user behavior, and manage internal economic activity in a predictable and programmable way.

The concept of arcade tokens builds on familiar pre-Web3 mechanisms such as loyalty points, airline miles, or in-game digital currency, but with a critical innovation: they are open, interoperable, and composable onchain. This allows users to carry tokens across applications, participate in multiple ecosystem activities, and benefit from coordinated incentives without relying on centralized intermediaries (Kominers et al. 2025).

As of late 2025, several blockchain projects issue reward tokens for eco-friendly actions, such as recycling, reforestation, or supporting renewable energy. While these tokens provide recognition or incentives, most of them lack the key property of expendability: they cannot be freely spent within a self-contained ecosystem as a medium of exchange. As a result, they do not fully qualify as arcade tokens, which are designed to be fungible, spendable, and to circulate within an ecosystem to manage internal economic activity. Instead, a clear example that would fully fit the green arcade token concept is a stable token deployed within a blockchain-based sustainable marketplace. Users would earn those tokens for verified environmental actions and can spend them directly on eco-friendly products or services, or redeem them for additional rewards such as workshops, educational content, or premium platform features.

Green Tracercoins

Similar to flatcoins, a framework proposed by the Cogito Protocol introduces a novel asset subtype termed *tracercoins*—stable assets characterized by their reliance on artificial intelligence (AI) mechanisms and pegging to non-financial indices (Cogito Protocol 2025). The fundamental premise of tracercoins involves anchoring their value to indices encompassing a spectrum of non-financial indicators and metrics. These indices extend beyond the conventional financial realm to encompass dimensions such as social or environmental progress. For instance, Cogito Protocol envisions a Green Coin (GCOIN) that will be expressly designed to trace and mirror the performance of a green index (Cogito Protocol 2025). This index functions as a quantifiable measure of societal advancement toward the ambitious goal of achieving a net-zero economy. The aim of GCOIN is to establish a correlation between its value and this socioecologically beneficial objective.

The operational mechanics of Cogito Protocol's tracercoins are anchored in algorithmic stabilization techniques that use both AI and conventional mechanism design. To safeguard the stability of its assets under diverse circumstances, Cogito proposes a risk-weighted reserve composed of liquid and illiquid assets. The management of the reserve is overseen by an algorithmic stabilization protocol (ASP), which employs a blend of AI techniques referred to as "autonomous stabilization functions" (Cogito Protocol 2025). The ASP operates according to dynamic rules that adjust the risk-weighted reserve, as well as periodic adjustments such as minting and burning tokens (among other mechanisms). Cogito posits that this orchestrated approach collectively maintains the integrity of the soft peg and maintains a high degree of tracercoin stabilization. Despite these claims, like flatcoins, the novelty of tracercoins demands additional research at this time.

INDEXES, ETFs & PORTFOLIO FUNDS

Green crypto ETFs, portfolio funds, and indexes function as curated asset baskets aligned with environmental or climate-related themes. Structurally, they provide diversified exposure to any combination of assets simultaneously.

Beyond asset selection, what defines index architecture is how they are maintained and rebalanced over time. Unlike static portfolios, these instruments are designed to adapt—through pre-defined rules, governance processes, or algorithmic triggers. Rebalancing strategies vary widely. They can be fully automated, using smart contracts to enforce time-based rebalancing (e.g., every 30 days) or threshold-based logic (e.g., if a token deviates 20% from its target weight). Others follow performance-based or volatility-based rules, dynamically adjusting weights to manage risk or reward momentum. Human-operated portfolios (often stewarded by fund analysts) can leverage discretionary or semi-automated processes, such as voting to include or exclude assets based on governance participation, ESG score changes, or updated climate data. Performance-based impact triggers (e.g., verified carbon retirements or biodiversity metrics) can play a direct role in rebalancing decisions, showing how environmental performance (not just price) can reshape portfolio composition.

Tokenized funds differ from traditional mutual funds and ETFs in several key operational aspects. Mutual funds often require end-of-day net asset value (NAV) processing and settlement periods of two to three days; tokenized funds are near instant and 24/7. ETFs provide greater liquidity than mutual funds and are commonly used as collateral in broker environments, but tokenized funds expand this functionality by allowing real-time collateralization through smart contracts. Similarly, while only select ETFs and few mutual funds are used as underlying assets for derivatives, tokenized funds are structurally suited for integration with smart derivative contracts (Chan et al. 2024).

Unfortunately, in late 2025, many high-scoring ESG funds are at a historic low point in terms of profit and interest. One cannot ignore the poor returns: the BNP Ecosystem Restoration Fund, for example, has lost nearly 70% of its value since its origination (BNP Paribas 2025). For green indexes to succeed, their "risk-adjusted returns… must be competitive with those currently offered within conventional settings" (HBAR Foundation 2025).

CRYPTOECONOMIC SYSTEMS: TOWARDS NOVEL USE CASES

As mentioned earlier in this chapter, cryptocurrency's hyper-composability allows for the production of cryptoeconomic systems that transcend present-day finance. Here, we introduce two fictional design sketches, where green crypto-assets are used to illustrate overall system synergies.

CARBON-BACKED PARAMETRIC INSURANCE

Figure 6.7 visualizes the carbon-backed parametric insurance system: In this design, from left to right, carbon credits are issued and tokenized as representations of greenhouse gas emissions reductions from two local environmental projects. The carbon tokens are however of different subtypes: one is a counterfactual credit project, and the other is a removal credit. The two projects are bundled in a *carbon pool*—a cryptoeconomic primitive popularized by projects such as Toucan Protocol that "bundle[s] multiple project-specific tokenized carbon tonnes… into more liquid carbon index tokens" (Toucan Protocol n.d.).

A liquidity pool is established with a stablecoin (e.g., USDC) and the now fungible carbon index tokens. The stablecoin ensures that the LP tokens issued by the

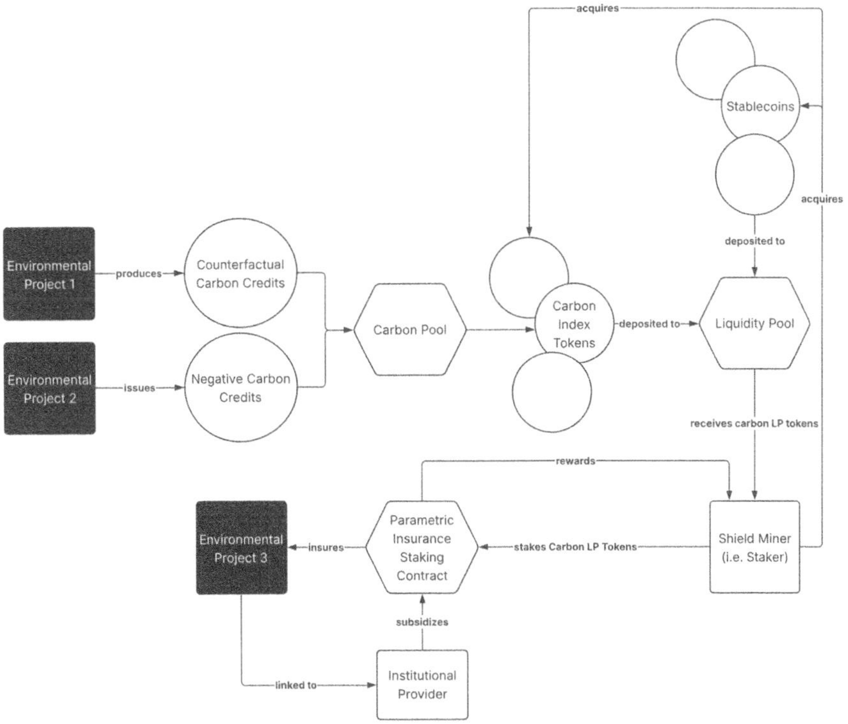

FIGURE 6.7 Visualization of the carbon-backed parametric insurance system.

***Source*: Diagram by the authors.**

liquidity pool (not to be mixed up with the carbon pool) will tend to be more stable than another volatile crypto-asset pairing, such as ETH. In the proposed design, these Carbon LP tokens represent ownership in the pool and its underlying assets (the tokenized carbon credits/stablecoin pair).

Carbon LP token holders may stake their tokens as collateral in a *parametric insurance staking contract*. The staked Carbon LP tokens act as a form of collateral, underwriting an insurance policy for a third local environmental project (in return for a reward subsidy issued by some institutional provider). The parametric insurance contract triggers a payout when specific environmental conditions are met, say, if a drought occurs according to the report of a climate oracle(s). The insurance was set up due to the co-dependencies between the three projects: should Environmental Project 3 fail, it would invalidate the credits issued by 1 and 2.

ENERGY-BACKED STABLECOIN

Figure 6.8 visualizes the energy-backed stablecoin system: From left to right, this design sketch starts by identifying a diverse portfolio of clean energy debt issuances, such as solar or wind power infrastructure, as well as an impact bond issuance that has

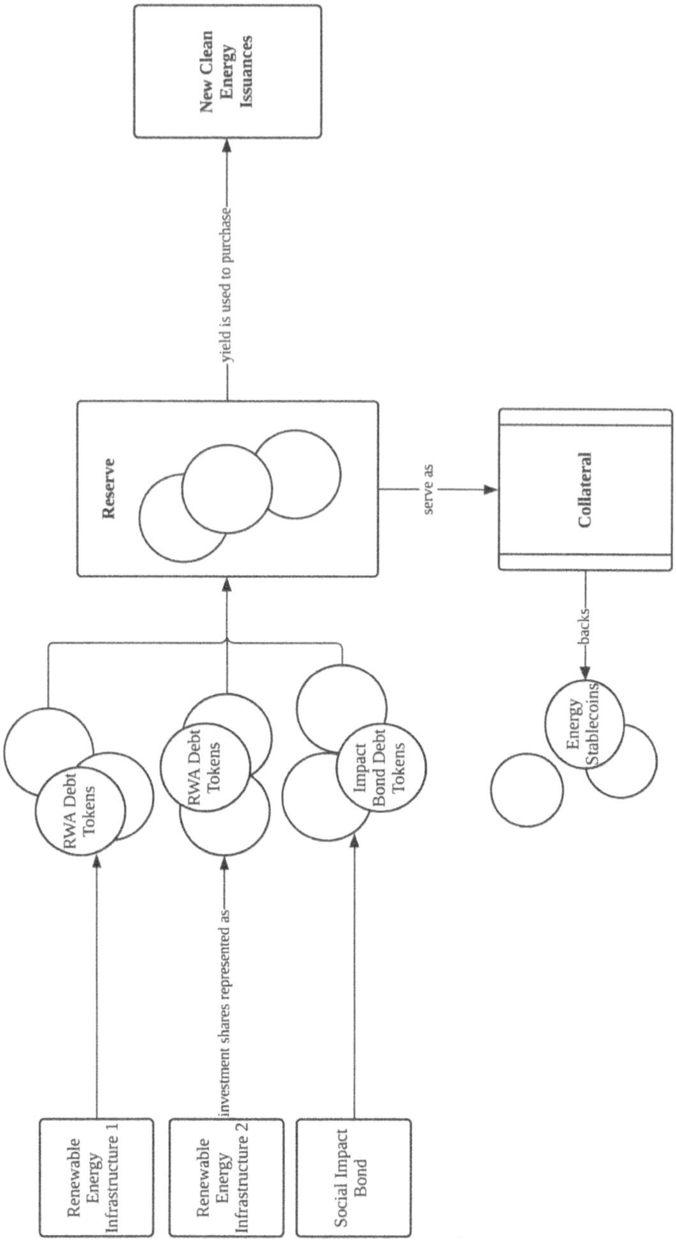

FIGURE 6.8 Visualization of the energy-backed stablecoin system.

***Source*: Diagram by the authors.**

incentivized the development of nearby social infrastructure as well. It then baskets these various RWA investments in a reserve that backs a "clean energy stablecoin." The yield earned by the debt basket is used for purposes of forward productivity, and is invested in new clean energy infrastructure investments. Through this system of forward purchases, the system encourages investments in green energy projects, which in turn benefits the environment and promotes renewable energy adoption, while stablecoin users can diversify their fiat holdings by utilizing a currency that aligns with sustainable values.

REFERENCES

1kx. 2023a. "Autonomous Worlds: The Case for Fully Onchain Games."

1kx. 2023b. "Digiphysical Goods: Bringing Programmable Utility to Physical Products." Mirror, June 14, 2023. https://mirror.xyz/1kx.eth. Accessed December 2025.

Agrotoken. 2020. "Agrotoken Whitepaper." https://agrotoken.com/Agrotoken_Whitepaper_ES.pdf. Accessed December 2025.

Ambios Network. 2025. "The First AI-Native Impact Protocol." https://ambiosnetwork.com/. Accessed December 2025.

Ando, Shah, Maureen Fonseca, Page Lewington, Louisa Durkin, Margaux Filippi, and Martin Wainstein. 2023. "Marine Biodiversity Credits: Technical Framework for Protection Credits." Zenodo, November 21, 2023. https://doi.org/10.5281/zenodo.10182712

Arbol. 2023. "What Is Reinsurance? The Types, Key Players, and Its Role in Modern Risk Management." Arbol Blog, November 17, 2023. https://www.arbol.io/post/what-is-reinsurance-the-types-key-players-and-its-role-in-modern-risk-management. Accessed December 2025.

Atlantis Labs. 2025. "Atlantis: A Nature Positive Lending Protocol." https://www.atlantislabs.io/. Accessed December 2025.

Azos. 2025. "Azos: Regenerative Finance." https://www.azos.finance/. Accessed December 2025.

Bardoscia, Niccolò, and Alessandro Nodari. 2023. "Liquidity Providers Greeks and Impermanent Gain." February 23, 2023. https://arxiv.org/pdf/2302.11942.pdf

Base. 2023. "Request for Builders." Mirror, March 23, 2023. https://paragraph.com/@base-8. Accessed December 2025.

Benkler, Yochai. 2007. The Wealth of Networks: How Social Production Transforms Markets and Freedom. Yale University Press.

BetaCarbon. 2025. "How It Works." https://www.betacarbon.com/#How-It-Works. Accessed December 2025.

Binance Academy. 2023. "What Is Data Tokenization and Why Is It Important?" April 27, 2023. https://www.binance.com/de/academy. Accessed December 2025.

Blanchard, Dominique, and Dominique Duval. 2020. "Crédit Agricole CIB Innovates, Bringing the First Green Interest Rate Swaps to the Asia-Pacific Capital Markets."

BlockScience. 2023. "Flatcoins: Inflation Adjusted Stablecoins." Medium, April 14, 2023. https://blog.block.science/flatcoins-inflation-adjusted-stablecoins/. Accessed December 2025.

BloombergNEF. 2022. "The Untapped Power of Carbon Markets in Five Charts." September 16, 2022. https://about.bnef.com/insights/finance/the-untapped-power-of-carbon-markets-in-five-charts/. Accessed December 2025.

BNP Paribas. 2025. "BNP Paribas Ecosystem Restoration: Fund Factsheet." https://docfinder.bnpparibas-am.com/api/files/63e923fb-9474-4f33-9cb5-b4e35d227a50/512. Accessed December 2025.

Borreani, Louise, and Pat Rawson. 2025. "Decentralising the Planet's Powerhouse: Promises of Blockchain Solar Production." CARBON Copy, March 24, 2025. https://carboncopy.news/content/features/decentralising-planet-powerhouse-promises-blockchain-solar-production. Accessed December 2025.

Boston Consulting Group. 2023. "BCG Enters Carbon Removal Credit Agreement with CarbonCapture." June 21, 2023. https://www.bcg.com/. Accessed December 2025.

BTCS Inc. 2025. "BTCS Inc. Arranges Financing to Buy up to $57.8 Million of Ether ($ETH) for Continued Strategy." Press release, May 14, 2025. Nasdaq. https://www.nasdaq.com/press-release/btcs-inc-arranges-financing-buy-578-million-ether-eth-continued-strategy-2025-05-14. Accessed March 2026.

Busch, Jonah, and Kalifi Ferretti-Gallon. 2017. "What Drives Deforestation and What Stops It? A Meta-Analysis." Review of Environmental Economics and Policy 11, no. 1: 3–23. https://doi.org/10.1093/reep/rew013

Carapella, Francesca, Grace Chuan, Jacob Gerszten, Chelsea Hunter, and Nathan Swem. 2023. "Tokenization: Overview and Financial Stability Implications." Finance and Economics Discussion Series, no. 2023-060: 1–29. https://www.federalreserve.gov/econres/feds/tokenization-overview-and-financial-stability-implications.htm. Accessed December 2025.

CarbonCredits.com. 2025. "Live Carbon Prices Today." https://carboncredits.com/carbon-prices-today/. Accessed December 2025.

Cassidy, Emily. n.d. "How Nepal Regenerated Its Forests." NASA Earth Observatory. https://science.nasa.gov/earth/earth-observatory/how-nepal-regenerated-its-forests-150937/. Accessed December 2025.

Chan, David, et al. 2024. "Tokenized Funds: The Third Revolution in Asset Management Decoded." Boston Consulting Group/Aptos Labs/Invesco, October 2024. https://web-assets.bcg.com/81/71/6ff0849641a58706581b5a77113f/tokenized-funds-the-third-revolution-in-asset-management-decoded.pdf.

Christensen, Rune. 2021. "The Case for Clean Money." MakerDAO, October 4, 2021. https://forum.makerdao.com/t/the-case-for-clean-money/10684. Accessed December 2025.

Clean Development Mechanism. 2025. "CDM Methodologies." https://cdm.unfccc.int/. Accessed December 2025.

Climate Bonds Initiative. 2021. "Climate Bonds Taxonomy." January 2021. https://www.climatebonds.net/. Accessed December 2025.

Climate Vault. 2025. "Carbon Reduction and Removal." https://climatevault.org/climate-vault-approach/. Accessed December 2025.

Cogito Protocol. 2025. "Cogito Protocol Whitepaper." GitBook. https://github.com/singnet/cogito-protocol/blob/master/Cogito_financial_model.pdf. Accessed December 2025.

Coorest. 2025. "Benefits of Coorest NFTrees." https://coorest.io/benefits-of-coorest-nftrees/. Accessed December 2025.

Crédit Agricole. 2023. "Crédit Agricole CIB and SEB Launch a Sustainable and Open Digital Bond Platform Built on Blockchain Technology."

Curmi, Elizabeth et al. 2023. Voluntary Carbon Markets: A Critical Piece of the Net Zero Puzzle. Global Perspectives & Solutions.

Curve Labs and Kolektivo. 2023. "Monitoring, Reporting, and Verification Methodologies in Regenerative Finance." April 2023. https://docsend.com/view/avd6hzqqhfs2hp2p. Accessed December 2025.

Curve Labs and Kolektivo Labs. 2022. "The Kolektivo Framework." August 2022. https://assets.website-files.com/5fcaa3a6fcb269f7778d1f87/63297723f700491a0698ab5a_Kolektivo%20Bluepaper.pdf. Accessed December 2025.

dClimate. 2025. "Unlocking the Power of Climate Data for a Sustainable Future." https://www.dclimate.net/. Accessed December 2025.

Echave, Cynthia. 2022. "Territorial Resilience: Pillars for a Holistic Approach of Resilience for Land Use Planning." Euro-Mediterranean Economists Association, March 2022. https://euromed-economists.org/. Accessed December 2025.
Ecosapiens. 2025. "Frequently Asked Questions." https://ecosapiens.xyz/faq. Accessed December 2025.
Energy Web Foundation. 2025. "Energy Web: Operating System for the Energy Transition." https://www.energyweb.org/. Accessed December 2025.
EthicHub. 2025. "EthicHub Abstract." https://docs-ethix.ethichub.com/v/english/. Accessed December 2025.
European Union Blockchain Observatory and Forum. 2022. "Blockchain Applications in the Energy Sector." Thematic report, June 2022. https://blockchain-observatory.ec.europa.eu/document/download/4ce6b8bf-8f22-4eef-acdc-99da056aeed8_en?filename=EUBOF-Thematic_Report_Energy_Sector_0.pdf. Accessed June 2025.
Fathom. 2025. "Risk Scores." https://www.fathom.global/product/global-flood-map/risk-scores/. Accessed December 2025.
Favre, Thibauld, Joris Delanoue, Victor Mimo, Adam Momen, and Alex Fong. 2025. "Open Cap Table Protocol Whitepaper." Fairmint. https://www.fairmint.com/whitepaper/open-cap-table-protocol. Accessed December 2025.
Flood, Chris, and Javier Blas. 2007. "Coffee Rises on Brewing Talk of Manipulation." Financial Times.
Ford, Helen V., Franziska Schrodt, Alexandra Zieritz, Daniel A. Exton, Geertje van der Heijden, Jonathan Teague, Tim Coles, and Richard Field. 2024. "A Technological Biodiversity Monitoring Toolkit for Biocredits." Journal of Applied Ecology 61, no. 9. https://doi.org/10.1111/1365-2664.14725
Frigg.eco. 2023. "Frigg Whitepaper." June 2023. https://content.frigg.eco/assets/01062023_frigg_whitepaper.pdf. Accessed December 2025.
Garba, Abba, and Derik Lu. 2023. "Tokenized REC on Celo via Arkreen AREC Bridging Protocol." Arkreen, Medium, December 4, 2023. https://medium.com/@arkreen/tokenized-rec-on-celo-via-arkreen-arec-bridging-protocol-60d84c850882. Accessed December 2025.
Garrido, José M. 2023. "Digital Tokens: A Legal Perspective." IMF Working Paper no. 2023/151. International Monetary Fund. https://doi.org/10.5089/9798400250149.001
Genuine Origin. 2021. "Coffee Prices Explained: A Beginners Guide to Green Coffee Prices." Medium, September 9, 2021. https://genuine-origin.medium.com/. Accessed December 2025.
Glow. 2023. "Glow: A Cryptoeconomic System for Producing High Additionality Carbon Credits." November 3, 2023. https://www.icrg.io/whitepaper.pdf. Accessed December 2025.
GoldFinch Finance. 2025. "Almavest Basket #7: Fintech and Carbon Reduction Basket." https://app.goldfinch.finance/pools/0x759f097f3153f5d62ff1c2d82ba78b6350f223e3. Accessed December 2025.
Gould, Gordon. 2022. "Introducing New Atlantis: Unlocking Marine Biodiversity and Blue Carbon." ReFiDAO, September 9, 2022. https://blog.refidao.com/introducing-new-atlantis-on-gr15-2/. Accessed December 2025.
Gradeckas, Simas. 2024. "Biodiversity Credits: For & Against." Bloom Labs, November 25, 2024. https://newsletter.bloomlabs.earth/. Accessed December 2025.
Green Finance Institute. 2025. "Quintana Roo Reef Protection (Parametric Insurance)." https://www.greenfinanceinstitute.com/hive/revenues-for-nature/case-studies/quintana-roo-reef-protection-parametric-insurance/. Accessed June 2025.
Gunarathna, Chathuri L., Rebecca J. Yang, Sajani Jayasuriya, and Kaige Wang. 2022. "Reviewing Global Peer-to-Peer Distributed Renewable Energy Trading Projects." Energy Research & Social Science 89: 102655.

Hahn, Thomas et al. 2015. "Purposes and Degrees of Commodification: Economic Instruments for Biodiversity and Ecosystem Services Need Not Rely on Markets or Monetary Valuation." Ecosystem Services 16: 74–82.

Handagama, Sandali. 2023. "Hong Kong Successfully Offered Inaugural 100m Tokenized Green Bond." CoinDesk, February 16, 2023. https://www.coindesk.com/policy/2023/02/16/hong-kong-successfully-offered-inaugural-100m-tokenized-green-bond/. Accessed December 2025.

HBAR Foundation. 2025. "The SIF Investment Thesis Part I: Making Climate Finance Auditable." https://www.hbarfoundation.org/blog-post/the-sif-investment-thesis-part-i-making-climate-finance-auditable. Accessed June 2025.

Helios. 2025. "Helios: Clean Energy for Everyone." https://helios.eco/. Accessed December 2025.

Holland & Knight. 2021. "Natural Asset Companies: A Nature-Based Solution to Unlock the Value of Natural Resources." Holland & Knight Energy and Natural Resources Blog, November 5, 2021.

IEA. 2023. "Fossil Fuels Consumption Subsidies 2022." February 2023. https://www.iea.org/reports/fossil-fuels-consumption-subsidies-2022. Accessed December 2025.

ImpactLabs 4 Earth and Nature Tech Collective. 2024. "Developing the Nature Tech Taxonomy Framework." Nature X Foundation, October 2024. https://drive.google.com/file/d/1IB0U0vkwqA5vyRUzgSdtyJ8ki2PAamQK/view. Accessed December 2025.

Inhabit. 2025. "Natural Capital Stewardship." https://www.inhabit.one/. Accessed December 2025.

International Carbon Registry. 2025. "Explore All Projects." https://www.carbonregistry.com/projects. Accessed December 2025.

Inuk. 2025. "Inuk: Nature-Positive Markets." https://inuk.co/. Accessed December 2025.

Kampakis, Stylianos, and Linas Stankevičius. 2023. "The Tokenomics Audit Checklist: Presentation and Examples from the Audit of a DeFi Project, Terra/Luna and Ethereum 2.0." The Journal of the British Blockchain Association 2, no. 6. https://jbba.scholasticahq.com/article/77551. Accessed December 2025.

Kazemifar, Farzan. 2022. "A Review of Technologies for Carbon Capture, Sequestration, and Utilization." Greenhouse Gases: Science & Technology 12, no. 1. https://doi.org/10.1002/ghg.2131

Khodai, Ela. 2022. "Tokenization of Carbon Credits — An Explainer." Toucan Medium, December 1, 2022. https://blog.toucan.earth/tokenization-of-carbon-credits-explained/. Accessed December 2025.

Kokonut Network. 2025. "Introduction." GitBook. https://kokonut.network/kokonut-framework/Introduction. Accessed June 2025.

Kominers, Scott D., Eddy Lazzarin, Miles Jennings, and Tim Roughgarden. 2025. "Arcade Tokens: The Most Underappreciated Token Type." a16z Crypto, November 13, 2025. https://a16zcrypto.com/posts/article/arcade-tokens/. Accessed December 2025.

Landua, Gregory. 2024. "To Credit, or Not to Credit." Medium, April 3, 2024. https://medium.com/regen-network/to-credit-or-not-to-credit-de48ba7da8c4. Accessed December 2025.

LandX. 2025. "World's First African Tokenized Farmland on Blockchain." Medium, May 20, 2025. https://medium.com/@landxfinance/worlds-first-african-tokenized-farmland-on-blockchain-landx-brings-south-african-farmland-3b9a727d4092. Accessed December 2025.

Lannoo, Karel, and Apostolos Thomadakis. 2020. Derivatives in Sustainable Finance. CEPS-ECMI Study, Centre for European Policy Studies.

LCX Team. 2023. "Tokenized Bonds vs. Traditional Bonds." February 20, 2023. https://lcx.com/en/tokenized-bonds-vs-traditional-bonds. Accessed December 2025.

Ledgard, Jonathan. 2022. "Interspecies Money." In The Promise of Frontier Technologies for Sustainable Development, edited by John W. McArthur, Homi Kharas, and Izumi Ohno. Brookings Institution Press.

Levin, Alana. 2025. "Crypto Trends Report: 2025 Edition." Variant Fund. https://docsend.com/view/8v8qrkrwbtfpjvta. Accessed December 2025.

Mac Naggar. 2023. "Real World Assets: The Bridge Between TradFi and DeFi." Binance Research, March 2023.

Mandel, James T., C. Josh Donlan, and Jonathan Armstrong. 2009. "A Derivative Approach to Endangered Species Conservation." Frontiers in Ecology and the Environment 8, no. 1: 44–49.

Marcus.limo. 2023. "Methodology Lifecycle Governance for Environmental Assets." August 9, 2023. https://www.marcus.limo/posts/methodology-lifecycle/. Accessed December 2025.

Maseer Finance. 2025. "Maseer Finance: Tokenized Carbon Issuances." https://maseer.finance/. Accessed December 2025.

Mercy Corps Ventures. 2024. "Pilot Insights | Anticipatory Action Leveraging Blockchain for Drought-Impact Pastoralists in the Horn of Africa." Medium, July 24, 2024. https://medium.com/mercy-corps-social-venture-fund/pilot-insights-anticipatory-action-leveraging-blockchain-for-drought-impact-pastoralists-in-the-e2d60d0f0f3d. Accessed December 2025.

Misra, Neeti et al. 2023. "Role of Blockchain Technology Integration for Green Bonds Issuance with Sustainability Aspect." International Journal on Recent and Innovation Trends in Computing and Communication (IJRITCC) 11, no. 6: 134–142.

Molecule Protocol. 2025. "The Future of Medicine Belongs to Everyone." https://www.molecule.to/. Accessed December 2025.

Nat5. 2025. "Nat5: Nature-Positive Technology." https://www.nat5.bio/. Accessed December 2025.

Nature Biotechnology. 2023. "The Community of the DAO." Nature Biotechnology 41: 1357. https://doi.org/10.1038/s41587-023-02005-1. Accessed December 16, 2025.

Natures Vault. 2025. NaturesGold Token and Pistol Lake NFT Litepaper. GitBook.

Nystrom, Mason. 2023. "DePIN and DeREN: Toward a Better Classification of Decentralized Infrastructure Networks." Variant Fund, July 20, 2023.

Obasi, Steve. 2023. "Yield Tokenization — How Pendle Finance Is Revolutionizing DeFi Strategies with Future Yield Trading." Medium, April 8, 2023.

OlympusDAO. 2025. "Convertible Deposits: Converting Stability into Strategy." Medium, September 3, 2025.

Open Earth Foundation. 2022. "Advanced Marine Ecosystem Credits." November 2022.

Open Earth Foundation. 2025. "OpenClimate." https://www.openearth.org/projects/openclimate. Accessed December 2025.

Open Forest Protocol. 2025. https://www.openforestprotocol.org/. Accessed December 2025.

Open Forest Protocol. 2024a. "Afforestation/Reforestation/Revegetation (ARR) Carbon Whitepaper. Version 1.1." April 2024. https://docsend.com/view/75zb4teqgzvvmyva. Accessed December 2025.

Open Forest Protocol. 2024b. "ReverdeC: The Roots of the World's First Fully Digital Carbon Credits in Colombia." February 13, 2024.

Ortlepp, Clemens. 2022. "Introducing the IP-NFT V2." Molecule, December 19, 2022. https://molecule.xyz/blog/introducing-ip-nft-v2. Accessed December 2025.

Paradigm. 2025. "DAO Legal Entity Matrix." https://daos.paradigm.xyz/. Accessed December 2025.

Plastiks. 2025. "Whale from Europe #55." https://app.plastiks.io/collections/. Accessed December 2025.

Polygon. 2024. "The Road to 100k Connected Cars: How DIMO is Revolutionizing the Auto Industry". September 12, 2024. https://polygon.technology/blog/the-road-to-100k-connected-cars-how-dimo-is-revolutionizing-the-auto-industry. Accessed March 2026.

Porsborg-Smith, Anders, Jesper Nielsen, Bayo Owolabi, and Carl Clayton. 2023. "Why the Voluntary Carbon Market is Thriving." Boston Consulting Group, January 19, 2023.

PRNewswire. 2020. "World's First Tradable Carbon Token Is Set to Democratize Access to the Most Important New Asset Class for Generations." December 1, 2020.

Purpose. 2022. "The Patagonia Structure in the Context of Steward-Ownership." Medium, September 22, 2022.

Regen Market. 2025. "CarbonPlus Grasslands Methodology." https://www.registry.regen.network/crediting-protocols/carbonplus-grasslands. Accessed December 2025.

Regen Registry. 2025. "Regen Registry Program Guide." https://www.registry.regen.network/. Accessed December 2025.

Reklev, Stian. 2023a. "Forecasters See Rapidly Growing Biodiversity Market as Nature Crisis Forces Response." CarbonPulse, January 10, 2023. https://carbon-pulse.com/186974/. Accessed December 2025.

Reklev, Stian. 2023b. "UPDATE – Swedish Bank Buys First European Biodiversity Credits." CarbonPulse, May 31, 2023. https://carbon-pulse.com/205424/. Accessed December 2025.

Reneum. 2025. "Marketplace: Fund the Future." https://reneum.com/marketplace. Accessed December 2025.

Reuters. 2023. "EU Gives Nod to 'World's First' Green Bond Standards." October 5, 2023. https://www.reuters.com/sustainability/eu-gives-nod-worlds-first-green-bond-standards-2023-10-05/. Accessed December 2025.

Rose, Janus. 2022. "Google's 'Democratic AI' Is Better at Redistributing Wealth Than America." Vice, July 2022.

Sahay, Apoorva, Shannon Hughes, and Josh Henretig. 2022. "Beyond the Buzz: What Can Blockchain Do for Carbon Markets?" Rocky Mountain Institute, November 11, 2022.

Schiller, Ben. 2018. "How a Bank of All the World's Genetic Codes Hopes to Save Nature." Fast Company, February 28, 2018. https://www.fastcompany.com/40534363/how-a-bank-of-all-the-worlds-genetic-codes-hopes-to-save-nature.

Sergeenkov, Andrey. 2021. "What Is a Perpetual Swap Contract?" CoinDesk, October 5, 2021.

Shamba Network. 2025. "Monitoring, Reporting, and Verification." https://www.shamba.network/. Accessed December 2025.

SimplexDNA. 2023. "Franklin by SimplexDNA." January 2023. https://36c42f49-dc4a-4009-82f5-a1245a4c3ffb.filesusr.com/ugd/a0b52e_09c46fa5be1047fd9a89d3cb31b21f06.pdf. Accessed December 2025.

Social Alpha Foundation. 2021. "Blockchain for Sustainable Energy and Climate in the Global South: Use Cases and Opportunities."

Solar Power Europe. 2025. "Asset Management Best Practice Guidelines (Version 2.0)."

SolarpunkDAO. 2025. "EARTH Token." https://www.solarpunkdao.earth/. Accessed December 2025.

SolidWorld. 2025. "CRISP-M Token Statistics." https://app.solid.world/pool/CRISP-M. Accessed December 2025.

Sovereign Nature Initiative. 2025. "Partnerships." https://sovereignnature.com/partnerships. Accessed December 2025.

Statista. 2025. "Games – Worldwide." https://www.statista.com/outlook/amo/media/games/worldwide?srsltid=AfmBOoobyB4B-wLxi0JYBprOsDqBLXAKq7didvFQbbeRYFro5pNwvuAC. Accessed December 2025.

Steger, Isabella. 2023. "Startup Tekkon Uses Crypto-Crowdsourcing to Spot Infrastructure Problems." Bloomberg, May 20, 2023.

Thallo. 2025. "Thallo Two-Way Carbon Bridge — Litepaper." https://www.thallo.io/litepaper-thallos-two-way-carbon-bridge/. Accessed December 2025.

Toucan Protocol. n.d. "Introducing Carbon Pools." Toucan Docs, GitBook. https://docs.toucan.earth/toucan/carbon-pools. Accessed June 2025.

Toucan Protocol. 2021. "Base Carbon Tonne (BCT): A New Web3 Building Block." Medium, December 21, 2021. https://medium.com/toucan-nest/base-carbon-tonne-bct-a-new-Web3-building-block-cae76bca25fd. Accessed December 2025.

Traditional Dream Factory. 2025. "Discover the Power of Regenerative Co-Living." https://www.traditionaldreamfactory.com/. Accessed December 2025.

UNFCCC. 2025. "The Clean Development Mechanism." https://cdm.unfccc.int/. Accessed December 2025.

Utrilla-Catalán, Rebeca, Rocío Rodríguez-Rivero, Viviana Narvaez, Virginia Díaz-Barcos, Maria Blanco, and Javier Galeano. 2022. "Growing Inequality in the Coffee Global Value Chain: A Complex Network Assessment." Sustainability 14, no. 2: article 672. https://doi.org/10.3390/su14020672. Accessed December 2025.

VeBetterDAO. 2025. "VeBetterDAO: Rewarding Sustainable Actions." https://vebetterdao.org/. Accessed December 2025.

Verbeek, Arnold, and Maria Lundqvist. 2021. Artificial Intelligence, Blockchain and the Future of Europe. European Investment Bank.

Verra. 2017. "Climate, Community, & Biodiversity Standards." June 21, 2017. https://verra.org/wp-content/uploads/CCB-Standards-v3.1_ENG.pdf. Accessed December 2025.

Verra. 2023. "SD VISta Nature Framework Now Open for Public Consultation." September 18, 2023.

VitaDAO. 2025. "VitaDAO — Decentralized Longevity Research Funding." https://www.vitadao.com/. Accessed December 2025.

Walodja1987. 2023. "DIVA Donate – Insights into Trigger Selection Methodology." DIVA Protocol Blog, November 6, 2023. https://www.divaprotocol.io/posts/diva-donate-trigger-selection-methodology. Accessed December 2025.

Waterford, Laura, Veda FitzSimons, and Olivia Back. 2023. State of Voluntary Biodiversity Credit Markets: A Global Review of Biodiversity Credit Schemes. Pollination.

WePower. 2018. "WePower Whitepaper." https://media.abnnewswire.net/media/en/docs/92627-WePower_Whitepaper.pdf. Accessed December 2025.

Witthaut, Markus, Henning Deeken, Philipp Sprenger, Petyo Gadzhanov, and Marcel David. 2017. "Smart Objects and Smart Finance for Supply Chain Management." Logistics Journal 2017: 1–10.

World Bank Group. 2021. "Toolkits for Policymakers to Green the Financial System." https://openknowledge.worldbank.org/entities/publication/b1897439-4fce-5466-b045-9a858b0273b3. Accessed December 2025.

World Bank Group. 2024. "State and Trends of Carbon Pricing 2024". https://openknowledge.worldbank.org/entities/publication/b0d66765-299c-4fb8-921f-61f6bb979087. Accessed December 2025.

World Economic Forum. 2016. "Renewable Infrastructure Investment Handbook: A Guide for Institutional Investors." December 2016. https://www3.weforum.org. Accessed December 2025.

Xu, Xun, Yuqian Lu, Birgit Vogel-Heuser, and Lihui Wang. 2021. "Industry 4.0 and Industry 5.0—Inception, Conception and Perception." Journal of Manufacturing Systems 61: 530–535. https://doi.org/10.1016/j.jmsy.2021.10.006. Accessed December 2025.

7 Market Layer
Blockchain Infrastructures and Opportunities in Green Cryptomarkets

Green cryptomarkets—platforms where green crypto-assets with verifiable material impact can be freely exchanged—span several evolving domains in Web3. These domains include regenerative finance (ReFi), decentralized science (DeSci), and decentralized physical infrastructure networks (DePIN). As seen in Table 7.1, what unites these approaches is their emphasis on the material intersection between green assets and the tools and practices of decentralized finance (DeFi):

Ultimately, the successful production and use of green crypto may come down to the conditions of its exchange in the global financial system. This chapter begins by summarizing the state of green markets. It then examines the added value that cryptomarkets introduce, ending with an analysis of trends and opportunities for practitioners to pursue.

For sustainability professionals, the timing is consequential: as AI increasingly automates knowledge work, ownership of productive assets will matter more relative to labor. Green cryptomarkets offer practitioners a means to democratize that ownership—ensuring the green transition expands access to infrastructure capital rather than concentrating it further.

STATE OF GREEN MARKETS

The green transition requires financing at unprecedented scale—regardless of political orientation or preexisting market structure. The cost of doing nothing or moving too slowly is too high. Faster capital deployment means greater avoided losses. Over $9 trillion has been spent globally in the last decade on wind, solar, electric vehicles, energy storage, electrified heat, and power grids—yet the renewable share of final energy consumption advances only 0.3–0.6% per year (Cembalest 2025).

Studies, including those by the Swiss Re Institute and the Network for Greening the Financial System, predict macroeconomic losses due to warming could reach 18% of GDP by 2050 (Buchner et al. 2023). These estimates, focusing on direct economic impacts like increased weather-related damages and health costs, likely fall short of capturing the full spectrum of consequences, including biodiversity loss, stranded assets, and the societal upheavals from increased conflict and migration. The urgency to fund the green transition is paramount; without swift action, accumulating damages and risk will escalate beyond manageable thresholds.

 DOI: 10.1201/9781003748472-7

TABLE 7.1
Key Web3 Domains Intersecting with Green Cryptomarkets

Domain	Goals
ReFi	Aligns finance with sustainability, environmental regeneration, and social equity. Unlike traditional profit maximization, ReFi supports economic activities that restore ecosystems, communities, and local economies through circular economy principles, renewable energy, and regenerative agriculture.
DeSci	Makes scientific knowledge more open, transparent, and accessible by addressing paywalls, opaque peer review, and publisher dominance. Improves research transparency and reproducibility through secure, blockchain-based records.
DePIN	Redefines infrastructure deployment through participatory models where growth is bootstrapped through active engagement and incentivization, empowering users through autonomous governance and rewarding contributions to network health.
DeFi	Recreates and improves traditional financial services—loans, savings, trading, insurance—without central authorities. Offers transparent, accessible financial ecosystems with permissionless access, full custody, and service interoperability.

Source: Table by the authors.

The financing of this transition requires new ways of thinking that move beyond previous waves of capital expansion and extractive resource development. Negative externalities are not reflected in market prices or represented as green assets. Unpriced externalities accumulate until they destabilize the systems that ignored them. When these hidden costs are made explicit, they sum to $12.7 trillion for global agrifood systems (FAO 2023); similarly, electricity supply systems generate an estimated $11.6 trillion annually in unpriced externalities—roughly equivalent to 28.7% of global GDP when combined with transport (Sovacool, Kim, and Yang 2021). At a macroeconomic level, this indicates that many economic activities have exceeded sustainable thresholds—human civilization is drawing down its ecological capital.

History shows that rapid industrial transitions are possible—the shift from open hearth furnaces to basic oxygen and electric arc furnaces in steel production occurred in just 20 years during the 1970s (Cembalest 2025). The key difference: those transitions financed themselves via returns accruing to innovators and early adopters. In contrast, most renewable technologies do not entail comparable improvements in cost or energy efficiency—they reduce carbon footprints without creating substantial economic incentives in a world without a universal price on carbon. This is why the renewable transition requires new financial infrastructure that can mobilize capital at scale without relying solely on market returns.

These concerns highlight a growing opportunity for cryptomarkets to provide new infrastructure for green markets. With this understanding, the collective challenge becomes one of generating USD trillions in green crypto-assets whose material claims are backed by trust-minimized, fair, and open-source accounting mechanisms—i.e., Web3.

Existing green markets offer reason for optimism. Recent literature covers these markets well, including *The Value of a Whale* (Buller 2022), *The Blue Commons:*

Rescuing the Economy of the Sea (Standing 2022), or the series of "Nature Market" publications by the Taskforce on Nature Markets (Taskforce on Nature Markets 2023). With this background, we can explore how blockchain integration enhances market efficiency, transparency, and scalability.

FIRST PRINCIPLES: MATERIALITY MEANS LEGITIMACY

The key to unlocking green asset markets is to ensure each green asset's claims are verifiably tied to real-world outcomes. Green assets must be fully auditable, transparent, and credible about their underlying material claims. Well-intentioned and capitalized institutions want to meet climate targets, but rightly fear reputational damage. Take, for example, the voluntary carbon market (VCM), where buyers face reputational risk if the material activities they finance are later shown to have been ineffective. As Citi GPS observes, corporate buyers will not participate if they perceive reputational risk from opaque or ineffective markets (Curmi et al. 2023). Consequently, the VCM remains a relatively small market valued at only a few billion USD in 2022 (Curmi et al. 2023), lacking big market players that can ultimately jumpstart the virtuous flywheel needed to scale.

SCALE IS DEMAND CONSTRAINED

The goal of dramatically expanding green asset markets confronts a stark reality: annual climate finance reached approximately $1.3 trillion in 2021–2022, but must scale to $8–9 trillion annually by 2030—a roughly five- to sixfold increase (Buchner et al. 2023). From 2031 to 2050, estimated needs exceed $10 trillion per year. Progress toward 1.5°C-aligned targets remains inadequate across nearly all sectors (Boehm et al. 2023).

Bridging this gap requires substantial private sector participation, but market expansion remains demand-constrained, as profitability drives private investment. Indeed, demand remains the primary constraint on CDR market growth. Scaling the market requires not only more buyers but exponentially increasing purchase volumes from existing participants. The nearly 50% crash in EU carbon futures during 2023–2024 underscores how easily supply can outstrip demand, and how early market projections proved overly optimistic (Investing.com n.d.).

KEY TECHNOLOGIES AND PROCESSES ARE GETTING CHEAPER

Green markets are challenged by the scarcity of projects that meet investment-grade criteria—a situation exacerbated by high initial project capital requirements and transaction costs. However, there are signs that these markets are becoming more accessible and affordable. Rapid, nonlinear cost declines are reshaping key sectors: solar PV generation costs fell 80% over the prior decade, onshore wind dropped 65%, and battery storage declined 89% since 2010. Electric vehicles reached approximately 20% of global new passenger car sales by 2024. These reductions have made renewables the most cost-effective option for new electricity generation across two-thirds of the world (Boehm et al. 2023; Cembalest 2025). Battery costs are also converging across sectors—a sign of market maturity as storage becomes more liquid and fungible (BloombergNEF 2023). Renewables are poised to double by 2030, although a tripling is needed (Altieri et al. 2023).

Falling MRV costs—increasingly enabled by digital and Web3 tools—are expanding the investable universe of green assets. Since its inception, the MRV framework for carbon markets has been characterized by manual processes, subjective assessments, and a complex network of stakeholders. Digital tools for conducting MRV—like those discussed in Chapter 2—are crucial for enhancing accuracy, transparency, and the capacity for high-integrity investments in emission reduction and removal activities. Take, for example, the shift to satellite-based monitoring, which is helping modernize many green assets—especially environmental assets:

> Despite remarkable advances in satellites and machine learning, many credit calculations as of the time of writing still rely on costly, labor-intensive methods. Field crews measure individual trees by hand… and cost tens to hundreds of thousands of dollars… Satellite-based carbon mapping offers a scalable, cost-efficient approach to crediting. Satellites are also essential to enhancing credit quality, because they can observe forest change both within a project and the surrounding region, enabling a data-driven approach to computing a project's emissions impact. Without a satellite view of the landscape, status quo crediting can rely on assumptions that can lead to accusations of over-crediting.
>
> **MRV Collective, Serena, and Nature4Climate (2023)**

With these technological gains, most CDR suppliers see costs drastically decreasing over the next 25 years (CDR.fyi 2024). When factoring in inflation, this trend points to a lower real cost of high-quality carbon assets.

TRANSITION SPENDING IS NOT ADEQUATELY DIVERSE

Inaction on the green transition includes failing to invest in the right combination of solutions. A wide material focus must acknowledge the interconnectedness of ecological systems and the multitude of environmental services they provide. Green assets addressing water quality, soil health, biodiversity, and other ecosystem services are emerging—but remain significantly underrepresented relative to carbon products. CDR investments pale in comparison to clean energy—the former measured in billions and the latter in trillions (Chen 2024). Even within CDR, significant room for innovation remains. The traditional focus on forestry and land use is expanding to include a variety of technological and nature-based solutions, from biochar and ocean fertilization to enhanced weathering techniques. By structuring products around these diverse methods, markets have the potential to cater to specific environmental needs and regional capacities.

- **The focus on environmental process assets like carbon credits obscures the need to green the upstream commodities and infrastructure that generate them.** Commodities, land, and energy-producing assets make up trillions in value and more work needs to be done to improve their sustainability at the source. The growing emphasis on differentiating Scopes 1–3 emissions is a good first step.

- **Renewable energy dominates green investment flows.** But this raises questions about optimal allocation and whether current investment patterns support a just transition. As discussed later in this chapter, renewable energy technologies are uniquely poised to democratize ownership: a solar panel is a far more decentralized energy-producing technology than a gas plant.
- **Venture capital allocation reveals stark mismatches between investment levels and emissions reduction potential.** Analysis of IPCC Working Group III data shows that over 2020–2021, $16 billion flowed into electric mobility subsectors with a combined annual reduction potential of approximately 1.7 GtCO2e, while ecosystem restoration—with nearly double the reduction potential at 2.9 GtCO2e—received only $200 million (IPCC 2022). This means ecosystem restoration receives roughly 140 times less investment per unit of emissions impact than electric vehicles, underscoring the need for capital allocation mechanisms that better align with mitigation priorities.
- **Cryptomarkets are uniquely poised to scale many types of green assets.** Crypto can catalyze entirely new green asset classes, such as digital collectibles, digiphysicals, or green currencies. Crypto also benefits existing assets that rely on sophisticated data management—such as ecological data rights, performance-based instruments, and green bonds (see Chapters 3 and 6). This chapter closes by covering these opportunities at length.

IMPROVING GREEN MARKET INFRASTRUCTURE WITH BLOCKCHAIN

Cryptomarkets and public blockchains offer a novel path forward to bridging the climate financing gap. At their core, these systems offer immutability, transparency, and decentralization—properties essential to green markets where provenance, materiality, and accountability are paramount. Cryptomarkets afford broad access and the accelerated capital formation a just and rapidly scaling climate transition requires. They are a level playing field, where capital can form and flow freely. They are global, 24/7, universally accessible, and drive settlement costs toward zero. Cryptomarkets represent both a qualitative and quantitative departure from existing infrastructure, opening new frontiers for social, technical, and financial innovation. As Table 7.2 shows, their extension to the material, environmental, and ecological is a natural progression driven by need.

At the time of writing, blockchain-based finance has achieved undeniable scale. Public blockchains are among the fastest-scaling technologies in history. Ethereum reached $10 billion in annual revenue in 7.5 years—faster than Meta and far faster than Microsoft's 19 years (Caleb and Brown 2023). Stablecoins alone processed $46 trillion in total transaction volume in 2025—nearly three times that of Visa—with adjusted volume (filtering out artificial activity) exceeding $9 trillion, more than five times PayPal's throughput (Matsuoka et al. 2025). Regulators are also helping

TABLE 7.2
Seven Needs for Green Asset Markets Addressed by Web3

Need	How Web3 Addresses It
Aligning economic and financial architecture with an equitable, global nature economy	Smart contracts and DAOs automate and decentralize financial transactions and governance, ensuring equitable distribution and access to information and resources. Local players can participate on a level playing field in existing financial systems.
Policy alignment of central banks and supervisors	Public smart contracts provide binding arrangements that ensure commitments are followed through, addressing the lack of coordination among central banks.
Aligning public finance with the needs of an equitable, global green economy	Tokenization facilitates transparent assets programmatically aligned with sustainability goals. Blockchain-based funding platforms and nature-backed currencies enable widespread adoption of materially impactful money.
Making food commodity markets accountable	Blockchain-based supply chain technologies provide end-to-end visibility, ensuring fair prices for producers and minimizing environmental impact.
Securing economic benefits for nature's stewards	Tokenized green assets—collectibles, phygitals, environmental process tokens—offer direct financial incentives to individuals and communities protecting natural resources.
Addressing nature crimes	Public blockchains record and verify transactions securely to prevent, track, and penalize illegal wildlife trade and other nature crimes through transparent markets.
Converging measures of nature's state	Decentralized ledgers aggregate environmental data from diverse sources in a trustless manner, providing unified and accurate measures to inform policy and investment decisions.

Source: Table by the authors. "Seven needs" adapted from Taskforce on Nature Markets (2023); "How Web3 Addresses It" by the authors.

accelerate adoption: in the United States, the SEC's "Project Crypto" initiative proposes an "innovation exemption"—new business models could launch immediately if they meet principles-based policy conditions (Atkins 2025). Token standards like ERC-3643 embed compliance features directly into tokenized securities, enabling automated enforcement of transfer restrictions and investor verification while preserving the composability that makes DeFi powerful (Atkins 2025). These developments signal a maturing regulatory environment where green asset innovation can proceed with greater certainty and eco-entrepreneurs can pursue new green forms of capital accordingly, broadening the existing climate market's base and impact potential.

As researchers from the European Central Bank and Columbia University note, public blockchains offer properties uniquely suited to green finance: "immediacy, omni-asset capability, programmability" and through disintermediation, the "ability to flatten the financial architecture," allowing issuers and investors to transact directly with transparent, algorithmic price discovery (Bindseil and Malekan 2025). These are not theoretical advantages—they represent a fundamental departure from traditional market infrastructure. Traditional capital markets impose substantial friction on their users, starting with the issuer: IPO underwriters typically capture a 7% fee on funds raised, plus an estimated 20% underpricing loss as offerings are systematically priced below market-clearing rates—a combined 27% value extraction (Chen and Ritter 2000; Loughran and Ritter 2004). Further along the value chain, DeFi innovations drive down the operational cost of capital allocation and management. These lowered costs are especially pertinent to environmental asset markets, whose public good attributes make them difficult to structure and expensive to deploy (Whitten et al. 2003). Crucially, the IPCC's Sixth Assessment Report indicates that approximately 30% of emissions reduction solutions are already cost-competitive with fossil fuel alternatives—these "deployment-ready" technologies require scaling capital rather than innovation capital (IPCC 2022). Web3 infrastructure is particularly well-suited to mobilizing this deployment capital through fractionalized ownership, programmable incentives, and reduced intermediation costs that enable broader participation in financing proven climate solutions.

Since Hayek's time, economists have understood that the price mechanism distributes knowledge, enabling adaptation and the emergence of socioeconomic order (Potts 2019). Distortions in the price mechanism hinder technological innovation and sectoral adoption. This is especially true in green markets—carbon markets in particular—where effective price discovery remains elusive. Crypto plugs existing price discovery gaps by democratizing once-exclusive utilities like collateral-backed minting of currency, globalizing market access, and enforcing market transparency. Nobel laureate Nordhaus's The Spirit of Green notes that most experts agree "the carbon price should be equal in every sector and every country." (Nordhaus 2021); coincidentally, effective carbon pricing requires uniformity across industries and geographies (Buller 2022). This ideal is hard to meet when trading primarily occurs through opaque OTC desks. As the Rocky Mountain Institute & Climate Collective observe, credit quality depends on both data integrity and process integrity—yet information on prices and contracts remains private, paywalled, and exclusive to intermediaries, complicating price discovery (RMI and Climate Collective 2023).

The opacity of transactions and an overreliance on brokerage systems have allowed a small group of intermediaries to exert disproportionate influence on price setting through opaque margin-setting and fee structures. Academic research estimates that intermediation fees in traditional voluntary carbon markets consume 10–20% of the total carbon offset price, though the actual figure may be substantially higher due to opaque fee structures where intermediaries sometimes pay project developers a fixed fee and capture all surplus themselves (Swinkels 2024). Investigations by Unearthed and SourceMaterial documented brokers capturing disproportionate margins, particularly from small-scale projects in the Global South (Swinkels 2024). Documented through interviews and leaked correspondence, these findings highlight the need to bring these assets onto public blockchains that enhance their transparency and data availability. More importantly, real price discovery cannot happen until these issues are resolved. Liquidity, the lifeblood of any market, suffers in this shadowy exchange environment; the voluntary carbon market has historically exhibited the characteristics of illiquid markets: wide bid-ask spreads, infrequent trading, and price opacity (Swinkels 2024).

As discussed in Chapter 5, decentralized exchanges (DEX) and automated market makers (AMM) are two public blockchain primitives that offer solutions for these market challenges. AMMs, in particular, represent a significant shift from traditional financial markets by using a bonding curve algorithm to determine asset prices based on supply and demand, ensuring transparent, efficient trading without order books or intermediaries. Independent market makers can use these algorithms to inject liquidity and uphold market efficiency, eliminating reliance on centralized intermediaries with conflicting incentives. This democratizes market making while enabling fairer price discovery. AMMs are composable and can be combined with other Web3 pricing primitives, such as batched auctions, to further optimize fair price discovery.

The theoretical foundations of AMMs are well-established. Recent peer-reviewed research demonstrates that properly designed AMMs satisfy key axiomatic properties: "anonymity" (prices depend only on contributions, not identities), "coalition-proofness" (groups cannot manipulate by merging or splitting trades), and "individual rationality" (participants receive better prices than their outside options) (Fabi et al. 2025). These properties formalize fairness guarantees that make AMMs suitable for markets where trust is limited and manipulation risk is high. Beyond theory, the scale of AMM adoption validates their utility. Uniswap, the largest decentralized exchange, has processed over $2.5 trillion in cumulative trade volume as of late 2024, with tens of thousands of unique trading pairs and permissionless creation of new markets (Matsuoka et al. 2025).

AMMs offer unique benefits to green assets, particularly in smaller, long-tail markets where traditional liquidity provision is uneconomic. For example, AMMs are being adapted for physical commodities, such as energy sharing communities, where "concentrated liquidity" enables prosumers to trade surplus renewable energy at prices between grid buy and sell rates—automatically, transparently, and without intermediaries (Fabi et al. 2025). The key challenge for such physical applications is oracle/sensor integrity: ensuring that the data fed into smart contracts accurately reflects real-world energy flows. Beyond energy, Automated Regression Market Makers (ARMM) are AMMs that evaluate high-dimensional attribute spaces, enabling buyers to evaluate the data-rich characteristics of green "semifungibles" (BlockScience 2021). This is useful for nature-based assets, whose complex attributes may include asset origin, development methodologies, and third-party validator identities. The complexity inherent to NbS makes measuring biodiversity and proving outcomes difficult; when outcomes are proven, they refer to many different attributes simultaneously (MRV Collective, Serena, and Nature4Climate 2023). With ARMMs and emerging AI-integrated pricing mechanisms, reported attribute outputs can directly influence asset prices through more-efficient grouping of like assets.

EMERGING GREEN CRYPTO OPPORTUNITIES FOR SUSTAINABILITY PROFESSIONALS

Achieving a more sustainable global economy requires green cryptomarkets to continue iterating, and for practitioners to continue to grow a multi-faceted toolkit of skills and domain awareness as illustrated in Figure 7.1. While early-stage financing

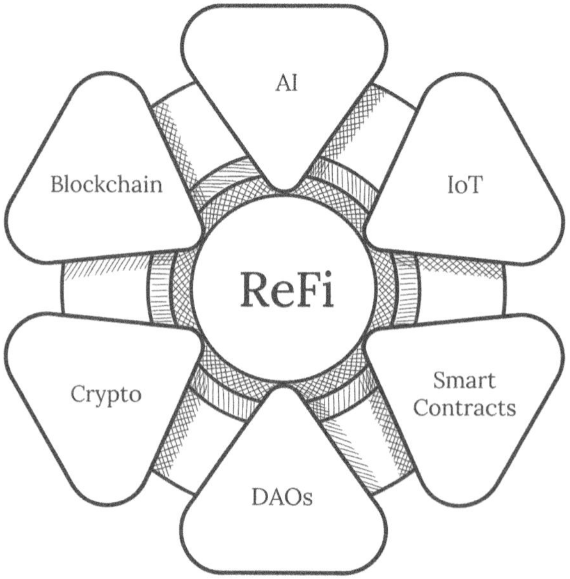

FIGURE 7.1 As noted earlier, emerging trends and opportunities in green crypto broadly fall under the ReFi, DeSci, or DePIN banners, with ReFi being predominant. ReFi denotes Web3-powered socioecological impact—taking the available Web3 solutions (blockchain, cryptocurrency, smart contracts, and DAOs) and combining them with other modern technologies to build solutions that address systemic issues.

***Source*: CARBON Copy. The State of ReFi 2025: The Latest from Web3 Regenerative Finance. CARBON Copy. https://carboncopy.news/content/reports**

from pre-seed to Series B rounds in Nature Tech is on the rise, subsequent funding phases are not keeping pace, indicating that the market is waiting for a new cohort of technologies to mature (MRV Collective, Serena, and Nature4Climate 2023). Many green blockchain projects remain at proof-of-concept stage as of late 2025, but this nascent state signals opportunity. Most tech start-ups begin to realize their value only after a decade in the market (Currier 2022). With this understanding, newly established DAOs and Web3 projects are laying groundwork for environmental and sustainability progress that may take years to materialize. The concluding section evaluates these opportunities for interested practitioners, discussing how they can be harnessed to catalyze significant, positive change and innovation.

ECOTECHNIC KNOWLEDGE COMMONS

Economist Jason Potts describes Innovation Commons as collaborative frameworks where resources and knowledge are pooled to facilitate entrepreneurial discovery under uncertainty. These commons operate as both material resource pools and repositories of entrepreneurial information, helping overcome market failures in innovation (Potts 2019).

Building on the framework of Innovation Commons, the authors introduce the concept of Ecotechnic Knowledge Commons (EKC) that focuses specifically on the integration of ecological and technological knowledge. Sociologist Martin Arboleda envisions a "lost unity between algorithmic knowledge and folk knowledge" that can be "restored within the context of an advanced technological future," where rural cultures produce alongside international advocacy networks "their own organic intellectuals" and "vernacular scientific knowledge." (Arboleda 2020) These collaborative spaces should aggregate, share, and enhance the connections between sustainable practices and the latest in open-source technologies. They could include cooperatives, eco-villages, homesteads, urban maker spaces, seed banks, fab labs, or even forest schools. These spaces should enhance access to technological innovation resources that can be applied to green use cases. Indeed, EKC should be hotbeds for citizen science, and facilitate network collaboration among innovators, researchers, scientists, financiers, legal experts, and global enterprises. Ultimately, they have a pivotal role in incubating and accelerating the early adoption of Web3, AI, and IoT ecotechnologies, helping reduce discovery costs and the challenges of large-scale deployment.

EKC are required due to the growing complexity of managing ecosystems and the urgent need to integrate specialized, often hyperlocalized knowledge into Web3. With the rapid transformation and intensification of agricultural systems, there's been a significant loss of traditional ecological knowledge (Gómez-Baggethun et al. 2010), highlighting the importance of preserving and integrating this knowledge into modern innovations that ensure their continued survival and usage. Artisanal skill shortages are chronic as well in various industries, including engineering and technology (Govender and Davidson 2019). Bioregionalist Joe Brewer describes well these types of integrated knowledge spaces in his *Design Pathway for Regenerating Earth*:

> Of particular importance is the need to create bioregional learning centers for each regenerative economy... there must be ways to retain and pass on knowledge about native species, understanding of how to build houses in the local climate using locally-sourced materials, comprehension of... sustainable food systems in this particular place [...] There are current efforts to combine these kinds of data from sensor networks with digital ledgers that track the creation of value...
>
> **Brewer (2023)**

By proliferating the intersection of ecotechnical and place-based epistemologies, EKC can support small-scale, sustainable enterprises, and contribute to territorial-scale institutional adaptations. EKC can support rural job shifts as labor-intensive work such as retrofitting, micropower generation, commons-based peer production and regenerative agriculture play a larger role in society. Comprehensive toolkits and playbooks offer valuable resources in this direction. Ekonavi—a Web3 ecological impact network—offers free resources on agroforestry and regenerative practices in their multilingual e-library (Ekonavi n.d.). The Traditional Dream Factory published a guidebook on *How to Build a [DAO] Regenerative Village* (Traditional Dream Factory n.d.). Organizations such as

LexDAO, Kolektivo, the ReFi Summit, and Crypto Commons Association have been working to integrate technology with place-based design, organizing workshops, clinics, and events that disseminate knowledge and establish vital connections with local communities.

This being said, significant gaps have been revealed by these early interactions, such as the intersection of law and DAOs and crypto-assets. Education around legal frameworks and the integration of environmental Web3 projects within existing systems is paramount to mitigating regulatory and securities risks, ensuring that novel, place-based ventures can flourish (Morgan 2023). Everything from designing and drafting agreements (leases, licenses, mutual aid, membership, co-ownership, etc.), structuring entities, the taxation of exchange, land use, employment, production, and crypto-asset regulations must be navigated by EKC, as mutualist legal professionals already know (Orsi 2013). Some promising directions are moving forward, though—consider the proposal by Delphi Labs for cybernetic, DAO-adjacent entities deemed "BORGs":

> Each BORG has a relatively specialized purpose, is incorporated in an appropriate, purpose-appropriate jurisdiction, utilizes DAO-connected smart contracts as much as possible, publishes its governing documents, and, beyond smart-contract-based checks/balances, creates accountability by giving limited legal rights to the DAO or DAO members [...] Because these BORGs are business entities, they can comply with regulations, can enforce agreements (whether governance-related and internal or commerce-related and external), pay workers, and pay taxes.
>
> **Delphi Labs (2023)**

As these legal models become replicable over time, the opportunities for place-based DAOs, crypto-assets, and token-based fundraising will in principle increase.

ECOLOGICAL AND SPATIAL DATA PRIMITIVES

Web3 Geographic Information Systems (Web3GIS) hold promise as a future area of R&D and market opportunity. Web3GIS would provide decentralized, transparent, and verifiable ecological and spatial data services. In his book Shared Governance for Sustainable Working Landscapes, ecosystem markets expert Tim Gieseke outlines the high-level specifications of such a hypothetical platform:

> [A] geographical-based platform [...] delineating the landscape into accessible units with the capacity to calculate ecosystem services [...] These eco-services become a geo-referenced index package and... simplify measurement, ownership, valuation and transactional processes.
>
> **Gieseke (2016)**

As discussed in Chapter 3, many primitives need to be developed in this direction, such as private, secure, and reliable data storage and management primitives for handling sensitive, asset-linked ecological and geospatial data. Data privacy is especially important, as biodiversity (e.g., endangered species) and human locations must be generalized to protect them from harm. Today, many regulators ban the "collection, use, and sale" of precise human location data without informed consent (Federal Trade Commission 2024). These examples point to a broader challenge: building market infrastructure that can use location data for value creation while protecting sensitive information.

A well-designed Web3GIS should unlock new GIS functionalities such as geographic or bioregional liquidity formation. With this, capital could form or be efficiently allocated with specific spatial, ecological, or logistical network parameters. Transitioning rural land management from linear to holistic approaches, which produce natural assets and public goods like water, soil, and biodiversity, demands precise measurements by verified observers, risk-minimizing oracle primitives, and smart incentives targeting material impacts (UNCTAD 2013). The next logical step beyond current trends in smart logistics that make "each component in the production process… able to communicate" sharing their "position and state" (Srnicek 2017) is co-incentivization by the components as transacting agents themselves. Geographic positioning is today an issue of economic concern, as liquidity is sociospatially biased, generally flowing from rural areas to urban ones. Could a Web3GIS better manage this flow, helping load balance capital between expanding "cosmopolitan, green and smart cities" and the "polluted towns, shanty towns, and overcrowded camp sites" that aggregate at new resource frontiers (Arboleda 2020)?

Web3GIS should enable collaborative geoprospective scenario creation, allowing for the modeling and anticipation of future territorial developments. It should aid stakeholders in efficiently allocating adaptation funding through participatory institutional methods, like those discussed in Chapter 4. To ensure impartiality and accuracy, there's a growing consensus in environmental asset markets that Validation and Verification Bodies should be independent from standard-setting entities. It's suggested that a significant budget, ranging from 10–25%, be allocated towards independent MRV (MRV Collective, Serena, and Nature4Climate 2023). Web3GIS systems could simplify the process by incentivizing a decentralized array of place-based participants to provide these sorts of services through geopinned bounties and other trust-minimized mechanisms. To this end, Web3GIS should not be approached as a mere tool for observation, but a multi-sided stakeholder platform that provides foundational geographical and ecological data, business, and liquidity formation services for the production of high-quality green crypto-assets.

AI/ML TECHNOLOGIES

Consider how companies today are adopting satellite imagery and machine learning to detect forest change across carbon credit projects. Where field crews once measured individual trees by hand at costs reaching hundreds of thousands of dollars, AI-driven analysis now monitors millions of hectares continuously, flagging anomalies in near real-time (Huang, Gong, and Pang 2022). This level of automation is the present state of environmental AI, and it intersects with green cryptomarkets in three distinct ways: as an *observational layer* that monitors ecosystems at a planetary scale; an *evaluative layer* that quantifies environmental outcomes for markets; and an *economic layer* where AI agents become market participants themselves.

As an observational tool, AI uncovers complex interactions and correlations within socioecosystems, enabling solutions for large-scale resource optimization, fleet management, and climate disaster response. By identifying trends and forecasting threats, AI helps prevent environmental harm—detecting illegal deforestation, tracking poaching networks, and monitoring pollution in real-time. The logical endpoint of this trajectory is publicly accessible digital twins of ecosystems and networks—tools through which corporations, investors, governments, and civil society could model historical and future Earth states interactively, running scenarios to test interventions before committing resources.

A handful of foundation models have already been released that support these observational use cases: the Large Nature Model focuses on ecological data (Dataland n.d.), NASA's Prithvi GeoAI model, which tracks changes in land use, monitors natural disasters, and predicts crop yields (Blumenfeld 2023), and ClimateGPT, a task-specific LLM that synthesizes interdisciplinary climate change research (ECI n.d.).

As an evaluative tool, AI delivers machine-verifiable assessments that provide high-integrity, science-based quantification of a project's historical and projected performance. Such rigorous assessments help stakeholders make critical funding decisions, and sustainability practitioners implement scientifically validated practices with more immediate feedback loops. Recall Gieseke's vision of "geo-referenced index packages" that simplify measurement, ownership, and valuation; AI-generated indexes such as the Human Impacts Index (HII) proposed by Martinez-Rivera et al. push this idea further:

> [HII uses] publicly available and spatially explicit panel data (i.e. structured and regularly published such as monthly or annual datasets) to quantify the marginal effect of a specific event… on human-centric measures such as changes in suicide rates, substance abuse, excess mortality, and unemployment… [It's] essentially modular in that the type of event and unit of analysis are adaptable.
>
> **Dias et al. (2023)**

Nonetheless, it would be a mistake to view AI solely as an observational and evaluative technology. With Web3, AI takes on an economic role, enabling the development of incentivized inferences and independent economic agents. Buterin (2024) describes four categories of AI-Web3 integration that map directly onto green crypto opportunities:

- The first category—**AI as a participating onchain agent**—introduces a new class of economic actors native to Web3. These agents can create wallets, transact with services and people, measure risk, optimize yield, and even draft and deploy smart contracts autonomously. For sustainability applications, imagine product passport-carrying smart objects that, as agents, optimize their green logistics through autonomous incentive issuance. This design space remains largely speculative, but its potential for automating green market participation is substantial.

- **AI as interface to the onchain** positions AI as a mediator between users and blockchain infrastructure. Buterin emphasizes AI's potential to protect users by interpreting and identifying dangers in the digital environment. But the inverse is equally compelling: AI can identify and create opportunities. Imagine an AI that comprehends the intersection of material reality and its liquidity potential. A user photographs terrain or provides a proof-of-presence; the AI translates this into an opportunity to mint or receive a crypto-asset, then guides the user through the process.
- **AI as an onchain decision-maker** holds perhaps the most immediate potential for green cryptomarkets. Here, AI enforces institutional protocols by providing evaluation or curation functions. An AI could determine whether a user-submitted impact report qualifies for the issuance of new impact tokens, or whether evidence provided by a collective satisfies the constraints of a performance-based asset. This raises provocative questions: could rules be implemented for nonhuman species acting as their own economic loci? Could users submit proposals to improve an ecosystem in return for minting that ecosystem's token? Such mechanisms would create new classes of green assets effectively independent from human economic decision-making.
- Buterin's fourth category—**recursive, self-improving onchain AI**—is the most speculative but potentially the most significant. This category is of interest to projects attempting to produce emergent planetary or biospheric intelligence that can become self-producing and self-coordinating. To reach this scale, such an AI would need to identify coordination gaps between socioecosystemic actors and incentivize their co-production.

Across all three layers—observational, evaluative, and economic—there remains ample room for innovation. The tools are maturing rapidly, but the design space is largely unexplored. Practitioners entering this intersection will find that the most impactful applications have likely not yet been imagined.

SUSTAINABILITY AND SUPPLY CHAIN PROVENANCE

In 2024, an investigation by Le Monde and Radio France revealed that Nestlé and other food industry players had been illegally treating bottled water to conceal contamination. Nearly 30% of bottled water brands were non-compliant—all Nestlé brands used forbidden treatments—and leaked documents showed the French government initially chose not to inform judicial or European authorities (Dupin 2024).

This case study draws attention to the opacity of supply chains that today reinforce corporate market dominance and prioritize market position over transparent product information—even for products as essential as water. Such dynamics can lead to regulatory capture, where institutional oversight fails to protect public interests. Blockchain's capacity for traceability and transparency (see Figure 7.2) offers a path toward supply chains free of products linked to pollution, unsustainable land use, and labor violations (Taskforce on Nature Markets 2022). A public blockchain system for water supply chain transparency would create accountability by recording

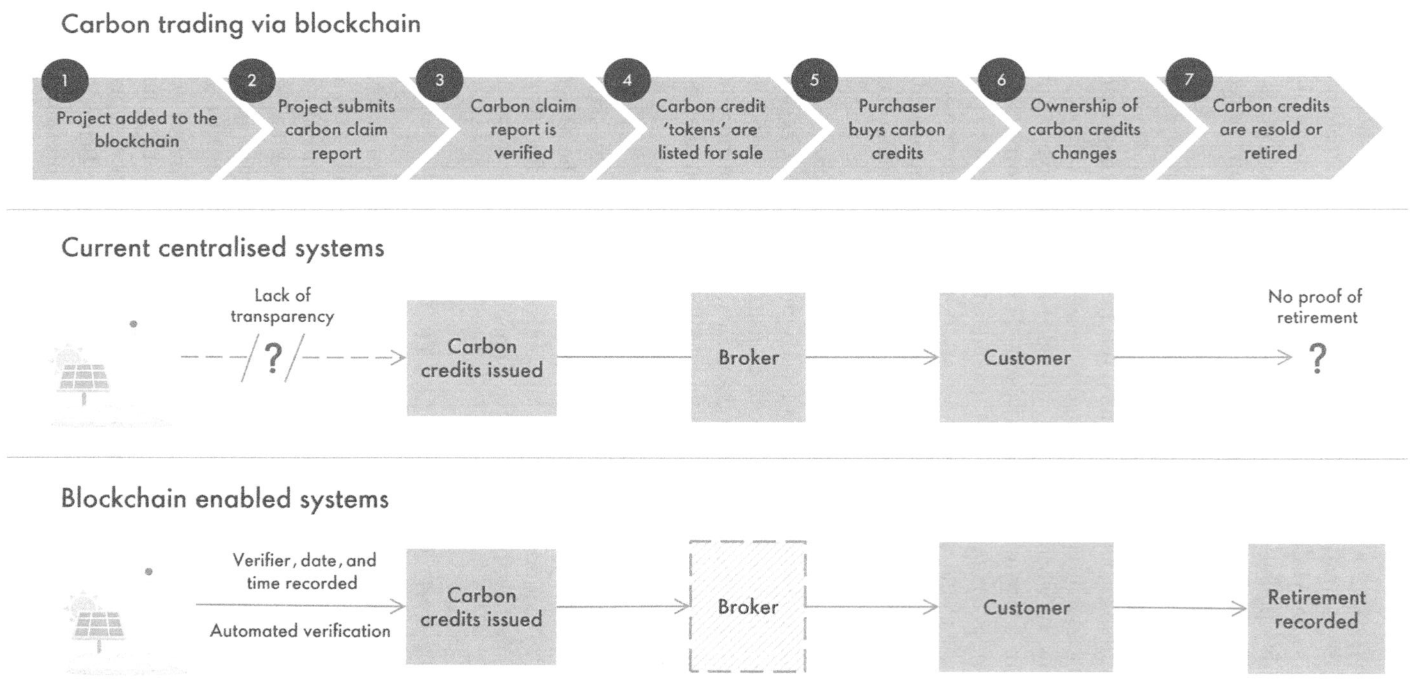

FIGURE 7.2 While current centralized systems do not offer any proof of retirement, demonstrate lack of transparency and need for a broker, public blockchains offer more rigorous proofs—i.e., the retirement is recorded onchain, and the MRV data is verified, automated and time recorded—and do not require brokers.

***Source*: Sipthorpe et al. (2022). Licensed under Creative Commons. https://www.sciencedirect.com/science/article/pii/S2590332222003256**

each batch of bottled water, from source to shelf, cradle-to-cradle, detailing critical data points such as source location, treatment processes, quality control measures, transportation, and final distribution. Each stage would be immutably timestamped, and any attempt at data manipulation would be easily detectable. Armed with immutable records, consumers could make informed purchasing decisions. They could, for instance, scan a QR code on a bottle of water to access the entire chain history of that specific batch—information that is currently difficult or impossible to obtain.

Smart contracts provide a secure and automated means of managing the ownership and control of both digital and physical assets. Phygital (physical-digital) designs support self-coordinating networks of smart objects that structure and economize their own "distributed, multisegment, [and] intermodal transport" within a more efficient "open supply web" (Rifkin 2022). Combined with AI, phygitals become foundational primitives for emerging agent-to-agent economies. As these transparent systems proliferate across supply chains, they combine programmable assets and provenance tracking into new markets and use cases.

Supply chain transparency enhances both investability and logistics efficiency. In the latter case, by applying operational research techniques (e.g., linear, nonlinear, integer, and dynamic programming, network analysis and optimization models, game, queuing, and inventory theory...) across entire supply chains running on blockchain, one can optimize processes and resource flows with the intent of reducing overall carbon footprints and reaching higher levels of local, circular efficiency (Mishra 2020). Decentralized used goods and secondhand marketplaces can achieve higher economic efficiency by lowering platform take rates (Dixon 2024). A recent report by Bank of America expects that "DLT/BCT-powered infrastructure" will optimize "inventory management and shipping routes, as well as enhance the detection of fraud and counterfeit items, which accounted for 3.3% of global trade in 2016" (Bank of America Institute 2023).

GREEN REAL-WORLD ASSET TOKENIZATION

The market for tokenized real-world assets has reached a significant inflection point. As of 2025, the total market for tokenized RWAs sits at $30 billion, up nearly 4x in the last two years (Matsuoka et al. 2025). This growth reflects institutional confidence in blockchain-based asset representation and the operational efficiencies it enables.

BCG and ADDX project the tokenized real-world asset (RWA) market will grow to $16t by 2030, but is still a mere fraction of the reported $126t of existing global assets (Kumar et al. 2022). Green RWAs (GRWA) correspond inglyrepresent tokenization of already existing physical or tangible assets that offer environmental benefits or positively contribute to the underlying material reality. GRWAs offer the same tokenization benefits of any RWA: enhanced accessibility, transparency, liquidity, and reduced transaction costs (Sipthorpe et al. 2022). GRWAs include most assets discussed in Chapter 6, e.g., climate company equities, renewable energy PPAs, sustainable forestry and agriculture, genomic IPs, natural assets, green infrastructures such as wind farms, solar installations, hydroelectric projects, etc. Some GRWAs already exist, including experiments with tokenized natural asset commodities via Agrotoken (Agrotoken n.d.) or Helios' funding of solar projects (Helios n.d.).

GRWAs bear the additional benefit of being able to disintermediate data associated with a tokenized real-world good. Imagine dynamic NFTs that embed relevant data like their associated Scope 1–3 emissions, or associated climate risks. These types of NFTs should automatically append new metadata around their direct energy and emissions costs, as well as shifting supply, transport, distribution, and consumption costs. Markets of RWA tokens that enshrine their material metadata would represent a thousandfold improvement over today's voluntary disclosure regime, and unlock many new use cases across the sustainability sector when paired with DeFi.

COMPLEX GREEN ASSETS AND DERIVATIVES

Complex green derivatives facilitate investment strategies aimed at fostering sustainable development while managing risk over time, such as the carbon assets in Figure 7.3. These financial instruments, such as perpetual options, swaps, or bespoke insurance products, are tailored to offer highly customized risk-return objectives, especially in initiatives like renewable energy projects, conservation efforts, or clean technology advancements. Ultimately, these instruments yield returns while embedding incentives for meeting environmental targets. Complex green asset products include:

- **Indexes, baskets, and token pools** that represent everything from micro-carbon credits to ecological assets, impact certificates, dMRV proofs, bespoke RECs, and more (Morgan 2023). As Scotland's Nature Agency observes, "project aggregation through investment funds or aggregation vehicles" can "improve cost efficiencies and facilitate replication" (Finance Earth and Economics for the Environment Consultancy 2021). Tokenized yieldcos, climate tech ETFs, and bundled solar leases/loans hold potential, especially when integrated with the broader DeFi ecosystem—specifically, DeFi vault mechanisms as discussed in Chapter 5.
- **Hedging assets and tools, such as green perpetual futures contracts (perps).** In environmental finance, the timeframe from project idea to implementation can be unpredictably long. This underscores the necessity for dynamic risk management strategies that accommodate evolving project landscapes. These instruments significantly mitigate durability risk—for example, planted forests burning down before maturity. Perps—a unique Web3 offering—offer corporate buyers and project developers an innovative asset for hedging, speculating, or leveraging positions without the constraints of traditional futures contracts. Using perps, a corporate buyer could engage in tokenized forward carbon contracts with significantly discounted rates for future delivery, lowering risk premiums (Finance Earth and Economics for the Environment Consultancy 2021).
- **Insurance products and tooling.** Previous economic transitions have required the conversion of uncertainty into risk, such as the development of marine insurance, initiating the process of Western globalization. The green transition is no different and will require many new forms of climate insurance to transform climate uncertainty into calculable risk. Consider

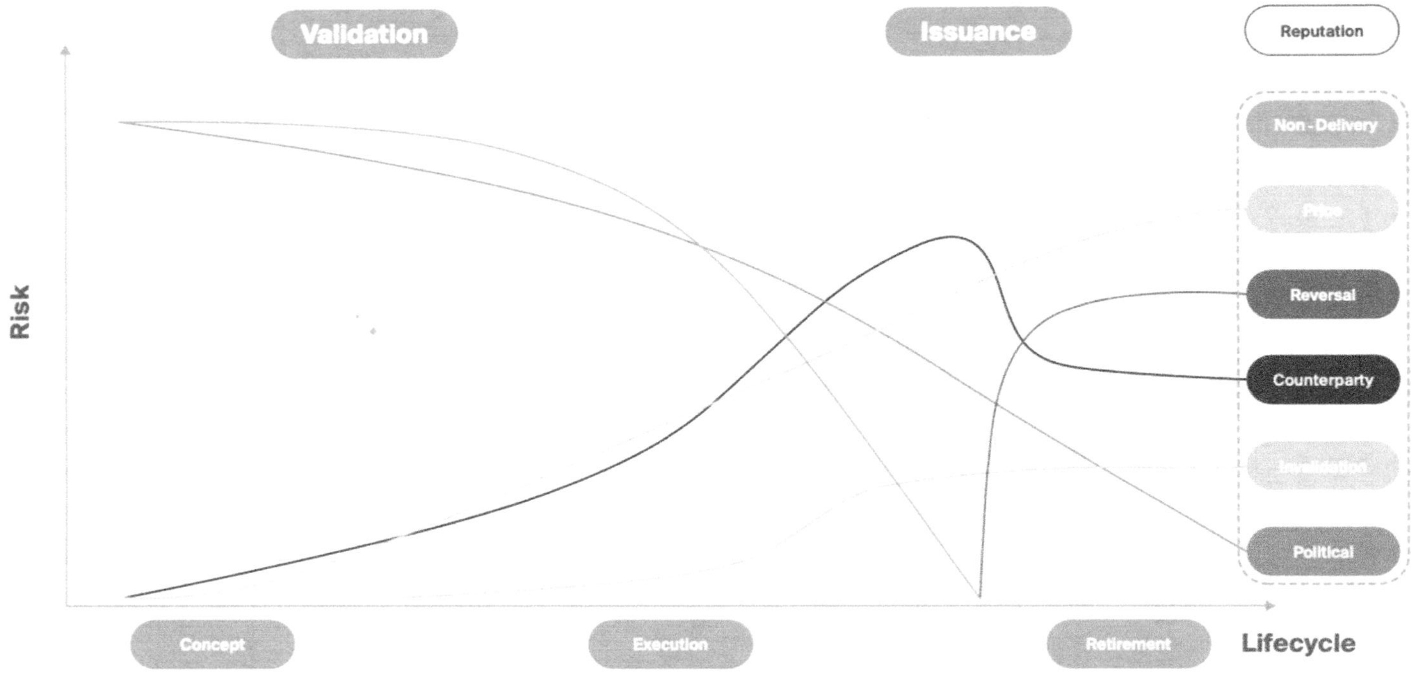

FIGURE 7.3 The risk profile of carbon assets changes over time, requiring different insurance solutions for different risk outcomes.

Source: **Kita and Oxbow Partners (2024).**

the emergence of specialized insurance for environmental assets. Biochar company PYREG and carbon insurer Kita aim to launch the largest durable biochar carbon removal project pool globally, "protecting offtake agreements from the risk of under-delivery of projected CO2 credits" (Doneva 2023). Automated parametric insurance—which pays out based on environmental conditions—holds particular potential as ecological stress periods of record heat, storms, and flooding become more common.

AUTOMATING PERFORMANCE-BASED ASSETS

Automated settlement of green, performance-based assets is pivotal to ensuring accountability and effectiveness. An automated design approach would mandate that incentives are disbursed upon meeting verifiable material targets or outcomes. As discussed throughout this book, for green financial assets to be effective, there must exist a direct link between the assets and the underlying material reality. This also affects price discovery: for assets like carbon credits, on average, ratings quality is becoming increasingly correlated to price (BeZero Carbon 2024). Consider a few examples:

- **Green bonds** could automate penalties for failing to meet material targets, enhancing commitment through guaranteed punishment. This is conceptually similar to the notion of slashing, where proof-of-stake validators lose their stakes for dishonest or malicious behavior.
- **The growth of PES programs** demonstrates the role of performance-based financing in supporting ecosystem services. However, the diversity and complexity of these programs demand comprehensive and reliable data for effective implementation and scaling. Automated escrow systems, where funds or tokens are held until predefined conditions are met, are a practical tool for enforcing conditionality in PES. Similarly, X-to-Earn models where users mint cryptocurrency in return for completing green activities such as beach cleanups or recycling require automated performance checks to scale.
- **In carbon asset markets,** leakage and reversal events—where intended environmental benefits are negated or reversed—require new forms of insurance and retroactive accounting. Scope 3 emissions evolve dynamically across product lifecycles, and would benefit from equally dynamic financial mechanisms that mirror their shifting materiality. Today, mechanisms such as buffer pools are used to deal with impermanence, where a "reserve of credits" is "set aside to protect against unforeseen carbon losses due to events like wildfires or disease" (Badgley 2023). These mechanisms can be automated, permanently enhancing the whole lifecycle value of any tokenized carbon asset. Alternatively, "performance risk scores" like models that evaluate durability risk could dynamically adjust premiums and payout mechanisms for holders of carbon assets if scoring evolves over time (Probst et al. 2024).

Note that automation need not execute solely based on discrete Boolean events. *Dynamic parameter tuning* can optimize system performance in real-time based on environmental outcomes and changing conditions. With it, asset or market parameters would continuously adjust depending on a material state. Such adaptive mechanisms enable more responsive and flexible financing models that can better cope with the complexities and uncertainties of environmental efforts.

NETWORK NEGOTIATION INTERFACES

Traditional commerce operates bilaterally: a buyer negotiates with a seller, they agree on price, and the transaction concludes. This model systematically excludes affected parties who bear costs but have no seat at the table—downstream communities, ecosystems, future resource users. Blockchain enables a fundamentally different mode of commerce: multilateral coordination where diverse stakeholders negotiate outcomes collectively, and where environmental constraints can be embedded as parameters rather than externalized costs.

The infrastructure for such coordination is maturing. AI Agent-to-Agent (A2A) communication protocols provide open standards for autonomous entities to discover, negotiate, and reach agreement without requiring shared internal architectures (Google 2025). In sustainability contexts, this matters because collective processes—carbon credit verification, resource allocation, supply chain certification—require coordination across organizations with different systems and incentives. Agents represent stakeholder interests in automated negotiations, from individual prosumers to environmental monitoring systems. Complementary onchain infrastructure like reputation registries enables verification not only of creditworthiness but of ecological trustworthiness. ERC-8004, proposed in August 2025 by teams from MetaMask, the Ethereum Foundation, Google, and Coinbase, introduces three onchain registries—Identity, Reputation, and Validation—allowing participants to discover, evaluate, and interact with agents across organizational boundaries without pre-existing trust (De Rossi et al. 2025). For sustainability applications, this means the reliability of oracles providing emissions data, the track record of counterparties in meeting commitments, and the integrity of certification bodies can all be verified onchain before the initialization of commerce. The opportunity for practitioners lies in building negotiation protocols where environmental parameters function as binding constraints—systems where transactions settle only when material conditions are verified.

The corresponding platforms and coordination mechanisms that are possible leveraging these new negotiation protocols are many. Renewable peer-to-peer energy trading demonstrates this concretely: in Germany, simulations of automated local energy trading have demonstrated potential household electricity bill reductions of 4–20%, depending on the scale of community participation (Grid Singularity 2023). The efficiency gain is not merely cost reduction but reduced leakage—energy produced locally consumed locally, revenue circulating within communities, grid infrastructure optimized for actual regional flows rather than centralized distribution assumptions. Grid Singularity concludes that "market platform models should be researched and developed to ensure holistic operation of P2P electricity markets, enabling the operational and regulatory framework to control, protect and settle financial transactions" (Grid Singularity 2023). Every local energy collective is effectively a decentralized organization trading energy resources, offering a compelling infrastructural template for regional prosumer coordination platforms and community energy networks.

In sustainable food systems, Community-Supported Agriculture (CSA) represents a prototype of multilateral commerce that predates blockchain but whose core logic can be incorporated into smart contracts. In CSA models, consumers commit capital in advance, sharing production risk with farmers; in return, they receive transparency about sourcing and cultivation practices. The relationship is participatory rather than purely transactional:

> Preorders... reinforce the cooperative and participatory culture. There are two 'rounds' to the preorder process. Members submit the first round of orders on the Monday before Market day... An email is then sent... with details on what has been ordered, and how much more for each item must be acquired to receive the greatest bulk discount. Members can then choose to buy more, or recruit family and friends to add to their original order, so that everyone can receive the lowest possible price for their food.
>
> **Figueroa (2015)**

Blockchain extends this logic by being able to address persistent coordination failures in wholesale procurement. The commodities sector faces well-documented risks, such as transportation damage to goods during transport, delivery failures where quality falls short of specification, and credit risk from unpaid invoices despite successful delivery. These risks are conventionally managed through intermediaries—clearinghouses, insurers, trade finance banks—who extract fees while adding friction. Smart contract escrow and onchain reputation systems offer pathways for improvement: transactions that settle automatically when verified conditions are met, counterparty histories that are transparent and immutable. Blockchain platforms that scale CSA logic to wholesale procurement, supply chain traceability systems, and collective bargaining tools that give small producers leverage would all be demonstrable improvements to the status quo.

At bioregional scale, for commons management and the institutional concentration of control over natural resources, there are structural challenges that existing coordination mechanisms have proven poor at resolving. Large trading companies dominate commodity sectors in ways that impede equitable land use and environmental sustainability (Taskforce on Nature Markets 2022). Their high concentration of control has led to adverse ecological impacts and constrained adaptation efforts (Moreira 2022). The green transition requires negotiation platforms where stakeholders can coordinate around equitable resource access in a transparent, decentralized manner that resists market centralization. For practitioners, this represents the most significant long-term opportunity: open-source platforms enabling collective coordination around resource governance, and transparency tools that make commodity sector concentration visible and actionable.

COMMONS CAPITAL PLATFORMS

New platforms for capital formation in green cryptomarkets that address ongoing challenges faced by impact investors are necessary. Democratization of finance through coin offerings and platforms that facilitate fractional ownership should allow anyone with minimal capital to contribute to the environmental movement. ICOs and token warrants (privately negotiated agreements of token sales) have already demonstrated their prowess for green crypto-asset capital formation: one survey of Web3's carbon sector found that "the highest TRLs" for projects at the time of writing were financed by "private investment and initial coin offerings" (Sipthorpe et al. 2022).

That said, ICOs have yet to prove effective for patient or performance-based capital formation. Token sales struggle to align investment timelines with the prolonged duration environmental projects require. This temporal mismatch is exemplified by forestry carbon issues highlighted in recent U.S. climate legislation (Coulston et al. 2023). Long-duration contracts are essential to address the risks that unfold over time, and strategies for wildfire reduction and forest planting illustrate the interplay between short-term impacts and long-term benefits—underscoring the need for flexible financing structures (Finance Earth and Economics for the Environment Consultancy 2021).

The balance between ecology, extraction, and profits is delicate. Timberland Investment Management Organizations (TIMOs) manage substantial forest investments, seeking financial returns while protecting ecological value through sustainable forestry and conservation easements—restrictions that protect land indefinitely while still permitting financial gains (Finance Earth and Economics for the Environment Consultancy 2021). Some economists advocate a parallel approach for non-renewable resources, treating mineral proceeds as shared inheritance and distributing dividends to citizens as beneficial owners (Basu and Pegg 2020).

The key insight: agreements and financing must evolve alongside the work. Long-duration timeframes and ecological variability demand sophisticated capital formation protocols that raise, retain, distribute, and release capital to the right stakeholders at the right time. Such protocols must specify land-based rights, divide revenues effectively, and streamline easements and temporary licensing (Prewitt and Henderson 2024). They should incorporate automated mechanisms—financial guarantees, first-loss capital, and preferred returns—enabling real-time adjustment of risk-return profiles. By embedding strong, code-enforced guarantees that address standard investment evaluation criteria as detailed in Table 7.3, these features simplify due diligence and enhance investability.

INTERSPECIES EXCHANGE

The concept of interspecies exchange proposes a new approach to environmental conservation by using blockchain to facilitate direct interaction and representation of nonhuman agents. This paradigm acknowledges the intrinsic value of ecosystems and their constituents, proposing mechanisms for their participation in financial systems and institutional governance. The development of autonomous agents capable of banking themselves represents a significant advance, illustrating the potential for these agents to hold, manage, and transact value independently or on behalf of other entities. Such capabilities highlight the limitations of traditional banking systems in serving AI, positioning crypto as the preferred infrastructure for AI entities

TABLE 7.3
Evaluation Criteria for Green Asset Investments. A Practical Framework for Sustainability Professionals Assessing Green Crypto Opportunities

Dimension	Evaluation Focus	How Web3 Contributes
Market Context	Strength of policy and regulatory environment	Smart contracts and onchain compliance tools streamline regulatory reporting and auditability.
	Signals of market demand and adoption trajectory	Transparent blockchain data (e.g., wallet activity, onchain economic flows) reflects real-time demand and investor sentiment.
	Ecosystem readiness and infrastructure maturity	Web3 infrastructure (e.g., decentralized storage, DAOs, oracles) creates composable, interoperable open-source environments for rapid deployment.
Project Fundamentals	Revenue potential and financial resilience	Tokenized cash flows, performance-linked bonds, or programmable yield enable novel revenue streams and financial experimentation.
	Capacity for replication or scale	Modular architecture and permissionless composability support rapid cloning, adaptation, and scaling of successful projects.
	Clarity and credibility of socioecological outcomes	Verifiable impact data can be recorded onchain using oracles, IoT sensors, or third-party attestations (e.g., MRV protocols).
	Exposure to risk and presence of mitigation measures	Algorithmic escrows, insurance primitives, and diversified staking models can reduce counterparty and project risk.
Financial Structuring	Projected returns relative to risk	Onchain risk models and open data can allow dynamic pricing, automated rebalancing, and continuous risk assessment.
	Alignment between capital timeline and project duration	Token vesting, streaming payments, and dynamic governance can adjust capital flow to project lifecycles.
	Investment size relative to opportunity and portfolio fit	Fractional tokenization and microfunding platforms enable precision allocation and entry at any scale.
	Fee structures and transaction costs	Reduced intermediary overhead and programmable fees via smart contracts drive efficiency.
	Collateralization or downside protection mechanisms	Onchain collateral, slashing conditions, and decentralized insurance markets can protect downside.
	Defined pathways for liquidity or exit	Secondary markets for tokenized assets enable earlier exits and better liquidity, even for traditionally illiquid assets.
Management Team	Operational capability and domain expertise	Reputation systems, verifiable credentials, and public contribution histories build trust and transparency in team performance.
	Sufficient resources and governance mechanisms	DAOs, multisigs, and treasury transparency tools enable more accountable and adaptive management structures.

Source: Table by the authors.

(ian@syndicateio 2023). This opens the possibility of autonomous agents representing the economic interests of nonhuman actors in cryptomarkets.

Futurist Jonathan Ledgard envisions "interspecies money" that will be "held by nonhumans" and become "a significant financier of conservation" (Ledgard 2022). AI interpretability techniques are deepening appreciation for nonhuman intelligence—research into sperm whale communication patterns, for instance, reveals surprising sophistication. This raises a design question: how might economic interfaces render nonhuman needs legible to financial systems? Nonhuman species provide valuable ecosystem services and perform economically beneficial work, yet their contribution remains invisible to markets. The Plantoid art project is one early prototypical model for how interspecies agents can incentivize human counterparts. The Plantoid's main goal is to reproduce itself by encouraging people to purchase and trade its cryptocurrency, with fees from minting and exchange funding its replication (Automata 2014).

In parallel to technical efforts, advancements toward recognizing the Rights of Nature and establishing *Locus Standi* for ecosystems are ongoing, helping establish a legal basis for nonhuman legibility. The movement to grant legal recognition to species and ecosystems challenges traditional property law, but the shift toward acknowledging these entities as beings with distinct lives and relationships helps ensure their contributions are recognized and protected. Until such legal changes are implemented, corporations will enjoy a *de jure* and *de facto* advantage in courts: corporations can sue for lost revenues due to conservation enforcement, but nonhuman actors cannot sue for destroyed habitat (Tómas 2024). These legal mechanisms complement blockchain and AI advancements—no technical solution alone can advance this emerging paradigm.

INCENTIVIZED INFRASTRUCTURES (DEPIN)

DePIN networks facilitate a participatory model where their growth and deployment are rapidly bootstrapped through the active engagement and incentivization of their participants, its "primary goal is to replace the monopolized coordinator and use native tokens to transform participants into stakeholders of the network" (Gate Learn 2024). This approach contrasts starkly with traditional infrastructures by empowering users through autonomous governance mechanisms or rewarding contributions toward network health and data richness. These networks challenge a long market history of infrastructures, where "small numbers of major shareholders seeking to maximize their dividends" (Saito 2024) have been pre-eminent vis-à-vis collaborative consumption patterns.

The scale of opportunity is immense. The World Economic Forum projects DePIN will grow to $3.5 trillion by 2028, encompassing everything from decentralized wireless networks to distributed energy grids (World Economic Forum 2025). This reflects not just technological possibility but structural demand: traditional infrastructure financing faces bottlenecks that participatory token models can help resolve. Green DePIN, as a subset, spans sectors where physical infrastructure supports the green transition: decentralized renewable energy grids in industry; sustainable supply chains and circular economy initiatives in commerce;

sensor networks monitoring tree health and ecological indicators in urban environments; smart eco-homes optimizing energy efficiency, water harvesting, and greywater recycling at the household level; and EV charging infrastructure in transportation.

Among DePIN's possibilities, carbon dioxide removal networks (CDR Networks) remain untested, but should be considered by sustainability professionals. A CDR-DePIN would likely involve deploying multiple CDR methods across distributed, locally managed sites rather than centralized, large-scale facilities. Envision a network of CDR hubs, each tailored to harness the environmental and socioeconomic strengths of its locale—urban centers with innovative DAC and biochar projects; rural landscapes flourishing via NbS implementations; coastal communities culturing seaweed and employing mineralization techniques. Rather than operating in isolation, these hubs would be linked by a digital platform enabling seamless data exchange and coordination across continents. This digital backbone would support real-time monitoring of carbon sequestration efforts, facilitate a marketplace for originating carbon assets, and share breakthroughs and best practices.

DePIN's scaling potential in green cryptomarkets is enhanced by infrastructure miniaturization—centralized systems like industrial agriculture and energy production giving way to market gardens and distributed solar networks. Bruce Usher notes in *Investing in the Era of Climate Change*:

> Solar panels are a form of distributed power generation, as PV panels can be placed in almost any location and at any scale… Solar power can also be used off-grid, providing electricity in locations too remote or too costly… This stands in contrast to traditional centralized power generation […] Solar could provide nearly 40 percent of U.S. power needs simply by installing panels on every rooftop.
>
> **Usher (2022)**

Infrastructure miniaturization affords more decentralized, local, and efficient resource management. These technologies complement each other: solar PVs can be combined with smart batteries that arbitrage grid loads or EV-to-grid systems that shift energy; solar farms can be co-designed as biodiversity habitats. Most importantly, these infrastructures scale well through voluntary collectivization, pairing strongly with Web3 DAO primitives in governance and data management—that same EV could be rented or co-owned through a Web3 product service platform.

Rifkin, a popular green economist and futurist, speculates in his book *Age of Resilience* on use cases DePIN is poised to develop (though not using the term): a "water internet made up of… smart meters and sensor monitoring," "ecosystem coordinators, tracking wildlife and providing data," and sensor networks "helpful in monitoring air pollution" (Rifkin 2022). He believes these technologies should make each of us "a node in the nervous system of the biosphere" (Rifkin 2022). As discussed in Chapter 3, this vision becomes far easier on an immutable, interoperable substrate. Though DePIN is still evolving, several use cases relevant to green crypto can be identified (see Table 7.4).

TABLE 7.4
DePIN Network Types and Green Crypto Applications. A Taxonomy of Decentralized Physical Infrastructure Networks Relevant to Environmental Markets

Network Type	Definition	Green Crypto Applications	Impacted Asset Types
Geospatial Networks	Utilize location-based data and technologies for mapping, positioning, and environmental monitoring.	Asset tracking for renewable energy installations; environmental monitoring for protection/restoration projects.	RECs, Renewable RWAs, PPAs, carbon issuances, carbon credits, non-carbon credits, ecological data rights, green bonds
IoT Networks	Connect physical devices with sensors and software to exchange data and perform tasks efficiently.	Monitoring and optimizing energy usage in smart homes and buildings; integration of IoT sensors in renewable infrastructure for real-time monitoring. Environmental monitoring for environmental protection and/or restoration projects.	RECs, Renewable RWAs, PPAs, carbon issuances, carbon credits, non-carbon credits, ecological data rights, green bonds
Mobility Networks	Enable connectivity and services within transportation systems, fostering innovations in EVs.	Direct connections between EV users and service providers for maintenance, insurance, and sales; promoting EV adoption.	Renewable RWAs (specifically EVs), digiphysical goods, ecological data rights, some output rights
Supply Chain Networks	Enhance efficiency, transparency, and traceability of supply chains in green markets.	Distribution and tracking of renewable energy components; ethical and sustainable sourcing of materials for green products.	Commodity derivatives, ecological data rights, some output rights
Energy Networks	Innovations in energy production, distribution, and management leveraging decentralized networks.	Decentralized energy trading and management; incentivizing renewable adoption through tokenized reward mechanisms; addressing curtailment.	Ecological data rights, RECs, Renewable RWAs, PPAs
Wireless Networks	Provide wireless communication infrastructure to support connectivity of decentralized networks.	Enabling connectivity and data exchange between IoT devices in renewable infrastructure; supporting decentralized energy trading platforms; remote monitoring and control of sensors and equipment.	All green assets
CDR Networks	Decentralized networks for carbon dioxide removal using distributed, locally managed sites and multiple CDR methods.	Coordinating diverse CDR methods (DAC, biochar, NbS, ocean-based); real-time sequestration monitoring; carbon asset origination and marketplace.	Carbon credits, carbon issuances, ecological data rights

Source: Table by the authors.

CONCLUSION

This book began with a practitioner's problem: sustainability professionals are increasingly asked to evaluate blockchain-based environmental finance tools without a framework for telling substance from jargon. The Environmental Finance Stack was our answer. Read from the bottom up, it grounds every claim in the biophysical world and traces its ascent through data, institutions, protocols, assets, and finally markets. Each layer poses a different question, and skipping any of them is where greenwashing takes hold. A carbon credit is no better than the measurement beneath it; a protocol is no better than the institution that authored it; a market is no better than the assets it circulates. Blockchain does not change this hierarchy—it only makes each layer legible, auditable, and, when properly designed, harder to corrupt.

The Market Layer, which closes the Stack, is where the preceding layers meet liquidity. It is also where the frontier of green crypto is most visible. The evaluation criteria for green asset investments introduced in this chapter, the emerging possibility of interspecies exchange, and the rapid scaling of decentralized physical infrastructure networks all point in the same direction: markets that can register forms of value—nonhuman contributions, distributed generation, long-duration stewardship—that legacy finance has historically rendered invisible. These are not speculative curiosities. They are structural responses to a climate finance gap exceeding five trillion dollars per year, and to a legacy infrastructure that concentrates authority while excluding many of the communities and ecosystems doing the underlying work. Whether the tools described in this book actually help close that gap will depend less on the technology than on the rigor with which practitioners apply the Stack's questions to each new project they encounter.

We wrote this handbook for those practitioners. The frameworks, taxonomies, and cases collected across these seven chapters are not a verdict on green crypto; they are an instrument for reaching your own. Used honestly, the Stack should make some projects look worse than their marketing suggests and others look considerably better. It should also, we hope, make the conversation between sustainability and blockchain communities more precise—replacing the binary of enthusiasm and dismissal with the harder, more useful work of layer-by-layer due diligence. The transition to a regenerative economy will require financial infrastructure we have not yet built. Building it well requires practitioners who can tell the difference between infrastructure that serves ecological reality and infrastructure that merely tokenizes the appearance of it. That distinction is the task this book has tried to equip you for. The rest is your work.

REFERENCES

Agrotoken. n.d. "Llevá la revolución digital del agro a tu negocio." https://www.agrotoken.com/. Accessed June 2025.

Altieri, Katye, Dave Jones, Uni Lee, and Oya Zaimoglu. 2023. "Tracking National Ambition Towards a Global Tripling of Renewables." Ember, November 2023. https://ember-energy.org/app/uploads/2024/10/Report-Tracking-national-ambition-towards-a-global-tripling-of-renewables-1.pdf. Accessed March 2026.

Arboleda, Martín. 2020. Planetary Mine: Territories of Extraction Under Late Capitalism. Verso Books.

Atkins, Paul S. 2025. "American Leadership in the Digital Finance Revolution." Speech, U.S. Securities and Exchange Commission, Washington D.C., July 31, 2025. https://www.sec.gov/newsroom/speeches-statements/atkins-digital-finance-revolution-073125. Accessed March 2026.

Automata. 2014. Plantoïd 15. Primavera De Filippi. https://www.automata.art/works/plantoid-15/. Accessed March 2026.

Badgley, Grayson. 2023. "Nearly a Third of California's Forest Offset Buffer Pool Has Gone Up in Smoke." CarbonPlan, November 29, 2023. https://carbonplan.org/blog/buffer-update-three. Accessed March 2026.

Bank of America Institute. 2023. "Beyond Crypto: Tokenization." July 29, 2023.

Basu, Rahul, and Scott Pegg. 2020. "Minerals Are a Shared Inheritance: Accounting for the Resource Curse." The Extractive Industries and Society 7, no. 4: 1369–1376. https://www.sciencedirect.com/science/article/abs/pii/S2214790X20302410. Accessed March 2026.

BeZero Carbon. 2024. "Towards Efficiency: Carbon Credit Pricing and Risk — Establishing Price-rating Correlation for Carbon Credits." January 16, 2024. https://bezerocarbon.com/insights/towards-efficiency-carbon-credit-pricing-and-risk. Accessed March 2026.

Bindseil, Ulrich, and Omid Malekan. 2025. "Public Crypto Networks as Financial Market Infrastructures." SSRN, February 14, 2025. https://papers.ssrn.com/sol3/papers.cfm?abstract_id=5138052. Accessed March 2026.

BlockScience. 2021. "Introducing Automated Regression Market Makers (ARMMs): A New Price Discovery Mechanism for Semi-Fungible Assets." Medium, October 27, 2021. https://medium.com/block-science/introducing-automated-regression-markets-arms-a-new-price-discovery-mechanism-for-semi-fungible-935d31ca457c. Accessed March 2026.

BloombergNEF. 2023. "Lithium-Ion Battery Pack Prices Hit Record Low of $139/kWh." November 27, 2023. https://about.bnef.com/insights/clean-energy/lithium-ion-battery-pack-prices-hit-record-low-of-139-kwh/. Accessed March 2026.

Blumenfeld, Josh. 2023. "NASA and IBM Openly Release Geospatial AI Foundation Model for NASA Earth Observation Data." EarthData, August 3, 2023. https://www.earthdata.nasa.gov/news/nasa-ibm-openly-release-geospatial-ai-foundation-model-nasa-earth-observation-data. Accessed March 2026.

Boehm, Sophie et al. 2023. "State of Climate Action 2023." World Resources Institute, November 2023. https://www.wri.org/research/state-climate-action-2023. Accessed March 2026.

Brewer, Joe. 2023. The Design Pathway for Regenerating Earth. TCP Press.

Buchner, Barbara, Baysa Naran, Rajashree Padmanabhi, Sean Stout, Costanza Strinati, Dharshan Wignarajah, Gaoyi Miao, Jake Connolly, and Nikita Marini. 2023. "Global Landscape of Climate Finance 2023." Climate Policy Initiative, November 2023. https://www.climatepolicyinitiative.org/wp-content/uploads/2023/11/Global-Landscape-of-Climate-Finance-2023.pdf. Accessed March 2026.

Buller, Adrienne. 2022. The Value of a Whale: On the Illusions of Green Capitalism. Manchester University Press.

Buterin, Vitalik. 2024. "The Promise and Challenges of Crypto + AI Applications." Vitalik.eth.limo, January 30, 2024. https://vitalik.eth.limo/general/2024/01/30/cryptoai.html. Accessed March 2026.

Caleb & Brown. 2023. "Weekly Rollup – September 26, 2023." Caleb & Brown Blog, September 26, 2023. https://calebandbrown.com/blog/weekly-rollup-september-26-2023/. Accessed March 2026.

CARBON Copy. 2025. The State of ReFi 2025. CARBON Copy Research Report. https://carboncopy.news/reports/state-of-refi-2025/. Accessed March 2026.

CDR.fyi. 2024. "2024+ Market Outlook Summary Report." January 17, 2024. https://www.cdr.fyi/blog/2024-market-outlook-summary-report. Accessed March 2026.

Cembalest, Michael. 2025. "Heliocentrism: 15th Annual Energy Paper." J.P. Morgan Asset & Wealth Management, March 2025.

Chen, Hsuan-Chi, and Jay R. Ritter. 2000. "The Seven Percent Solution." Journal of Finance 55, no. 3: 1105–1131.

Chen, Tank. 2024. "2023 Investment Landscape in Carbon Removal." CDR.fyi, January 11, 2024. https://www.cdr.fyi/blog/2023-investment-landscape-in-carbon-removal. Accessed March 2026.

Coulston, John W., Grant M. Domke, David M. Walker, Evan B. Brooks, and Claire B. O'Dea. 2023. "Near-Term Investments in Forest Management Support Long-Term Carbon Sequestration Capacity in Forests of the United States." PNAS Nexus 2, no. 11. https://doi.org/10.1093/pnasnexus/pgad345

Curmi, Elizabeth, Jason Channell, Ying Qin, and Andrea Fleming. 2023. "Voluntary Carbon Markets: A Critical Piece of the Net Zero Puzzle." Citi GPS: Global Perspectives & Solutions, July 2023.

Currier, James. 2022. "The Durability Formula – How It Will Determine Your Startup's Future Value." NfX, February 2022. https://www.nfx.com/post/durability-formula-will-determine-your-startups-future-value. Accessed March 2026.

Dataland. n.d. "A Museum and Web3 Platform Dedicated to Data Visualization and AI Arts." https://dataland.art/. Accessed March 2026.

De Rossi, Marco et al. 2025. "ERC-8004: Trustless Agents." Ethereum Improvement Proposals, August 2025. https://eips.ethereum.org/EIPS/eip-8004. Accessed March 2026.

Delphi Labs. 2023. "Assimilating the BORG: A New CryptoLegal Framework for DAO-Adjacent Entities." Medium, April 20, 2023. https://delphilabs.medium.com/assimilating-the-borg-a-new-cryptolegal-framework-for-dao-adjacent-entities-569e54a43f83. Accessed March 2026.

Dias, Philipe A, Thomaz Kobayashi-Carvalhaes, Sarah Walters, Tyler Frazier, Carson Woody, Sreelekha Guggilam, Daniel Adams, Abhishek Potnis, and Dalton Lunga. 2023. "GeoAI for Humanitarian Assistance." In Handbook of Geospatial Artificial Intelligence, edited by Song Gao, Yingjie Hu, and Wenwen Li. CRC Press.

Dixon, Chris. 2024. Read Write Own: Building the Next Era of the Internet. Random House.

Doneva, Dimana. 2023. "PYREG and Kita To Collaborate on Biochar Carbon Insurance Structure." CarbonHerald, November 23, 2023. https://carbonherald.com/pyreg-and-kita-to-collaborate-on-biochar-carbon-insurance-structure/. Accessed March 2026.

Dupin, Marie. 2024. "Nestlé et d'autres industriels ont purifié illégalement de l'eau contaminée pour continuer de la vendre." France Inter, January 30, 2024. https://www.radiofrance.fr/franceinter/nestle-et-d-autres-industriels-ont-purifie-illegalement-de-l-eau-contaminee-pour-continuer-de-la-vendre-6817370. Accessed March 2026.

ECI. n.d. "ClimateGPT." https://www.eci.io/climategpt. Accessed March 2026.

Ekonavi. n.d. "Library of Ecological Resources." https://ekonavi.com/biblioteca. Accessed March 2026.

Fabi, Michele, Viraj Nadkarni, Leonardo Leone, and Matheus V. X. Ferreira. 2025. "Automated Market Making for Energy Sharing." HAL Preprint hal-05424478, December 2025.

FAO. 2023. "The State of Food and Agriculture 2023 – Revealing the True Cost of Food to Transform Agrifood Systems." November 2023. https://www.fao.org/3/cc7724en/cc7724en.pdf. Accessed March 2026.

Federal Trade Commission. 2024. "FTC Order Prohibits Data Broker X-Mode Social and Outlogic from Selling Sensitive Location Data." FTC Press Release, January 9, 2024. https://www.ftc.gov/news-events/news/press-releases/2024/01/ftc-order-prohibits-data-broker-x-mode-social-outlogic-selling-sensitive-location-data. Accessed March 2026.

Figueroa, Meleiza. 2015. "Food Sovereignty in Everyday Life: Toward a People-Centered Approach to Food Systems." Globalizations 12, no. 4: 498–512. https://www.tandfonline.com/doi/abs/10.1080/14747731.2015.1005966. Accessed March 2026.

Finance Earth and Economics for the Environment Consultancy. 2021. "Facilitating Local Natural Capital Investment: Literature Review." NatureScot Research Report No. 1260. https://www.nature.scot/sites/default/files/2021-02/Publication%202021%20-%20NatureScot%20Research%20Report%201260%20-%20Facilitating%20Local%20Natural%20Capital%20Investment%20-%20Literature%20Review.pdf. Accessed March 2026.

Gate Learn. 2024. "Critiquing DePIN: False Hope or Real Dawn?" Gate Learn, February 25, 2024. https://www.gate.com/learn/articles/critiquing-depin-false-hope-or-real-dawn/1870. Accessed March 2026.

Gieseke, Timothy M. 2016. Shared Governance for Sustainable Working Landscapes. CRC Press.

Gómez-Baggethun, E., S. Mingorría, V. Reyes-García, L. Calvet, and C. Montes. 2010. "Traditional Ecological Knowledge Trends in the Transition to a Market Economy: Empirical Study in the Doñana Natural Areas." Conservation Biology 24: 721–729. https://doi.org/10.1111/j.1523-1739.2009.01401.x

Google. 2025. "Announcing the Agent2Agent Protocol (A2A)." Google Developers Blog, April 9, 2025. https://developers.googleblog.com/en/a2a-a-new-era-of-agent-interoperability/. Accessed March 2026.

Govender, T., and I. Davidson. 2019. "Artisan Development and Training – An Analysis of the Apprentice, Learnership and ARPL Trade Test Results of Candidates Tested at TEK-MATION Training Institute." Southern African Universities Power Engineering Conference/Robotics and Mechatronics/Pattern Recognition Association of South Africa (SAUPEC/RobMech/PRASA): 643–647. https://ieeexplore.ieee.org/document/8704795. Accessed March 2026.

Grid Singularity. 2023. "A Vision of a Decentralised Energy Market for Germany in 2030." Medium, November 30, 2023. https://gridsingularity.medium.com/a-vision-of-a-decentralised-energy-market-for-germany-in-2030-66463e87fac6

Helios. n.d. "The Evolution of Solar, Open to Everyone." helios.eco/. Accessed March 2026.

Huang, Chengquan, Weishu Gong, and Yong Pang. 2022. "Remote Sensing and Forest Carbon Monitoring—a Review of Recent Progress, Challenges and Opportunities." Journal of Geodesy and Geoinformation Science 5, no. 2: 124–147. https://doi.org/10.11947/j.JGGS.2022.0212.

ian@syndicateio. 2023. "AI Agents That Can Bank Themselves Using Blockchains." Mirror, November 16, 2023. https://mirror.xyz/0x16de9a0d10EFc67EF575e72E40FD4a2A826fdEA7/yBj-fWQxrueXNs8jEjUo-Ozu_Nwt04GaXf1D8LjemtM. Accessed March 2026.

Investing.com. n.d. "Carbon Emissions Futures – Dec 24 (CFI2Z4)." investing.com/commodities/carbon-emissions-streaming-chart. Accessed December 2024.

IPCC. 2022. "Climate Change 2022: Mitigation of Climate Change." In Contribution of Working Group III to the Sixth Assessment Report of the Intergovernmental Panel on Climate Change, edited by P. R. Shukla, J. Skea, R. Slade, et al. Cambridge University Press. https://doi.org/10.1017/9781009157926

Kita and Oxbow Partners. 2024. Gross Written Carbon: Are Carbon Credits the Next Billion-Dollar Insurance Market? February 2024. https://static1.squarespace.com/static/61b1112b32e4550980845d3b/t/65c1044bc26b200c6c57846c/1707148371756/Kita+Oxbow+-+Gross+Written+Carbon.pdf. Accessed March 2026.

Kumar, Sumit, Rajaram Suresh, Bernhard Kronfellner, Aaditya Kaul, and Darius Liu. 2022. "Relevance of On-chain Asset Tokenization in 'Crypto Winter'." Boston Consulting Group and ADDX, September 2022. https://web-assets.bcg.com/1e/a2/5b5f2b7e42dfad2cb3113a291222/on-chain-asset-tokenization.pdf. Accessed March 2026.

Ledgard, Jonathan. 2022. "Interspecies Money." In Breakthrough: The Promise of Frontier Technologies for Sustainable Development, edited by John W. McArthur, Homi Kharas, and Izumi Ohno, 77–102. Brookings Institution Press. https://www.brookings.edu/wp-content/uploads/2021/12/Chapter-Five_Breakthrough.pdf. Accessed March 2026.

Loughran, Tim, and Jay Ritter. 2004. "Why Has IPO Underpricing Changed Over Time?" Financial Management 33, no. 3: 5–37.

Matsuoka, Daren, Robert Hackett, Jeremy Zhang, Stephanie Zinn, and Eddy Lazzarin. 2025. "State of Crypto 2025: The Year Crypto Went Mainstream." a16z crypto, October 22, 2025. https://a16zcrypto.com/posts/article/state-of-crypto-report-2025/. Accessed March 2026.

Mishra, Mukesh K. 2020. "Application of Operational Research in Sustainable Environmental Management and Climate Change." ZBW – Leibniz Information Centre for Economics. https://www.econstor.eu/bitstream/10419/215782/1/Application%20of%20Operational%20Research%20in%20Sustainable%20Environmental%20Management%20and%20Climate%20Change.pdf. Accessed March 2026.

Moreira, Assis. 2022. "EU New Rules Against Deforestation Reach 80% of Brazil's Agricultural Exports". Valor International, September 15, 2022. https://valorinternational.globo.com/agribusiness/news/2022/09/14/eu-new-rules-against-deforestation-reach-80percent-of-brazils-agricultural-exports.ghtml. Accessed March 2026.

Morgan, Thomas. 2023. "RWA x ReFi: Real World Positive Impact Using Web3 and Blockchain Technologies." February 16, 2023. https://docs.google.com/document/d/1IyHX8b_M9MjKG6UyXE6T53IMaP42BzZzXk-T6zY3cWY/edit. Accessed March 2026.

MRV Collective, Serena, and Nature4Climate. 2023. "The State of Nature Tech: Building Confidence in A Growing Market." https://nature4climate.wpenginepowered.com/wp-content/uploads/2023/10/N4C-The-state-of-nature-tech-final.pdf. Accessed March 2026.

Nordhaus, William D. 2021. The Spirit of Green: The Economics of Collisions and Contagions in a Crowded World. Princeton University Press.

Orsi, Janelle. 2013. Practicing Law in the Sharing Economy: Helping People Build Cooperatives, Social Enterprise, and Local Sustainable Economies. American Bar Association.

Potts, Jason. 2019. Innovation Commons: The Origin of Economic Growth. Oxford University Press.

Prewitt, Matt, and Jack Henderson. 2024. "PCO: A New Model of Ownership." RadicalxChange, February 20, 2024. https://www.radicalxchange.org/media/blog/pco-a-new-model-of-ownership/. Accessed March 2026.

Probst, Benedict S. et al. 2024. "Systematic Assessment of the Achieved Emission Reductions of Carbon Crediting Projects." Nature Communications 15. https://doi.org/10.1038/s41467-024-53645-z

Rifkin, Jeremy. 2022. The Age of Resilience. St. Martin's Press.

Rocky Mountain Institute and Climate Collective. 2023. "Voluntary Carbon Market (VCM): Landscape Guide." August 1, 2023. https://static1.squarespace.com/static/6155af7da5675116403c9136/t/64de45efdea3513d1cfc2fbc/1692288502204/VCM%2BLandscape%2BGuide%2BFull.pdf. Accessed March 2026.

Saito, Kohei. 2024. Slow Down: The Degrowth Manifesto. Astra House.

Sipthorpe, Adam, Sabine Brink, Tyler Van Leeuwen, and Iain Staffell. 2022. "Blockchain Solutions for Carbon Markets Are Nearing Maturity." One Earth 5, no. 7: 779–791. https://doi.org/10.1016/j.oneear.2022.06.004

Sovacool, Benjamin K., Jinsoo Kim, and Minyoung Yang. 2021. "The Hidden Costs of Energy and Mobility: A Global Meta-Analysis and Research Synthesis of Electricity and Transport Externalities." Energy Research & Social Science 72: 101885.

Srnicek, Nick. 2017. Platform Capitalism. Polity Press.

Standing, Guy. 2022. The Blue Commons: Rescuing the Economy of the Sea. Penguin Books UK.

Swinkels, Laurens. 2024. "Trading Carbon Credit Tokens on the Blockchain." International Review of Economics and Finance 91: 720–733.

Taskforce on Nature Markets. 2022. "Making Nature Markets Work: Shaping a Global Nature Economy in the 21st Century: Extended Report." October 2022. https://www.naturefinance.net/wp-content/uploads/2023/10/MakingNatureMarketsWork EXTENDED.pdf. Accessed March 2026.

Taskforce on Nature Markets. 2023. "Making Nature Markets Work: Extended Report." October 13, 2023. https://www.naturemarkets.net/publications. Accessed March 2026.

Tómas, Ragnar. 2024. "Hvalur Files Claim Against Icelandic State Over Whaling Ban." Iceland Review, January 26, 2024. https://www.icelandreview.com/politics/hvalur-files-claim-against-icelandic-state-over-whaling-ban/. Accessed March 2026.

Traditional Dream Factory. n.d. "How to Build A Regenerative Village." traditionaldreamfactory.com/how-to-build-a-regenerative-village. Accessed March 2026.

United Nations Conference on Trade and Development. 2013. "Wake Up Before It Is Too Late: Make Agriculture Truly Sustainable Now for Food Security in A Changing Climate: Trade and Environment Review 2013." United Nations. https://unctad.org/system/files/official-document/ditcted2012d3_en.pdf. Accessed March 2026.

Usher, Bruce. 2022. Investing in the Era of Climate Change. Columbia University Press, Columbia Business School.

Whitten, Stuart M., James Salzman, Dave Shelton, and Wendy Procter. 2003. "Markets for Ecosystem Services: Applying the Concepts." 2003 Conference (47th), Australian Agricultural and Resource Economics Society.

World Economic Forum. 2025. "Technology Convergence Report." June 2025.

Index